THE PRACTICAL GUIDE

Marvelous and maddening,
full of secrets and surprises,
peopled with the whole spectrum
of humanity. . . .
This is Cairo, my home.
Please come in and enjoy it.

Omar Sharif

THE PRACTICAL GUIDE

Compiled by
Claire E. Francy

New Revised Edition
Updated and Edited by Lesley Lababidi

Fifteenth Edition
Original 1975 edition edited by
Deborah Cowley and Aleya Serour

THE AMERICAN UNIVERSITY IN CAIRO PRESS

Cairo • New York

First Edition 1975   **Compiled & Edited by D. Cowley & A. Serour**
Second Edition 1977   Revised & Edited by Aleya Serour
Third Edition 1981   Revised & Edited by S. Arulantham & J. O'Hanlon
Fourth Edition 1984   Revised & Edited by Arunkumar Pabari
Fifth Edition 1986   Revised & Edited by Marianne Pearson
Sixth Edition 1988   Compiled & Edited by Cassandra Vivian
Seventh Edition 1997   Compiled & Edited by Claire Francy
Eighth Edition 1998   With updated directory
Ninth Edition 1999   Revised by Michael McCain
Tenth Edition 2000   With updated directory
Eleventh Edition 2001   Revised by Mandy McClure
Twelfth Edition 2001   With updated directory
Thirteenth Edition 2002   Revised by Alex Dessouky
Fourteenth Edition 2004   Revised by Abigail Ulman

Fifteenth Edition © 2006 by
The American University in Cairo Press
113 Sharia Kasr el Aini, Cairo, Egypt
420 Fifth Avenue, New York, NY 10018-2729
www.aucpress.com

Dar el Kutub No. 23754/05
ISBN 977 416 017 7

Design, layout, and maps by Penguin Advertising Agency, Cairo

Printed in Egypt

Contents

ARTS, ENTERTAINMENT, AND NIGHTLIFE   79

SPORTS AND FITNESS   84

PREFACE

More than a thousand years of history are mirrored, and mired, in the blooming, buzzing confusion of modern Cairo. Evidence of thousands more loom at the city's doorstep and beyond: the stark grandeur of the Great Pyramids, Alexandria, city of dreams, the marvels of Luxor and Aswan. Throughout the city, remnants of ancient Egypt abut reminders of the caliphs and sultans who made medieval Cairo the hub of Arab commerce and culture. Elegant souvenirs of eighteenth- and nineteenth-century French and British influence form graceful counterpoints to superb mosques. More recent history shows up in stylish examples of the Art Deco look Cairo wore in the 1930s.

The spectacle is clear evidence that through the ages, Cairo has been a magnet for foreigners and Egyptians alike. Today, it is bursting at the seams with both, reaching ever further out into the desert and up and down the Nile to accommodate us all. Making sense of modern Cairo's sheer size and complexity calls for this new edition of *Cairo: The Practical Guide*. Like its predecessors, it offers English-speaking visitors and residents verbal and visual maps to the how-tos of life, work, and leisure in Cairo. But it differs in providing more selective listings to help sort out the unprecedented boom in goods, services, and culture over recent years. To make the *Guide* less of a catalog and more of a companion, we have expressed opinions—our own and others'—to entertain and perhaps provoke both wide-eyed newcomers and jaded old-timers.

The best place to start is with what you know and are familiar with. This guide assists in the process of helping you become familiar with your immediate surroundings, after which, there are suggestions of how to branch out and begin to explore Cairo.

Cairo's magic contradictions—its minarets and pop musicians, its vastness and surprising intimacy, the dust of its past and the cacophony of its present—can best be savored step-by-step. Walk! (But watch the traffic and the potholes.) Meander the Byzantine alleyways, parks, and markets—all surprisingly safe and genuinely friendly. And when a Cairene stranger says "Welcome in Egypt," smile in return, and thank whatever fate brought you to al-Qahira ('The Vanquisher'), 'Mother of the World,' whose diversity, mystery, and warmth will touch your heart if you let them.

HOW THIS BOOK IS ORGANIZED

No guide is all things to all people. As its title suggests, *Cairo: The Practical Guide* focuses on the nitty-gritty realities and practicalities of life in Cairo. The audience? Short-term visitors who want more than a tourist's perspective, foreign residents new and old who need help with making a life and a home in Cairo, and Cairenes themselves who, for business or personal reasons, want to tap the pulse of the large foreign communities of Cairo.

To make the publication as useful as possible for these three groups, we have divided it into two stand-alone units:

1. The *Guide* itself, including:
   Welcome to Cairo (arrival, health, basic background, restaurants and lodging, shopping and sightseeing)
   Leisure and Learning (entertainment, sports, kids' activities, the arts, hobbies)
   Living in Cairo (househunting and furnishing, schools, neighborhoods, household help, cooking and cleaning, shopping lists in Arabic)
   Work and Research (office etiquette, doing business, permits, privatization, job-hunting)
   Cairo Arabic (the basics one really needs)
   Directory (a consumer listing of goods, services, and interests, with phones and addresses, by category and neighborhood; in the chapters, Directory categories are cross-referenced in bold, e.g., **Banks, Museums, Shoes**)
   Subject Index
2. The *Maps* booklet

Readers who have comments, corrections, or ideas they would like to see reflected in the next edition of *Cairo: The Practical Guide* are cordially invited to submit them by mail (*Cairo: The Practical Guide*, AUC Press, PO Box 2511, Cairo 11511, Egypt) or by e-mail (aucpress@aucegypt.edu).

ACKNOWLEDGMENTS

For their expertise, ideas, effort, encouragement, patience, and sheer entertainment, grateful thanks to Aleya Serour, Anita Girgis, Ann Owen, Anne and Curt Beech, Anne Dorra, Bessie O'Rourke, Beth Miller, Bob Kingsley, Bridget and Rob McKinney, Carol Sidky, Carole King-Reed, Cetra Rees, Chris Bell, Colette Belanger, Cosima Lukashevich, Delores Clardy, Diana Digges, Dr. Ehab Fayek, Dr. Karim Shaalan, Dr. Sherif Zakher, Ennas Omar, Gini Stevens, Hamida and Menem Moafi, Hanan Shouman, Hassan Ahmed, Ian Portman, Jacki Sutton Shirbini, James and Elham MacIntyre, Jane McCarthy, Jo Nessim, Jon Hill, Josse Dorra Fiani, Judi Holtze, Larry and Polly Cunningham, Leslie Zehr, Lorraine Chittock, Luanne Napoli, Maria and Peter Hartmann, Mark Linz, Mike Dixon, Nagwa Kami, Neil Hewison, Nicola Kutner, Patricia Lawrence, Peter Reynolds, Remah Talaat, Simon O'Rourke, Soha El Gawali, Tessie El Gabi, Wael Salem. Thanks to Daney, Kusuma, Brad, and Marina. Special thanks to Saad Dakkak, Mahmoud Youssef, and Dr. Lisa Sabbahy.

CHARTS

RAINFALL   Cairo 2.5 cm (1 in.) per year, usually Dec–Mar; Alexandria 18 cm (7 in.) per year, Oct–Apr; Aswan and Luxor almost none.

TEMPERATURE   Cairo hottest June–Sept (normal daily maximum 35–38°C, 95–100°F), coolest Nov–Feb (normal daily maximum 10–18°C; 50–65°F), with very significant nighttime drops, especially in winter and spring.

HUMIDITY   30–60 percent.

KHAMSIIN   This hot sandstorm blows variably, usually Feb–Apr, lasting 3–8 hours, but rarely more than once a week.

2006 / 2007 / 2008 HOLIDAYS AND BUSINESS HOURS

Banks, government offices, and most businesses are closed on public holidays. Banking hours are 8:30 am to 2 pm Sun–Thurs; some hotel banks are open 24 hours. Many shops are closed on Sundays; most do not open until at least 10 am, but stay open until late at night. Government shops close during Friday prayers. Normal office hours, government and private, are approximately 8:30 am to 4 pm, with great variations, and all normally close on Fridays. Many private businesses also close on Saturdays, including foreign embassies and consulates. Ramadan in 2006 is expected to begin on 24 September, in 2007 on 13 September and in 2008 on 2 September.

PUBLIC HOLIDAYS

Fixed holidays: Coptic Christmas, Sinai Liberation Day, Revolution Day, Egyptian Armed Forces Day.

Movable: *Eid al-Adha* (Great Feast); *Eid al-Fitr* (Small Feast); Islamic New Year; Prophet Muhammad's Birthday; *Shamm al-Nisim*

2006

6 October	Armed Forces
23–26 October*	*Eid al-Fitr,* the Small Feast
31 Dec 2006–3 Jan 2007	*Eid al-Adha,* the Great Feast

2007

7 January	Coptic Christmas
20 January*	Islamic New Year
31 March*	*Al-Mawlid al-Nabawi,* the Prophet's Birthday
9 April	*Shamm al-Nisim* (spring festival)
25 April	Sinai Liberation Day

1 May	Labor Day	
23 July	Revolution Day	
6 October	Armed Forces Day	
13–16 October*	*Eid al-Fitr,* the Small Feast	
20–24 December*	*Eid al-Adha,* the Great Feast	

2008

7 January	Coptic Christmas
10 January*	Islamic New Year
20 March*	*Al-Mawlid al-Nabawi,* the Prophet's Birthday
25 April	Sinai Liberation Day
28 April	*Shamm al-Nisim* (spring festival)
1 May	Labor Day
23 July	Revolution Day
2–5 October*	*Eid al-Fitr,* the Small Feast
6 October	Armed Forces Day
9 December*	*Eid al-Adha,* the Great Feast

Dates of Islamic holidays are approximate
Orthodox Coptic Easter (Eastern Easter) is not a public holiday; however, *Shamm al-Nisim* is a public holiday and is always celebrated the day after Coptic Easter.

8 April, 2007	Coptic Easter
27 April, 2008	Coptic Easter

ARABIC NUMBERS

0	٠	Sifr
1	١	waaHid / waHda
2	٢/٢	itneen
3	٣/٣	talaata
4	٤	arba'a
5	٥	khamsa
6	٦	sitta
7	٧	sab'a
8	٨	tamanya
9	٩	tis'a
10	١٠	'ashara
11	١١	Hidaashar
12	١٢	itnaashar
13	١٣	talattaashar
14	١٤	arba'taashar
15	١٥	khamastaashar
16	١٦	sittaashar
17	١٧	sab'ataashar
18	١٨	tamantaashar

19	١٩	tis'ataashar
20	٢٠	'ishriin
21	٢١	waaHid wi 'ishriin
22	٢٢	itneen wi 'ishriin
30	٣٠	talatiin
40	٤٠	arba'iin
50	٥٠	khamsiin
60	٦٠	sittiin
70	٧٠	sab'iin
80	٨٠	tamaniin
90	٩٠	tis'iin
100	١٠٠	miyya
101	١٠١	miyya wi waaHid
120	١٢٠	miyya wi 'ishriin
125	١٢٥	miyya khamsa wi 'ishriin
200	٢٠٠	miteen
273	٢٧٣	miteen talaata wi sab'iin
300	٣٠٠	tultumiyya
356	٣٥٦	tultumiyya sitta wi khamsiin
400	٤٠٠	rub'umiyya
500	٥٠٠	khumsumiyya
600	٦٠٠	suttumiyya
700	٧٠٠	sub'umiyya
800	٨٠٠	tumnumiyya
900	٩٠٠	tus'umiyya
1,000	١٠٠٠	alf
2,000	٢٠٠٠	alfeen
3,000	٣٠٠٠	talattalaaf
10,000	١٠٠٠٠	'ashartalaaf
100,000	١٠٠٠٠٠	miit alf
1,000,000	١٠٠٠٠٠٠	milyoon

CONVERSION TABLES

CURRENCY

Effective July 2006

US$1 = LE5.74   1 Euro = LE7.27   UK£1 = LE10.63   J¥1 = LE0.05   Aus$1 = LE4.34

TEMPERATURE

To convert degrees Celsius to Fahrenheit, multiply by 9, divide by 5, then add 32,
e.g., 20°C x 9 = 180, 180 ÷ 5 = 36, and 36 + 32 = 68°F.
To convert degrees Fahrenheit to Celsius, subtract 32, multiply by 5, then divide by 9,
e.g., 68°F – 32 = 36, 36 x 5 = 180, and 180 ÷ 9 = 20°C.

COOKING TEMPERATURES

Oven Description	Temperature in °F and °C		Gas
Very Cool	225°F	110°C	1/4
	250°F	120/130°C	1/2
Cool	275°F	140°C	1
	300°F	150°C	2
Warm	325°F	160/170°C	3
	350°F	180°C	4
	375°F	190°C	5
	400°F	200°C	6
Hot	425°F	220°C	7
	450°F	230°C	8
	475°F	240°C	9

In the case of thermostatically controlled electric ovens, it is usually found that the thermostat scale is marked in either degrees Fahrenheit, or in serial umbers (1, 2, 3 etc.) corresponding with 100°F, 200°F, 300°F, (38°C, 93°C, 150°C etc.)

IMPERIAL MEASURES AND EQUIVALENTS

Distance

1 inch	2.54 centimeters
1 centimeter	0.394 inches
1 foot (12 inches)	0.3048 meters
1 meter	3.28 feet
1 yard (3 feet)	0.9144 meters
1 meter	1.094 yards
1 mile (1,760 yards)	1.609 kilometers
1 kilometer	0.621 miles

Weight

1 ounce	28.35 grams
1 pound (16 ounces)	0.454 kilograms
1 kilogram	2.2 pounds

Liquid Measure

British

1 pint (20 fluid ounces)	0.568 liters
1 liter	1.76 pints
1 gallon (8 pints)	4.456 liters
1 liter	0.22 gallons

American

1 pint (16 fluid ounces)	0.473 liters
1 liter	2.11 pints
1 quart (2 pints)	0.946 liters
1 liter	1.05 quart
1 gallon (4 quarts)	3.785 liters
1 liter	0.26 gallons

TRAVEL INFORMATION

DISTANCES BETWEEN CAIRO AND MAIN EGYPTIAN CITIES

	kilometers		kilometers
Abu Simbel	1,235	Ismailiya	135
al-Alamein	293	Kharga	578
Alexandria	217	Kom Ombo	881
Asyut	386	Luxor	679
Aswan	929	Marsa Matruh	473
Damietta	295	Minya	235
Edfu	818	Saint Catherine	378
Esna	755	Siwa	700
Fayoum	100	Sharm al-Sheikh	350
Heliopolis	24	Port Said	212
Helwan	26	Suez	129
Hurghada	510		

LONG-DISTANCE BUSES

Fares are one-way and some vary slightly depending on time of day and amenities; check on air-conditioning in summer.

Superjet: Cairo—579-8181; Almaza (Heliopolis)—290-9017; Turgoman (off Gala St.)—578-8181; Tahrir—575-1313; Sharm al-Sheikh—(069) 366-1622; Alexandria—(03) 428-9092; Hurghada—(065) 355-3499. Check *http://www.touregypt.net/busses.htm* for Superjet schedule for Agami, Mamoura Beach, Marsa Matruh, North Coast.

East Delta Bus Co.: 482-4753, 419-8533. To: Ismailiya, LE10; Suez, LE10; al-'Arish, LE28.50–38.50; Sharm al-Sheikh, LE55–65; Nuweiba, LE50–75; Dahab, LE70–86; St. Catherine, LE39.00; Taba, LE55–76. Stations: Turgoman (off Gala' St.), Almaza and Tagnid (Heliopolis) for Ismailiya and Suez; Sinai Bus Station in 'Abbasiya for al-'Arish, Sharm al-Sheikh, and Nuweiba.

Upper Egyptian Bus Co.: 431-6723. To: Hurghada, LE50; Safaga LE50; Luxor LE70; Aswan LE60; Oases LE18–35. Buses depart from Turgoman Station, 'Abud (Shubra), Tasnid, Almaza, Munib (Giza).

Buses to Oases 576-0261.

For up-to-date bus timetables, see: *www.egypttourism.org/New%20Site/info/bus.htm*

TRAINS

Information Ramsis Station: 574-9274, 574-9474, 575-3555, 575-1954.

It is best to go to Ramsis Station for the most up-to-date schedule. Check at *www.toure-gypt.net/trains.htm* for information (not current). Also, you can buy your tickets on the sleeper train, Cairo to Luxor, from Carlson Wagon Lit (795-6571) at the Shephard Hotel (commission added) or directly from Ramsis Station. Always check the train times at each city of embarkation. Egyptian trains offer four classes of accommodation: 1st class air-conditioned; 2nd class air-conditioned; 2nd class ordinary; 3rd class.

1st and 2nd air-conditioned classes are available on express trains. Ordinary 2nd class is much more basic and 3rd class is uncomfortable; both classes are available on slower trains. If you are a student and/or resident, take identification as there may be a discount.

CAIRO–ALEXANDRIA

There are three types of trains running between Cairo and Alexandria: (1) Ordinary trains with very basic 2nd and 3rd class; (2) Express trains—"Spanish" train, with air-conditioning (2.5 hours) and "French" trains making several stops; and (3)Turbini trains, non-stop (2 hours).
Fares: A 1st class one-way ticket for an air-conditioned express from Cairo to Alexandria costs about LE 25.

Turbini trains depart 6 am, 8 am, 2 pm, 7 pm. "Spanish" trains depart 9 am, 12 pm, 5 pm, 10:30 pm. "French" trains (stopping at Banha, Tanta, and Damanhur) depart 6 am, 8:15 am, 9:30 am, 11 am, 4 pm, 6:10 pm.

CAIRO–LUXOR/ASWAN

There are four ways to travel by train between Cairo and Luxor/Aswan:(1) Day-time air-conditioned express train with comfortable 1st and 2nd class seating; (2) Overnight air-conditioned express train with comfortable 1st and 2nd class seating; (3) Overnight deluxe sleeper, now run by a company called Abela Egypt. For more information on the Abela Egypt sleeper train, check *www.sleepingtrains.com*; (4) 2nd and 3rd class slow trains.

CAIRO–PORT SAID

Ordinary trains with 2nd-class air-conditioned and 3rd class non-air-conditioned compartments depart from Port Said at: 6:25 am, 8:45 am 11:30 am, 2:35 pm, 7:10 pm.

PLANES

Information: EgyptAir, National Call Center—09007 0000 (50p a minute); mobile—1717 (LE1 a minute).

Roundtrip fares (prices fluctuate according to season): Aswan, LE2060 foreigners, LE820 residents; Hurghada, LE1020 foreigners, LE517 residents; Luxor, LE1520 foreigners, LE587 residents; Sharm al-Sheikh, LE1020 foreigners, LE512 residents.

FERRY BOATS

Ferry Boat Schedule: Sharm al-Sheikh to Hurghada—every Saturday, Monday, Tuesday, Thursday at 6 pm.

To give directions, or to get them from passers-by, you will be more successful if you say or show the name in Arabic. Cairo is often better navigated by landmarks than by actual addresses. For explanation of transcription, see Chapter 5.

Abbas Bridge	kubri abbas	كوبرى عباس
Abdeen Palace	'aSr 'abdiin	قصر عابدين
American University	il-gam'a il-amrikiya	الجامعة الامريكية
	(specify Tahrir or Zamalek)	
Al Azhar Park	Hadiiqat il-azhar	حديقة الأزهر
Botanical Garden	gineent il-urmaan	جنينة الأورمان
Cairo Tower	burg il-qaahira	برج القاهرة
Cairo University	gam'at il-qaahira	جامعة القاهرة
Camel Market	suu' il-gimaal	سوق الجمال
Citadel	il-'al'a	القلعة
City of the Dead	il-'araafa	القرافة
Coptic Cairo	maSr il-'adiima	مصر القديمة
Downtown	wust al-balad	وسط البلد
Duty Free Shop	il-suu' il-Hurra	السوق الحرة
Egyptian Museum	il-matHaf il-maSri	المتحف المصرى
Fish Garden	gineent il-asmaak	جنينة الاسماك
Gezira Club	naadi giziira	نادى الجزيرة
Heliopolis	maSr il-gidiida	مصر الجديدة
International Gardens	il-hadiqa il-dawliya	الحديقة الدولية
Islamic Cairo	il-Huseen	الحسين
Islamic Museum	il-matHaf il-islaami	المتحف الإسلامى
Qasr al-Nil Bridge	kubri 'aSr il-nil	كوبرى قصر النيل
Manial Palace Museum	matHaf 'aSr il-manyal	متحف قصر المنيل
Ministry of Foreign Affairs	wizarit il-khargiyya	وزارة الخارجية
Mogamma	il-mugamma'	المجمع
Old Cairo	maSr il-'adiima	مصر القديمة
Opera Complex	daar il-ubra (fi-l-giziira)	دار الاوبرا
Pyramids	il-haram	الهرم
Ramsis Train Station	maHattit ramsiis	محطة رمسيس
Ring Road	id-da'iri	الطريق الدائرى
Roxy	ruksi	روكسى
Shooting Club	nadi iS-Seed	نادى الصيد
Swissair Building	mabna swiseer (fi-l-giiza)	مبنى سويس أير
Tahrir Square	midan it-taHriir	ميدان التحرير
Television Building	mabna it-tilivizyoon	مبنى التليفزيون
World Trade Center	markaz it-tigaara	مركز التجارة
Zoo	gineent il-Hayawanaat	جنينة الحيوانات

BOOKS

TRAVEL GUIDES AND TRAVELOGUES

Egypt Pocket Guides. A. Siliotti. Cairo: AUC Press, 2000–2002. A series of handy pocket guides covering Sinai, Islamic Cairo, The Valley of the Kings, Abu Simbel, Alexandria, the Pyramids, Luxor, and Aswan and the Nubian Temples.

The Illustrated Guide to the Egyptian Museum. Cairo: AUC Press, 2001. Gorgeous photographs accompany this comprehensive yet undaunting itinerary around the museum.

Insight Guides: Egypt. (5th updated ed.) Michel Rauch, ed. 2002.

Insight Guides: Cairo. (2nd updated ed.) John Rodenbeck, ed. 2000.

Let's Go: Egypt. J. Shabot, ed. London: Macmillan. Great for budget travelers and anyone wanting a cheerfully jaded-youth perspective as well as the lowdown on prices. Updated annually.

National Geographic Traveler Egypt. Andrew Humphreys ed. 2002. Well-illustrated travel guide with in-depth site descriptions and background information with insights on history, culture, and contemporary life. Includes detailed maps with walking and biking tours.

The Rough Guide to Egypt. (4th ed.) Dan Richardson and Daniel Jacobs. Rough Guides, ed. 2000.

Jim Antoniou. *Historic Cairo: A Walk through the Islamic City*. Cairo: AUC Press, 1998. A charming illustrated walking guide through one of the most fascinating areas of Cairo.

Amitav Ghosh. *In an Antique Land*. Vintage Books, 1994. Ghosh skillfully weaves travel account with medieval history, highlighting forgotten parts of Egypt's ancient and modern past.

Ahmed Hassanein Bey. *The Lost Oases*. Cairo: AUC Press, 2006. A classic about desert exploration in 1923 through Egypt's Western Desert.

Jocelyn Gohary. *Guide to the Nubian Monuments on Lake Nasser*. Cairo: AUC Press, 1998. The only guide available to this area.

R. Neil Hewison, *The Fayoum: History and Guide*. Cairo: AUC Press, 2001. A revised edition of this indispensable guide to one of Egypt's most beautiful regions.

Jenny Jobbins and Mary Megalli. *Alexandria and the Egyptian Mediterranean*. Cairo: AUC Press, 2006. Discover the northern Egyptian coast from Sallum to Sinai.

Jill Kamil. *Coptic Egypt: History and Guide*. Cairo: AUC Press, 1993.

Lesley Lababidi, in collaboration with Lisa Sabbahy. *Cairo: The Family Guide*. Cairo: AUC Press, 2006. The only guide to Cairo specifically geared to families with children. Activities and itineraries for all ages.

Edward Lane. *An Account of the Manners and Customs of the Modern Egyptians*. Cairo: AUC Press, 2003. A new printing of the definitive 1865 edition of this classic work.

Edward Lane. *Description of Egypt*. Cairo: AUC Press, 2000. A previously unavailable book by the great 19th-century scholar.

Bonnie Sampsell. *A Traveler's Guide to the Geology of Egypt*. Cairo: AUC Press, 2003. A very clear introduction to Egypt's geology and how it formed the country's physical landscape and influenced its human culture.

Anthony Sattin. *The Pharaoh's Shadow: Travels in Ancient and Modern Egypt*. London: Orion, 2000. Sattin tracks down extraordinary examples of ancient survivals in modern Egypt.

Alberto Siliotti. *Guide to Exploration of the Sinai*. Luxor: A. A. Gaddis & Sons, 1995. The best guide on Sinai so far, with especially good inland coverage.

Alberto Siliotti. *The Illustrated Guide to the Pyramids*. Cairo: AUC Press, 2003.

Caroline Williams. *Islamic Monuments in Cairo: The Practical Guide*. (5th ed.) Cairo: AUC Press, 2002.

Cassandra Vivian. *The Western Desert of Egypt: An Explorer's Handbook*. Cairo: AUC Press, 2000. Vivian's book is completely up to date, and is a major resource with excellent maps. An essential guide for anyone planning a trip to Egypt's last frontier.

Susan L. Wilson. *Culture Shock! Egypt: A Guide to Customs and Etiquette*. Portland: Graphic Arts Center, 2002. Provides anyone moving to Egypt with the information needed to make their stay in the country more comprehensible and meaningful.

ECONOMY AND POLITICS

Nicholas S. Hopkins and Saad Eddin Ibrahim, eds. *Arab Society: Class, Gender, Power, and Development*. Cairo: AUC Press, 1997. A useful sourcebook with papers by a variety of leading authors on diverse aspects of modern Arab society.

Saad Eddin Ibrahim. *Egypt, Islam, and Democracy: Twelve Critical Essays*. Cairo: AUC Press, 2002 (paperback). A fascinating collection of essays on modern Egyptian politics and society by one of Egypt's leading analysts. A new edition with new postscript.

Paul Ayoub-Geday, Mandy McClure, et al. *Egypt Almanac: The Encyclopedia of Modern Egypt*. Egypto-*file* Publications, updated annually. An excellent resource for up-to-date facts and figures about life in contemporary Egypt, plus a review of all the major news stories of the year.

COOKBOOKS

Samia Abdennour. *Egyptian Cooking: and other Middle Eastern Recipes*. Cairo: AUC Press, 2005. *Middle Eastern Cooking: A Practical Guide*. Cairo: AUC Press, 1997. Have a certain matter-of-fact charm as if a busy Egyptian mother-in-law were showing her son's foreign bride how to cook while skimping on essential details—perhaps intentionally so!

Nora George. *Nora's Recipes from Egypt*. Clovis, CA: Nora George, 1995. Presents easy-to-follow recipes that the author learned and practiced while growing up in Cairo.

Magda Mehdawy. *My Egyptian Grandmother's Kitchen: Traditional Dishes Sweet and Savory*. Cairo: AUC Press, 2006.

FICTION

Ibrahim Abdel Meguid. *No One Sleeps in Alexandria*. Cairo: AUC Press, 1999.

Ibrahim Abdel Meguid. *The Other Place*. Cairo: AUC Press, 1997. Winner of the 1996 Naguib Mahfouz Medal for Literature.

Ibrahim Aslan. *Nile Sparrows*. Cairo: AUC Press, 2004. A drily humorous slice of the life of Cairo's underclasses.

Alaa Al Aswany. *The Yacoubian Building*. Cairo: AUC Press, 2004. This multi-layered novel of life in a downtown Cairo apartment building caused a great stir on its publication in Arabic because of its straightforward treatment of relationships based on power and sex, both straight and gay. Now available in this English translation.

Noel Barber. *A Woman of Cairo*. London: Coronet Books, 1984. A painless overview of the turbulent politics of Egypt from 1919 to 1953 in the cloak of an enjoyable romantic saga.

Lawrence Durrell. *The Alexandria Quartet*. Various editions.

Michael Ondaatje. *The English Patient*. Bloomsbury Publishing. Poetic and epic WWII love story, parts of which are set in Cairo. Winner of the 1992 Booker Prize.

Sonallah Ibrahim. *Zaat*, Cairo: AUC Press, 2001, and *The Committee*, AUC Press, 2002 (paperback). Two blackly satirical novels from one of Egypt's most iconoclastic novelists.

Yusuf Idris. *City of Love and Ashes*. Cairo: AUC Press, 2002 (paperback). Winner of the 1997 Naguib Mahfouz Medal for Literature. A superb novel set against the backdrop of unrest in Cairo just before the Revolution.

Naguib Mahfouz. Any of thirty titles by Egypt's Nobel laureate, published in Cairo by the AUC Press, and in the United States and Britain by Doubleday.

Samia Serageldin. *The Cairo House*. A semi-autobiographical novel by an Egyptian woman who has spent a large part of her life in the West. A family saga which shows the changes in Egyptian life from the time of the Pashas to Nasser and after.

William Shakespeare. *Antony and Cleopatra*. Many editions. The tragic romance of boy-meets-girl, or rather Rome-meets-Egypt, imagined and recounted by the Bard himself.

Ahdaf Soueif, *In the Eye of the Sun* and *The Map of Love*. Two outstanding and very popular novels by this London-based Egyptian writer.

Latifa al-Zayyat, *The Open Door*. Cairo: AUC Press, 2002 (paperback). Winner of the 1999 Naguib Mahfouz Medal for Literature. A landmark of women's writing in Arabic.

ANCIENT HISTORY

Robert A. Armour. *Gods and Myths of Ancient Egypt*. Cairo: AUC Press, 2001. One of the clearest guides available to the complications of the ancient Egyptian pantheon.

John Baines and Jaromir Malek. *Atlas of Ancient Egypt (revised edition)*. Cairo: AUC Press, 2002. Maps, plans and descriptions of the ancient sites of Egypt.

Erik Hornung. *History of Ancient Egypt*. Edinburgh: Edinburgh University Press, 1999. A vivid and concise chronological history of the civilization of ancient Egypt from its foundation to the era of Alexander the Great.

Salima Ikram and Aidan Dodson. *The Mummy in Ancient Egypt: Equipping the Dead for Eternity*. Cairo: AUC Press, 1998.

T. G. H. James. *Ancient Egypt: The British Museum Concise Introduction*. Cairo: AUC Press, 2005. Basic introduction to everything about ancient Egypt.

Mark Lehner. *The Complete Pyramids*. Cairo: AUC Press, 2004. Everything you wanted to know about Egyptian pyramids and more.

Jaromir Malek. *Egyptian Art*. New York: Phaidon Press, 1999. A clear and concise introduction to the art of ancient Egypt from an internationally respected authority.

Béatrix Midant-Reynes. *The Prehistory of Egypt: From the First Egyptians to the First Pharaohs*. Oxford: Blackwell Publishers, 2000. One of the few books on Egypt before the pharaohs.

Donald Redford, ed. *The Oxford Encyclopedia of Ancient Egypt*. 3 vols. Cairo: AUC Press, 2001. A wonderful reference source.

Nicholas Reeves and Richard H. Wilkinson. *The Complete Valley of the Kings*. Cairo: AUC Press, 1996.

Ian Shaw and Paul Nicolson. *The British Museum Dictionary of Ancient Egypt*. Cairo: AUC Press, 2002. A handy book to check for anything about ancient Egypt.

Richard H. Wilkinson. *The Complete Temples of Ancient Egypt*. London: Thames and Hudson, 2000. Together with the other "*Completes*" in the list, these books provide a fully-illustrated and authoritative history of ancient Egypt.

Richard Wilkinson. *The Complete Gods and Goddesses of Ancient Egypt*. Cairo: AUC Press, 2004. Good source for understanding the multitude of ancient Egyptian deities

BIOGRAPHIES AND AUTOBIOGRAPHIES

Leila Ahmed. *A Border Passage*. New York: Penguin Books, 2000. The author recounts her struggle for personal identification as a woman, a Muslim, an Egyptian, and an Arab.

Anna and Pierre Cachia. *Landlocked Islands: Two Alien Lives in Egypt*. Cairo: AUC Press, 1999. The double memoir of a mother and son, taking us from Anna's childhood in Russia and subsequent arrival in Egypt in 1901 to Pierre's enrollment at the American University in Cairo in the late 1930s.

Virginia Danielson. *The Voice of Egypt: Umm Kulthum, Arabic Song, and Egyptian Society in the Twentieth Century*. Cairo: AUC Press, 1997.

Katherine Frank. *A Passage to Egypt: The Life of Lucie Duff Gordon*. New York: Houghton Mifflin, 1994. Moving and informative biography of this nineteenth-century writer who came to Upper Egypt to cure her tuberculosis. Sadly, it didn't work, but in the meantime, she conveyed through letters home her love for and fascination with rural Egypt and its people. An evocative legacy well worth reading.

Midhat Gazalé. *Pyramids Road: An Egyptian Homecoming*. Cairo: AUC Press, 2004. A humorous but telling account of a childhood in pre-revolutionary Egypt, and of a bewildering return from exile many years later.

Hassan Hassan. *In the House of Muhammad Ali*. Cairo: AUC Press, 2000. A beautifully written and fascinating account of growing up inside Egypt's royal family in the second quarter of the twentieth century.

Denys Johnson-Davies. *Memories in Translation: A Life Between the Lines of Arabic Literature*. Cairo: AUC Press, 2006.

Naguib Mahfouz. *Echoes of an Autobiography*. Cairo: AUC Press, 1997. Brief remembrances of Egypt's winner of the Nobel Prize for Literature.

Ahmed Zewail. *Voyage through Time: Walks of Life to the Nobel Prize*. Cairo: AUC Press, 2002. The autobiography of the Egyptian winner of the 1999 Nobel Prize for Chemistry.

NON-FICTION

For the general, eclectic reader rather than the scholar.

Nadje Al-Ali. *Secularism, Gender and the State in the Middle East: The Egyptian Women's Movement*. Cambride: Cambridge University Press, 2000. An examination of women's activism in Egypt that challenges the usual stereotypes of Arab women.

Galal Amin. *Whatever Happened to the Egyptians?* and *Whatever Else Happened to the Egyptians?* Cairo: AUC Press, 2000, 2004. These two books together take a wry look at some of the more disturbing phenomena that underlie Egyptian society today.

Nayra Atiya. *Khul-Khaal: Five Egyptian Women Tell Their Stories*. Cairo: AUC Press, 1984. From the mouths of mostly poor women, narratives of their own lives with perspectives at once philosophical, humorous, devout, cynical, resigned.

Beth Baron. *Egypt as a Woman: Nationalism, Gender, and Politics*. Cairo: AUC Press, 2005. Examines how gender shaped the Egyptian nation between 1919 and 1940.

Donna L. Bowen and Evelyn A. Early, eds. *Everyday Life in the Muslim Middle East*. Bloomington: Indiana University Press, 2002. Excellent anthology from a wide range of social-anthropological sources, many from Arabic translations, and including customs, fiction, poetry, rituals, and reflections on exactly what the title says.

Artemis Cooper. *Cairo in the War 1939–1945*. London: Penguin, 1989. A fascinating portrait of Cairo during World War II.

Agnieszka Dobrowolska. *The Building Crafts of Cairo: A Living Tradition*. Cairo: AUC Press, 2005. A study of traditional arts and crafts in Egypt, such as stone masonry, marble work, wood turning, and glass blowing.

Arthur Goldschmidt, Jr. *A Concise History of the Middle East* (5th ed.). Cairo: AUC Press, 1997.

Gianni Guadalupi. *The Discovery of the Nile*. Cairo: AUC Press, 1997. Magnificent coffee-table tome crammed with rare pictures and interesting tidbits showing how the Nile has been perceived down the ages.

Sonallah Ibrahim and Jean Pierre Ribière. *Cairo: From Edge to Edge*. Cairo: AUC Press, 1998. The Mother of the World as seen through the lens of French photographer Jean Pierre Ribière and the pen of Egyptian writer Sonallah Ibrahim.

Edward Lane. *Description of Egypt*. Cairo: AUC Press, 2000. Lane's 'forgotten' manuscript, recently resurrected and published for the first time, nearly 170 years after it was written. A fascinating portrait of the Egypt that was.

Lesley Lababidi. *Silent No More: Special Needs People in Egypt*. Cairo: AUC Press, 2002. Focus on Egypt's advancement in the field of special needs.

Britta Le Va and Gamal al-Ghitani. *The Cairo of Naguib Mahfouz*. Cairo: AUC Press, 1999. A collection of outstanding visual images of historic Cairo, each complementing a verbal image selected from Mahfouz's writings.

Samia Louis. *Kallimni 'Arabi*. Cairo: AUC Press, 2006. Textbook of intermediate Egyptian colloquial Arabic.

Cynthia Myntti. *Paris Along the Nile: Architecture in Cairo from the Belle Epoque*. Cairo: AUC Press, 1999. A loving photographic portrait of an often overlooked part of Cairo's architectural heritage.

André Raymond, (ed.). *The Glory of Cairo: An Illustrated History*. Cairo: AUC Press, 2002. A stunning collection of photographs coupled with authoritative texts covering Cairo's urban, artistic, and architectural history.

Max Rodenbeck. *Cairo: The City Victorious*. Cairo: AUC Press, 2000. An insider's history of Cairo; well-written, comprehensive, and highly entertaining—a portrait both epic and intimate of this indomitable city.

Maria Sole Croce and Marcello Bertinetti. *In the Eye of Horus*. Cairo: AUC Press, 2001. Gorgeous coffee-table book featuring bird's-eye views of Cairo and Egypt accompanied by fascinating textual tidbits.

Sherif Sonbol and Tarek Atia. *Mulid! Carnivals of Faith*. Cairo: AUC Press, 1999. A celebration of both the riotous color and the vivacity of the mulid.

James Steele. *An Architecture for People: The Complete Works of Hassan Fathy*. Cairo: AUC Press, 1997. Comprehensive critical overview of the entire output of the famous Egyptian architect, whose championing of affordable, local designs was way ahead of its time.

Desmond Stewart. *Great Cairo, Mother of the World*. Cairo: AUC Press, 1996. A first-class history of the city that reads like a good novel.

Denis Sullivan and Sana Abed-Kotob. *Islam in Contemporary Egypt: Civil Society vs. the State*. Boulder: Lynne Rienner, 1999. An accessible account of the complex relationship of Islamic political movements and the Egyptian government.

RELIGION

The Message of the Quran. Muhammad Asad, translator. Cited by the Blue Guide as "a superb English interpretation of the Arabic text." Kazi Publications, 1997.

The Koran Interpreted, translated with an introduction by Arthur J. Arberry (Oxford and New York: Oxford University Press, 1983) is a version widely preferred by students of Middle East Studies.

Two other good English translations are Marmaduke Pickthall's and Yusuf Ali's.

Karen Armstrong. *Islam: A Short History*. Modern Library, 2002. A concise history of the religion from its inception to the present day.

Karen Armstrong. *The Battle for God: Fundamentalism in Judaism, Christianity and Islam*. London: Harper Perennial, 2004.

Gawdat Gabra, ed. *Be Thou There: The Holy Family's Journey in Egypt*. Cairo: AUC Press, 2001. Traces the Holy Family's stay in Egypt in words and pictures.

Suzanne Haneef. *What Everyone Should Know About Islam and Muslims*. Library of Islam Ltd., 1995 (12th ed.)

Jill Kamil. *Christianity in the Land of the Pharaohs: The Coptic Orthodox Church*. Cairo: AUC Press, 2002.

Ruqaiyyah Waris Maqsood. *Teach Yourself Islam*. London: TeachYourself, 2003 (2nd ed.).

Otto F.A. Meianardus. *Two Thousand Years of Coptic Christianity*. Cairo: AUC Press, 2003.

Mark J. Sedgwick. *Sufism: The Essentials*. Cairo: AUC Press, 2003.

1 WELCOME TO CAIRO

BASIC FACTS AND STATISTICS

Although this is a practical guide, Egypt elicits a touch of the poet in anyone remotely susceptible to its charms. So we precede our bare-bones statistics and facts by urging the reader to first picture a large, nearly square expanse of desert. Superimposed on the square is an eternally blooming lotus flower with a very long curling stem, the River Nile, stretching from south to north. The Delta is the triangular lotus flower, just below which is one large nodule, the city of Cairo, and in the far south, near the Sudanese border, is another, Lake Nasser.

The Delta and the banks of the Nile are almost the only arable land in all of Egypt's one million square kilometers. Nearly all of the country's 77.5 million people (95 percent) live within this three percent of the land, a good quarter of them (19–22 million) in Cairo. No single flower could feed so many, and in fact Egypt imports over half the food it needs for its burgeoning population.

Egypt, or Misr (pronounced 'masr' by its people), is officially known as the Arab Republic of Egypt. It occupies the northeastern corner of Africa, with the Mediterranean Sea its northern border and the Red Sea and its gulfs (of Aqaba and Suez, with the arrowhead of the Sinai Peninsula between them) occupying the bulk of its eastern border. Israel and the Gaza Strip touch Egypt's northeastern corner, Sudan lies to the south, and Libya to the west. Egypt's coastline is nearly 2,500 kilometers long, with the Suez Canal linking the Red Sea to the Mediterranean—a marriage of geographical accident and human technology vital to both Egypt and the world.

PEOPLES AND CULTURES

According to 2005 estimates, the population of Egypt is 77.5 million. The National Center for Mobilization and Statistics states that an Egyptian is born every 23.4 seconds, which accounts for why over a third (37.7 percent) of the population is under fifteen years old, while 40.8 percent is aged between 15 and 40. With its youth and its fertility rate of 2.88 children per woman, it is not surprising that Egypt's annual population growth rate is nearly 1.78 percent. This means that every year, despite some of them dying (on average, at age 69 for men, 73 for women), the number of people in Egypt increases by more than 1.3 million.

Who are the Egyptians? The progeny of peasants and pashas alike assert half-jokingly but nevertheless proudly that they are descended from the pharaohs. The boast is not intended literally; it signifies that they consider themselves ancient Egyptian rather than Arabs or Africans. (Given the fecundity and polygyny of some of the pharaohs, though, the claim may well have some genetic merit!) Throughout Egypt's history, though, and particularly in the urban centers, its people have influenced, been influenced by, and intermixed with people from the east, north, and south as well.

Southward toward Sudan, the tall, dark-skinned Nubians are more evident. Upper Egyptians who are not Nubians refer to themselves proudly as Sa'idis. FellaHiin is the general term for the agrarian peasants, many of whom have migrated from the countryside to the cities to find work. In the deserts and oases there are Bedouins and Berbers. Cairo's mix is notably harmonious, showing little or no overt prejudices, although stereotypes, biases, and plenty of good-natured jokes based on differences abound. The deep divide in Egyptian society is neither racial, geographic, nor religious. It is economic, and it is profound.

In addition, Egypt has always been hospitable to foreigners—sometimes to its detriment. Today, there are approximately 15,000 Americans, 3,000 Britons, 4,500 French, 5,000 Germans, and thousands of other Europeans and Africans living and working in Egypt. There are also many Latin Americans and larger numbers of Middle Easterners, who maintain residences and do business in comparatively freewheeling Cairo, plus Asians from India to the Philippines.

RELIGION

Islam's profound influence is visible—and audible—at every turn: the haunting calls to prayer five times a day from every minaret (now mostly a matter of loudspeakers rather than the unadulterated song of the muezzins) . . . the minarets themselves, spiraling to the skies and putting modern skyscrapers to shame by their beauty . . . the sight of men in gallabiyas or Brooks Brothers suits, on sidewalks, in shops, and in office buildings, breaking to prostrate themselves in prayer . . . the incantations of *in sha'allah* ('God willing') and *il-Hamdulillah* ('praise be to God') punctuating all conversations as naturally as breathing . . . the sudden and total absence of food, drink (even water), and cigarettes all during the days of Ramadan, and the nightlong revels that follow . . . the blood of sacrificed animals on the doors of new homes in hovels and high-rises alike. All exert their undeniable effects on Muslims and on non-Muslims as well, demanding our attention and respect.

Reliable estimates place the percentage of Egyptians who are Muslim at 94 percent, virtually all of whom are Sunni rather than Shi'a Muslims. The divide between these two branches dates to shortly after the death of the Prophet Muhammad (AD 570–632). When he died, the heirs and devotees of the charismatic Prophet, who named no successor, began a family squabble of epic proportions, replete with assassinations and counter-assassinations. Adherents of the Prophet's son-in-law, Ali, became the Shi'a, while those who sided with a series of elected factional leaders became the Sunnis. During all this internecine intrigue, though, Islam spread far and fast, partly as a result of the power of the message of the Quran, partly due to the Prophet's and his followers' military and political stratagems.

The Quran is regarded by Muslims as immutable and infallible. It is the recorded collection of God's revelations given to the Prophet by the angel Gabriel. These the Prophet passed on orally to his followers, who eventually codified them in AD 651; since then no changes whatever have been introduced. In addition, there are two other important bodies of work: the Hadith, the sayings of the Prophet; and the Sunna, precepts based on the example of the Prophet's life. Islamic law (Shari'a) is based mostly on the Quran, partly on the Hadith and the Sunna.

All Muslims are required to follow the Five Pillars of their faith: to declare publicly and sincerely that "There is no god but God and Muhammad is His Prophet" (anyone thus proclaiming is immediately accepted as a Muslim); to pray five times daily toward Mecca; to fast during the month of Ramadan, which was when the Prophet received his first revelations; to make one pilgrimage to Mecca during one's lifetime, given physical and financial ability; and to give alms to the poor or for the defense of Islam.

In principle, Islam is a highly tolerant religion. Both Moses and Jesus are regarded as prophets under Islam, and Jews and Christians are respected as "people of the Book." In practice as well, the vast majority of Muslims, particularly in Egypt, are tolerant of other religions. It is illegal, however, for foreigners to attempt to proselytize, and deportations have been known.

Modern Egyptian law is based partly on the Napoleonic Code and partly on the Shari'a. The center of Islamic jurisprudence is in Cairo at al-Azhar University, the oldest in the world. Muslims from all over the world congregate to study here as they have for over a thousand years. The Grand Imam of al-Azhar is Shaykh Muhammad Sayyid Tantawi, appointed in 1996. He is well regarded by President Mubarak and is considered moderate compared to his highly conservative predecessor.

In addition to Islam, Coptic Christianity (an Orthodox rite) has had a long and enduring influence in Egypt. Current estimates put the number of Coptic Christians at six to ten million, spread throughout the country, with large concentrations in Middle Egypt around Minya and Asyut. The number of Coptic monasteries thriving today, including those at Wadi al-Natrun north of Cairo, provide fascinating glimpses of Coptic Egypt past and present. Six percent of Egyptians are Coptic or members of other Christian denominations. Other Christian sects, including Protestants and Roman and Greek Catholics, are evident in the many crosses that mingle in neighborly fashion with the minarets spanning the skyline. Most of Egypt's substantial and influential Jewish community left the country (along with large numbers of Italians, Greeks, and Maltese) in the adverse political climate of the 1950s. The total Jewish population of Egypt today numbers a few dozen.

MODERN GOVERNMENT AND POLITICAL PARTIES

Egypt's strongly centralized government operates in principle as a political democracy with executive, legislative, and judicial branches. In practice, and along with official democratic features such as a multiparty system, free elections, and a bicameral National Assembly, power resides heavily in the office of the president, supported by a large military bureaucracy, ministry heads

appointed by the president, and a heavily nationalized industrial complex as part of a huge public sector–based economy.

President Muhammad Husni Mubarak is serving his fifth six-year term (through 2011), and is the head of the ruling National Democratic Party (NDP). There are several legal opposition parties, the strongest of which are the Wafd Party (center-right) and the Tagammu Party (leftist). More influential in some senses is the outlawed Muslim Brotherhood. In an unexpected show of electoral success during the 2005 parliamentary elections, independent candidates affiliated to the Muslim Brotherhood won 88 out of the 444 contested seats; the remaining independents won 24 seats, the NDP won 311, the Tagammu Party two, the Wafd Party six, and the Ghad Party one. The 12 remaining seats are still contested. Although the NDP continues to dominate the National Assembly by a two-thirds majority, the new assembly is quite different from that of previous years when the NDP won landslide victories.

Egypt is divided into twenty-six governorates, each with a governor, local councils and ministerial representatives, and other appointed and elected officials. Greater Cairo is divided among three governorates, Giza (west of the Nile), Cairo (east of the Nile), and Qalyubiya (in the northern districts).

ECONOMY

Ever since President Anwar Sadat's 'Open-Door Policy' was introduced in 1974, Egypt has been shifting slowly from a public to a private sector–driven economy. The shift to privatization and foreign investment poses real and imagined threats to the labor force and to the status quo of the powers that be— threats that to date have been effectively staved off by regulations, paperwork, and a legalistic framework that tends to thwart rather than support these changes.

Recent estimates report that 35 percent of the work force of 20 million are employed in the public sector, including the government itself and the military. The private sector accounts for a further 44 percent and the informal sector accounts for 19 percent. Included in the informal sector are the 2.5 million Egyptians working abroad whose remittances are the country's largest sources of foreign currency. Revitalizing the economy might well stem the 'brain drain' of professionals and skilled labor, whose contributions are sorely needed at home. Income from the Suez Canal and tourism follow expatriate remittances as the major sources of foreign currency.

Egypt's most important natural resource is its people—too much of a good thing at present, but representing an enormous labor force and a huge market for local and foreign goods. But since Egypt is otherwise relatively resource-poor as a major world market supplier of anything except cotton (and to a lesser extent gas and oil), the economy is in something of a vise: Egypt produces far more people than it can support and too many of them lack the skills to support themselves. The Central Authority for Public Mobilisation and Statistics (CAPMAS) states that 88 percent of the unemployed are aged between 15 and 30 and that most of them are educated. The average number of workers entering the job market each year exceeds 600,000, yet the Egyptian economy has created only 450,000 jobs per annum during the last decade. The 2004 Egypt Human Development Report emphasizes that jobs for unskilled workers make up as much as 66 percent of employment demand, while the demand for people with higher education is only 17 percent. Unless both these situations change, this resource cannot be 'exploited' to its own advantage.

One more vital natural resource needs to be mentioned: location. Egypt's position on the geographical and political map has always been of paramount significance, but never more so than today. Hence the health of the Egyptian economy is closely monitored—and in fact supported—by the major world powers. Egypt is near, or at the top of the list of international foreign aid recipients overall, and, after Israel, is the largest recipient of US foreign aid. The goal of much of this aid is to help Egypt become economically self-sustaining. It is a goal that will be extraordinarily difficult to reach, in no small part because it is at cross-purposes with another: the donor nations' desire to assure political alliances with Egypt through partial economic dependence.

GEOGRAPHY AND TOPOGRAPHY

Very simply, Egypt is a desert and Egypt is the Nile. The Nile's banks and its Delta are among the richest agricultural land in the world, and beyond is desert almost everywhere.

Each area of the country has its own character. The Sinai Peninsula is perhaps the most dramatic in terms of color and topography, with wadis, mountains (including Mount Catherine, the highest in Egypt, at 2,642 meters), and massifs or high plateaus. The Eastern Desert is largely stony sand punctuated by crags revealing eons of striations to the naked eye and low-lying purple and black mountains set back from the Gulf of Suez. The Western Desert is by far the largest. Parts of it are below sea level and it is here that the major oases are found. The Nile Valley, no more than ten kilometers wide on average, is the narrow, fertile ribbon that, along with the Delta, supports the vast majority of Egypt's population. The Nile Delta is the green fan beginning just north of Cairo where the Nile splits into its remaining two distributaries, the Rashid (Rosetta) and the Dumyat (Damietta) branches. The Fayoum is a fertile depression in the Western Desert watered by an offshoot of the Nile, the Bahr Yusif.

The Aswan High Dam, completed in 1971, is largely a blessing, partly a curse. It created Lake Nasser, one of the world's largest artificial lakes, but drowned villages and archaeological sites. It allowed for controlled irrigation and hence increased the growing season, but raised the water table throughout the Nile Valley, lifting buried salts to the surface that are gradually poisoning the land. The people of the river are now subject less to the whims of nature, but more to the effects, both good and bad, of human technology. And rarely, as if to reassert its dominance, Mother Nature cries long and hard. It rains, even in the deserts, flooding ancient tombs, washing away roads and villages, and reconfiguring the land.

The Toshka Project, initiated in 1996, reclaims approximately 1.5 million acres of land in the Western Desert by pumping 5.5 billion cubic meters of water a year from Lake Nasser. The reclamation of land aims to relieve the Nile Valley and create employment in the areas of agriculture, industry, and tourism. Again, as before the building of the Aswan Dam, the land and its people rely on nature's generousity to provide the rains that will water the Nile for years of plenty rather than drought.

EGYPT PAST

Assuming that most visitors and residents will explore their particular interests in Egypt's vast history with more detailed guides, the following is a brief chronological introduction to the main periods in Egyptian history, contributed by Dr. Lisa Sabbahy.

ca. 5000 BC Predynastic cultures with agriculture and domesticated animals settle in both Upper and Lower Egypt.

ca. 3300 BC Upper and Lower Egypt share a single, unified culture under early kings, and the earliest hieroglyphic writing appears.

ca. 3100 BC Pharaonic history begins with Dynasty I under the rule of King Menes, and Memphis is founded as Egypt's capital.

The three main periods of ancient Egyptian civilization are referred to as kingdoms. These were times when Upper and Lower Egypt were united under one king. The periods that come between the kingdoms are times of instability and political disunity. Kings are divided into dynasties, which for the most part indicate a family bloodline.

ca. 2696–2181 BC Old Kingdom (Dynasties 3–6) Highly centralized state centered on the king, who ruled from Memphis and was buried in a pyramid nearby at Giza, Saqqara, Abu Sir, or Dahshur. This kingdom is often referred to as the "Pyramid Age." By the end of the Old Kingdom, provincial officials rival the power of the king, and climate change brings about drought and famine.

ca. 2041–1786 BC Middle Kingdom (Dynasties 11–13) A Theban king, Nebhepetre Mentuhotep reunites Egypt by military force. Under the 12th Dynasty, art and literature flourish, Egypt expands to the south, colonizing Nubia. Toward the end of the Middle Kingdom, nomads from Syro-Palestine, called the Hyksos, begin settling in the Delta. The kings of the Middle Kingdom still build pyramids. They can be seen at Dahshur, and further south at Lisht, Lahun, and Hawara.

ca. 1552-1069 BC New Kingdom (Dynasties 18–20) This is the best-documented period of ancient Egyptian history, and the time when Egypt ruled a great empire in the Near East, extending from northern Syria south to Sudan. The New Kingdom begins with the expulsion of the Hyksos invaders by King Ahmose. The kings who follow in the 18th Dynasty include: Hatshepsut, the queen who became pharaoh; Tuthmose III, the great builder of the Empire; Amenhotep III, the great temple builder; Akhenaten, who moved to Tell al-Amarna to worship his deity the Aten; and Tutankhamen, famous for his tomb. The best-known king of the later New Kingdom is the great Ramesses II of the 19th Dynasty. Thebes becomes an important religious center, with the temple of Amen at Karnak on the east bank of the river at Thebes, and the royal burials and funeral temples on the west. By the end of the New Kingdom the empire has been lost, civil war rages in Thebes, and the High Priest of Amun eclipses the power of the king.

Following the New Kingdom are 700 years of political stability, as well as foreign invasions and warfare. Egypt is invaded by Libyans, Sudanese, Assyrians, Persians, and finally Greeks, when Alexander the Great is victorious in 332 BC. Alexander spends about a year in Egypt, during which time he designs his city, Alexandria, and consults the oracle in Siwa Oasis.

323–330 BC Ptolemaic Period Upon the death of Alexander the Great, his general Ptolemy takes Egypt and rules as Ptolemy I. He and Ptolemy II are responsible for the building of Alexandria, famous for its lighthouse and library. Cleopatra VII rules as the last of the Ptolemies, and struggles to retain her rule with the support, first of Caesar, and then Mark Anthony.

30 BC–AD 641 Roman and Byzantine Periods Emperor Augustus seizes Egypt after the deaths of Cleopatra and Mark Anthony. Egypt is heavily taxed by the Romans, and supplies the grain for Roman bread. There are rebellions against Roman rule, particularly in Upper Egypt, and the Roman Emperors add to the great temples of Upper Egypt begun by the Ptolemies, portraying themselves as traditional pharaohs of Egypt. In AD 395 Egypt becomes part of the Eastern Roman, or Byzantine, Empire.

AD 640–1805 The Arrival of the Arabs and Islam The Arabs camped at Fustat besiege and take the fortress of Babylon in 642. Egypt is ruled by a succession of caliphates: Umayyad (658–750), Abbasid (750–868),

Tulunid (868–905), Abbasid (905–935), Ikhshidid (935–969), Fatimid (969–1171), Ayyubid (1171–1250), Bahri Mamluk (1250–1382), Burgi Mamluk (1382–1517), and Ottoman (1517–1805).

1805–1952 The Egyptian Royal Family Muhammad Ali becomes governor of Egypt under the Ottoman Turks in 1805. He soon declares independence and begins a ruling dynasty, which lasts until the abdication of King Farouk in 1952. His son the Khedive Ismail transforms the city of Cairo during his period of rule, 1863–1879. The area that is now downtown is changed from a swampy plain into midans (squares) and boulevards echoing the city of Paris. The British occupy Egypt militarily in 1882, and in 1922 Egypt becomes a British protectorate. From that time on there are three main forces engaged in a political struggle: the British, the king, who is beholden to the British, and a strong Egyptian nationalistic movement. This struggle culminates in the Egyptian revolution of 1952, led by Gamal Abd al-Nasser.

EGYPT PRESENT

Nasser solidified his power and his heroic stature by successfully nationalizing the Suez Canal and resisting the joint British–French–Israeli invasion that resulted in 1956. The windfall, economic and political, allowed him to build the Aswan High Dam with the help of the Soviets, to whom Nasser leaned but never capitulated. Although he was tarnished in his own eyes by the loss of the Sinai Peninsula to the Israelis in 1967, he retained his esteem and his presidency until his death in 1970. The country's economy, however, took a nose-dive during Nasser's rule thanks to his autocratic form of socialism. Takeovers of private lands and industries alienated aristocrats and industrialists, many of whom left Egypt for good, and created the ponderous state and military bureaucracies that still shackle Egyptian society.

Egypt's third president, Anwar Sadat, had a more international and democratic outlook than his predecessor. He enhanced his power at home greatly by recapturing part of the Sinai Peninsula from the Israelis during the October War of 1973. But in 1977, when he made the overtures to Israel that produced the Camp David Accords in 1978, Sadat's fate was sealed in the Arab world. He became a pariah. And despite massive infusions of Western aid, the plight of Egypt's poor worsened. His 'Open-Door' economic policies did not make up for the loss of food subsidies, and the hungry poor were ripe prey for the blandishments of Islamic nationalism and militarism.

Sadat's assassination in 1981 brought the current president, Muhammad Husni Mubarak, to power. He was elected to an unprecedented fifth term in 2005. Mubarak has adroitly managed a series of domestic and international crises. Relations with Egypt's Arab allies in the Middle East, though tense, are holding, and the country's preeminent position among them has been firmly reestablished. This despite Mubarak's continuing efforts to broker the peace between Israel and all its neighbors, including the Palestine National Authority.

The same pragmatism that characterizes Mubarak's regime in the region appeared to be working internally as well. Partly as a result of a 1991 agreement with the International Monetary Fund, inflation and trade tariffs have been reduced considerably. More importantly, Egypt was the beneficiary of one of the biggest foreign debt write-offs in history as a direct result of Egypt's alliance with the West during the 1990–91 Gulf War. Egypt was also required as part of the deal to revert to a privately fueled capitalist economy. Despite these measures, however, Egypt's unemployment rate remains high and the gap between rich and poor ever-growing.

EGYPT FUTURE

Egypt's path toward 'progress' at the opening of the twenty-first century is beset by some enormous boulders, political and socioeconomic. The definition of progress itself is a key one. Will it be based upon a largely secular democratic model, or upon a conservative Islamic model with strongly socialistic overtones? Each view ignores the other at its peril. And each will ultimately have to accommodate the other to devise palpable solutions to severe problems. Among them: overpopulation; a true unemployment rate of at least 10 percent plus endemic underemployment; a rise in headline-grabbing terrorist attacks; severe degradation of the environment, whether land, air, or water; tremendous income disparities between rich and poor; and illiteracy rates of 53 percent among women and 31.7 percent among men. To put this catalog into perspective without minimizing any of it, it might be noted that many of these problems are shared by a number of 'highly developed' countries as well.

With financial and technical help from its foreign allies, Egypt is making some headway in addressing its problems. To bolster the economy overall, both foreign investment and privatization of much of the public sector are being pursued more aggressively than in the past. And to offset the economic and social upheavals these moves entail, the Social Fund for Development (SFD) was inaugurated in 1991 to address five interlinked issues: family planning, health, education, women in development, and poverty alleviation. The idea seems to be that the SFD will cushion the blows of economic reform until its benefits trickle down to the poor, while simultaneously empowering them to influence their own lives through education, training, micro-enterprise development, and so on. Untold numbers of non-governmental organizations, plus many charitable organizations (including the Muslim Brotherhood), also work directly on these development projects.

CAIRO TODAY

Tourists in Egypt sometimes ignore its capital. A quick ride from the airport, two nights in a lowdown or upscale hotel, one at each end of the trip, a nod, if that, at the Egyptian Museum—more likely shopping in Khan al-Khalili instead—and then off to Luxor and Aswan for cultural enlightenment or to the Red Sea resorts for fun in the sun. But Cairo, marvelous and maddening, and always throbbing with life, is well worth exploring for its own sake.

Cairo is a city-lover's city. Its most obvious asset is the river that runs through it, its genuinely accessible banks dotted with cafés and gardens everywhere. Then there is the architecture: Cairo is home to some of the world's most splendid Islamic monuments. Museums and galleries? There are plenty more than those listed in most guidebooks. Although Cairo may not rate as a gourmet's paradise, there are hundreds of appealing places to get a good meal, a few in the 'splurge' category, but many more quite reasonable. Night owls will be relieved to find the nightlife hot and heavy if one knows where to look. Sports fanatics find themselves in good company in Cairo, with the weather and wealth of facilities cooperating fully. A daunting and unique array of shopping, the Opera complex, green enclaves, a 'neighborhood' feel, contrasts galore—are all at one's doorstep in Cairo.

Cairo has its 'too much' problems as well, with one significant exception—and that is crime, of which until now there has been mercifully little. But there is too much noise, pollution, traffic, and dirt, and far too many people. Overall, though, Cairo works, and it is working on its problems as well. Lead-free gasoline and emission controls have been introduced to make the air cleaner. Trucks are banned from the city's streets during the day. Most of the garbage in middle-class neighborhoods gets picked up by the *zabbaliin* garbage-collectors, and an army of street-sweepers keep the dirt at bay—barely. And the Metro is a marvel—clean, quiet, and safe—which, as it expands its tentacles, will further alleviate the traffic.

Less successful is the attempt to get the Cairenes out of Cairo and into the new desert cities. Cairo dwellers are a gregarious and urbane lot, unwilling in the main to exchange their crowded but lively and familiar conditions for the starkness and isolation of raw new cities in the desert. Thirty years ago, though, all of Giza was a suburb—the sticks—and look at it now. The comparison is not fully apt, however, as the new cities lack something that exerts a powerful psychological pull: the Nile. But because Cairo changes with dizzying speed, see pages 98–99 for information about new areas: 10th Ramadan, 6th October, and Qattamiya.

We hope this new edition of *The Guide* persuades you to share the belief of the majority of Cairo residents both native and expatriate: that modern-day Cairo is an eminently livable and even lovable city.

PRACTICAL MATTERS FOR ALL VISITORS

CLIMATE—AND AESTHETICS

The **Climate** chart at the front of the book gives the hot and cold facts. But what newcomers want to know is how the weather feels and how to dress for it. Many visitors are chagrined to find they have not brought remotely the right clothing for the climate, weather-wise or culture-wise. We therefore address both here.

Fall and early spring are touted by many guidebooks as being the best seasons in

Cairo, but in fact they are almost nonexistent in terms of temperature moderation. Winters are marvelous—crisp, breezy, and invigorating, sometimes stretching from late October into April. You will, believe it or not, probably appreciate having a winter coat for this season—maybe not fur or down, but warm nevertheless. Fortunately, Cairo shops carry a good selection of coats and jackets, thereby obviating the stuffed-sausage look caused by excess layering. A turtleneck shirt plus a sweater over it suits warm-blooded mammals of both sexes, both indoors and out, as do cozy bathrobes and slippers inside the house. Handy additions and alternatives might include that old fifties standby, the sweater set, or leggings with long tunics. For women's feet, socks plus boots work well with skirts or slacks and are easy to dust off with a brush. Since Cairo's sidewalks and streets are incredibly dusty at best, filth-strewn at worst, you will stay not only warmer but cleaner in these get-ups than with pantyhose and pumps. Men can have their shoes shined on any corner for a song, but we've never seen a woman having it done.

Summer in all its sullen heat and humidity can suddenly smack right up against winter. For Cairo, this definitely does not mean a blithe baring of the flesh for either men or women. Although Cairenes are accustomed to seeing foreigners wandering their city, the dress code on the street is largely conservative. Foreign women, especially, should leave the spandex bike shorts and midriff-baring tank tops at home, unless, of course, you want to be hassled endlessly with cat-calls, car horns, and declarations that you are "beyoodiful, very very beyoodiful." Settle instead for loose, comfortable cotton clothing with highish necklines and hems below the knee. Men, meanwhile, can don light-weight sport shirts or t-shirts, and slacks. The sleeveless issue for women is a matter of personal taste and comfort, with many expatri-

ate residents prudently advising against it, and other chic Cairenes saying modest sleeveless-ness is fine in the city. One can comfortably straddle the issue by carrying a short-sleeved shirt or shawl.

Outside Cairo, it's another matter entirely. There is almost no shade anywhere, and the sun is punishing, so make your own, winter or summer. If you have the élan to carry off a parasol, do so; otherwise, some sort of floppy hat plus a loose, light-colored jacket or long-sleeved blouse work well. But since the temperature plummets late afternoon through early morning the further you go into the desert, warm sweaters are vital except perhaps in high summer. The modesty factor increases in the countryside as well, with men, as usual, having more leeway than women.

A note on shoes: the best foot forward is not sandal-clad except at home or perhaps at a beach resort. Feet get sunburned and filthy very fast, and sand is gritty and uncomfortable. We hate to admit it, but sneakers are a practical alternative. If you deplore the look, though, rubber-soled loafers, espadrilles, and rubber-soled ballet flats for women work well. They look okay, can be slipped off easily for mosque visits, and allow for a reasonable amount of clambering about pyramids and monuments.

Rain is usually a non-issue in Cairo except for rare, brief, and welcome showers in winter and early spring (though on rare occasions the city can suffer sudden down-pours that flood the streets). But the *khamsi-in,* the hot southerly wind from the desert, is another matter. When it pays a visit, usually between February and April, it gusts and whistles into every nook and cranny—doors, windows, eyes, nose, and mouth. The skies turn a murky yellow with sand and dust. For fans of strange weather phenomena, it is quite appealing and dramatic in its way. The *khamsiin* can blow for seven or eight hours at a time, but two or three is more common, and it is rare to have more than one or two a week. Do not go into the desert during a *khamsiin,* obviously. It is dangerous. And even in the city, beware of loose signboards, rickety scaffolding, and dancing garbage.

Pollution, too, affects the weather and one's lungs, nose, eyes, and skin. A couple of large cement plants near Cairo spew their cloying dust into the air. Cairenes smoke like fiends indoors and out, but a few restaurants now actually have non-smoking areas. Traffic fumes are unpleasant and unhealthy; Cairo traffic cops' blood has among the highest lead levels in the world, and their sperm counts are consequently among the lowest. Airborne sand particles from the desert are the housekeeper's bane, but also contribute to Cairo's magnificent sunsets. In all, Cairo is not ideal for contact lens wearers, and sensitive skin suffers some here. Coping mechanisms include eye drops at the ready, heavy-duty all-over moisturizers, and sunscreen always.

Finally, although they are rare, earthquakes do occur. A very bad one hit Cairo in 1992, causing significant damage and loss of life. A milder one struck in November 1995 near Sharm al-Sheikh, but shook up Cairo considerably as well, with aftershocks lasting into the next week. Supposedly, buildings constructed in Cairo after 1992 are quakeproof: they'll shake, rattle, and roll, but not tumble. You are supposed to head for a reinforced corner or stand under a doorway during earthquakes. But realistically, they are over so fast that there is barely time to do so.

TRAVEL AND TRANSPORT

ARRIVAL BY AIR
Airfares from Europe and North America to Cairo vary wildly depending on season, political climate, and your bargain-hunting skills. Budget travelers know to check the fine print in the travel sections of major

newspapers for the best deals, and then to check again carefully before forking over any money. Recent economy class round trips New York–Cairo have fallen in price as GATT changes are slowly introduced, hovering between $850 and $1,400. London–Cairo round trips are generally in the region of £400. And Europeans on organized tour can get great deals on airfare and hotel rates direct to Sharm al-Sheikh: around £500 for a week.

Cairo International Airport, twenty kilometers northeast of the city, is undergoing major expansion. It improved by leaps and bounds when the new Terminal 2 for international flights opened in 1980 (before that, it vied with Bombay's airport as one of the world's least pleasant airports). Today, however, the airport complex has been completely remodeled, with two new terminals added. What is still known to the public as "the old airport" has been renovated and is a pleasant and easy facility with a superb duty free section, good restaurants, and coffee bars. Terminal 3 opened in 2005. It is spacious, comfortable, and easy to move through. Now, Terminal 2 (and still referred to as the "new airport") is run-down, and renovations have begun. Because of this, the road to Terminal 2 has been diverted to a parking lot where you are encouraged to board a bus that will take you there. However if you are in a private car or a taxi, you can go directly to the terminal. Soon, another terminal, 4, will open, but it is not clear for which airlines. Because of all these changes, the roads and parking areas are confusing, *and it is essential to check with your airline the exact terminal you fly into and out of.* There are plans for a new airport at 6th of October but not in the near future.

You can certainly get through customs and into Cairo on your own, but if you are short on patience or pluck, or cannot meet Aunt Ida yourself, you can opt for a meet-and-assist service (**Airport Meet-&-Assist**) like

American Express's. Charming people will whisk you through passport control and customs and deposit you into a limo car for a hassle-free ride to your destination. For meet-and-assist services and transportation to downtown Cairo, American Express charges LE75 for one person. You will pay LE20 more if you are going to Heliopolis and LE120 if you are going to Maadi. If you are willing to pay for the convenience, it is a godsend. No lines, no excessive pawing of luggage, no haggling with taxi drivers.

If you do take a taxi, LE50 or 60 (per trip, not per passenger) is the going foreigner rate to downtown, the lower figure only for those with well-honed bargaining skills and enough patience to indulge in the pastime. Age, sex, clothing, skin color, facility in Arabic, number of passengers, amount of luggage, and time of day may all be involved in the taxi driver's reckoning. When traffic is light (before 7 am, very late at night, or on Fridays), you can be at the Nile in twenty minutes, but otherwise, count on close to an hour. And during the pilgrimage-to-Mecca season, which lasts for about two weeks around the Eid al-Adha, seventy days after the end of Ramadan, it could take nearly that just to get into or out of the airport, as carloads of wellwishers waving white flags cram the roadways to joyously send off or greet the departing or returning pilgrims. It is best to have a reservation made or the name of a hotel in mind, to avoid being driven to a hotel owned by the driver's brother, uncle, or second cousin twice removed, or one that offers the driver a hefty commission for your patronage but may not be to your taste or price range.

Buses and minibuses from the airport are also available. Private mini-buses offering door-to-door service cost LE60 plus a tip. Limousines range between LE115 and LE125. Inquire at the airport or consult one of the more budget-oriented guides for details. One can, of course, jump right into the fray by renting a car at the airport. However, we strongly advise against it, unless you speak and read Arabic. Also it is expensive—about $40–85 per day depending on the car model—and an international driver's license is necessary. Read the section on **Cars in Cairo** (Chapter 3) before making your decision.

Reconfirming airline reservations for both domestic and international flights, by the way, is taken somewhat seriously in Egypt. Overbookings and flight cancellations are commonplace, and reconfirming may give you a competitive edge and a seat. (See **Airlines**.)

GETTING IN AND OUT BY OTHER MEANS

You can still travel overland by bus to Jordan and to Jerusalem from Cairo reasonably comfortably and very inexpensively. But border crossing formalities can take forever, especially to/from Israel.

Travel to Israel may necessitate either a second passport or an Israeli visa stamped on a separate piece of paper, as having an Israeli visa in your 'real' passport could cause difficulties when entering certain Arab countries. Check with both the Israeli Embassy and your own (**Embassies & Consulates**) for the most up-to-date details.

VISAS AND PERMITS

Put off your introduction to Egyptian bureaucracy for as long as possible by getting visas when you arrive at the airport (Cairo, Luxor, or Hurghada). It is cheaper and easier than getting them at Egyptian consulates abroad. All that anyone except diplomats can get is a thirty-day visitor's visa initially. Your passport must be valid for six months, and you can get a multiple-entry stamp, but it costs more than double the price of the single entry visa ($15 currently). If you are staying longer, or plan to work and live here, the necessary visa extensions and changes are done here, not from abroad. Even if you are Mr. or Ms. Hotshot from MegaCompany with reams of paper and letterheads that show your official status, either let your company handle the visa or do it here yourself. Otherwise, you can spend long hours and more money and make numerous return visits for absolutely nothing more than you will get more quickly on arrival. For temporary residents, you can easily extend your tourist visa up to one year at the Mugamma.

The formality of foreigners having to register at the local police station upon arrival was suspended for many nationalities (including US and UK citizens and most Europeans) in late 2000. Check with your hotel or your company to ascertain current regulations.

In a government move to entice more foreign tourism, Germans and Italians are now allowed to enter Egypt carrying only a valid ID card.

THE MUGAMMA

This daunting pre-revolutionary monstrosity on the south side of Midan al-Tahrir strikes terror in the heart of any Kafka fan. But fear not: it can be efficiently negotiated with a bit of know-how, and all sorts of complexities have been considerably streamlined. Just the same, if your company or educational institution offers support in obtaining visas and passport registration, by all means take advantage of it. The Mugamma is open from 8 am until 3:30 pm, except Thursdays and Fridays when it is closed, but individual windows can close at any time, especially after 1:30 pm. Go early to avoid the crowds.

To extend a tourist visa or pay fines, head straight upstairs to the first floor and turn right. Proceed directly to the 'forms' section and buy the proper paperwork before going to the visa windows. This will save a lot of time. A visa application with all the stamps will cost around LE8–15. Currently, a one-year tourist visa extension costs LE38. Fees for a one-year, resident, work permitted visa are LE158.15; for a one-year, no work permitted visa, the fee is LE83.10; and

for a three-year resident visa with an Egyptian spouse, the fee is LE98.10. For the most common infractions, fees are LE103.40 for overstay fine and late registration fine (some nationalities) LE73.40. To give you that in-the-know veneer of confidence, here are the functions and numbers of various windows:

	Windows
Temporary residence for work-permit seekers/non-Arab	40
Temporary residence for tourist visa extensions	38–39
Payment of fines	37
Form purchase	50
Stamp purchase	43–44
Lost passport	42

Why this emphasis on residence, temporary or otherwise? Because as a resident, you pay Egyptian rather than foreigner rates for in-country airfares and hotels throughout Egypt—for example, LE587 versus LE1091 for a Cairo–Luxor roundtrip air ticket.

If you are lucky, you may find someone who speaks some English at the Mugamma. A patient Arabic-speaking friend or a Mr. Fixit makes things easier. And certainly go armed with reams of passport photos. Some small remuneration will be in order if you decide to avail yourself of the services of the 'guides' outside who offer their Mugamma expertise, but the negotiations involved in doing so might be more protracted and ultimately unpleasant than just doing it yourself.

CUSTOMS—CAVEATS AND CURIOSITIES

Alcohol is seen as *Haram*—forbidden, a sin—by most Muslims but its consumption is tolerated here more than in many other countries of the Middle East. Hence the fairly moderate approach described below with respect to its importation.

Currently, adults may bring one liter of alcohol and two cartons of cigarettes in their luggage. Presumably, this includes what you buy from the duty-free airport shops abroad, and you are liable for customs duty and/or confiscation on the excess. At the duty-free shop in Cairo Airport, you may purchase an additional four cartons of cigarettes and four liters of alcohol. If you don't take advantage of this, you can also take your passport to one of the **Duty-Free Shops** in Cairo within twenty-four hours of arrival, where you can purchase yet more cigarettes, but only three liters of alcohol, not four. (Or you can do both if they neglect to stamp your passport at the airport duty-free.) A carton of imported beer can be substituted for one liter of alcohol at any of the duty-frees.

If you will be living and working in Cairo and are sending air or sea shipments of household effects, or if you have diplomatic status or some of the privileges thereof, these restrictions do not apply. Depending on your nationality, you may be able to ship as much wine and other spirits as you like. But do inquire first with your shipper (see **Movers or Relocation Consultants** for Cairo-based ones) and your employer, as these regulations change frequently. (More details on shipment of household goods are found in Chapter 3.)

Cellular telephones no longer require permits, as long as you only have one, but color printers do, even the most basic model. Fax machines and photocopiers do not require import permits, but they are problematic—although computers (including laptops) and normal telephones are not. CDs and videocassettes, but not video games, may attract the attention of customs agents and censors, but then again, since censorship does not officially exist, they might not. If all this seems arbitrary and vague, it is—at least to the newcomer. To be on the safe side, declare major items of electronic equipment when you enter the country or on your shipping lists.

The pros and cons of your many options for transport in and about Cairo are reviewed here.

Walking: This is the best—the most fun—and, over walkable distances, the fastest. Do consider it once you have recovered from your alarm at the chaotic traffic and the condition of most sidewalks. Crossing the streets encircling Midan al-Tahrir is the best way to practice the art of pedestrian survival; it doesn't get any worse, and once you have mastered it, you are a pro. Simply wait for a crowd or a bus crossing where you want to cross, and blend right in. The crowd or the bus will be your buffer against certain death. After a few successful crossings, you will be ready to take on the Leader of the Pack role yourself. Then reward yourself with a cold Stella at the shisha terrace of the Nile Hilton (there is now a minimum charge during the day, but believe us, you'll feel you deserve it). There are also underground Metro tunnels crisscrossing Midan al-Tahrir, but then you miss the astounding patter of the potato-peeler salesman, the flirting of the AUC students, and the throbbing hubbub of this one of Cairo's many hearts.

The Metro: Cairo's miracle. LE1 ($0.17) will take you from one corner of Cairo to the other. The metro is clean and extremely easy to move through. Maps are available in the *Cairo: The Practical Guide Maps* and most other guidebooks or on the Internet at *www.urbanrail.net/ af/cairo. htm.* The metro is open from 5:30 am to midnight in the winter, with trains running at peak times every 5–6 minutes and every 8–10 minutes at other times. In the summer the metro is open until 1 am. There are now two lines: one north–south, on the east bank of the Nile, with 34 stops between Helwan and El Marg; the other, running north–south–west, from Shubra via Tahrir to Giza. There are stations in Maadi, Coptic Cairo, Midan al-Tahrir, Ramsis Train Station, and Saray al-Qubba, within easy reach of Heliopolis. A third line is underway from Imbaba and Mohandiseen to the airport. The Metro is clean, safe, cool, and relatively quiet. The first two cars are reserved for women, but women can also ride in the others, mostly without being bothered. If someone annoys you, a loud shout of *'eeb* ('shame!') will do the trick. In sum, riders of London's Underground and New York City's subways will think they have died and gone to heaven. But remember that the Metro caters to workers and residents, not tourists; hence, with few exceptions, it does not stop at prime tourist spots. And remember to keep your ticket for exiting. If not, you'll quickly be slapped with an LE10 fine.

Some useful stops

Helwan—Marg/Helwan: Although dilapidated, the sites are unusual—wax museum, Japanese Garden, and sulfur spa popular in the 1920s.

Maadi—Marg/Helwan: Has tree-lined streets, a popular shopping street, Road 9, and in the springtime, the Tree Lovers Association has an annual Maadi tree appreciation walk-about.

Mar Girgis—Marg/Helwan: These are Cairo's roots. Visit the remnants of a Roman fortress, ancient churches, synagogues, mosques, the ancient site of Fustat, handicraft workshops, and, by 2009, the Civilization Museum.

Mubarak—Shubra/Giza and Marg/Helwan: for Ramsis railway station.

Sadat–Shurbra/Giza and Marg/Helwan: for Midan al-Tahrir, the Egyptian Museum, and Downtown.

El Matareya—Marg/Helwan: for the ancient Obelisk of Senusert I and the temple of the god of the Sun, Ra. It's also a short taxi ride to the Virgin's Tree.

Opera—Shubra/Giza: as of 2006, this metro stop is closed due to security concerns but one day it may open again, providing easy access to the Opera House.

Cairo University—Shubra/Giza: a short walk to the Giza Zoo and Orman Botanical Gardens.

Heliopolis Metro: An above-ground trolley system known as the Metro in Heliopolis still functions, just.

Buses: One look at Cairo's old municipal buses—rusted sardine-cans on wheels—will put off anyone with more than a few piasters in their pocket. Avoid them unless you want a vivid reminder of what many resilient Cairenes cheerfully put up with. And if you do decide to try the buses, wear sneakers, carry no money, and steel yourself for a world-class athletic event to board and exit. The older white buses are being replaced, and green buses are beginning to dominate the streets. A ride in the former costs 50 piasters, while the green buses (sometimes air-conditioned) are cleaner and cost LE1–2. Destination boards and route numbers are written in Arabic at the front and side of the bus. Useful routes: Tahrir to airport #400 (terminal 1 and 2); Tahrir to Pyramids/Mena House #997; Tahrir to Citadel/Ibn Tulun #951 and #154. Air-conditioned coaches run from the Pyramids to the airport (#355, 357) and are a welcome introduction; #356 starts from Midan 'Abd al-Mun'im Riyad next to Ramses Hilton Hotel and is the most comfortable way to Heliopolis and the airport in summer.

Minibuses, microbuses, and service taxis: These are the choice of budget-conscious Cairenes and foreigners when their feet will not quite cover the distance. The government-run white-with-an-orange-stripe minibuses have fixed routes, fixed fares, and fixed stops; microbuses and service taxis are government-licensed, privately-owned vans and Peugeots that also operate on fixed routes but have scaled fares and no fixed stops—you just get in and get out where you want. You can get to the Pyramids from 'Abd al-Mun'im Riyad on minibuses #82 and #83 for less than LE1 in the same time it will take a taxi for LE5–10. Also from 'Abd al-Mun'im Riyad, you can ride minibuses #155 to Maadi and #49 to Zamalek. If you are living in one part of town but working in another, find the nearest minibus stop or just look for the microbus vans on main thoroughfares and shout out your destination to fellow passengers. This is the cheapest plausible way to get to Roxy in Heliopolis (minibus #35 from 'Abd al-Mun'im Riyad for LE1).

River buses: These stop at various spots on both banks of the Nile between the Television building and Old Cairo, as well as going north to the Nile barrages at weekends, when they're crammed with noisy revelers. They only operate up to 4 pm.

Taxis: Since most foreign visitors and residents will use taxis exclusively, as do many middle- to upper-middle-class Cairenes, some exposition of this subject is required. In March 2006, a new fleet of yellow, air-conditioned taxis, Capital Taxi, City Cab, and Cairo Radio Cab, were introduced into Cairo. They are metered: LE3.50 base fare with LE1 per kilometer. For the time being, you hail the taxi but there will be taxi stands as well as a number to call. Blue Cab offers quality and reliable service with door to door service, for reservations and inquiries phone: 760-9717 or 760-9616. The complete price list for destinations throughout Cairo is at *www.thebluecab.com*.

Hotel taxis generally charge a lot more than a taxi you hail on the street. A kilometer away: LE10; airport: LE100; Saqqara round-trip: LE150. If you are rich and a temporary visitor to Cairo, it doesn't matter, but if you live here, it does. On the other hand, some of the most useful people you will meet initially come from the hotel taxi ranks. Most know their way around, have decent cars, and speak at least a bit of English. The older drivers tend to have more foreign language skills and far better manners than the younger ones, some of whom are surly and aggressive once they have wheedled you into their car and then act unable to get you anywhere but where they want you to go. In their defense, though, they have very tough jobs—dependent on the ups and downs of tourism, having to cope with maddening traffic, in competition with their colleagues, and regularly dispensing baksheesh to the pashas who rule the hotels' driveways and curbsides.

Once you have an idea of what to pay, it is easier and cheaper to hail the black-and-white taxis on the street. What to pay depends not only on the distance traveled but also on time of day, state of the traffic, and number of passengers: as a rough guide, most journeys within the Dokki–Mohandiseen–Zamalek–Downtown area normally fall in a LE4–10 range; Downtown to Heliopolis or Maadi LE15–20; Downtown to the Airport LE40–50. During rush hours, don't hesitate to share. Just call out your destination to any cab, occupied or not. Disregard the meter, even if it is on. Since meters are rarely used, neither is tipping. Don't haggle over the price before getting in; it is a futile pastime that will last the entire length of the ride and beyond. Just get in knowing about what to pay, and pay when you exit. If the driver asks beforehand, tell him what you will pay—and if he balks and you know it is fair, hail the next cab. Women should avoid sitting in the front seat.

Taxi drivers the world over are a cynical lot, with good reason, and Cairo's are no different. But the bulk of them are surprisingly kind, affable, and patient. For every negative anecdote you will hear, there is a corresponding one about a guy who returns a stranger's full wallet untouched, makes sure his passenger does not get swindled in the markets, or watches over a cranky toddler with good humor, skill, and affection while Mama confers with the butcher. Many drivers have mobile phones, and once you establish a relationship, you can call them up for efficient, reliable service—and an opportunity to practice your growing Arabic vocabulary. Finding a few good taxi drivers early on may help your adjustment to Cairo.

Limos: They sound like a glamorous and expensive alternative, but they are neither. Limousine Misr (**Taxi & Limousine Services**), for example, charges LE168 plus mileage for six hours' Cairo running, in good, air-conditioned cars with English-speaking drivers. To rent a Toyota for 12 hours, the cost is approximately LE345 plus mileage after 50 kilometers and a relatively new Mercedes LE660 plus mileage. These amounts are doubled for 24 hours and longer distances.

CAIRO FOR PEOPLE WITH PHYSICAL DISABILITIES

. . . is murder! Major hotels and a few of the major tourist attractions are getting better in this regard, but it is tough getting around. The sidewalks and streets are hard on pedestrians, period; those using wheelchairs or canes require even more determination than usual. If you have a hearing loss, you must be extraordinarily attentive to traffic. Likewise for the blind, although people are generally very accommodating when you want help. But it is probably unwise to submit a seeing-eye dog to the general mayhem.

Generally, dogs are not acceptable in public areas and most people are not comfortable with dogs. It is more important to have a companion as an escort through the chaotic traffic and maneuvering over the sidewalks (if any) and pavement. However, Egyptians are willing to help, which makes up for lack of facilities.

If you are traveling in Egypt, airports are equipped with ramps and lifts. Cairo airport has toilets for the disabled, which may not be the case in airports in other areas of the country. For trips and transportation advice, contact a specialized agent such as Egypt for All, *www.egyptforall.com.*

Most five-star hotels are disabled-friendly, having special rooms with wide doors for wheelchairs, and bathrooms with support bars next to the toilet and showers. However, most three and four star hotels are not equipped for the disabled, with the exception of Camel Dive hotel in Sharm al-Sheikh, Domina Nuweiba hotel in Nuweiba, Shams Safaga hotel in Safaga, and Three Corners Rihana Resort in al-Gouna. Hotels that are on ground level are good choices for wheelchair users as is investigating special wheels that make mobility possible on the sand.

Most of the major museums have ramps and elevators. It may take investigating and planning, but sightseeing in Cairo is possible. The pyramids, citadel, and even Khan al-Khalili are accessible by bus. Internationally, for information about traveling with a disability within Egypt, contact Barbara Jacobson at Flying Wheels Travel, *www.flyingwheelstravel.com.* Locally, contact Dr. Mohamed Gamal at Enjoy Tours in Cairo *www.enjoytours.org.* They provide specialized attention for travelers with special needs: wheelchair, dialysis, impaired vision, the deaf, and travelers with oxygen cylinders.

NAVIGATING BY LANDMARKS

Street names sometimes get revamped to honor this or that politician, and the same street can also change names from one end to the other. Furthermore, the giving and getting of directions, seemingly regardless of whether you speak Arabic, results in a great many well-meant social exchanges, but not usually in getting you where you want to go. Finally, terms like 'next to,' 'behind,' 'across from,' and so on, can be very broadly—like, a kilometer broadly—

interpreted. What to do? Navigate by landmarks. The **Landmarks** chart at the front of the book gives the most familiar ones in English, Arabic transcription, and Arabic script. As you create your own cognitive map of Cairo, learn how to pronounce the names of landmarks relevant to you so that you can at least give directions. Also ask your friends to give you directions referring to common landmarks in addition to their street addresses. Old Cairo hands already do this as a matter of course.

Lastly, a thought that might cheer you up as you are on the verge of tears after being hopelessly lost for an hour exactly a few blocks from where you know you have to go: if you were to ask in perfect Arabic for the Villa Borghese Gardens or the Empire State Building or the Little Mermaid in Rome, New York, or Copenhagen, the locals would be just as stymied as they are here when you ask in English. Learn the names of 'your' landmarks in Arabic.

GETTING OUT OF TOWN

Wonderful as Cairo is, you will want to leave it briefly sooner or later. Despite the city's enormous size, it is delightfully easy to escape to the countryside for a dose of nature, peace, and quiet (which you can also find without leaving it; see **Green Cairo**, page 59). A few means of transport are evaluated below, and the **Travel Information** chart at the front of the book gives stations, times, prices, and amenities.

Buses: These are a great alternative to the trains or more expensive private transport for destinations outside of Cairo. You can book a seat in advance, some buses are air-conditioned, and some have videos blaring to help wile away the journey.

Trains: The trains are also good and cheap, but they are limited to the north–south line of the Nile—Port Said, Alexandria, Cairo, Luxor, Aswan, and stops in between.

Reserved seats or berths are essential in first class and must be purchased in advance—at Ramsis Station, through a travel agent for a commission. Carlson Wagon Lits office (795–6571) at the Shepheard Hotel can assist in booking and purchasing tickets on overnight trains to Luxor only. You can also buy tickets for major destinations at (centrale) telephone exchanges from 8 am to 4 pm—Bab al-Luq, for example, near the American University in Cairo. Although the train station is beautiful from the outside and the crowds offer great people-watching fodder, you will not want to spend much more time there than strictly necessary. The café, where service is poor and a cup of coffee expensive, is unappealing.

Planes: Egypt Air underwent a transformation in 2005. It is now customer-service oriented, with new airport facilities, better staff, and multi-lingual, friendly operators who efficiently book air-travel arrangements over the telephone. Egypt Air Call Center—0900-70000 (50 piasters a minute), and from the mobile, 1717 (LE1 a minute). Or on the Internet, find schedules at *www.egyptair.com.eg*. If you plan to travel with Egypt Air (the prices are often better than European airlines), it is worth signing up with their mileage program. Egypt Air is changing its image from an airline notorious for lateness and poor service to a serious world competitor. For all arrival and departure flights, updated every 3 minutes, at Cairo airport, check out *www.cairo-airport.com*.

For flight information from a landline, call 0900-7777; from a mobile, 2777. Information desk at Terminal 1, 265-5000/1/2/3; Terminal 2 departures, 265-2222, arrivals, 265-2077.

Tourist buses: Very comfortable but comparatively expensive—for example, a trip to the Pyramids is $35–45 per person. These afford the opportunity to strike up temporary new acquaintances as well as excessive forced 'opportunities' to stop at the perfume-bottle factory, rug shop, kebab restaurant, and so on. The destinations are strictly limited to the major tourist attractions. Contact any travel agent or hotel for what's on when.

Organization-sponsored trips: Cairo's many community and other **Organizations** always have a large roster of interesting trips in and around Cairo. The Community Services Association (CSA), American Research Center in Egypt (ARCE), the Women's Association (WA), and the British Community Association (BCA) are among the most active in this regard. Their trips are always reasonably priced, well-planned and guided, and usually anyone can sign up. These outings are an excellent way to get your feet wet, meet people, and learn something. But you do have to sign up ahead of time. Just call, or see the "In Cairo" section in *Egypt Today* magazine for a very thorough listing.

Taxi and limousine services: For privacy and convenience, these are ideal. You do have to know where you want to go, and to make sure the driver knows as well. For any place off the beaten track, this can be problematic, but not insurmountably so with a little persistence. Unless you are able to resist very politely, you will also be subject to visits to Ali's uncle's alabaster shop and his sister-in-law's restaurant.

Travel to the oases: The major oases of the Western Desert—Kharga, Dakhla, Farafra, Bahariya, and Siwa—are all major jaunts requiring three to four days minimum, good planning, and a fair amount of cash until you are experienced enough to venture on your own. Contact CSA or WA (**Organizations**) to see if any trips are planned, or call one of the travel agents specializing in desert-and-oases travel—specifically MAX Travel, Abercrombie & Kent, Saad Ali, Isis Travel, TRAUCO, or SIAG Travel. Just be aware that these agencies charge between $100 and $200 per day all-in, except for Isis,which is closer to $55 per day. Mr. Hany Amr offers first-rate

safaris to the desert oases with an added personal touch and wonderful, healthy cooking (**Desert & Diving Safaris**). Most Cairenes, even those who regularly travel the globe, have never been to the oases. Their allure seems to appeal more to foreigners, some of whom even live there. Check out the prospects for oasis travel carefully beforehand, as it can be restricted from time to time.

STAYING HEALTHY

BASIC PRECAUTIONS

The first and best advice is preventive: make sure family immunizations, especially children's, are up to date before you come, as not all vaccines are always available here. Contact the Center for Disease Control, *www.cdc.gov/travel/nafrica.htm*, or its equivalent in your country to ascertain the most current recommendations regarding health precautions and immunizations for travel in Egypt. Currently these are: hepatitis A, hepatitis B, rabies, typhoid, booster doses for tetanus-diphtheria and measles and a one-time dose of polio vaccine for adults. Note especially the preexposure rabies vaccinations with Imovax, which involves three shots over a one-month period. You can also have this done in Cairo by a doctor or a pharmacist. The preexposure shots (imported from Merieux of France and available locally at As-Salam pharmacy in the hospital of the same name) confer almost indefinite immunity in three shots at LE70 each.

We do not wish to sound alarmist, but since rabies is common among stray animals in and out of Cairo, caution is warranted, especially for children. As you probably know, rabies is inevitably fatal unless treated very quickly. Postexposure treatment involves first and foremost washing the scratch or bite (or even a preexisting cut that may have been licked by a stray animal) for at least ten minutes with soapy water, then immediately getting started on postexposure injections. But the postexposure treatment with injections of RIG (Human Rabies Immunoglobin) is not consistently available in Egypt, which means you might have to leave the country to get treated—so it is well worth having the preexposure treatment.

Yellow fever is only required if you plan on traveling to sub-Saharan Africa or to Thailand. It is available at the Airport Clinic.

The Family Health Care Clinic on Road 9 in Maadi has vaccinations for children's immunization and immunizations for travel. Also, contact Vacsera in Mohandiseen on 761-1111.

You will also need to be tested for HIV if you are planning to work here. An HIV certificate is required by the Ministry of Labor when issuing a work permit for the first time and for subsequent renewals. HIV certificates issued abroad are accepted providing they are legalized by an Egyptian consulate in the country in which they were issued; you can also have HIV tests in Cairo. Tourists do not need to have an HIV certificate.

Upon arrival, two simple rules suffice for tourists, plus one more for residents: be moderately careful about food, carry a small bottle of water everywhere, and, if you will be living here, find the most decent hospital closest to your home and make sure everyone in the family knows how to get there. Another way to guarantee quick access is to rent your flat from a doctor who also lives in the building; he or she will have a direct financial interest in keeping you healthy!

Much is made of 'pharaoh's revenge'—diarrhea—and dehydration in Cairo. Rule one above will probably not prevent one short bout of diarrhea shortly after arrival, but will keep it mild. Dose yourself and your loved ones with Kapect rather than Immodium should the pharaoh strike; both are available at all pharmacies, but Immodi-um should not be given to small children. Take along a packet of Re-hydrant that mixes with water—excellent for infants and adults. Obviously one carries water in the desert to prevent dehydration, but it is also easy to get dehydrated trekking around the Pyramids and throughout Cairo. It is a law of nature that exactly when you feel faint from thirst after hours of shopping or exploring, there is not a place in sight from which to buy water—even in the heart of downtown Cairo.

Although Baraka is the most common brand of bottled water, its very high mineral content gives it a taste some people don't like. The market is awash with competing brands, many offering lower mineral content. Siwa, Schweppes, and Safi, to name just a few, come recommended.

Tap water in Cairo is fine, but highly chlorinated and very occasionally an unappealing beige color. Accustom yourself to it in small doses gradually, and you will be far better off than visitors who keep their systems virginal and end up sicker than they need be from a sudden fall from grace in a five-star hotel.

Details on hygienic food handling are in Chapter 3 for people living, cooking, and buying food here. Eating out involves the usual commonsense precautions: no raw unpeeled fruit and vegetables; meat fairly well cooked; hot food hot and cold food cold. Also, try to eat where food handlers are more likely to wash their hands. Lastly, and discreetly or not, immediately spit out anything that tastes funny, especially seafood or alcoholic beverages.

SEAFOOD AND ALCOHOL

As two prime sources of potential health problems, these need to be addressed separately. The Nile is polluted and carries both giardia and schistosomiasis, both nasty things you do not want to get. Don't eat fish from the Nile and don't swim in it. And because of variations in storage and cooling, don't eat any seafood from anywhere that has even a faint off-taste. Shrimp are particular culprits here.

Because of the very high price and limited availability of imported alcohol, people who drink do drink the local wine and beer. In this area, privatization has worked wonders. Stella, the old public-sector stand-by, is now produced by Al-Ahram Beverages (ABC), which has also recently been distributing its locally brewed version of the Dutch beer, Heineken. Gone are the days when your Stella was served flat with tiny unrecognizable particles swimming in the bottom. ABC is also producing the Sakara and Meister lines and converting tried-and-true Stella fans. With the beer market itself growing by leaps and bounds, there are sure to be more developments in the not-too-distant future.

Stella Local is around LE5.50 in stores where it is sold (especially good are the Al-Ahram-owned depots that will deliver round the clock), and ranges from around LE6 to LE12 per bottle in restaurants of various categories.

Local wines have also benefitted—though less so—from privatization. The Gianaclis line includes Omar Khayyam, Cru des Ptolémées, and Rubis d'Egypte in red, white, and rosé respectively. Gianaclis has also produced the more premium Grand Marquis line of wines, as well as a sparkling wine, Aida. Another contender is the Obélisque line of white and red wine. All are moderately decent table wines, but still nothing to rave about. Remember the comments on soil salinity earlier on? Apparently the vineyards are among its first victims, resulting in the ruination of what was once palatable Egyptian wine. Although efforts are being made to improve the quality of grapes, it is an uphill battle.

Locally made hard liquor still has a long way to go and has been clearly implicated in a number of cases of methanol (wood alcohol) poisoning that causes death especially among teenagers. Avoid all but clearly imported hard liquor purchased from a traceable source—duty-free shops or trustworthy bars. Do not give empty liquor bottles to the garbage collector, the housekeeper, your friendly bootlegger, or anyone. Instead, break and discard them. Include a bottle-cutter among your household goods if you live here, or at least soak off labels before discarding bottles. Because adulterated wine caused one of the deaths, wine is now being sold less openly than before. If you want to drink it, do so gingerly, in moderation, and make sure it is from a reputable source. This last is relative, since a vaguely clandestine air surrounds all alcohol purchases other than at the duty-free shops.

MOSQUITOES

Egyptian mosquitoes can produce pyramid-sized welts on the tender flesh of the susceptible. Some sources swear that garlic pills and vitamin B-12 supplements ward off mosquitoes. You can also avoid them by using insect repellent on the skin and plug-in vapor repellents (which stink, but work) in the bedroom. Mosquito nets are effective too, but work and look best with a four-poster bed and a net big enough to puddle on the floor. Don't believe people who say that living high up in a highrise is a deterrent. Mosquitoes easily ascend to at least the tenth floor. In the summer and on a weekly basis, Cairo's streets are sprayed for mosquitoes. Go indoors when you hear or see the pesticide truck coming down a street, to protect yourself from the chemicals.

COMMON AND UNCOMMON AFFLICTIONS

Following the relatively low risks of diarrhea and dehydration given sensible precautions, the Cairo cough or cold caused by low humidity and pollution is more common and less avoidable. We are not at the gas mask stage as in Bangkok or Mexico City, but when you drive south on the Corniche toward Helwan, you will think twice about it. The dust from the cement is noticeable. People susceptible to allergies will notice them flaring up more here. As suggested earlier in the **Climate** section, those with dry skin and those who wear contact lenses will have to make the appropriate moisturizing adjustments. Instant hand sanitizer is widely available at Egyptian pharmacies and will definitely come in handy. Finally, and again, sunscreen is always vital, especially for the fair-skinned.

MEDICAL CARE IN CAIRO

Overall, medical care in Cairo is good. Doctors train here by doing two years of pre-med in the Faculty of Science of their university followed by six years of medical school in the Medical Faculty, followed by a one-year internship and then two to four years of residency, depending on specialization. A license to practice medicine is awarded after completion of the internship phase. Internships and residencies are done abroad (UK, Germany) by many, and the great majority of doctors in Cairo speak good English.

Egyptian nurses may have either a government diploma (which is somewhat equivalent to a Licensed Practical Nurse's degree in the United States) or a Faculty of Nursing degree (four years) involving much more theoretical knowledge, but less patient-care practice. Egyptian doctors—and most patients, too—fault the low standard of nursing care as a major problem in Egyptian hospitals. Clearly the doctors themselves, as well as the Ministry of Health and the Medical Syndicate, could and should actively address this, as might the nurses themselves. But as elsewhere, 'women's work' is undervalued, and nurses have traditionally come from the lower classes, although that is beginning to change. Experienced nurses with Higher Institute degrees are paid LE450 per month in the government hospitals. It is customary, therefore, as you might well imagine, to tip everybody below doctors when you stay in hospital or have an operation. Doctors often prefer to work in private hospitals because there they can treat private patients, and charge private-patient fees for their services.

If you do have to spend time in hospital, it is quite normal to take in a companion. He or she can plump up your pillow, make sure that a needle dropped on the floor does not go into your arm, and keep an eye on you when the busy doctor is away from the hospital. Many people recommend using a foreign-trained nurse to monitor post-operative progress; your embassy should have a list, or contact the Community Services Association (CSA) in Maadi to get theirs (**Nurses; Organizations**).

More and more, the better hospitals are trying to attract foreign directors of nursing to upgrade and professionalize nursing care. One recently offered such a position to a well-qualified candidate at a very high Egyptian salary, LE2,000 per month, but it was not high enough by the foreigner's standards; an international oil company paid her far more.

Pharmacists are the buffer zone between the people and the rest of the medical establishment. They too are generally well trained, most speak English, and all in all, they are a godsend. Find a good one in your neighborhood if you live here, and your life will be much simpler. They deliver (medicines, not babies), they consult and diagnose intelligently, and they even make housecalls to give injections to you, your kids, and your pets. Veterinarians do the same for pets. Some pharmacies stay open 24 hours. It is important to find out which pharmacy offers this service near your home and post the phone number with other emergency numbers.

Alternative or holistic medicine is booming in Cairo, as it always has in the countryside. A large number of foreign and Egyptian practitioners of everything from acupuncture to yoga ply their specialties formally and informally, and have large and devoted followings (**Alternative Therapies**). Egyptians have always used herbalists as well, who fall into the 'can't hurt, might help' category, and certainly they have centuries of practice from cosmetics to embalming to call upon in Egypt. The Harraz Herb Shop in Bab al-Khalq is reputed to be the best in Cairo for all sorts of advice and remedies in this line.

However interesting and unique this shop is, you need to speak and read Arabic as well as be familiar with hundreds of herbs and their properties. Customers either know what they want or explain their ailment to one of the herbalist who prescribes a remedy.

Foreigners notice two big differences about medical care in Cairo. One is hygiene standards, which are distinctly lower than most Westerners are used to. It is not common even in the fanciest clinics, for example, for the doctors to wash their hands as a matter of course before examining or touching a patient. Although you might feel reluctant, you should nevertheless diplomatically request that this be done. You can and should also request disposable needles for injections; this is pretty standard by now anyway. The other big difference is access:

ACCESS TO DOCTORS

Do not get sick in the morning or the afternoon if at all possible! Doctors traditionally keep only evening hours, saving the daytime for teaching and hospital attendance, and many jump from clinic to clinic. Hence tracking them down can be frustrating. Some of them also cancel or do not show up for their two-hour stint at Clinic X

if there are not enough appointments scheduled to make it worth their while. Call just before leaving to make sure the doctor is due. Waiting times will vary depending on the luck of the draw. Patients may be better off seeing younger but well-qualified doctors who have not yet built up their reputations. The Anglo-American Hospital already has doctors attending in the morning.

When making an appointment, clarify whether your appointment is am or pm. All doctors have mobile phones. Ask your doctor for his/her mobile number and another number that would be important in case of emergency.

MEDICAL FEES AND INSURANCE

A prominent Cairo physician acknowledged that the sight of a foreigner conjures up dollar signs in many a doctor's eyes. At the very first visit, clarify exactly what the fees are for a range of clinic and laboratory services. Make clear whether or not you have insurance, and whether you have a residence visa stamp in your passport, which should make you eligible for Egyptian fee rates. Some hospitals expect a cash guarantee that you will be able to pay their fees, often a minimum of LE1,000. Many companies working here issue a payment card for use in such a case, and in a few cases you can use an AMEX or VISA card, though you will probably have to pay the 5 percent extra commission on the card.

For Egyptians, medical insurance is supplied by the government, by employers, and through private insurers. Foreigners working here often have some form of insurance through their companies, but not always.

The International Association for Medical Assistance to Travelers (IAMAT), a Canada-based organization, has member clinics in and around Cairo, *www.iamat.org*. Fees are set by the organization and tend to be comparable to overseas medical fees—for example, $55 for an office visit, $75 for house calls, and $95 for holiday/Sunday house calls; residents may be eligible for lesser fees. One IAMAT doctor, Dr. Nabil Ayad al-Masry, specializes in tropical diseases and fevers; his IAMAT Clinic is conveniently located near the Coptic Hospital off Sharia Ramsis just north of Ramsis Station.

Foreign-based medical insurance for independent travelers or residents is also available, but in general is quite expensive, as it usually includes medical evacuation options. For this kind of insurance, consult classified ads in the international newspapers or your embassy's consular section.

EMERGENCY CARE

The best emergency care is the closest. You realize this the first time you are caught in a major traffic jam and you hear the blare of an ambulance siren—and nothing moves! Including, of course, the ambulance. Inquiries to taxi drivers regarding this phenomenon yielded the observation that 'big shots' commandeer ambulances when they want to get somewhere fast. So of course everyone ignores them. Whether or not this belief has any validity, the result is the same as if it were true. In addition, ambulances in general do not have paramedical professionals or life-support apparatus on board, but there are exceptions: specifically, As-Salam and Nile Badrawi hospitals in Maadi send emergency room physicians with their ambulances. Some clinics, such as Family Health Care Clinic in Maadi, have a hotline for emergencies, including heart attack and head trauma (See **Medical Emergencies**, front of Directory.)

Please note that telephone lines in Cairo are overloaded, including those at hospitals, clinics, and particularly emergency rooms. So in a real emergency, don't bother calling. Just go as quickly as you can.

PLASTIC SURGERY

To bring you down from emergency alert to a more frivolous level, a word on plastic surgery in Cairo. If you have been considering the odd nip and tuck, you have come to the right place. Cairo is becoming something of a center for plastic surgery among well-heeled Egyptians as well as among Europeans and Middle Easterners, men as well as women. Face lifts, liposuction, collagen treatments, laser and sclerotherapy for varicose veins, radial keratotomy for the nearsighted on an out-patient basis—all are available at considerably more reasonable cost than abroad. If you are curious but feeling tentative, ask to interview a few patients after you have discussed your requirements with a plastic surgeon.

Please keep in mind that plastic surgery can deform and be life-threatening. Thoroughly investigate the doctor and his/her qualifications before opting for a procedure, and check out the hospital and facilities for intensive care and recovery.

BEST HOSPITALS AND CLINICS

We have listed in the Directory only hospitals, doctors, laboratories, and clinics that come well recommended by foreigners and Egyptians. For additional recommendations, consult any of the **Nurses** in the Directory or your embassy, but note that some embassies tend to be impractically limited or perhaps hidebound in their recommendations. The US Embassy recommends the following hospitals: al-Salam and the Shalaan SurgiCenter. The Qasr al-'Aini Teaching Hospital, the post-modern brick-and-aluminum fortress on the Corniche in Garden City that opened in March 1996, is the best public hospital. Its great potential rests heavily on the government's ability to keep up its state-of-the-art equipment, which is currently being serviced under contract with France, who funded the hospital.

BRAND NAMES FOR COMMON DRUGS AND PHARMACEUTICALS

Trade names for reliable Egyptian-made brands are given below, preceded either by their common American names or by their effects. They are much cheaper than imports, and often made under license to a foreign pharmaceuticals company. New drugs, imported and locally produced, come on the market every day, so consult with your pharmacist on what is available and best. Prescriptions are rarely necessary, even for some controlled substances like codeine, Valium, and Prozac. Warning: This does not mean that our readers or anyone else should self-medicate.

Ibuprofen: Brufen; comes in 200, 400, and 600 mg coated tablets and in syrup for children

Tylenol: Paracetamol.

Aspirin: Rivo (original and micronized formulas), Aspocid, Asponasr.

Antidiarrheals: Kapect, Lomotil, Entocid, Streptoquin.

Worm treatments: Flagyl, Fluvermal.

Antifungal creams: Canesten, Dactarin.

Rehydrators: Rehydrans (sold in packets of powder to be mixed with juice or water).

Antihistamines: Claritine, Flurest, Allergex, Hismanel, Histadine (most come in both sedative—for sleeping—and non-sedative formulas).

Topical analgesics: Xylocaine (2 percent and 5 percent), Lignocaine.

Anti-inflammatories: steroidal: Diprosole, Betaderm, Dermatop, Fucicort; non-steroidal: Voltaran, Olfen, Feldene (both come in tablets and ointments).

Antibacterial ointments, creams: Fucidin, Garamycin, Fucicort.

Antibiotics: Septrin, Taravid, Ceclor, Peflacin, Augmentin (note, please, that antibiotics are only effective against bacterial infections, not viruses, and that they must be taken for five to ten days to work, and so as not to build up an immunity to them; don't self-medicate, especially with antibiotics, but if you cannot reach a doctor, rely on careful consultation with a pharmacist).

Antivirals: NoVirus (tablets and ointments, intended for herpes and other viral infections).

Multivitamins: for adults: Vitamax, Supravite, Geriatric Pharmaton, Theragran; for children: Theragran liquid, Multisenestol; for all: Seven Seas brand vitamins in a large range of formulations.

Mosquito repellents: Off Spray (contains 15 percent DEET).

Tampons: the only brands available so far in Egypt are Tampax and Ria and they are hard to find. Egyptian women generally resort to sanitary pads, but the cultural prohibitions against tampons may lessen in the face of advertising and education, thereby inreasing market choice.

Baby wipes: Fresh Ones brand comes in big boxes, and now also in pocket- and purse-sized dispensers; very convenient anywhere and everywhere.

Please check the Directory under the specific appropriate heading for anything you need or want to investigate—for example, **Alternative Therapies**, **Doctors** (under which each specialty is listed alphabetically), **Clinics**, **Pharmacies**, **Veterinarians**, etc.

MONEY MATTERS

CURRENCY AND CURRENCY EXCHANGE

Cairo (and more so the rest of Egypt) is still largely a cash economy as soon as you descend from five-star altitude. The best place to change foreign currency is at the innumerable exchanges throughout the city. They have much better hours, better rates, and shorter lines than the banks, and they do not charge any commission. The rate you see posted is what you get. Travelers' checks limit your flexibility in this regard, as many exchanges—and banks—will not take them, or will charge a lot for doing so. Carry cash instead, with caution. ATMs are now widespread throughout the city, allowing you to withdraw cash (in Egyptian pounds) directly from your home bank account, using Visa, Mastercard, or Cirrus debit or credit cards. Hotel personnel can also usually be trusted, by the way, to change foreign currency for you when the hotel's exchange service is closed, as it often is. They just go to an exchange or a bank, get the cash, and bring you the receipt, deserving, of course, a tip of a pound or two for their trouble. Just make sure the person who does this for you is traceable.

You will need something other than a normal wallet to carry your wads of Egyptian pounds *(gineeh)*. Some sort of make-up case with dividers works well. The two largest denominations, LE50 and LE100 bills, are now ubiquitous, and are fairly easy to change. Denominations of LE20, LE10, LE5, and LE1 are more common. It's wise to get at least LE100 in singles and fives from a bank or exchange as soon as you can for taxis and so on, to save yourself the nuisance involved in making change. One hundred piasters (singular,*'irsh)* make one pound, and paper currency also comes in 5, 10, 25, and 50 piaster notes. Coins of smaller denominations are rare, often superseded by matches, gum, and candy for change from a purchase. The **Currency Conversions** section at the front of the book gives Egyptian equivalents of major foreign currencies.

A FEW CURRENT SALARY SAMPLES

Before proceeding to tipping (baksheesh), the humanitarians among our foreign readers might be interested in what some Egyptians earn. The 2005 estimated per capita GDP hovered at $1,400 per year, or $116 (LE670)

per month. Look around at prices, consider inflation and the likely devaluation of the Egyptian pound, and then imagine raising a family on monthly salaries like the following:

Cairo University tenured professor, Ph.D. with twenty years' experience: LE1,500

Egyptian housemaid, full-time: LE800

Accountant, recent university graduate, large private international accounting firm: LE1,000

Government schoolteacher; mid-level public servants: LE600

Laborer at Stella bottling plant: LE500

Driver at private company: LE700

Bawwaab (before tips): LE400–500

Sales clerk, mid-range clothing shop: LE400

Tea boy, private company: LE450

TIPS ON BAKSHEESH

There are a lot of people in Cairo. Quite a number are obscenely rich. But the vast majority of them are poor, or barely scraping by. You will probably note that wealthier Cairenes tend to tip generously. If you are a foreigner, who most likely falls into this same relative category, you might do the same. We note, for example, that Cairenes who can afford it routinely tip 10 percent over the restaurant bill directly to the waiter, who theoretically receives the 12 percent service charged at most places, but in all likelihood does not.

'Parking attendants'—both the ones who really do guard and move your car, as well as those who suddenly appear out of the woodwork—expect 50 piasters or a pound, depending on how long you have been parked, how bad the parking situation is, whether they have cleaned your windshield, and so on. If you are taxi-ing, notice that the taxi driver tips these fellows, and take that into account when you pay him. One Egyptian acquaintance routinely waves off the out-of-the-woodwork parking attendants, another routinely—but ever so discreetly—tips a pound to her neighborhood traffic cop as he stops traffic for her. Watch, figure out what the locals do, and let your conscience be your guide, along with the specifics below:

If you are a weekend guest, it is traditional to tip the domestic help of your hosts; LE20 is generous and fair for foreigners.

When someone carries your packages, tip them 50 piasters or a pound. When it takes three people to carry the same packages, tip a pound altogether. Bellhops in the big hotels get more—LE2–5 depending on the number of bags.

Avoid self-appointed 'guides' at museums and monuments. They are the bane of tourists in Egypt, expert at nothing except haranguing you. If you succumb, agree on a price before beginning the tour.

If you are at a hotel for a considerable length of time, about LE10 per week for the person who cleans your room is good. Prorate for other services from doormen and concierges.

It is not uncommon to tip the fellow who fills your petrol tank or the man who prepares your deli order at the supermarket. Supposedly this assures you of continued good service. The much more complex baksheesh issues that arise when you live here are covered in Chapter 3.

BEGGARS

Beggars are a fact of life throughout Egypt. The elderly poor, the handicapped, mothers with fly-bespecked babes in arm, and children, children everywhere. And as usual, rumors abound of beggar kings and beggars' auctions and drug involvement in the whole business. Whether the rumors are true or false, the pathos and plight of many beggars are obvious, of some others, not so. Since it is one of the Five Pillars of Islam to give alms to the poor, and since a strong

streak of fatalism runs through Egyptian society, there is little shame, if any, associated with begging. It is just the beggars' lot in life, with which they cope quite cheerfully in the main.

Be aware of one strong deterrent to giving money to beggars: you will frequently and immediately be surrounded by ten more, especially when children are involved. And the old ploy of giving food rather than money to someone mimicking eating with a hands-to-mouth movement is usually met with derision and scorn, so don't attempt to control the process in this fashion (although we did witness one enterprising young girl of eight or so, under her mother's watchful eye, deftly and with great aplomb scooping hearty leftovers from the tourists' plates during Ramadan in Khan al-Khalili; not begging at all, but recycling).

If you feel that you cannot face it on a daily basis and decide to simply ignore all beggars, you might consider salving your conscience by a generous donation of food, toys, clothing, time, or money to the many charities that help the poor, or to take one neighborhood family discreetly under your wing in some useful fashion—shoes, books, and vitamins for the kids; food, especially meat, for one of the feasts. This is a customary, practical, and personal form of charity here in Cairo.

PRICES AND BARGAINING

A number of sources we contacted, particularly among expatriates, claimed that bargaining is on the wane in modern-day Cairo. They must have been referring to Cairo, Illinois!

Virtually everything is negotiable in Cairo and throughout Egypt, from airline tickets to hotels, a length of fabric from any shop in any price category, to a kilo of tomatoes at the corner grocer's. Arabs the world over are known for the trading skills and wiles they have honed over centuries, and the Egyptians are no exception. However, be observant, don't haggle over a few pounds.

Even where prices are clearly marked, and even in upscale shopping venues like Citystars, some people bargain to good effect. 'Discounts' are often made available to 'friends.' Doctors' fees are negotiable. And of course, bargaining is *de rigueur* in all the *suuq*s (markets), the epitome of which is the tourist-infested but nevertheless wonderful Khan al-Khalili. Are there any rules of thumb? Probably not. Knowing exactly what one wants to pay is the only possible advantage the buyer can claim over the seller. If you enjoy the complex dance steps of bargaining for its own sake, you offer far less than you will actually pay and then gradually spiral up to agreement with the seller. If not, you state and then implacably stick to your price, but this may well be regarded as so crude that sellers will cut off their noses to spite their faces rather than sell to an ignoramus who seems oblivious to the whole concept of 'face.' Remember, this is supposed to be fun; it is the social heartbeat of the Middle East.

A few unusual aspects of pricing and commerce that may run counter to some foreigners' intuition: A whole lamb—head, eyes, hooves, wool, and all—will cost the same per-kilo price as a choice cut, at least at the numerous butchers we have patronized. Volume discounting, unlike discounting by any and every other rationale, does not seem to be the norm here. Returning merchandise is also frowned upon, although it can be done. It is a question of more-persistent-than-thou, and of stressing your value as a customer to the management. Customer relations and consumer activism are fairly new concepts in Egypt, so caveat emptor is the rule

MISCELLANEOUS POINTERS ON MONEY

Learn the Arabic number symbols immediately if not sooner. Some establishments

have no qualms about rounding up even well-marked prices if they think it will fly.

Travelers' checks are a real nuisance in Egypt. Avoid them.

Don't be alarmed if your restaurant bill is higher than you calculated from the menu. Service and taxes are added on at the end of the meal. If, on close scrutiny, you still believe you've been overcharged, politely consult your waiter.

Look at the menu. It is all too common for the gullible *khawaga* to be soaked by the friendliest waiters and managers of charming restaurants. If they say they do not have a menu or that it is in Arabic only, leave or ask the price first.

Don't accept torn or otherwise mutilated bills from banks or exchanges, as shopkeepers will not accept them.

BANKING IN CAIRO

Even if you live here as a foreign resident, you can almost avoid banking here. Cash rather than checks are used to pay bills. Checking accounts are used mostly by companies with payrolls. Individuals should be able to satisfy all of their banking needs through the use of a savings account. ATM machines are now widespread throughout Cairo, via which you can withdraw Egyptian pounds from your savings account even if the account is in dollars. You cannot, however, withdraw dollars from an ATM machine. Each bank requires a minimum deposit, though not a minimum ongoing balance, to start a savings account. These vary from bank to bank.

With a Visa or American Express (preferably gold) credit card you can, by maintaining a positive balance on the card account, withdraw money readily from hotels that honor those cards. It's free!

Savings accounts and fixed deposits (CDs) are available in Egyptian pounds and dollars at most banks, as stated above. The interest rates for these in mid-2006 were hovering around 0.50 percent for dollar savings accounts (1–2 percent for CDs with one- to twelve-month maturities). For Egyptian- pound accounts, these options were more interesting: 10.5 percent for savings accounts and about 9.5 percent for CDs.

Historically, banking in Egypt has tended to be a time-consuming and inefficient process, regardless of the bank. However, there are moves afoot by even some of the worst offenders in this regard, to provide convenient retail banking solutions to customers. Gone are the days, almost, when each slightly different transaction required going to a different department. Simple transactions like cashing a check can now be handled with relative ease at many banks, though it is still advisable to stay away from the large Egyptian institutional banks when possible. International banks like (but not by any means limited to) Citibank charge reasonable fees for the privilege of getting your foreign-bank check (even from another Citibank) deposited into your local account. It also takes a minimum of two weeks, and more commonly four weeks, for a check from abroad to clear, so remember this when calculating your cash-flow needs. Finally, do not assume that because you have an account at one branch of a bank, you can simply wander into another branch of the very same bank to cash a check. At many banks you cannot—well, you can, but you have to go through a lot of rigmarole with the manager of each branch first. Banks' branches are slowly becoming electronically connected to each other, but it is a work in progress.

If you must bank, it is the same situation as with hospitals, for similar reasons: the best bank is the one closest to home or work. And the best time to hit the bank is shortly after it opens at 8:30, when most customers are still sleeping but employees are in place. MIBank, HSBC, and the Egyptian–American Bank come well recommended within the context of the comments above.

CRIME IN CAIRO

This section can be mercifully brief: Cairo is an astonishingly safe city, considering its size and the poverty of many of its inhabitants. There is virtually none of the horrifying, anonymous violence that plagues some of the world's major metropolises. The first reason given in response to "Why do you love Cairo?" by a veteran foreign journalist (female) living here was: "I feel safe. I can walk anywhere, any time, alone, without feeling threatened."

That said, here are a few caveats and observations worth considering, as petty non-violent crime seems to be on the rise of late.

Foreign pedestrians of either sex should be wary of a few pickpocketing scams: being approached by a playful 'drunk' who is bobbing and weaving too closely; the old "There's mud—or pigeon dirt, or ice cream—on your leg/back" ploy; and, of course, being targeted in crowded bus or train stations or in the conveyances themselves where foreigners stand out. Should you suddenly find yourself being victimized, quickly shout "IlHa'uuni! Haraami!" meaning 'Help! Thief!' You will be helped, not ignored, by passersby.

If your car breaks down—even (or especially) in Maadi, we hear—don't fall prey to the 'helpful' stranger who lifts the hood to have a look and may walk off with the vital part he has just removed, only to have his 'brother' appear a short time later to sell the part back to you at an exorbitant price. Such ruses are rare, though; more typically, Egyptians of all classes will genuinely and competently help you charge the battery or replace the flat tire and absolutely refuse any money for it.

And now a note on sexual harassment, a

topic on which there is little consensus among the women we interviewed. Many feel violated, at least symbolically, by the hisses, stares, and sotto voce comments one sometimes gets on the streets of Cairo. Others barely notice it, or just ignore it if they do. Although harassment, sexual or otherwise, is a punishable crime in Egypt, do not expect much sympathy from those who should know better. The magazine *Egypt Today* in March 1996 published a frankly hair-raising piece quoting such eminent personages as the vice-head of a department and a (female!) AUC professor, who seriously opined that really 'decent' women do not get harassed or attacked. The rest of the article makes very clear that they do. Advice: be friendly but on guard in response to friendliness; totally ignore rude stares and comments; react with loud outrage the moment an unwelcome male hand is placed upon you; and do not sit in the front seats of taxis.

Finally, the police: it is unlikely you will ever have to resort to them, but if you must, you are in for a pleasant surprise. Real policemen, English-speaking or not, are unfailingly courteous and as helpful as they can be on the whole. Please keep this in mind as you digest the following paragraph. For Tourist Police, call 390-6028.

Unfortunately, there also seems to be a number of people—real but renegade policemen or impostors, who knows?—who use their uniforms to first intimidate and then rob their victims of money, passports, and jewelry, sometimes with the unpleasant twist of having first planted an alleged drug like hashish or cocaine on them. *Do not* get into an unmarked car or taxicab with anyone in a police uniform. *Do not* hand anything over to them. *Do not* give them your address or take them to your home. Insist politely, and then loudly, that you must first walk to a telephone to call the local police station and talk with an English-speaking officer, and ask them to give you the number. Act cool or act clueless, but attract an audience and be stubborn. Your persistence will eventually drive these creeps away unrewarded. Then, to reduce the frequency of this new phenomenon, report it to the real police and to your consular section.

TERRORIST ATTACKS

On November 17, 1997, the world was shocked and saddened by a horrifying attack on tourists visiting Queen Hatshepsut's Temple in Luxor. Since this tragic event, the Egyptian authorities seem to have changed their approach to terrorism with some measure of success, although there have been other attacks on tourist sites since then. This has prompted security authorities to close streets around major hotels to parking, while at hotel parking garages you will be asked to surrender your car license until you depart. It remains to be seen how effectively the updated policy works in averting this very serious threat to Egypt's vital tourism dollars. In the recent past, the response has been swift and hard. For this, both residents and tourists in Egypt must be grateful while they, and Egypt at large, wait for an enduring end to the myriad conflicts in the Middle East.

COMMUNICATIONS

MAIL SERVICES

The good news is that, basically, the postal system in Cairo works. However, pity the poor postal workers. They have to sort mail written in two different alphabets. Given that, they do a pretty good job. To enhance the chances of your in-Cairo mail arriving, print the address very clearly or type it, and allow a week for delivery, although lots of things take only a day—amazing! You can put it in the red (local mail) mailboxes one finds around town, but it is probably better off taken to your local post office. Many Cairo residents, local and foreign, advise against using the local mail, but from our experience, this is unwarranted. We and other people we know routinely receive flyers, notices of meetings, and even letters from overseas unscathed. It helps in any case to develop a personal relationship with your mail carrier and tip him regularly.

Letters for overseas can be successfully mailed from any big hotel, which may work better than from a post office or the blue airmail mailboxes. Overseas stamps, available from hotel newsstands and the post office, are LE1.50; letters take 3–5 days to Europe and 5–7 days to North America and Australasia. For your regular overseas correspondents, you could send them address labels written in both Arabic and English—a handy present to family and friends and a gentle reminder to write. Larger **Stationery Stores** along Sharia 'Abd al-Khaliq Sarwat downtown can make such labels for you. To guarantee your letter send it registered; for a fast and reliable service to international destinations, look for Express Mail Service (EMS). It is more expensive than airmail but much less than courier services. Most post offices provide this service.

Receiving packages or well-stuffed envelopes from overseas is dicey and a nuisance at best. They are inspected by customs officials and censors—CDs, videocassettes, and computer games especially—and hence rarely arrive intact, if at all. You receive a notice and must go to the dusty, cavernous customs clearing house downtown or out near the airport to pick up the package, run around to various windows, and very possibly pay duty worth more than the package's contents. This is true even if packages are sent to a business address, by the way. All in all, not worth it.

COURIER SERVICES

To send important mail, and especially packages, with the greatest expectation of its getting through, you will probably have to resort to expensive courier services (**Couriers**). Federal Express's charges from Cairo are typical, and even competitive: a minimum rate of LE326 for anything up to 500g. A full kilogram (2.2 lbs), by comparison, is 'only' LE434. For this, though, you are promised (but almost never get) 24-hour door-to-door delivery to anywhere in the Middle East, Europe, and the United States. Lower rates can be negotiated if you set up an account.

The state-operated Express Mail Service (look for the blue and orange EMS sign outside post offices) is considerably cheaper and actually quite reliable. They promise 1–3 days' delivery to the United States and most places in Europe. A half a kilo (500 grams) to the US and other countries, such as Thailand, Nigeria, and Italy costs LE117 plus LE30 for every 0.5 kg thereafter. To France, the first 0.5 kg costs LE137 and every 0.5 kg thereafter is LE45. The EMS telephone number is 272-5562.

TELECOMMUNICATIONS

Telephone density throughout Egypt is low: roughly 10 telephones per 100 people—but much higher in Cairo—compared to 66 per 100 in the United States. But service in Cairo is, at long last, relatively good. Egypt ranks among the five most expensive countries in the world for international calls. Nevertheless, Egypt's telecommunications infrastructure is excellent (*www.telecom-egypt.com.eg*). As of 2006, there are two mobile phone companies, Vodafone and MobiNil.

Under each heading below, we first cover those aspects of the topic relevant to visitors, and then move on to considerations for residents. But first off, we strongly advise all new residents to do a thorough hands-on check of their telephones and phone lines before signing a lease on an apartment. Just because there is a telephone physically present on the premises does not guarantee that it works, that the number is valid, or that it has the long-distance or international capacities promised by either lease or landlord. Particularly important is to make sure your phone can dial trunk calls (any number in Egypt beginning with zero). This allows you to make domestic long-distance calls, and, more importantly, calls to mobile phones.

DIRECTORY ASSISTANCE AND DIRECTORIES

Telephone service in Cairo is not like it use to be. Egypt Telecom's service has come into the twenty-first century by providing an informative web site in Arabic and English, *www.telecomegypt.com.eg/english/Home.ht m* with directory assistance and emergency numbers, billing information, prepaid card service, and much more.

There is a free, much improved English/ Arabic *Cairo Yellow Pages* (*www.yellow-pages.com.eg*). For business, the American Chamber of Commerce in Egypt's *Membership Directory* is useful. Egypt Trade *www.egtrade.com* and Kompass Directory *www.kompassegypt.com* list major company with the latter is the most comprehensive.

There are several publication and pamphlets available at bookstores such as Diwan, AUC Bookstores, El Shorouk First Mall, and Volume I, which provide information about hotels, restaurants, nightlife, shopping, travel, culture, and so on. Look for *The Croc* (free) as well as pamphlets such as *School and Nursery Directory 2006* and *the Good Times Guide*. Most magazines provide directories that support their reader's interests such as *Mother & Child*, *Egypt Today*, and *Community Times*.

However, the Internet is your best source to keep informed about cultural events and places of interest. Put your name on this web site for up-to-date exhibitions, parties, band performances, opera's, movies, new openings, restaurants, workshop, special events: *http://groups.yahoo.com/group/ wazzup_in_cairo/*

Here are a few more sites:

www.yallabina.com lists restaurants, travel, events, movies

www.cairokids.com lists things to do, places to go, and listing of schools

http://egycalendar.com for monthly schedule of conferences

www.worldswitch.com/Countries/Egypt/ Directories.html for a list of 20 directories from information on ancient Egypt to the Red Sea, and five search engines.

Cairo: The Practical Guide's Directory is trying to fill the large gap for consumer listings; we hope that community-minded readers will send their additions and corrections to AUC Press, PO Box 2511, 113 Sharia Kasr el Aini, 11511 Cairo. E-mail: aucpress @aucegypt.edu.

LONG-DISTANCE AND INTERNATIONAL CALLS

Long-distance calls within Egypt and overseas calls can be made from any of the big hotels, but at considerable mark-ups over the already high rates. Use an international calling card like MCI or AT&T when calling from hotels. Calls can also be made from any telephone exchange (known as 'centrales') either by purchasing time in advance (with a minimum of three minutes) or, better, by purchasing prepaid calling cards. Purchasing time from the centrale operator costs about LE15 for three minutes to Europe or North America; when using the operator you must pay for at least three minutes if you connect, including to wrong numbers and answering machines. And, of course, in using centrales, be prepared for long waits and lines; the low telephone density means that many Cairenes must use the centrales. See the front of the Directory for neighborhood centrale numbers. Prepaid calling cards are much cheaper and are not subject to a minimum amount of time; LE15 gives 2.5 minutes. The cards do not work from some phones, though, even for long-distance calls within Egypt. Nile Telecom sells prepaid telephone cards under the name of Ringo and ElNile. There are 'Ringo' telephones throughout Cairo, while ElNile telephones are mainly found outside of Cairo. Buy a prepaid card for LE10, 15, 20 at any kiosk. For more information go to *www.internetplus.com.eg*. Trunk calls can also be made from home but require a trip to the centrale first to pay a deposit, usually a percentage of the estimated length of the call.

CALL-BACK SERVICES

Call back companies act as long-distance wholesalers. First, register for their service and pay a down payment. Call a local or toll-free number to the call-back company; it will recognize your number and call you back then dial the international number. Magic Service in Zamalek has an Egyptian origination system in place, with rates under $1 per minute for long-distance calls to the US. They also deliver the bills in person. Call-back services require a touch-tone phone. For more information on international call-back services look on the Internet: *www.escapeartist.com/internet/callback.htm*

Another option is calling computer to computer, such as SKYPE, *www.skype.com*. Both parties to the conversation need to be signed up to SKYPE for free calls.

LOCAL AND IN-EGYPT CALLING

These are fairly straightforward procedures, but there are a few bleeps. In 2006, the following is unlikely, but still possible in smaller cities or rural areas. It is not uncommon for lines to get crossed so that Mr. Mustafa across town is getting your calls and you his. Your line, unbeknown to you, may actually be the *bawwaab*'s line 'temporarily' being run up to your flat from the basement. And unless you specify — and check — beforehand, you (rather than the landlord) might get hit with the hook-up charges for long-distance service.

CENTRALES, BILLING, REPAIRS, AND SERVICE

Each neighborhood in Cairo has its own centrale, which is responsible for all repairs and service problems, billing and purchase of new or additional lines, and long-distance calls. Phone bills are issued every three months for local service. Bills are mailed, as well as accessed over the phone; or simply go to any centrales, give your number, and pay. If you are renting, your landlord will know when the bills are due. It may be advisable to allow him or her to handle payment, or to have a Mr. Fixit or your *bawwaab* make the payments and thereby save you a lot of standing around at the centrale. See your local and international bill at *www.telecomegypt.com*.

Complaints and requests for repairs can be made by calling 188 or by calling your centrale directly.

MOBILE PHONES

The Egyptian mobile phone market has boomed in recent years. Two companies, Vodafone and MobiNil, offer a wide range of services. Rates are competitive and both comp-anies offer personal, business, and corporate packages. Mobile phones purchased in Egypt use a GSM operating system, which is compatible with European networks but not with systems in the United States (**Mobile Phones**). Vodafone Directory 2121, MobiNil 8000.

TELEPHONES AND ANSWERING MACHINES

International brand-name phones with all the bells and whistles are available here—the Ogail stores, Radio Shack, and Carrefour have a good selection—but make sure you are buying what you want: for example, a real Panasonic rather than a Panesonic or a Panasunic, which are cheaper Chinese knock-offs without warranties (**Appliances, Small**).

If you are bothered by crank callers, an answering machine with a male-voice phone message is a good way of warding them off. Or buy a caller ID device at Radio Shack.

FAX SERVICES

All hotel business centers and **Business Service Centers** provide fax, all at a hefty price. If you do a lot of personal or business communicating to overseas destinations, or even locally, strongly consider getting your own fax machine or fax modem set-up. The convenience is invaluable.

INTERNET AND E-MAIL

In October 1993, Egypt started full Internet services. Today, using the Internet from a landline is almost free. By dialing a supplied dial-up number—all beginning with 0777 or 0707—you can access 294 free Internet numbers. The charge is LE1 per hour, with the ISP collecting 70% and the remainder for the government. Free Internet Providers with the highest market share are LinkdotNet (0777-0777), Super Net (0777-0500), Internet Misr (0777-5000). Super Net and Internet Misr Free Internet Numbers are powered by Nile-Online while LinkdotNet number is powered by Linkdot-Net. Broadband lines can be rented from Telecom Egypt for a yearly fee of LE1,200. Total cost varies according to the Bandwidth rate requested. The higher the Bandwidth rate carried, the faster the service, the higher the cost.

Free internet service provides fast and easy access. Those who use the Internet primarily for e-mail and browsing the web should find this service sufficient. For those seeking faster connections and expanded services, commercial ISPs also offer paid subscriptions to a variety of services. Most also provide server space, website design, software development, training, and cybercafés. Leased lines are also available, which are dedicated copper lines on which Internet & Data (VPN-Data Transfer) Services are delivered. It costs LE15,000 for a yearly connection of a 512Kbps Internet Leased Line Connectivity, while that of a 1Mbps Speed is almost LE35,000 a year.

Dialup access telephone numbers in Cairo can always be accessed from any other Egyptian city provided you have a long distance connection, although this is not recommended unless you have a good line. Access to major providers such as America Online and Compuserve is possible through some local providers.

Class A Internet providers are network service providers: they are carriers that are directly connected to international service providers and they built the backbone that provides the service to ISPs. There are four providers in Egypt: Nile-Online, EgyNet, TE Data, and Link dotNet

Class B Internet providers: There are five in Egypt: Raya Telecom, Noor, Yalla Online, Batelco, and Mena Net. They are provided with international connectivity through Class A providers.

Class C Internet providers: There are 208 Providers, such as The WayOut, Internet Egypt, RITE etc. These are ISPs that are provided with Internet service through Class A & Class B providers (through international links).

Class A providers provide Internet service through dedicated leased lines, dial-up ports, ISDN service. They also provide the VPN connectivity used to connect any head office to its branches. (See **Internet Service Providers** in the Directory.)

Wireless Connectivity and Voice over IP (VoIP) is the up and coming technology of great interest to the Egyptian Market. Voice Over IP has been permitted for internal calls only and not yet for international calls. To learn more, consult the Egyptian Regulatory Authority at *www.ntra.gov.eg*.

CYBERCAFÉS

One of the best bets for access to the cyber-world and its denizens. Cybercafés are everywhere as part of the internet gold rush; if you're in any reasonably affluent part of Cairo or indeed Egypt the chances are you'll be near one. In Cairo (Garden City, Mohandiseen, Zamalek, Heliopolis, Nasr City, and Maadi), cybercafés are operated by Internet Egypt, The WayOut, Data Care, and Connet. The cost per hour as of April 2006 is approximately LE5 to LE20, depending on where the cybercafé is. Sometimes you may use the service for a fraction of an hour. Operating hours vary but are typically 9 am to 11 pm. There is wireless service at coffee houses such as Cilantro, and in hotels.

MEDIA

The scope and variety of English print and other media are improving. International daily newspapers usually arrive only one date late on Cairo newsstands. For residents, it is cheaper and more convenient to get subscriptions to these, and they really do arrive most of the time. The local English-language daily *(The Egyptian Gazette)* is not up to par, but a few weeklies and some magazines, plus television, radio, and the World Wide Web keep ignorance at bay. Note that unless one is in an expat neighborhood or tourist area, international publications are hard to find.

NEWSPAPERS AND MAGAZINES

Here's a hint: if you want to keep track of interesting people, places, and events in Egypt, get a loose-leaf binder and a hole puncher from the stationery shop; as you read the publications described below, cut out whatever interests you and file it in your binder to spare yourself the 'now-where-was-that-great-article-on-the-Camel-Market' syndrome. See **Newspapers** and **Magazines** in the Directory.

If you read Arabic, up-to-the-minute local and international news and commentary are available, with lively coverage from all points on the political spectrum. If not, you will probably resort to *The Egyptian Gazette*, a daily that purports to offer international and local news.

The *Gazette*'s annual subscription for twelve months is LE355 in Egypt, $160 in the Arab world, and $310 in Europe. The *Gazette*'s sister newspaper, the French daily, *Le Progres Egyptian*, also originates here and the annual subscription is LE360 in Egypt, LE960 in Arab countries, and $280 elsewhere.

Al-Ahram has two weekly foreign-language papers: *Al-Ahram Weekly* in English and *Al-Ahram Hebdo* in French. Annual subscripton to *Al-Ahram Weekly* costs LE52 in Egypt, $50 in the Arab world, and $100 elsewhere. Both Al-Ahram weeklies offer sophisticated items of regional and local news plus good cultural coverage listings and features.

The International Herald Tribune/The Daily Star Egypt is currently the only international newspaper that is available on the same day. It can be bought at major bookstores and hotel newsstands, or subscribe and it will be delivered to your door. On newsstands the cost is LE9; for subscription, the cost is LE5.64 per copy. For twelve months, the cost is LE1,760.

Ask the *bawwaab* about the possibility of newspapers being delivered daily and weekly to your building. The following is a list of newspapers available in Egypt.

Al-Ahram—state-owned, Arabic-language daily, the oldest newspaper in the Arab world.

Al-Ahram Weekly—English-language weekly.

Al-Ahram Hebdo—French-language weekly.

Egyptian Gazette—English-language daily.

International Herald Tribune and Daily Star—English-language daily.

Middle East Times—English-language, weekly.

Al-Jumhuriyah—state-owned, Arabic-language daily.

Al-Akhbar—state-owned, Arabic-language daily.

Al-Ahali—opposition, Arabic-language weekly.

Al-Wafd—opposition, Arabic-language daily.

Al-Messa—pro-government, Arabic-language daily.

The general-interest, English-language magazine market includes *Egypt Today, Community Times,* and *Business Today.* Glossy, well written, and even mildly provocative on occasion, each has the hands-down best listings on events, activities, and organizations relevant to its audience. For *Egypt Today*, it is the cosmopolitan Cairene and for *Business Today*, anyone doing business in Egypt. Subscriptions are much cheaper than newsstand prices and the magazines come unscathed and on time monthly.

The rest of the local English-language magazine scene is somewhat fickle; new magazines spring up and disappear sometimes within a matter of weeks. The best on offer at the moment include *Enigma* and *Cleo.*

Business Monthly, the publication of the American Chamber of Commerce, is distributed for free on a monthly basis and contains excellent coverage of the Egyptian business and economic scene. For subscription details contact the American Chamber of Commerce (**Organizations**).

TELEVISION AND RADIO

As one might infer from the satellite dishes that now far outnumber minarets on the skyline, television is rapidly altering not only the silhouette but the culture of Cairo and Egypt. Cairo was long the hub of television and film production in the Middle East, but the advent of satellite broadcasts as a direct result of the Gulf War has changed all that. Big battles backed by big money, largely Saudi, are shaping up over who will control this megamarket and whether secular or Islamic influence will prevail.

Satellite and cable television offer a variety of programming, but satellite usually offers a few more channels (albeit in Turkish or Russian). Check with several companies to see who has the best programming. Cable television is available through Cable Network Egypt (CNE) (see **Television**) for around LE20–200 a month, which includes MNET, CNN, K-TV, MTV, and SuperSport. A number of other services originate by satellite from London (MBC—Middle East Broadcasting Company), Italy (ART—Arab Radio & Television), and Cyprus (Orbit, which includes a number of English and French channels). Currently the best satellite programming on offer is Showtime and Orbit, also available through CNE. It shows a variety of western entertainment including movie and sport channels, as well as CNN, the Discovery Channel, MTV, Nickelodeon, and various channels showing the latest American serials, as well as many Arab channels. For CNE and any others, though, you must also purchase a decoder box; a digital decoder with remote control is LE950. Satellite is available from a number of different companies. Tarek Radwan, owner of Queen SAT (519-7606, 010 141-4982), speaks excellent English and can walk you through this maze of options. His service is reliable and his engineers come to your house even on holidays to correct a problem. Flats rented to expatriates in Cairo now frequently include satellite dishes as part of the furniture—but to get a wide variety of channels via satellite, you need the remote that turns the satellite dish. (Whew! Our advice: read books instead.)

Avoiding cable and satellite, couch potatoes still have a reasonable choice, including Nile TV, which broadcasts in English, Hebrew, and French. Channels 1 and 2 are the national channels emanating from the Television Building on the Corniche, with Channel 2 having news in English and French. Channel 3 is the Cairo local channel, and 4 through 8 are broadcast from Ismailiya, Alexandria, Tanta, Minya, and Aswan respectively. Dream TV targets young viewer and Dream 2 is an entertainment channel. All channels carry a variety of programming, including foreign language films and serials. Foreign serials appear often but tend to change frequently so check scheduling to see what is currently available.

FM 95 carries Cairo's European service radio, and features programming in English, French, German, Italian, Greek, and Armenian. The news is available in both French and English in the mornings. NILE FM 104.2 is the newest English language rock station. For more easy listening tune into FM 98.8

The BBC World Service is also available throughout the day on several different AM frequencies. The *Middle East Times* prints a weekly schedule and a list of frequencies. Additional BBC information and schedules are available from the British Council (**Organizations**).

MANNERS, MORALS, AND CUSTOMS

Egypt is a complex blend of Mediterranean and Arab with respect to its manners, morals, and customs. Anyone coming from these traditions will find it easy to adapt; others may not. But Egyptians are quite open-hearted and open-minded (even if occasionally confused and amused) about the foibles of foreigners. Arrogance and bluntness, especially on the part of foreigners, though, are not well tolerated, and people who display these traits are rightly regarded as boors. It is also considered extremely gauche to criticize or display anger in public; the concept of saving face is as strong here as in many Asian countries. Most Egyptians, in other words, display considerably higher levels of tact, sensitivity, and good manners than certain Westerners do. Our advice: When in Cairo, do as the Cairenes do. Watch how they talk, watch their body language, observe the interactions among guests and hosts, men and women, adults and children, and follow suit. Mostly, you will find yourself becoming more civil and civilized as a result. Below, we describe general customs, manners, and morals, and give a few specific pointers on how foreigners can make a positive impression for their own and their compatriots' sakes.

HOSPITALITY WITH A CAPITAL H

Even among the hospitable and generous Arabs, Egyptians take pride of place. They entertain lavishly or not at all—and up to, sometimes beyond, what they can afford. At no dinner parties in Cairo will you find anything remotely resembling nouvelle cuisine with its minimalist selections and starvation-ration portions. Instead, expect at least two or three offerings of every course, often served buffet-style, and heavy on the sweets Egyptians adore. To please your hosts, come with a hearty appetite, dieting for days ahead if necessary. Cairo is no place for finicky eaters, so mind your manners and try a little of everything. If you really cannot stomach liver or kubeeba or pigeon or mulukhiyya, just pray they are not all served at the same dinner, and say, "I love most Egyptian food, but I'm allergic to X, I'm afraid."

It is polite to refuse the first offer of tea or a drink or hors d'oeuvres. Your host will press you, and you then graciously accept the second or third time. You will note quickly that two minutes after you are invited to an Egyptian home, even just to borrow a screwdriver, you will be offered something to eat or drink. You may refuse graciously, but do make the same offer yourself when people are in your home. This holds for business meetings as well, by the way.

Children are far more in evidence on social occasions than in the West, including those that go on until all hours. Your little darling will occasion the kind of acceptance and affection that nothing else can. The only place it is not appropriate to bring kids is to an official or semi-official party or an obviously adults-only event. When in doubt, ask three ways: "Shall we bring the children?"—But of course!—"Will any of the other children be there?"—Oh, a few.—"We have a baby-sitter anyway."—Oh, well, if you'd really rather not . . . .

You are not expected to show up on time to any social event, except the Opera or an *iftar* meal (see **Holidays** below). If you are invited for 8 pm, arrive between 8:30 and 9, but not much after. If it is for dinner, dinner may be served between 11 and 12 anyway. It is also likely that the men and women will eat and socialize quite separately at parties; the more traditional the home, the more likely this is, but even among Westernized Cairenes, it is common. Invitations are issued primarily by telephone. If you are entertaining, it is not untoward to call a few days ahead to remind your guests of the invitation.

Potluck dinners are not an Egyptian custom, nor is offering guests 'doggie bags' to take home or offering to bring something for the dinner, except to the closest of friends. On the other hand, one never ever shows up empty-handed for dinner at someone's home—even Mom's. Foreigners may wonder what their Egyptian hosts do with all the flowers, candy, and pastries they are laden with. Wonder on, if you will, but bring them nevertheless. A fancy cake from a fancy bakery is the safe, chic thing. If you know for certain that your hosts drink alcohol, a bottle of scotch, or some exotic liqueur—imported only—is a welcome alternative. Wine—again, imported only—is less so unless you are sure of your hosts' tastes. Fruit is not acceptable except among close friends, as it might suggest that the hosts cannot afford to buy their own.

If you spend the weekend as someone's guest, it is considerate to tip any household help. LE50 is generous unless you have made a real mess or they have gone above and beyond the call of duty in the care and feeding of your children. And don't bring Fifi or Fido; even if your hosts adore the little mutt, some of their other guests or neighbors might well not.

EGYPTIAN FAMILY LIFE

The importance of this cannot be overemphasized, particularly to Northern Europeans and North Americans, many of whose upbringings lead them to prize independence over family ties. Exactly the opposite is the case here. It is almost unheard of in Egypt, for example, for family members to go for months without seeing each other as adults. The cradle-to-grave family bond is not only inescapable, it is inconceivable that one could live otherwise.

An Egyptian's children, parents, and spouse—usually in that descending order—are exalted above all else. Egyptian mothers are at least as avid, for example, in their attention to their children's studies as Japanese women, this even if they are holding down full-time jobs themselves. It is not uncommon for little Ahmad's mother to learn German herself, say, in order to help Ahmad with his German homework. In the countryside and among the poorer classes, when a mother bears her first son she is proud to be called, for example, Umm Mustafa, 'mother of Mustafa,' and does not remotely view this as a negation of her own identity; on the contrary, it enhances and ennobles it. The mother–son bond is traditionally closer than any other, and, as in many other cultures, is paralleled by the father–daughter bond, although fathers generally play a less active role in their children's upbringing.

The job of Egyptian parents is to set their offspring up for life. They do everything they possibly can financially and socially to make sure their children marry well, get good jobs, and—very important—have a home and its many accouterments to embark on and renew the cycle. For all but the wealthiest, these efforts entail great sacrifices, which are usually undertaken more than willingly. Without a home of his own, usually paid for by his parents, a young middle-class man cannot hope to attract a suitable bride. If the parents of the young lovers (a strictly poetical term) cannot agree on exactly where the home is located and who pays for what bit of the furnishings, the marriage is off. Hence among the middle and upper classes, a broken engagement or two is not uncommon before the right personal and financial terms are reached to produce marriage.

We see, then, that the emotional stake parents have in their children's welfare is intensified by their considerable financial stake all up and down the economic ladder. As in much of the world, arranged marriages are the norm. That is not to say that romantic love does not enter the picture, but it is frequently a secondary consideration. Divorce is certainly not unheard of among Muslims, especially in Cairo, but it is comparatively rare and regarded as a calamity, except, perhaps, among the jaded nouveaux riches. The Coptic church does not allow divorce. An unmarried child is almost as much of a tragedy, childlessness a curse. Much is made of all this on the very popular Egyptian soap operas.

Although Islam permits the taking of up to four wives, this is rare now, particularly as one climbs the social and economic ladder.

SOCIAL CLASS AND MOBILITY

Is Egypt a class-conscious society? Yes, very much so, according to rich and poor alike. But especially since the 1952 Revolution, there are two routes to upward mobility: a military career and education. None of Egypt's four presidents was born to wealth or aristocracy, but they reached the acme of success through their military, and hence political, ambitions and connections. And some lucky few of the poor whose intelligence is recognized and fostered in school can also jump the class barriers to illustrious careers. Top civil servants, for example, are no longer necessarily of the aristocratic class as they invariably were before 1952, nor are members of the professional classes. 'Marrying up,' though not unheard of, is a less common ticket to a different life, given that marriages are more or less arranged.

Nevertheless and overall, despite the postrevolutionary increase in social mobility, Egypt's social structure retains many of its feudalistic divisions, and the Quran teaches all to accept their given stations in life. A couple of examples of how these class divisions work on a daily basis might illustrate the point: upper-class mothers do not take their children to the many public amusement parks appealingly scattered around Cairo—they take them to 'the club' instead. And the bulk of the café–casino–restaurants dotting the banks of the Nile, with their ideal settings, shade, and charm, are frequented only by the odd foreigner and the lower-middle classes—at least according to a number of upper-class Egyptians who would not be caught dead there.

THE BIRDS AND THE BEES

Cairo is much like the rest of Egypt and the Arab world with regard to relations between men and women. Marriage is the sole permissible venue for sexual relations, and platonic friendships between the sexes are rare. Light flirtation, though, is quite commonplace, as long as its limits are made eminently clear, and Egyptians are famous for their bawdy jokes and earthy sense of humor. But public displays of affection beyond a little clandestine hand-holding among young lovebirds are greeted with censure and even downright hostility. An Egyptian friend who gave her fiancé a quick peck in the car when he told her he had finished his doctorate was spat on by the middle-aged couple in the car next to them! (Our friend later used this experience to her advantage when she wanted street lights installed in her midan; she explained to the local council that her aim was to prevent the leafy street from being used as a 'lover's lane'—and quickly got her street lights.)

Adultery is illegal and can carry severe penalties, especially for the adulteress. Homosexuality is illegal too, but generally a blind eye is turned. Women of all classes are expected to be virgins at marriage. An Arabic saying loosely translated warns: 'A girl is like a match—you can only light it once.' To make sure the match lights on the wedding night, for the poor there is chicken blood, for the rich, re-virginization operations—and for the great bulk of brides there is genuine chasteness. Engaged couples can go out alone, in public, but the Western practice of dating prior to engagement does not exist; in effect, the couple only begin getting to know each other after they have committed publicly to marriage—another reason that broken engagements are not uncommon.

Males are circumcised with great fanfare among country people between ages five and ten, although among wealthy urban dwellers it is commonly done in infancy. And yes, female circumcision is practiced to a considerable extent in Egypt among both Muslims and Copts.

The removal of all bodily hair (including that of the head) was regarded by the ancient Egyptians as an act of spiritual purification for men and women. Today, men tend to limit it to shaving the underarm and sometimes the pubic hair, but fastidious women regularly have their bodies depilated completely using a sugar-and-lemon taffy-like substance called *halaawa*. Many a Western bride has been somewhat chagrined to learn that her Egyptian husband views this as an essential aspect of his wife's toilette, as do her mother- and sisters-in-law.

WEDDINGS AND FUNERALS

Egyptian weddings are wonderful and exceedingly noisy bashes, whether held on the village street or at the Nile Hilton. Invariably, they are joyous, raucous, open-handed affairs designed in part to demonstrate the wealth and generosity of the families involved. And like Western weddings, they frequently break the bank of the parents. The groom's family usually pays for the wedding, the couple's house or flat, kitchen, lights, and electrical appliances. The bride's family handles the engagement party, furniture, and carpets. But the groom also has to come up with 'bride money,' or *mahr*, usually equaling one room of furniture, and a wedding gift, usually gold, for his bride, called the *shabka*; in rural areas, it is the *kir-daan*, or wedding necklace, and it has to be 21 or 24 carat gold, whereas in the city one can get away respectably with only 18 carats.

Foreigners are frequently invited or mere-ly dragged along most welcome to Egyptian weddings. Your only obligation if dragged along is to enjoy yourself, dance, and be gracious. If you are invited, a gift is required. Gifts of cash are not appropriate, unless for a driver or bawab. Silver tea sets, ashtrays, vases, and the like are also wel-come. For the wedding of friends, it is per-fectly all right to ask what they would like. Gifts are delivered to the couple's or fami-lies' home, not taken to the wedding, and they are not formally acknowledged.

Funeral customs are comparatively sim-ple, but there are a few things to be aware of. Among Muslims, women receive women at home and men receive men either at home or in a specially-erected tent nearby on the day of the burial and for the follow-ing two days. It is customary to offer condo-lences then sit quietly for half an hour or so before leaving. Sugarless coffee is tradition-ally served. Only the men go to the mosque, where prayers are said, then they walk to the cemetery or part way carrying the bier. If one cannot attend a funeral when it is expected that one should—and this is an obligation to which great weight is given—it is customary and virtually required to send a telegram, fax, or note of condolence right away to the family of the deceased. An important commemoration takes place on the fortieth day after the death, and if you were not able to pay your respects at the time, you should certainly do so now. Cop-tic funeral customs differ slightly in having a church service, attended by men and women, but otherwise condolences are paid in the same way on the three days at the time of the death and on the fortieth day after.

HOLIDAYS AND HOLIDAY CUSTOMS

Although Egypt is not the country with the most holidays in the world (Sri Lanka holds that distinction), it is up there—thanks to the mix of secular, Muslim, and Coptic traditions. Egypt also uses three dif-ferent calendars for different purposes: the Gregorian or Western calendar is used for most secular purposes, the Islamic for Muslim religious events, and the Coptic, the ancient pharaonic calendar, for farming and Coptic observances. Each is slightly different in duration, and each starts at a different time of year, so some holidays shift considerably on the Gregorian calen-dar from year to year. In our description below, public holidays are indicated; banks, schools, government offices, and many businesses close on these days. The holidays are given in 2006 Gregorian cal-endar order. (See also the **Holidays** chart at the front of the book.)

Ramadan. 24 September–24 October, 2006; 13 September–13 October, 2007. See below for a full description.

Laylat al-Qadr (Night of Power). 27th night of Ramadan, commemorating the Prophet's receiving of the first chapter of the Quran. It is believed that prayers are answered on this night.

Eid al-Fitr, or the Small Feast (public). 24–27 October, 2006 and 13–16 October, 2007*. Three-day holiday feast marking the end of Ramadan. Many people take off for the country or seaside, so travel reser-vations need to be made well ahead of time, and the roads to and from Cairo are packed. Tourists take heed—not the ideal time for a spontaneous visit. This Eid is also one of the two annual sale times, when everyone is supposed to get a new set of clothing. At this feast, it is traditional to give one's Muslim domestic help, building employees, etc., gifts of food and/or money, as much as a month's salary if not dispersed piecemeal during other holidays. This is much more vital than Christmas baksheesh, which will nevertheless also be solicited.

Coptic Christmas. 7 January. Copts attend midnight mass. Monasteries are closed for fasting during the 43 days preceding.

Eid al-Adha, or the Great Feast (public). 31 December, 2006–3 January, 2007*. This four-day feast, occurring seventy days after the end of Ramadan, marks the prophet Abraham's sacrifice of a sheep in place of his son. It is celebrated by the slaughter of sheep, naturally, the meat of which must be shared with those who cannot afford to slaughter their own. Hence the streets are filled with temporary pens holding the sheep until they are slaughtered. Like the Small Feast, this is not the ideal time for spur-of-the-moment travel.

Islamic New Year (public). 30 January, 2007*.

Sinai Liberation Day (public). 25 April.

Eastern Palm Sunday. Coptic Christian holiday.

Labor Day (public). 1 May.

Eastern Easter.

Shamm al-Nisim (public). 2 May. The pharaonic rite of spring, Shamm al-Nisim or 'sniffing the breezes,' is the origin of some Western Easter practices, including the dyeing of eggs.

Mulid al-Nabi, the Prophet's Birthday (public). 31 March, 2007*. Great festivities countrywide, with a big, colorful procession held at al-Azhar.

Evacuation Day. 18 June. Celebrates the evacuation of the last British troops from Egypt in 1956.

Revolution Day (public). 23 July. Anniversary of the 1952 Revolution.

Coptic New Year. 11 September (12 September in leap years).

Armed Forces Day (public). 6 October.

*Dates of Islamic holidays are approximate.

Ramadan, the holiest month and holiday of Islam, celebrates the beginning of the revelation of the Quran to the Prophet through the Archangel Gabriel. Business and schooling come largely to a standstill, starting late and ending early. Devout Muslims fast totally (no food, drink, cigarettes, sex, or impure thoughts) from sunrise to sunset, in accordance with one of the Five Pillars of Islam. The streets empty completely just before sunset, when everyone breaks the fast with a festive meal called *ifTaar*. Then, in the very early morning (1–2 am), a second meal, *suHuur*, is taken, often in restaurants with friends.

Tents and tables line the streets of the city as wealthy merchants and philanthropists lay out night-long feasts for the poor every single evening—an amazing and impressive logistical and charitable feat. The wealthy congregate in special tents set up outside fashionable restaurants and hotels and in the Opera House gardens to eat, socialize, and smoke shiisha. Some restaurants close during the day, except for those in large hotels, which remain open. Alcohol is removed from the shelves of all stores, and people carrying Egyptian passports will not be served alcohol anywhere, day or night. As a mark of respect, foreigners should refrain completely from eating, drinking, or smoking in public during the day in Ramadan; if they do not, they will hear about it, usually politely, from the taxi driver or passersby.

Since they do not get much sleep during Ramadan, some people tend to get a bit cranky during the day, especially when Ramadan falls during the summer with its long hours of daylight and high temperatures. Young children, travelers, the sick, and pregnant and menstruating women are exempt from fasting, although many women fast a few days beforehand to account for the days of their menstruation during Ramadan. Stores are laden with special foods, especially nuts and sweets, in anticipation of the nightly feasts, and special Ramadan lanterns decorate all the highways and byways. Husayn Square and Khan al-Khalili are packed from dusk to dawn with revelers—an amazing riot of noise, music, entertainment, food, and shopping, but only for the sturdy and crowd-tolerant.

During Ramadan of 2006, the Ministry of Culture selected several ancient monuments for musical entertainment. Free of charge, the evenings gave the local communities and guests a wonderful way to spend the evening after a day of fasting. Keep an eye out for the schedule when Ramadan rolls around.

All in all, Ramadan reveals a unique set of contrasts: piety and gaiety, charity and ostentation, sacrifice and indulgence. Especially for foreigners interested in Islam, Cairo during Ramadan is fascinating—and exhausting. Tourists should note that the streets are very noisy at night, that businesses keep odd hours, and that sustenance during the day is hard to come by.

YET MORE HOLIDAYS!

Fathers and mothers, farmers and doctors, artists and engineers also get their special days marked in Egypt, but on these, life goes on an usual. Another type of feast, the *muulid*, is celebrated by Copts and Muslims to honor their special saints. They are colorful religious celebrations involving dense crowds, parades, food stalls, animal acts, whirling dervishes—the works. Well worth seeing, but keep a very low profile, as religious zeal as well as great merriment runs high during a mulid. The biggest ones in Cairo are al-Husayn and Sayyida Zeinab, but women are strongly advised to stick to the smaller, local mulids.

HOW TO DRESS, DRINK, AND COMPORT ONESELF IN GENERAL

Egyptian movies from the thirties through the sixties reflect an Egypt that embraced Western ideals. In real life, too, affluent couples danced the night away in the smoke-filled boîtes of Cairo and Alexandria, and women copied the latest fashions from Paris and New York. Now, their daughters and granddaughters voluntarily veil themselves, join Islamic study groups, and take great pride in their religious heritage. Young men whose fathers have huge stocks of Johnny Walker Black at home spend their nights in vigil at the mosque and work for Islamic reform. So what is a foreigner to do?

You will generally avoid embarrassing yourself and others by keeping one thing uppermost in mind at all times: Egypt is a predominantly Muslim country in which Islamic ideals are becoming more and more the yardstick for behavior. It might also be useful to remember that most Egyptians' ideas about foreigners are colored much more by what they see on television and at the movies than by what they experience directly. Hence the average Westerner has love affairs and illegitimate children, takes drugs, carries a gun, has money to burn, and dresses just like they do on *The Bold and the Beautiful*.

To dispel these myths is not easy, particularly as some tourists perpetuate them by their dress and manners. Foreign residents, especially women, should dress considerably more modestly than they might at home, as detailed in the **Climate** section early in this chapter. For men and women, shorts are for sports and resorts, period.

Alcohol is another source of pitfalls. Obviously, many Muslims drink, just as many Christians ignore some of the tenets of their faith. But it is best to assume they do not until one has evidence to the contrary. If you are hosting a man with a prayer bruise on his forehead or a woman wearing the 'Islamic' head-covering, don't offer alcohol, and drink orange juice yourself if you need the contract. Even where alcohol is offered, imbibe moderately; this is especially important for women. One foreign consultant quickly lost her job in Cairo, in no small part because she mistakenly assumed she could slug 'em back with the boys at cocktail parties just like she did back home.

Muslims do not eat pork and would not knowingly relish anything cooked with alcohol, so save the bacon, grandemère's soufflé Grand Marnier, and your famous lasagna with pork sausage and red wine for compatriots.

EXCEPTIONS AND CONTRADICTIONS

Some of what has been said above might suggest to Westerners in particular a strait-laced, restrictive, intolerant society. Nothing could be further from the truth. Egypt, and Cairo in particular, embraces many exceptions and contradictions to the basic (and basically conservative) rules. A few examples. The extraordinary courtesy that prevails overall occasionally gives way to public screaming matches of epically obscene proportions. Young and old Egyptian cosmopolites of both sexes dance, smoke, drink, and even get drunk in the trendy bars. Hordes of Gulf Arabs out for a good time pack the belly-dancing clubs on the Pyramids Road and along 26th of July Street downtown. Prostitutes from all parts of the world including Egypt ply their trade in special 'hooker bars' scattered around town. Drugs are all too readily available, with wealthy (often foreign) teenagers being frequent targets of the dealers. For some rich men, a mistress is as essential to the wardrobe as an Armani suit. And the shop selling headscarves and long dresses is flanked on one side by a display of daring lingerie, on the other by sequined cocktail dresses of even more daring dimensions. In other words, Cairo is a big city. Don't expect consistency. And if you choose to explore the seamier side of its many-faceted personality, do so prudently.

A FEW SPECIFIC DOS AND DON'TS

Do see your guests to and beyond the door at the close of an evening. It is rude to abandon them before the elevator door closes.

Don't ask for 'Turkish coffee' in Egypt. Until barely a hundred years ago the Ottoman Turks ruled the Egyptians, who are still a tad touchy about it. Ask for *'ahwa* ('coffee') instead.

Women's Lib has not had quite the same impact in Egypt as it has in some Western countries. This produces some charmingly chivalrous behavior toward women on the part of men—opening doors, carrying packages, etc.—but can also cause the poor things acute embarrassment if a woman offers to or insists upon paying for dinner. Defer to the custom of the country or your male companion's sensibilities on this issue.

Don't send flowers when someone dies. Flowers connote happiness and are therefore inappropriate on sad occasions.

Don't wonder aloud why your colleague is washing his or her feet, hands, ears, and face in the lavatory so often. It is done by devout Muslims before each prayer. Neither should a woman put a man in the awkward position of having to shake hands, as a woman's touch must also be washed away before prayer. Wait for him to make the first move. Egyptians are big kissers, but in public it's mostly same-sex greeting and departure kisses.

Don't barge in and discuss money. These are not safety precautions: it is simply considered extremely rude to be hasty or frank about money. This holds regardless of the facts that many Cairenes think nothing of asking foreigners what they have paid for their flat, their dress, their kids' school, or their laundry detergent.

Don't direct the soles of your feet at someone when crossing your legs and don't put your feet onto a stool with the soles facing someone, it is considered extremely rude.

When greeting an Egyptian, take time to address them with a salutation, smile, and inquiry of their family. There is no rush to jump immediately into business. Take a few minutes to be friendly before proceeding with your business.

In the office, do not have your secretary call a colleague of the same level; call yourself.

If an Egyptian brings a plate of food to your home, return the plate with some goodies on it, as well.

Be complimentary, but not unduly so, about other people's possessions. Excessive admiration attracts the evil eye and puts the owner in the position of having to follow the Egyptian custom of offering the item to the admirer with a gracious "Here, take it." A lengthy exchange of "Oh, no, I didn't mean . . . ," "But I insist . . ." must then follow.

Likewise, don't gurgle and coo over an adorable infant or toddler. Au contraire: either say nothing or, if you know the parents well, say something like, "Oh, what an ugly baby; this is the ugliest baby I have ever seen!" They will understand that you mean exactly the opposite and appreciate your thoughtfulness.

Unless you want to advertise that you have just had sex, don't go out of the house with wet hair.

ACCOMMODATIONS

Cairo has a huge number of restaurants and hotels, the range and variety of which, however, are somewhat less than dazzling for a city of this size, diversity, and crossroads-of-the-world location. The novelty-seeking sybarites among our readers should adjust their expectations accordingly. For the rest of us, good beds and good food in a wide range of prices are easily found throughout Cairo. Rather than supplying an exhaustive review, we highlight here the main five-star hotels and some less expensive, well-recommended alternatives in different areas of town.

Although the high-end hotels are managed by major international chains, most are government-owned by the Housing, Tourism, and Cinema Holding Company under the direction of the Ministry of Public Enterprise. Hotel staff members generally reflect the friendliness for which Egyptians are justly famous, but service standards overall are comparatively low—undelivered newspapers and messages are common, telephones calls go unanswered or misdirected, restaurant service is slow to inept, and so on. You will find exceptions, certainly; when you do, bring them to the attention of the management, reward them with good tips, and they might become the rule.

Belly-dancing fans who want to go to bed before the wee hours will lament the lack of shows that finish by 10 or 11 pm. As it is, the only early-evening venues are the Nile riverboat cruises, which are fine, but a bit constrained on space and variety.

THE MAIN FIVE-STAR HOTELS

All of these have the usual amenities, including some with 24-hour casinos, executive floors, and basic to state-of-the-art health clubs. Sample rack rates for non-residents: $300 for executive floor singles, $275 for doubles with Nile views, $250 for city views, $210 for regular rooms. But don't be alarmed by these unduly high prices: corporate, government, tour-group, resident, and long-term rates are half or less, with seasonal and bargaining skill variations. Or check hotel websites for bargains.

CENTRAL CAIRO

Cairo Sheraton: Despite its other-side-of-the-river location in Giza, this is a strong favorite among business and embassy types. There is a duty-free shop on site.

Photo of the Sonesta Star Goddess "Beethoven Suite"

ABC Bank

بنك المؤسسة العربية المصرفية

هدفنـا التميـز

سهوله التعامل

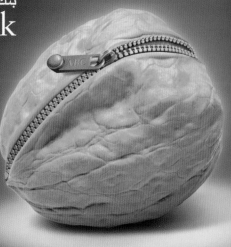

ATM locations

Cairo:
Grand Hyatt Hotel
Cairo Marriott Hotel
Nile Hilton Commercial Annex
Gezira Sheraton Hotel
Talaat Harb Mall
Arkadia Mall
Maadi Grand Mall
Maadi City Center- Carrefour
City Center - Nasr City
Geneina Mall
New Airport (Arrivals Hall)
10th of Ramadan (HiPack Co.)

Alexandria:
City Center - Carrefour
Green Plaza

Sharm El Sheikh:
Marriott Hotel
Fayrouz Hilton
Naguib Commercial Center
Radisson Hotel

ATMs are also available at all ABC BANK Branches

www.arabbanking.com.eg

ABC Bank

HEAD OFFICE
1, El Saleh Ayoub St., Zamalek, Cairo
Tel.: (202) 7362756 - 7362684
Fax: (202) 7363614
Email: abcegypt@arabbanking.com.eg
Website: www.arabbanking.com.eg

Branches

ZAMALEK
1, El Saleh Ayoub St., Zamalek, Cairo
Tel.: (202) 7362756 - 7362684
Fax: (202) 7363614
Email: zamalek@arabbanking.com.eg

MOHANDESEEN
32, Syria St., Mohandeseen, Giza
P.O. Box 237 Embaba 12411
Tel.: (202) 3366758 - 7492200
Fax: (202) 7615760
Email: mohand@arabbanking.com.eg

CAIRO (BOSTAN)
18, Youssef El Guendi St., El Bostan Center,
Bab El Louk, Cairo
Tel.: (202) 3911973 - 3956084 - 3955859
Fax: (202) 3926467
Email: cairo@arabbanking.com.eg

MAADI
8, 257 St., New Maadi
Tel.: (202) 7057026 / 7
Fax: (202) 7057028
Email: maadi@arabbanking.com.eg

HARAM
400, Al Haram Street, Giza
Tel: 02 5879831/ 5879832
Fax: 02 7815112
Email: haram@arabbanking.com.eg

NASR CITY
62, Makram Ebeid St., Area No.6, Nasr City
Tel.: (202) 2755270 / 1
Fax: (202) 2877532
Email: nasrcity@arabbanking.com.eg

OBOUR BUILDINGS
3, Obour Buildings, Salah Salem St.
Tel.: (202) 4033095 - 4033075
Fax: (202) 2616860
Email: obour@arabbanking.com.eg

HELIOPOLIS
105, Merghany St., Heliopolis
Tel.: (202) 2906345 - 2906782
Fax: (202) 2910393
Email: heliopolis@arabbanking.com.eg

SHERATON
2, Khaled Ibn Elwaleed Street, next to
El Sedeek Mosque, Sheraton Heliopolis.
Tel: 02 2673128/ 2673129
Fax:02 2673117
Email: sheraton@arabbanking.com.eg

10th OF RAMADAN
First Quarter Center, Building No.4, Entrance
No. 1, 10th of Ramadan City 44629
Tel.: (2015) 361697 / 8
Fax.: (2015) 364074
Email: ramadan@arabbanking.com.eg

6th OF OCTOBER CITY
Hamees Mall, Next to Misr University for Science
and Technology, El Hai El Motamayez,
6th of October City
P.O. Box 62 El Hai El Motamayez (12568)
Tel.: (202) 8367607 / 8
Fax: (202) 8367610
Email: 6october@arabbanking.com.eg

ALEXANDRIA
24, Bani El Abbas St., Bab Sharky, Alexandria
P.O. Box 313 (21111) Alexandria
Tel.: (203) 4840154 - 4879676
Fax: (203) 4879675
Email: alex@arabbanking.com.eg

SHARM EL SHEIKH
Marriott Hotel, Commercial Annex,
Sharm El Sheikh
Tel.: (2069) 3603742
Fax: (2069) 3603741
Email: sharm@arabbanking.com.eg

Call us at **19123** from Cairo and **(+202) 3003003** from outside Cairo

Four Seasons: With two branches, one at the First Residence in Giza and the other in the Nile Plaza in Garden City, this is by far the most expensive hotel in town, boasting that it has brought unprecedented five-star service to Cairo. Catering particularly to business travelers, it offers computer-friendly rooms and a full service business center. Both hotels have a spa service at international prices and high-end shopping malls.

Nile Hilton: Its 1960s-style aqua-and-white exterior lacks charm, but the rooms facing the Nile have delightful balcony views, and the secluded pool area may be the best in town. There is a small new upscale shopping arcade that is very agreeable, with a good coffee shop, Café Olé, that is ideal while waiting for the Egyptian Museum next door to open. With the Corniche traffic to the front and Midan al-Tahrir to the back, all rooms are quite noisy with the windows open. Ali's Alley, the shiisha terrace at the back of the hotel, is the place to see and be seen—and smoke shiisha—on a summer's afternoon.

Ramsis Hilton: Rising above a welter of flyovers and a bus station, this Hilton is more centrally located than those in search of peace and quiet might wish. Windows on the World, the top-floor restaurant, has the most spectacular views in town and is open after 6 pm. But the LE49 minimum charge deters the many local patrons who would otherwise pack the place to enjoy the sunset with tea or a beer. At night, Windows becomes a popular hangout with a jazz singer on hand, finally justifying the minimum. The Ramses Hilton has the largest shopping arcade of any of the hotels, in its separate annex. There is a good movie theater in the annex that shows Western films.

Hyatt and Grand Hyatt Cairo: Bar none, the best views of Cairo, thanks to the hotel's north-facing location at the tip of Roda Island. The hotel also has a shopping center and movie theater, as well as good Japanese, Indian, and Italian restaurants.

Semiramis Intercontinental: Very convenient to the many embassies in Garden City, and boasting one of the better lobby-lounge areas and overall layouts of the in-town hotels. The posh Grill Room restaurant has sweeping Nile views and good food. There is also an Italian restaurant that occasionally boasts live music. The Bird Cage restaurant reputedly has the best Thai food in Cairo.

Conrad: This opened in 1999 and is a hotel favored almost exclusively by business travelers. Its location next to the World Trade Center is a bit out of the way, making the atmosphere rather subdued. Guests are treated to excellent service in a calm environment with three very good, though highly priced, restaurants. All rooms have a Nile view.

HELIOPOLIS

Mövenpick Heliopolis is a popular community center for residents as well as being ideally located close to the airport and the many businesses that line the roads to it; it also holds frequent garage sales or flea markets as does the Mövenpick in Giza.

The *Meridien Heliopolis* is a favorite of Heliopolis's large French community; its Le 51 Bar is a favored watering-hole.

Rounding out the upscale choices are the *Sheraton Heliopolis*, *Concorde Cairo El Salam* and the older *Baron Heliopolis*, famous for its bakery.

Intercontinental Heliopolis Cairo: Located next to Citystars, the largest mall in Cairo, and only minutes from Cairo International Airport, this massive hotel caters for tourists who want to 'shop till they drop' and then relax by one of the three swimming pools.

QATTAMIYA

Mirage City JW Marriott Hotel: A new resort hotel near many schools and universities, JW Marriott Hotel is only 15 minutes away from Cairo International Airport and Cairo Conference Center. Further from central Cairo than tourists may like, it however offers an 18-hole golf course and a water park that has a wave pool and water slides.

6TH OF OCTOBER CITY

Thirty-eight kilometers from downtown Cairo, Sixth of October City is an up-and-coming government-planned community created to ease the congestion and overcrowding of Cairo. People are moving to large villas with gardens, and already the area is studded with amusement parks, international hotels, and mega-malls. The population is more than 500,000. One day there will be a new international airport, but for now it is a child's paradise, with many amusement parks—Magic Land, Dreamland Park, and Egypt Media Production City. Diamond Mall and Bahgat Stores are mega-malls with Renaissance 6th of October Cinema—a new cinema with two screens and surround sound (midnight shows on Thursday, Fridays, and Saturdays). There is already a well-equipped Gold's Gym. Modern Science Academy University, the sister school of University of Greenwich, is receiving students. Two international hotels are open for business: Movenpick Cairo Media City and Hilton Pyramid Golf Resort.

PYRAMIDS AREA

Le Meridien Pyramids: Close by the Pyramids and with eye-popping views of them from the pool and some of the rooms. Excellent tennis courts, a large pool with a swim-up bar, and an elegant lobby.

Mena House Oberoi: Rising in Moorish splendor at the foot of the Pyramids, this is the choice of many Cairenes for a weekend getaway in Cairo. Lovely gardens, a great pool, golf, tennis, and the Moghul Room for some of the best Indian food in Cairo. Since it is not in the heart of town, it does not attract the business crowd, but does get many tour groups. Service is similar to that of other hotels but the ghosts of all the greats who have stayed there, plus the spectacular decor and setting, make up for this.

Mövenpick Jolie Ville: Pyramid views from some rooms, good programs for kids and for Giza residents, from whom the hotel garners good customers in addition to its tour-group business. A popular flea market is held on Fridays in the parking lot.

Intercontinental Pyramids Park on the Alexandria Desert Road is pleasant with a large garden, pool area, and playground. It is a favorite weekend retreat for American expat families.

OTHER CHOICES AROUND TOWN

MAADI

Sofitel: Popular with the many oil companies in and around Maadi and for its advantageous pool membership with residents.

The *Cairotel* has the best pool, with reasonable membership rates as well.

The *Residence Hotel,* home to the popular La Cassetta restaurant, is a real residential hotel with large two- and three-bedroom flats, often used by incoming/outgoing expatriates for temporary living quarters. The hotel has recently been renovated.

ZAMALEK

Cairo Marriott Hotel: Ismail Pasha, ruler of Egypt from 1863–1879 built a U-shaped palace on the northern part of Zamalek island for house guests arriving for the opening of the Suez Canal in 1869. Around the palace, the gardens were used as a race course and polo field, aquarium, and even as an area for roller skating. Today, the Marriott still boasts the palace's original décor and architecture. On Friday afternoons, the garden restaurant is a favorite for long-time residents and Cairenes.

The *Hotel Flamenco* is deservedly a favorite for its food, service, and lovely views; its Florencia Restaurant on the tenth floor is rated the best in Cairo by many residents—superb steak au poivre, real paellas, great shrimp bisque—and there is an interesting cocktail lounge and a billiards room on the same floor.

The *President Hotel* is also highly regarded top to bottom—from the sixteenth-floor balcony rooms facing west, one can see the Pyramids in the mist, and the Cellar Bar is a good one. Also recommended is the *Safir Zamalek*, which rents apartments as well. And if you want to be literally on the water and get a taste of what houseboat-living might be like, the *Imperial Hotel* boat is a reasonably cushy way to experiment. Way down on the star scale, but perfectly okay, is the Pension Zamalek above the Meringo Bakery; for the budget-conscious young and young-at-heart, it cannot be beaten at LE50 single and LE80 per night with breakfast. *Horus House* (singles/doubles $52/$70) is a clean and friendly family-run hotel.

DOKKI AND MOHANDISEEN
We like three in this area: the *Hotel Nabila* right off Midan Sphinx on Sharia Gam'at al-Duwal al-'Arabiya is very clean and appealing with a nice little nook of a bar–coffeeshop outdoors. The *Atlas Zamalek* is nearby, not in Zamalek at all. Also it is right next door to al-'Umda for cheap, good Egyptian fare. Finally the *Jasmin Hotel* near Midan Libnan is a charmer.

DOWNTOWN AND GARDEN CITY
The best source for a thorough rundown on the many very cheap hotels around Midans Tahrir and Ramsis is Lonely Planet's *Egypt*. But for the more fastidious and/or over-the-hill who nevertheless eschew luxury in favor of 'atmosphere,' the same names keep coming up word-of-mouth: Windsor, Odeon, Cosmopolitan, Pension Roma, and Garden City House.

The *Windsor Hotel* (singles $38–$47; doubles $37–$56) behind Cinema Diana echoes its history from the moment you enter the welcoming portals and see a genuine old-fashioned switchboard in working order behind the reception desk. Formerly an annex to the Shepheard's of old, the hotel has been owned and managed by the Doss family since the 1950s; they keep the large rooms and baths clean. Although some may find the bar dreary, its time-warped, old-style atmosphere is the very attraction for its many devoteés.

The *Cosmopolitan Hotel* (singles $48; doubles $60) is another remnant of another world smack dab in the middle of today's, but mercifully quiet.

Garden City House (singles LE54–85; doubles LE63.5–83) is convenient to AUC and Garden City embassies.

The *Odeon Palace* is efficient, central, and reasonable (singles $40; doubles $50); like many others, it is amenable to discounts for longer-term stays, and the 24-hour rooftop bar is a popular Cairo institution.

Pension Roma (singles LE45, doubles LE85) has antique furniture, high ceilings, wooden floorboards, polite staff, and old-world charm.

Talisman: Boutique hotels are beginning to surface in Cairo and the Talisman is a gem. In the heart of downtown Cairo, the owners renovated a dilapidated building and opened this charming hotel in an authentic oriental atmosphere. With only 25 rooms, the hotel is quiet and elegant yet fitted with modern technology. The hallways are full of art, and open onto Arab salons where you can sip tea and read a favorite book. Breakfast is served in a mashrabiya room. The hotel provides information about good restaurants throughout Cairo for lunch and dinner. Should you travel to Damascus, look up the Talisman there, also a luxurious renovated house in the center of the old city.

FOOD AND DRINK

Cairo boasts some fine restaurants and new ones open every week to take advantage of Egypt's bounty of fresh, excellent produce available almost year round. Another plus: most foreigners will find that, except at the very highest levels, restaurant prices are mostly very reasonable.

For foreigners who prefer the tried and true, all the large hotels offer 'continental' cuisine like one finds the world over in their coffeeshops and plush restaurants. Breakfast buffets in particular are designed to satisfy the peculiarly wide range of what people eat in the morning: fish for the English and Scandinavians, cheese and charcuterie for the Germans, croissants for the French, scrambled eggs and cereal for Americans, plus steaming copper vessels of fuul, the Egyptian breakfast of champions. Note, though, that these buffets are not cheap—between LE100 and LE300—so if you indulge, eat heartily. Some of the hotels throw in breakfast with the room, which represents a considerable saving particularly when traveling with children, so do try negotiating this.

Continuing in the tried-and-true vein, foreign readers will be either relieved or appalled to see the familiar logos of McDonald's, Dominos, Fuddruckers, Pizza Hut, KFC, Baskin Robbins, Hardees, and local variants thereof on virtually every corner of Cairo. Well, not in Islamic and Old Cairo . . . yet. Will the Golden Arches rise up next to Bab Zuwayla one day? Perish the thought. These fast-food joints are wildly popular among Egyptians and foreigners, and the in thing for toddlers' birthday parties is for the little critters to invade one of these places with their harried mothers in tow. Curiously and most refreshingly, service at both the Egyptian and international fast-food and take-away restaurants is far superior to that found in many of the upscale places.

Nearly every kind of food is deliverable in Cairo, from groceries to fine restaurant cuisine and fast food. Check bookstores for the most recent dining guides, pick up *The Croc*, or go to *www.otlob.com* and *www.cairodining.com*.

EGYPTIAN FOOD

Before discussing what Egyptians eat, it is handy to know when they eat. Lunch at home or in restaurants other than those in hotels is usually not served until at least 2 pm and can start anywhere up to 5 pm after that. But some places close between 3:30 and 7 or 8 pm. For dinner, restaurants are deserted until at least 8, when tourists start trickling in, but 10 or 11 is when Egyptians start arriving, and it is not at all unusual for whole families to be working through their dinners at 1 or 2 in the morning. Office workers often have breakfast at their desks around 10, so 11 am might be the ideal time to approach government offices in particular so as not to disturb the morning's rituals.

Egyptian cuisine is a melange of Middle Eastern fare with local variations in spice. In general, the food is not overly hot-spicy, although it can be very salty. There are loads of good places around town to try, each with its own adherents who swear that this place has the best *kufta,* that stand the best *Ta'miyya*. We describe here some of the dishes you will encounter, and reliable places in which to do so, but we hope you will discover your own favorites and maybe even report back to us.

Breakfast often consists of a *fuul* sandwich—stewed broad beans with spices and salt added, slathered into *'eesh shaami* or *'eesh baladi*, respectively the delicious white and brown Egyptian versions of pita bread. The bread is sold in bakeries and supermarkets, but it is also hawked by children on every corner, and young boys wheel around Cairo on their bikes balancing huge piles of it on door-sized frames on their heads. *Ta'miyya*, fried patties of ground broad beans, parsley, coriander leaves, and other greens mixed with spices and sometimes egg, is also eaten at breakfast and throughout the day. Another way of preparing broad beans is to allow them to sprout and then marinate them in oil and spices: this is *fuul naabit*, a good snack often served free with drinks in bars (the Cellar Bar in the President Hotel is reputed to serve the best).

Speaking of bread, and to torture our readers who love it, the very best bread in Egypt, and perhaps in the whole wide world, is called *'eesh shamsi*—'sun bread.' Bread cognoscenti compare it favorably to France's *pain Poilane*. Left to rise on the hot sand in the sun, it is chewy and brown, with a crispy crust and a marvelous bite and aroma—divine. But you cannot get it in Cairo, so there! It is made only in Upper Egypt, a whole hour away by plane. Who will be first to make a mint by marketing *'eesh shami* in Cairo and Alexandria? In the meantime, leave an entire suitcase empty to carry loaves of it home with you from Hurghada, Aswan, and Luxor.

Lunch and dinner always begin with selections of *mazza*, or appetizers, which can in themselves make a great meal. *Babaghannuugh* and *TaHiina* dips are standard, the former being smoked mashed eggplant (aubergine) with garlic and oil, the latter a ground sesame seed paste with mild spices. Both are eaten with plain or toasted pieces of *'eesh baladi*, as are soft feta cheese dips with tomato and garlic. *Wara' 'inab* are grape leaves stuffed with minced meat and rice, served both hot and cold; our favorites are from Estoril downtown and Paprika on the Corniche. Sometimes you see *baTaarikh*, the semi-dry pressed Egyptian salmon roe—very strong, salty, and somewhat expensive, but otherwise not much like caviar—served with hard-boiled egg. *Tabbuula* is usually delicious in Egypt; either as

the salad course or part of the *mazza*, this mixture of parsely, tomato, onion, lime juice, oil, and usually bulgur wheat, tastes like health incarnate. *Mazza* also might include pickled carrots, radishes, onions, and olives. A few of the desert monasteries make and sell fantastic olives, but the ones in Cairo stores and restaurants tend to be more bitter than their European cousins.

More substantial fare includes *kufta*, spiced, grilled meatball fingers that kids love along with adults, and *kushari*, a great, cheap, and filling dish of rice, pasta, and brown lentils served with tomato sauce and dry-fried onions. The very best is said to be at Abu Tarek on Champollion Street, downtown, as is Kushari Tahrir near AUC. Kids also usually like kushari, and it is certainly healthy. *Mulukhiyya* (which is Jew's mallow, a leafy plant that somewhat resembles mint in appearance but not in taste) is a uniquely Egyptian dish, usually made as a soup served with rice. It is green, it is slimy, it is an acquired taste, but the amazing thing is that tots who normally refuse any remotely green food simply gobble up this unusual staple of the Cairene diet, so take note and try it. Stuffed pigeon is another popular delicacy; all those tall narrow mud-brick towers with holes in them one sees in the countryside are pigeon coops, whose little denizens, once nicely roasted, grace many a buffet table. More common still is simple spit-roasted chicken, sold at any number of holes-in-the-wall throughout the city and usually delicious. Andrea's on the Kirdasa road serves up a particularly good version in a more serene setting.

Meat, particularly lamb, can be excellent; the beautiful fat-tailed sheep one often sees being herded through Cairo's quieter streets make delicious eating and are highly prized during the many feasts, since the average Egyptian's diet is heavily vegetarian for economic reasons. The sheep's testicles are considered a great delicacy; Alfi Bey on

Sharia al-Alfi, Downtown serves some of the best. Beef and veal are very lean, hence healthy, in Egypt, although the veal is not milk-fed. In many places, beef tends to be less tender than its European and American counterparts, but Florencia, Angus, and Pub 28, all in Zamalek, serve superb steaks—juicy, tender, and cooked as ordered. Mixed grills served kebab-style on skewers are very popular, as are mountainous barbecued meat platters, but this cooking method tends to bring out the toughness and dryness of all cuts. Lovers of offal—kidneys, brains, and above all, liver—will find that many Egyptians also enjoy these delicacies; one of the best (and cheapest) places to try these is al-'Ahd al-Gadid on Sharia Muski near Khan al-Khalili or any Abou El Sid restaurant.

Fresh fish from the Mediterranean and the Red Sea is widely available, but restaurants catering to foreigners tend to limit their offerings to grouper, or sea bass, and shrimp (prawns) and calamari. Lobster is also available, but is generally unremarkable and always expensive. Shrimp tends to be expensive. Calamari is much cheaper, generally more reliable, and positively addictive when lightly fried and served with lime wedges. One of the best places for a delicious bouillabaise-like stew loaded with seafood is Tia Maria in Mohandiseen; their whole menu, in fact, is very good, and consequently this restaurant is almost always crowded. The Flying Fish in Agouza also serves excellent seafood; it is reputed to be Omar Sharif's favorite Cairo restaurant.

A favorite seafood restaurant, pre-1995, was Asmak Amir in Shubra. The restaurant has since changed its name to Malik el Gambary and opened a branch in Mohandiseen. If you are up for an adventure take a left onto Sharia Khulusi from Shubra bride-tunnel and follow Khulusi to its end in Midan Dawaran Shubra.

Last but certainly not least is dessert. Egyptians love sweets of all sorts and make

some delicious pastries. Wandering around Cairo, one immediately notices that pastry shops are nearly as prevalent as shoe stores, and that they are often quite glitzy and sparkling affairs, even in poorer neighborhoods. There used to be a clearer divide between pastry shops and bread bakeries, but some now overlap and offer both. Certainly try *kunafa,* a shredded wheat–like confection drizzled with honey, and *fiTiir,* a delicious and versatile soft puffed pastry with various fillings and toppings; much better, in general, than the baklava found throughout the Middle East and in Cairo as well. Perhaps the favorite dessert is *umm 'ali* ('the mother of 'Ali'), a soothing and subtle Egyptian version of bread pudding with rich cream, coconut, and nuts—not for the calorie-conscious, or at least not often; instead of as a dessert after a big meal, try it warm on a cold winter morning for breakfast. It is delicious.

Bottled water or soft drinks, including tonic water straight, are the beverages of choice with meals, all usually served at room temperature. A few delicious alternatives are *karkadeeh,* a hibiscus-flower infusion with a lovely ruby color drunk cool or warm, and in summer, fresh lime juice with sugar and water. Tea *(shaay)* and Turkish coffee *('ahwa),* both strong, are drunk prodigiously, usually with loads of sugar. For coffee with no sugar, ask for *'ahwa saada; 'ar-riiHa* is with very little; *maZbuut* is medium; and *ziyaada* is very sweet. More places are now offering filter coffee, called 'American' for some reason, but most places still have only one alternative to Turkish coffee—Nescafé.

Cairo has never lagged behind. There are plenty of espresso machines all over Cairo. The best coffee is at Café Greco on Road 9 in Maadi. Cilantro has branches throughout Cairo as do thirteen (and counting) other café chains. With dozens of independent coffee houses, there is always a chance to relax with a cappuccino and newspaper near your home. If you can't get away from the Internet and love coffee, Cilantro offers wireless Internet.

In addition to places we have already mentioned, another comes well recommended for authentic Egyptian food: Tab'i, with two branches, one on Sharia 'Urabi downtown and the other on Sharia Gam'at al-Duwal al-'Arabiya across from the Mustafa Mahmud Mosque in the same green-and-white building as Abu Shaqra restaurant, which is also good. Gad, on Gam'at al-Duwal al-'Arabiya in Mohandiseen, al-Alfy, downtown, and El-Tekkia, one of the oldest authentic Egyptian restaurants, are also very good.

To close our discussion of Egyptian cuisine, we suggest that adventurous readers try two irresistible street foods. First, all over the city and almost all year long, but especially in summer, you will see net bags of fruit, and carrots, suspended from the rafters or piled on the counters of little juice stands. Orange, banana, mango, apple, pineapple, apricot, pomegranate, sugarcane juice . . . go ahead and indulge in anything that grows off a tree or is peeled. If the carrots are peeled, they are probably okay, but it is probably wise, regrettably, to avoid the tempting strawberries, as they are notoriously hard to clean. Nothing beats these refreshing vitamin-packed juice treats after a morning of climbing up and down dusty minaret steps in the heat. Second, in winter, the aroma of roasting sweet potatoes wafts from donkey carts with small charcoal-fired ovens aboard. There is some suggestion that the charcoal or the lighter fluid the vendors use may be carcinogenic, but for those who take a so-what-isn't-these-days attitude, these treats comfort cold hands and stomachs.

MORE RESTAURANTS AND CAFÉS

INTERNATIONAL PLACES
On the international 'ethnic' food front, options are plentiful and constantly growing.

The five-star hotels all have their versions of ethnic restaurants, and they are generally about as authentic as one would expect, with a few exceptions. There are at least three really good Indian restaurants: the previously mentioned *Moghul Room* at the Mena House, and *Taj Mahal* and *Kandahar* in Mohandiseen. *Asia House* at the Shepheard is also praised for its Indian, but not its Chinese, food. There are a number of Chinese restaurants. Consistently cited favorites: *Peking*'s various branches, *Chin Chin* at Four Corners in Zamalek, *Dragon House* and *Maxie's Long Feng*, both in Maadi. There are other Chinese restaurants downtown as well.

There are several good Thai restaurants: *Bird Cage* at the Semiramis, *Lai Thai* at Four Seasons, Giza, and *Bua Khao* in Maadi. Restaurants specializing in Sushi are the rage in Cairo: *Jo Sushi* in Zamalek, *Sapparo* at the Sheraton Cairo, *Torili* at Cairo Marriott. Mexican food is hard to come by but one can find *Tex-Mex* at Planet Africa in Heliopolis and *Hard Rock Café* at the Grand Hyatt. Also try the superb *Fusion* on the Corniche al-Nil in Maadi, right next door to TGI Friday's, for a wide variety of southeast Asian cuisine.

It is logical that Lebanese food would be easier to come by, and there are a number of places offering it: *Taboula* in Garden City is excellent. *Papillon* and *Maroush,* both in Mohandiseen, are cited most frequently for food, atmosphere, and service.

For French and Italian food, choices are limited. There is one excellent French bistro, conveniently called *Le Bistro*, downtown. *Charwood's* in Mohandiseen has the look and feel of a French bistro, and serves delicious steaks and pizzas, with complimentary green salad and fresh bread. *La Trattoria* in Zamalek is an upscale Italian restaurant. Haute cuisine can be found at *Justine* and at *Revolving Restaurant*. Justine has a good reputation and high prices to match; it is the place to wine and dine someone you want to impress, and *Revolving Restaurant*'s views are worth a splurge. For Italian food, two places are pretty good: *Bella* at the Four Seasons, Nile Plaza, may be the best, along with *Restorante Splendido Tuscany* in the Cairo Marriott. *Tia Maria* and *Le Tabasco*, though not really Italian, have far better pasta dishes than some of the 'Italian' places, especially *La Casetta* and *Il Cortigiano*. The latter two have large portions of drab pastas, but are pleasant enough; don't automatically expect a glass of wine, though, as only the La Casetta in Maadi serves alcohol. *Da Mario* in the Nile Hilton is consistently reliable if not thrilling, with the additional plusses of very nice waiters, an agreeable outdoor café, and very good beef carpaccio. *Lucille's* in Maadi serves the best hamburger in Cairo. Best brunch is at the Four Seasons, Giza.

INTERESTING PLACES

For people-watching—Egyptians as well as tourists—and to soak up atmosphere and local color, here are a few of our favorites, and not-so favorites. We like *Estoril* downtown because: it looks like it has never changed, it has a lovely mashrabiya medallion on the ceiling, the Egyptian–continental food is consistently excellent, it is quiet but not lugubrious, and the owner and bartender recognize you in their low-key way after you have been in a few times. Both of the *Groppi*s are disappointing—dirty, dark, and sad; even nostalgia buffs would do well to simply take in the lovely tilework at the entrance to the one on Midan Tal'at Harb and have their pastry and coffee elsewhere. *Felfela* is okay and still attracts locals due to its convenient locations and reasonable prices, but there is a distinctly world-weary air on the part of the staff. All the places on the square in Khan al-Khalili make for great places to observe the human condition, as do the famous *Fishawi* café and the far ritzi-

er *Naguib Mahfouz Café* in the Khan itself. The food at Mahfouz is good, but expensive, operated as it is by Oberoi. *Malik el Gambary*, Shrimp King, in Shubra (see **Egyptian Food** above) is not only a great fish place, but a great vantage point from which to join Cairenes from all walks of life engaging in their favorite pastime. Great fish can also be had at the top of *Le Pacha 1901* in Zamalek. For late-night diners with a craving for kebab and kofta, *Al Rifai* just off Sayyida Zeinab Square behind the ornate wooden kuttab, offers alfresco dining in a lively, local setting. Be sure to try the *whiskey*, a pepper-flavored beverage served in a shot glass. Though it contains no alcohol the effect is equally spirited!

OUTDOOR PLACES

Sidewalk cafés abound in Cairo, but you will notice right away that women do not frequent many of them, with a few notable exceptions such as Zahrat al-Bustan and the ones around the Khan. But there are many other places for agreeable al fresco dining, for which Cairo's climate is ideal, except perhaps on the very hottest and coldest days. Mosquito repellent is the best perfume for outdoor dining, and a light shawl or sweater is almost always welcome at night, especially by the water.

Popular waterside spots include the *Sea Horse*, the top deck of *Le Pacha 1901*, the *Imperial Hotel*, and the *Meridien* terrace. Many agreeable, somewhat more local places dot the river—*Casino Cleopatra* and *Casino al-Nahr* in Zamalek, *Mamoura Torz* near the Manyal Palace on Roda, and *Casino Kasr al-Nil* on the Giza side of Gezira, but if you are a foreigner, do check the menu prices before tucking in. 'Casino,' by the way, is the term also given to riverside restaurants, many of which have belly-dancing in the wee hours.

The place to enjoy the outdoors is al-Azhar Park, which has four choices of restaurant.

Places with large or small gardens include *Five Bells* in Zamalek, *Maroush* in Mohandiseen, *Andrea's* and *Felfela Village*, both tour-bus-and-barbecue joints on opposite sides of the Maryutiya Canal heading toward Kirdasa, *Christo's* near the Pyramids and with great views of same (but the food is can sometimes be mediocre), and *Rossini's* and *Le Chantilly* in Heliopolis. The *Swiss Club* in Imbaba is delightful as well.

The very best outdoor restaurant of all is the one you make yourself: a home-made picnic, take-out from any restaurant or hotel, or even direct-to-the-dock delivery from Abu Shaqra on Sharia Qasr al-'Aini. Find a felucca with a nice table and comfy cushions, bring your own drinks, and for romance, a lantern and the partner of your choice. Mosquito repellent is a must at night unless you find itching irresistible. Heaven on the Nile from LE35–50 per hour. (And we have been asked to note that some of the felucca men prefer a liquid tip to money.)

Tea and coffee have brought people together in Egypt for centuries. Gathering at a sidewalk café to drink these hot delights, discuss politics, read a paper, or play backgammon has been a predominately male pastime, but since 2000 new coffee houses have opened throughout Cairo where everyone can pass the time of day over a good cup of coffee. *Café Greco*, on Road 9 in Maadi, serves the best coffee in Cairo. *Arabica, Costa Coffee, Coffee Roastery, Cilantro, Beano's*, and *Café Complete* also serve good coffee.

TRENDY PLACES

To rub shoulders with the young and the beautiful—and the old, rich, and famous or notorious—there are three places in Dokki, all within shouting distance of each other. The newest is *Abou El Sid*, an offshoot of the highly successful Zamalek restaurant. It has classic Egyptian décor replete with mashrabiya window boxes and engraved copper chandeliers. Umm Kulthum music blends effortlessly into the overall atmosphere. The kitchen serves delicious authentic Egyptian dishes such as *mulukhiyya* and pigeon with gourmet flair and beautiful presentation. The mezze is also impressive. A variety of drinks and shiisha are served.

Next door is one of Cairo's longstanding 'in' spots, *Le Tabasco*. Under the same management as Abou El Sid, it serves excellent food as well, with a menu stretching to many parts of the world. The music selection is great and dancing on the tables has been known to occur.

El Yotti is staid, comfortable, and elegant until about 11 and then rocks out with live music and dancing, serving up good quasi–French–Egyptian food throughout; ring the bell at the end of a lamp-lit passage to enter.

Across the street from the World Trade Center, on the Nile, are two of Cairo's newest offerings: *Sangria* and *Absolute*. *Sangria* operates upstairs with both indoor and outdoor seating. The décor is decidedly undecided but the end effect is quite pleasing. Good sushi is available. It is a beautiful riverside setting to see and be scene. *Absolute* suffers from a bit more attitude than its upstairs neighbor. But a house DJ does offer a good selection of music and there is ample space to dance. *The Cairo Jazz Club* is a great place to enjoy quality music. The club is famous for its choice of high quality performances. The only problem is the cigarette smoke. *After Eight* have live bands almost every night. *35* is a swank club, while *Bliss* is mainly for the younger crowd. *La Bodega* is definitely 'in.' El Sawy Culture Wheel in Zamalek is a wonderful place to enjoy various musical styles.

The best restaurant reviews are to be found in the *The Croc*. Their critics give detailed, balanced run-downs of both the well-known and out-of-the-way places. *Egypt Today*'s monthly Restaurant Guide is also good, but tends to repeat only the better-known places and to be glowing rather than balanced. Truly die-hard gourmets and gourmands will be pleased to know that there is an Egyptian branch of the international Chaîne des Rôtisseurs club in Cairo. It is notoriously difficult for foreigners to gain membership to this exclusive club, which is offered strictly by invitation or by examination for restaurant professionals.

SIGHTSEEING

A large number of books, especially those in the **Book List** on page xxiii, cover this ground in thorough detail. So, rather than reinvent the wheel, we confine ourselves here to worthwhile sights in and around Cairo that consistently come recommended by native Cairenes and expatriates.

PYRAMIDS

How could we start with anything other than the Great Pyramids at Giza? Nothing prepares even the most jaded traveler (Mark Twain excepted) for their grandeur, their sheer awesomeness. Go. Here are some don'ts, followed by dos, to make your pilgrimage to the Great Pyramids what it should be.

Do not let the incredible hassles from touts of every description spoil the experience; just look dazed and ignore them totally. Do not take a guided tour unless it is with an organization like the Egyptian Antiquities Organization (EAO) or the American Research Center in Egypt (ARCE). Skip the Sound and Light Show unless you are highly partial to such displays. Don't go early in the morning (early being anytime before 9:30 or so). One would think dawn would be the ideal time for the quality of the light and the tranquillity, but, especially in the cooler months, the pyramids are often shrouded in mist until 10 am—and regard-

less, the security people and ticket takers do not care to accommodate early risers and can be quite obdurate about it, even at dawn on New Year's Day. Don't bring a videocamera: the pyramids do not move. If you must go into a pyramid just to say you have done so or because you are an archaeology or architecture buff, go ahead, but it is quite a claustrophobic experience and there is nothing to see anyway. Only 150 tickets are handed out each morning and 150 tickets are handed out at noon for entry into the Great Pyramid. The moisture from perspiration and human breath damages the interior walls, hence the control on the number of daily visitors. Young visitors in particular like the Solar Boat Museum (from the outside an eyesore, as is all the touristic claptrap that infringes too closely on the pyramid complex).

Sunset and moonlight are the best times to go—when, of course, the pyramids are officially closed, the tourists being shooed out at 4 pm in winter, 6 pm in summer, to clear the premises for the Sound and Light Show.

Entrance to the pyramids is from Haram Street past the entrance to the Mena House. The road is one way to the Sphinx area. You cannot drive from the Sphinx to the pyramids. A ticket entrance to the Sphinx is from the southwest, near the garden.

Good riders can go all the way from the Giza pyramids to Abu Sir or Saqqara and back; for anyone else, this is arduous, but fantastic on a full-moon night; many of the clubs and associations in town arrange such parties now and then.

Many pyramid fans prefer the smaller, older, more isolated step pyramid complexes at Saqqara and Abu Sir and the one lonely pyramid at Maydum, near Fayoum, with its much more interesting mastabas. Saqqara is the only one of the three much frequented by tourists, but it is still far less of a hassle than the Giza pyramids, and, to many eyes, more beautiful. Abu Sir, off the road to Saqqara, opened in 1996 after a long closure to the public, it is an exquisite, magical place at sunset. Maydum, thought to be the first attempt to build a true pyramid, is quite splendid in its isolation, as a grand development scheme seems to have stopped for the moment. Only the very sure-footed should attempt the descent and ascent into the corbeled vault. It is "fifty-seven meters down, ten meters up," as your helpful guide will repeatedly reiterate and illustrate in the sand.

The museum at Memphis near Saqqara is on the tourist circuit, but is not a must-see. It is a rather paltry affair except for the fallen colossus of Ramesses II and the alabaster sphinx in the courtyard. It is sobering, though, to think that the site of the small dusty village that is modern Memphis was the seat of power for centuries during the Old Kingdom and after. What wonders must still lie buried in the sandy hills nearby. All around the routes to Memphis and Saqqara are dozens upon dozens of carpet schools and showrooms. Avoid them if you can.

THE CAMEL MARKET

Once, a visit to the Camel Market in Cairo dredged up images of ancient caravans gliding through the Sahara, but today the market is no more than the remnants of a once-important livelihood. This is not a zoo; camels are a commodity and are treated as such. If you are squeamish about the rough treatment of animals, this is not a good outing for you.

The market is located thirty kilometers northwest of Cairo, past the village of Birqash. It is open on Monday and Friday mornings, starting at 7 am. The entrance fee for foreigners is LE20, with LE10 charged for cameras and LE30 for video cameras.

Entering the Alexandria/Desert–Fayoum roundabout from the Pyramids Road, take the first road to the right (the second is to the Cairo–Alexandria Desert Road and the third is to the Fayoum road), and follow the sign for Kerdasa (turning left). Pass Kooki Park on your right and go under the bridge. From this point you continue straight on, going under a second bridge and continuing straight. There is a sign at 23 kilometers (on the left side of the road), just past it turn left at the sign for Nimos Farm nursery. Continue for approximately 5 kilometers; the road comes to an end (at this point you can ask any passer-by for the whereabouts of the camel market—*suuq al-gimal*). Take a left onto a sand and gravel surface, and from this point, whenever there is a choice of road, take the left.

You will come to a fork (keep the grocery store on your left); turn left. The road here is winding and goes through a small village, after which you come to another fork with a mosque without a minaret that separates the roads, turn left. Follow this road for about two kilometers along a cement fence that leads to the camel market on the left.

The Community Services Association, *www.livinginegypt.org*, organizes trips year-round to the Camel Market.

SOME MAJOR AND A FEW MINOR MUSEUMS

One realizes quite quickly that huge tracts of Cairo are in effect great outdoor museums, particularly the whole of Islamic Cairo. We give brief descriptions of some 'real' museums, then take a look at Old (Coptic) Cairo and Islamic Cairo, sketching the major sights therein.

THE EGYPTIAN MUSEUM
Literally hundreds of elegant, exquisitely decorated mummy cases stand as silent sentries over the thousands of visitors who daily pay homage to Egypt's treasures. The whole museum is overwhelming in its sheer volume, and is even more so with the

knowledge that in the basement lurk many more uncatalogued treasures than fill the public spaces. Although the traffic in the museum is heavy and very noisy at all times, with guides exhorting and enlightening their charges in a cacophony of languages, it is easy to wander off into near-isolated halls to contemplate parts of the collection in peace and quiet. For a first visit, it is worthwhile hiring a guide or going with a tour group to get an overall sense of the place, which takes about two hours. Depending on the level of detail you want while looking at displays, a guidebook like the museum's own or the Blue Guide is a necessity, as the legends are limited, illegible, or nonexistent. On subsequent visits, tourists' lunch time (12 noon–2 pm, except on Fridays, when the museum is closed), or late afternoon are good times to go. There is an additional fee for the Mummy Room, (LE70) high but well worth it, and the Tutankhamun display is duly dazzling, but always very crowded. Cameras and videos are not permitted in the museum. Buy postcards instead. The museum is open from 9 am to 6 pm. There are very few places to sit in the museum, but there is a decent restaurant outside on the second floor for relaxing and digesting what you have seen. The gift shop and T-shirt shop are okay, a bit pricey, but if you haven't time for Khan al-Khalili, both serve souvenir-seekers well enough. The sculpture and statuary garden in front of the museum is full of lovely things, but none are labeled.

THE MUSEUM OF ISLAMIC ART

This is a delight for lovers of exquisite ceramics, illuminated manuscripts, and mashrabiya art. The museum's objects are not only from Egypt, but from Turkey and other parts of the Ottoman Empire as well. At the time of writing, the museum is undergoing major renovations and is closed to the public.

THE COPTIC MUSEUM, OLD CAIRO, AND THE NILOMETER

The easiest way to reach the Coptic complex in southern Cairo is by Metro to the Mar Girgis stop or by river taxi to the Masr al-Qadima landing. Here you are walking on historic ground, for this area is what was once the Roman fortress of Babylon, and after that al-Fustat, the early Arab city. In addition to the museum, the area accommodates Egypt's first mosque ('Amr Ibn al-'As), a number of Coptic churches (the most famous of which are the 'Hanging Church' of al-Mu'allaqa and Sitt Barbara), the oldest synagogue in Egypt (Ben Ezra), and two Roman towers—all coexisting peacefully. Very little of what stands today is original, except for the Roman towers, but the area nevertheless has a wonderful feel to it.

The Coptic Museum is renewed, renovated, and beautiful. The museum exhibits some of the most important pieces of art, architectural, and writing in Christian history and in the world. Each room is organized by theme, and displays are labeled clearly in Arabic, English, and French. A morning spent in the district and the museum might conclude with lunch at the nearby al-Fustat Restaurant, on the corner between 'Amr Ibn al-'As Mosque and the ancient churches of old Cairo. Then cross over to Roda Island for a quick visit to the Nilometer at the southern tip. This column measuring the Nile's level determined flooding and harvest dates from the ninth century AD and was in use until the building of the Aswan High Dam, which put an end to the annual flood. Visit the Umm Kulthum Museum and peek into Monasterli Palace, the venue for International Center for Music hosting international musicians, monthly. Since the gardens receive few visitors, the area is an oasis of calm.

MANYAL PALACE AND MUSEUM
(NOT MAJOR, BUT A GOOD OUTING)

A short walk south from the Grand Hyatt Hotel on Roda is the vast former residence of King Farouk's uncle, Prince Muhammad 'Ali. Dating from the turn of the century, it houses an eclectic collection of weaponry, insects, china services, portraits, and mounted trophies. Very little is labeled, but it doesn't really matter as there are no historically significant treasures to speak of. Nevertheless, this museum is quite visitor-friendly, evoking the rococo-Oriental splendor in which the royal family lived and played. The gardens could use a lot more tending, but they are quite nice as they are. This is a good museum for tots, as the animal and insect displays intrigue them and they can gleefully run up and down the long esplanades and galleries, all on the ground floor.

THE POST OFFICE MUSEUM

Just off Midan Ataba is the Post Ofice Museum, a quirky philatelist's dream, with a unique collection of stamps and mannequins dressed in postmen-through-the-ages costumes. Nearby is Muktallat, at 14 al-Ataba al-Khadra, the philatelists' café, where priceless stamps are bartered and traded over coffee and shiisha.

ISLAMIC CAIRO

It would take a number of full-time months and a lot of energy to do a serious exploration of this fascinating area, which harbors not only a great many treasures of Islamic architecture, but a throbbing, endless parade of street life. To get an initial sense of both, look from on high from the Muqattam Hills, the Citadel, or the roof of the Ibn Tulun mosque. Then consult a detailed map to get an orderly perspective (SPARE, the Society for the Preservation of the Architectural Resources of Egypt, produces an excellent series of 3-D maps of Islamic Cairo). Also check the program calendars at the American Research Center in Egypt (ARCE) and the Arabic Language Institute (ALI) for listings of their guided walks through Islamic Cairo. Finally, go exploring, but a little at a time, especially in summer's heat. Go on foot only; the medieval streets were never intended for cars. Wear easily removed, comfortable, rubber-soled shoes. The ancient steps of many minarets are slippery, sandy, and dark, ideal for ignominious and even dangerous falls in leather-soled shoes, as we ruefully discovered. Carry a small bottle of water and your map, however discreetly, since it is unproductive to stand at the footbridge between Khan al-Khalili and al-Ghuriya asking ten people for directions to the Street of the Tentmakers in semi-perfect Arabic only to find not one who has a clue that it is less than five hundred meters away. (It is best to ask for Bab Zuwayla in this case, using the navigate-by-landmarks principle, and once there ask for Sharia al-Khayyamiya.) For women entering mosques, a headscarf is a respectful touch, but it is no longer expected, especially of foreigners.

The energetic can 'do' Islamic Cairo in three days, one each at the southern, middle, and northern sections. In the southern part, start at Amir Taz Palace, a Bahri Mamluk palace constructed in 1352, which is on Souffeya Street in the Khalifa district. Continue to the mosque of Ibn Tulun and the Gayer-Anderson House behind it, then proceed toward the Citadel. At Ibn Tulun, climb as high as you can and clamber about the roof for spectacular views of nearby minarets and of the impressive courtyard of the mosque itself. Everyone finds the Gayer-Anderson House (*Bayt al-kiritliyya*, 'House of the Cretan Woman') charming; it is a well-cared-for anachronism of the nineteenth and early twentieth centuries in the midst of all the medieval stones, full of art and artifacts lovingly collected by the owner and displayed in a fanciful series of rooms he designed.

Walking toward the Citadel on Sharia al-Saliba, and drinking in the sights and smells all the while, one comes to Midan Salah al-Din, which fronts the Madrasa of Sultan Hasan, a splendid example of Mamluk architecture, and the mosque of al-Rifa'i, which is lavish in the extreme but otherwise unremarkable. It gets loads of tour buses, though, as it houses the remains of Shah Reza Pahlevi of Iran (who was denied burial in Iran by the late Ayatollah Khomeini) in multi-marbled splendor. The last two kings of Egypt, Fouad and Farouk, plus their father and grandmother, are also buried here.

The fortress of the Citadel (al-'al'a) stands as the cynosure of Cairo, evoking from a distance visions of the Thousand and One Nights with its glistening domes and minarets. It was originally constructed with the labor of captured Crusaders under Sultan Salah al-Din in the twelfth century. Within the two enclosures, referred to as the Northern and Southern enclosures but more accurately east and west respectively, one finds a staggering array of mosques, palaces, and museums. The main mosques are the nineteenth-century mosque of Muhammad 'Ali, or the Alabaster Mosque, with its enormous square courtyard; the mosque of al-Nasir Muhammad (1335); and the mosque of Suliman Pasha (1528). In addition, there are the remains of many more historic buildings, and a number that have been converted into an odd assortment of museums: the Carriage Museum, the Military Museum, the National Police Museum, and the Jewel Palace, scene of a grand dinner after which Muhammad 'Ali slaughtered his four hundred Mamluk guests for dessert.

The middle section of Islamic Cairo is about a kilometer north of the southern part and can be reached from it by walking along Sharia Bab al-Wazir. Two areas, Bab al-Khalq and al-Ghuriya, comprise this section, which is home to many more mosques and lively markets. The better-known include the Blue Mosque of Aqsunqur (1347) and al-Azhar mosque and university. Between the two is the imposing Bab Zuwayla (1092), one of the gates of the Fatimid city; from its minarets one can get a great view of the whole area and then wander over to the nearby the Street of the Tentmakers.

For over a thousand years, al-Azhar has been the seat of Islamic scholarship. Roam around in the University's expansive courtyard, but do so well covered, as the women students do. Just to the west of al-Azhar is the old caravanserai of Wikalat al-Ghuri, an eye of calm amidst the hubbub of the streets surrounding it. Nearby is the Ghuri Palace, which houses art exhibitions and cultural events from time to time.

The northern section of the region begins across the green footbridge over Sharia al-Azhar. It is very easy—and highly recommended—to simply get lost here, keeping a few landmarks in mind: Sharia al-Azhar is the main east–west street coming from Cairo, worth avoiding in favor of the largely car-less side streets; just past and under the footbridge are the mosque, midan, and parking lot of al-Husayn, with Khan al-Khalili abutting it; and the main north–south street is Sharia al-Mu'izz li-Din Allah, on either side of which is a staggering array of mosques and madrasas in varying states of repair, but all a lovely counterpoint to the shops and shoppers jostling each other. If you are on a gawking rather than a shopping expedition, Sunday mornings are ideal for a relatively peaceful visit, as many of the shops are closed then. A full-moon night will find Sharia al-Mu'izz crowded, but it is also one of the best times to contemplate the stunning beauty of the place—a religious experience regardless of one's religion. The northern end of the street, known as Bayn al-Qasrayn, 'between the two palaces,' is the setting for the first volume of Naguib

Mahfouz's moving Cairo Trilogy, *Palace Walk*. In an alley off al-Mu'izz is the lovely Bayt al-Sihaymi, a seventeenth-century merchant's house that functions as a cultural center. The highlight of the area is the graceful complex of Qalawun, Barquq, and al-Nasir, just north of Khan al-Khalili on the left of Sharia al-Mu'izz. At the north end of the street is the mosque of the caliph al-Hakim (c. 1000), notable for its size (the second largest in Cairo). The Suuq al-Futuh, around the Bab al-Futuh ('gate of conquests') marking the northern boundary of Islamic Cairo, is the locals' as opposed to the tourists' Khan al-Khalili, where many of the same things can be found in a more authentic and lower-priced setting.

THE CITIES OF THE DEAD

Just east of the regions described above are the teeming Cities of the Dead, home to hundreds of thousands of alive-and-well Cairenes. A visit to the beautiful northern cemetery makes it easy to understand why: no high rises, no traffic, some stupendous architecture, low (no) rent, and some very quiet neighbors. Here are the mausoleum of Sultan Qaytbay with its large, lace-inscribed dome (1474) and the mausoleum of Barquq (1411), plus many lesser but nevertheless impressive ones. The southern cemetery is far less grand; in fact, it is a slum, but a unique and friendly one. The Friday morning flea market around the mosque of Imam al-Shafi'i draws the innumerable aficionados of broken bicycle parts, used gallabiyas, and plastic-mosque alarm clocks that deliver the call to prayer at the appropriate times. Go early; things get even more dusty, hot, and full of buses after 10 am.

GREEN CAIRO

One of the most surprising and wonderful aspects of Cairo is how green it is. Consid-

ering the rainlessness, the dust, and the pollution, every tree and garden is a tribute to the Cairenes' love of greenery. Much has been lost with development, with everyone except high-rise builders decrying the loss of the gardens and villas of Garden City, Zamalek, and Maadi, but an awful lot remains. When the noise and the heat get you down, head to the nearest park, many of which are often empty, for a jog or a contemplative walk, or just to let the kids run off steam.

Virtually all the parks, midans, clubs, and cafés offering respite are on the Giza side of the city, many on the island of Gezira (which includes Zamalek). The largest is the Gezira Club, which except for swimming can be used by non-members for an admission fee of LE50 (see **Sporting Clubs** in Chapter 2 for details on membership and amenities). Don't drive—or if you do, park at the Marriott or on a nearby street, as you can spend easily half an hour waiting in a car queue to enter the parking lots. The club is full of leafy glades, comfortable chairs and tables, and cheap refreshment stands, which is handy since no food or drink may be brought in. The Fish Garden has hilly grottoes that make it a favorite of young lovers. The lovely gardens on either side of Sharia al-Burg on the way to the Cairo Tower on Gezira are virtually deserted, but safe, with vine-covered arbors, walkways, and a couple of formerly grand but now ramshackle Victorian greenhouses. You can easily skip the Cairo Tower itself; with its foreign admission of LE50, it is underwhelming and annoying, even though the view from the observatory is spectacular. At the southern tip of Gezira is a nice, formally laid out garden which also appears to be a nursery is al-Riyada Gardens.

In Giza, the Orman Botanical Gardens at the south end of Sharia Dokki near Cairo University house a large array of rare trees and plants collected by Ismail Pasha, whose green thumb also expressed itself in the creation of the Gezira Club. The gardens are usually more peaceful than the nearby Zoo, but even that is fine except on Fridays, when it is overrun with schoolchildren playing boisterous games of soccer. Refreshments are available at both places, and though it is a bit run down, the Zoo is an oasis for humans—perhaps less so for the other animals. The Agricultural Museum in Dokki (first available right off the 6th October Bridge coming from Cairo) is neglected by most visitors, making it a terrific place to visit. There are three small, fun museums set in a lovely garden—another good place to bring small children. All around this area of Dokki, and in Mohandiseen as well, one finds a large number of residential areas surrounding lovely midans. Two particularly nice ones are Midan Ibn al-Walid, with a few nice shops and restaurants, just south of the Shooting Club (Nadi al-Seid), and a large jungle of a place at the corner of Sharia Midhat Abd al-Hamid and Sharia Fawzi Ramah in Mohandiseen. The Shooting Club itself is a vast sports and social complex similar to the Gezira Club, but it has very little shade.

Roda, the 'garden island,' no longer has much in the way of gardens except for those in the Manyal Palace, which suffice well. And Garden City, alas, has no gardens at all for walking, but a few of its tree-shaded boulevards recall Paris, traffic congestion included. At the American University in Cairo (AUC) right off the mayhem of Midan al-Tahrir, the students and anyone else who can pass for one or for a professor can enjoy its agreeable courtyard.

In Nasr City, there are two massive gardens, International Gardens, off Abbas al-Akkad Street, and Makatibit Gardens on Ahmed Fakri Street. Maadi is the greenest of Cairo's suburbs, but there is no real public park. The side streets, however, make for pleasant walks, as a great many avid gardeners show off their skills along the garden walls. Victory College Field has become a haven for recreational opportunities. Sports such as soccer, rugby, cricket, softball, remote control auto-racing, skateboarding, and a playground provide a chance to get outside and participate. If you like to explore the desert but not too far from home, go to Wadi Digla Protectorate just east of Maadi. Further afield, a visit to the Japanese Gardens in Helwan offers sanctuary to the serenity-starved, and further still, the Saqqara Palms Country Club and the Saqqara Country Club make an agreeable afternoon's outing.

Al-Azhar Park is the newest green area in Cairo and everyone is thrilled by this 74-acre oasis in the heart of the city. Bound on the west by Darb al-Ahmar and on the east by Sharia Salah Salim, the former landfill and military camps have been converted to the greenest, most spacious park in the city.

A COMPLETELY ARBITRARY COMPENDIUM OF FAVORITE PLACES

When we asked long-time residents about their favorite places to take visitors in or around Cairo, the answers were mostly outside of Cairo, reflecting the city-dweller's need to escape the city now and then. What topped the in-Cairo list was felucca rides any time of the night or day—but from late afternoon on is probably ideal. The Gezira Club was also popular, especially for mothers with small children; moms can talk and drink fresh lime juice while the kids run safely amok. Saqqara got high marks from many, much more so than the Pyramids at Giza. Picnics at Wadi Digla Protectorate; an afternoon walking through al-Azhar Park and stopping for coffee to look over the twelfth-century Ayyubid wall and the Giza pyramids; Ataba Market for varied sights and smells at bargain prices; having a beer and watching the river traffic at one of the Casino restaurant terraces; AUC's annual classic film series; taking advantage of the cultural offerings at the Opera complex and in the many galleries downtown and in Zamalek; a visit to the al-Zahraa Stud Farm near Heliopolis during the annual Arabian Horse auction in May; the Wissa Wassef studios for the indigenous architecture, the weavings, and fresh country air . . . . The list is long and varied, showing that for many, Cairo is a great place to live.

Going further afield, there are many high spots in addition to the obvious ones of Luxor and Aswan. Despite the far more numerous wonders of the former, many residents prefer the latter for its grandeur and isolation, particularly at Abu Simbel. Other highly recommended jaunts reflecting a variety of interests and effort: the Bedouin market at al-'Arish; antiquing in Alexandria, but only in the winter months; the elegant new resort of El Gouna (near Hurghada, and far preferable to it); day trips to Fayed on the way to Ismailiya; cheap weekend camping at Basata on the Gulf of Aqaba with the hippies; luxury in the Moorish simplicity of the Qusir Mövenpick, south of Hurghada; the water sports and nightlife at Sharm al-Sheikh; birdwatching at Lake Qarun; the terrible beauty of the British cemetery at al-Alamein; sunrise from the top of Mount Sinai; watching the canal traffic at Ismailiya; exploring all of the Sinai Peninsula; Farafra Oasis and the psychedelic sculptures of the White Desert; cruising Lake Nasser by houseboat *(dahabiya)*. This list, by no means comprehensive, nevertheless illustrates that there is no excuse for boredom in Egypt. Stamina, enthusiasm, and a good sense of humor are baggage essentials, though. Keep in mind the happy-go-lucky approach of one Cairo tour guide, Barbi Eysselinck: "The detour is the tour." This will save you much psychic wear and tear as you discover Cairo and Egypt.

SHOPPING

All of Cairo is an enticing bazaar that fascinates and confuses most newcomers. To help our readers make sense of it, we have used a few exclusionary criteria and an organizational system we hope makes sense to you as well.

There are two sections of this book devoted to the fine art of shopping. This one is more for shopping-as-entertainment—souvenirs, local handicrafts, clothing, and so on—whereas the one in Chapter 3 is for the more humdrum items that householders need. To clear up any confusion this may cause, the Directory lists categories alphabetically, with specific sources for each. We have concentrated on quality rather than quantity, so our comments, advice, and listings are by no means comprehensive. Instead, they reflect the eclectic recommendations garnered from our many Egyptian and foreign-resident informants. So check the Directory for listings after reading our general comments, then reread the **Bargaining** section earlier in this chapter, and—happy hunting.

THE MAJOR SUUQS OR MARKETS

Almost all the old *suuqs* sell almost everything under the sun, with some specializing. Except for Khan al-Khalili, they are all authentic marketplaces where Egyptians have done their household shopping in the same way for centuries. Even as one modern, lookalike shopping arcade after another is built, these will not change. Prices are lower than at supermarkets or arcades only if you are an experienced or Arabic-speaking shopper. The modern arcades, by the way, are also described in Chapter 3.

Khan al-Khalili: This bazaar dating from the fourteenth century may be a greater tourist attraction than the Pyramids. Look up at the glorious medieval stones and wood surrounding you as you browse and bargain. And go up—up the many often smelly, dungeon-like stairways, and up the not-so-secret stairways in many of the shops. It is there that many of the Khan's really interesting stuff is on offer. One unarguable benefit of tourism: the Khan also, unlike most of the non-tourist markets, offers even the footsore and hungry female many places to sit down, gather sustenance, and watch the world go by.

Al-Muski (Ataba Square to Khan al-Khalili): Everything; lots of small electrical shops, and lots of car fumes and traffic. Right off Husayn Square to the west and parallel to Sharia al-Muski is one full of paper products with nary a tourist in sight. Nearby are shops full of buttons, bangles, bows, sequins, bridal supplies and all kinds of sewing notions.

Suuq al-Futuh: At the northern end of Sharia al-Mu'izz li-Din Allah near Bab al-Futuh; very worthwhile. This is where the shiisha pipes that fill the cafés of Cairo are made and sold.

Perfume and Spice Market: Part of the Khan just north of Sharia al-Azhar where it meets Sharia al-Mu'izz li-Din Allah; sometimes called the Suuq Sudani.

Suuq al-Khayyamiya: The Tentmakers' bazaar behind Bab Zuwayla.

Note: All of the above suuqs, plus many more—gold, coppersmiths, etc.—are very near each other, but nevertheless distinctive. It takes more than a few trips to make your own cognitive map of the area.

Ataba Market (Downtown): Large, mostly indoor food market with household goods, clothing, and hardware on the fringes. Wear gaiters or something similar for sloshing through the fish and butcher stalls.

Bab al-Luq (near Falaki Square): Covered food market.

Dokki Market (Sharia Suliman Guhar): Small, shady, manageable indoor–outdoor market with all types of food, hardware, jewelers, etc.

Midan al-Tahrir: Airlines and tourist traps. Tal'at Harb and Qasr al-Nil streets off it to the northwest have mostly clothes, travel agents—and shoes, shoes, shoes.

Tawfiqiya Market (near 'Urabi Square): Outdoor food market.

Wikalat al-Balah: About half a kilometer south of the World Trade Center, a diagonal street branches to the right. Fabric, clothing, car covers, spare parts, and who knows what else.

OTHER SHOPPING STREETS AND AREAS

Heliopolis: Is turning into one giant shopping mall. In the Suuq al-'Ubur on Sharia Salah Salim are branches of every store imaginable. Midan Roxy, Kurba, and Sharia Baghdad are chockablock, too (don't drive; no parking). More everyday shopping is along Sharia Harun al-Rashid and on Midan al-Gami'.

Maadi: Road 9 for everything, with the places on the Nile side of the railroad tracks for interesting utilitarian shopping.

Midan Libnan area (Mohandiseen): Mostly upscale furniture and clothing stores and many restaurants.

Sharia Muhammad Farid (Downtown): Many carpenters and a colorful outdoor food market

Sharia 'Abd al-Khaliq Sarwat (Downtown): Stationery shops, printers, computer accessories, and electronics.

Sharia 'Abd Al-'Aziz (Downtown): All kinds of small and large appliances that is duty free.

Sharia Gam'at al-Duwal al-'Arabiya (Mohandiseen): Modern strip-mall street: mostly clothes, shoes, car showrooms, lighting shops, no shade whatsoever.

Shooting Club vicinity (Mohandiseen and Dokki): An up-and-coming shopping area. On and off Sharia al-Thawra on the north side of the club is Creek's Restaurant, the very chi-chi Mohammed Jr.'s beauty salon, and two elegant couturier-type women's clothing stores, Melodie's and Boutique Viola. On Suliman Abaza off the club's northwest corner are Clarine's antiques, Queenie's couturier clothing, La Beauté for cosmetics, Bunny's for kid's clothes, etc. Off the southwest corner between Sharia Nadi al-Seid and Muhi al-Din Abu-l-'Izz are fancy fabric and home accessories shops.

Zamalek: As befits its status as a foreigners' and diplomatic enclave, Zamalek has the most concentrated range of elegant shops and good restaurants in the city. Expensive, yes, but you save on cab fares by walking.

SHOPPING ITEMS

ANTIQUES

Zamalek is the antique-lover's stomping ground. There are no bargains here, but there are dozens of wonderful shops full of genuine antiques and excellent reproductions, mostly European and Egyptian in origin. Serious hunters favor Alexandria's 'Attarin district over Cairo for antiques; the rare mind-boggling bargain, like a Beidermeier chair for LE70, can still be unearthed there. As with furniture in general, many Egyptians prefer the lavish and ornate to the simple, and this is true of antiques as well, but art deco pieces are also popular. All the shops listed in the Directory are good, but a few that are mouthwatering, with gourmet prices to match, are Clarine in Dokki, Hamdy al-Dab' in Khan al-Khalili, Atrium and Mit Rehan in Zamalek, Morgana in Maadi, as well as the best shops downtown, including Mahrous, Hassan and Ali, Ahmed Zeinhoum, and Philippe Devlay. Other favorites for accessories, as opposed to furniture, are Nostalgia in Zamalek and Samia Imports in Mohandiseen, which both have charming owners and are wonderfully funky places to dig around in. The Old Shoppe in the Khan is more like a dusty warehouse,

but they have some great stuff, including an abundance of tables, mirrors, chests, and chairs with mother-of-pearl and wood inlays.

If you are already an expert, try Osiris Auction House downtown or Amr Mohamed Rashed Auction Hall in Zamalek to compete with the professionals. If not, take an antique shop tour, run by the Women's Association from time to time.

APPLIQUÉ WORK

The Street of the Tentmakers behind Bab Zuwayla is the place to find it all, concentrated in one place that is a riot of color. Cushion covers, bedspreads, wall-hangings, toaster covers(!), and yes, even tents for your wedding or your balcony can be found ready-made or custom-made. Colors tend to be bright to garish, and quality of work varies, but one place that has been recommended is Farghaly at 2 Sharia al-Khayyamiya. Dry-cleaning and ruthless bargaining strongly advised.

ARTS AND CRAFTS

Many places called galleries are either arts and crafts, furniture, or antique shops—a holdover from the French. Egyptian craftspeople used to be among the best in the Middle East, but many of them have either died or gone to greener pastures. Nevertheless, quite a lot of good work can still be found, much of it originating in the oases and among the Bedouin, where buyers go directly for their wares. Such items include rugs and weavings, silver jewelry, Bedouin shawls and wedding dresses, and baskets. With few exceptions, Khan al-Khalili is definitely not the place to go for good-quality handicrafts. Instead, try these, where quality and taste are on exhibit and representative crafts from around the country are well-displayed: al-Ain in Dokki; Oum el-Dounia on Sharia Tal'at Harb has a wonderful and unusual selection of Egyptian crafts, clothes, leatherwork, scarves, jewelry, books, and

CDs and DVDs. Nomad, whose lovely shop on Saray al-Gezira is like falling into a seraglio (the one in the Marriott around the corner is smaller and less enticing); Egypt Crafts on Yehia Ibrahim, and Tukul Crafts in St. Andrew's Church, Zamalek (non-profit outlet); Shahira Mehrez in Dokki; Khan Misr Touloun, opposite the entrance to the Ibn Tulun mosque; and Catacomb and World of Art in Maadi, and Khatun behind al-Azhar, featuring traditional crafts with a twist. Another good place to get an overview of the crafts scene is at the monthly meetings of the Women's Association held at the Marriott. The first hour is usually devoted to shopping from a varied roster of vendors selling some kitschy, some classy goods.

BASKETS
Really beautiful baskets come from the Nubians in Aswan; a common type is a round, flattish cone used for serving and protecting food, but it also makes an elegant sun hat. More pedestrian but highly utilitarian baskets can be found on donkey carts at many Cairo street corners; they usually come from Fayoum, where they are cheaper and there is more variety. Visit Bahariya Oasis and buy 'saddle-bag' baskets; they are great to carry things from place to place.

BEADWORK AND EMBROIDERY
Thanks to the belly dancers and to Egyptian women's penchant for dressing up, these needleworker's arts still thrive here. Bedouin women use both extensively on their dresses. For kinky dress-up fun, haggle with the belly-dance costume sellers in Khan al-Khalili. For the real thing at sky-high prices, go where Fifi Abdou goes, to Bekhita in the Marriott. More restraint and style, but still with plenty of dazzle, can be found at Boutique Viola in Mohandiseen (**Clothing, Women's Evening**).

Soutache-like embroidery *(itan)* with silk and metal thread embroidery *(sirma)* are

available by order from Atlas and Aseel respectively in Khan al-Khalili. These are unique couturier touches that one would pay a queen's ransom for in Europe, but are quite reasonable here. Another uniquely Egyptian craft, machine-woven ribbon called *'iqada,* can be found in a number of shops. You choose the colors and designs, and the ribbon is custom-made. It is a whole evening's entertainment to explore and haggle in one of the dusty ateliers, where you should end up spending LE150 for 6 meters, depending on width, with silk and wool being more costly. Use it to border cushion covers, gallabiyas, or curtains.

BRASS AND COPPER
Pardon the pun, but Cairo, specifically Khan al-Khalili, really shines here. Aspiring Julia Childs clones can form a complete batterie de cuisine with gorgeous copper cookware, all tin-lined, from the shops hidden away up a dank stairway near the Naguib Mahfouz Coffee Shop, and at prices far more reasonable than abroad—for example, about LE200 for a large oval casserole. The same is true for brass. Quality, as determined by weight and work, varies, but it is all pretty nice and makes for beautiful cache-pots for your houseplants.

BOOKBINDING
This art that is dying in the West is still going strong in Cairo. Abd al-Zahir behind al-Azhar (**Bookbinding**) does good work at reasonable prices.

BOOKS
Bibliophiles in search of the old and arcane are very well served in Cairo, especially at L'Orientale, Lehnert & Landrock, and Reader's Corner, all fascinating browsing grounds. Those in search of a really wide selection of modern literature and non-fiction are less well served, although Danielle Steele, John Grisham, and Tom Clancy

abound. Books in English and other foreign languages are expensive here, as most are published and printed abroad. Luckily, there are the two AUC bookstores, on the main Tahrir campus and in the Zamalek hostel, which are well thought of. Diwan, in Zamalek, is garnering much deserved attention for its very good collection of books, music, and video as well as its atmosphere. Volume One in Maadi is a clean, well-lit place with a good selection, and other worthwhile places are listed in the Directory (**Bookstores**). Used treasure can be unearthed at the bookstalls in the Azbakiya Garden near Opera Square and outside of Groppi's on Midan Tal'at Harb.

Oum el-Dounia has a good selection of books in French and English. You can order any French title and receive your order in less than two weeks. Shorouk Bookstore at First Mall has a good selection of titles in Arabic, English, and French. For the largest online bookstore in Egypt, for used and new books, visit *www.cairobookmark.com.*

CAMELS

Well, you never know when one might come in handy. The going rate is quoted by the kilo as between $300 and $600 (LE1750 to LE3500), with females being more valuable. The new camel market (directions in **Sightseeing** section) will give you the widest selection. Camel meat, by the way, is much eaten in Egypt, and is not only delicious but is said to be virtually cholesterol free.

CARPETS AND RUGS

For those in search of a bargain, Cairo is not the place to buy oriental carpets, although many beautiful shops selling them abound. However, richly colored Bedouin carpets and simple camel-hair moquettes are a buy—for example, less than LE100 for a 1 x 1.5 meter one of the latter at Kirdasa, handled by a hopeless non-bargainer. Cairo shops charge quite a bit for the Bedouin carpets, so it is better to go to al-'Arish or to the carpet markets west of Alexandria on the coast road. One is at al-Hammam (seventy kilometers west of Alexandria), the other at Burg al-'Arab (fifty kilometers). Since 2000, however, there have been fewer traders. Still, it is a fun trip, as what sells in Cairo for LE1,000 can be found there for around LE500. Finally, and to dispense with floor covering altogether, cotton rag rugs are a great buy here: LE30 for a really big bathmat from the Association for the Protection of the Environment (APE) in Heliopolis or through Egypt Crafts in Zamalek. El-Assiouty Carpets, with branches throughout Cairo, including Maadi and Zamalek, sell handmade Egyptian carpets with Persian design, at a fraction of the cost of Persian carpets.

CLOTHING, ETHNIC

Gallabiyas, the ubiquitous long, loose tunics worn by men and women, make wonderful nightshirts, loungewear, and evening wear. For the best quality in men's and women's gallabiyas go to Halowa, Downtown on the corner of Sharia Abd al-Khaliq Sarwat and Sharia Muhammad Farid. In plain cotton, they are less than LE50. Traditional Bedouin wedding dresses dripping with embroidery and coins are also fun for evening. The beautifully woven wool scarves that farmers wear wrapped around their necks all winter make surprisingly sophisticated, warm coat scarves for men and women; they are available throughout the Khan.

For really glamorous take-offs on ethnic Egyptian styles, there are several great places to go. Oum el-Dounia, Downtown has an excellent collection of Bedouin dresses, offering unique costumes that are stylish. Abbas Higazi in Khan al-Khalili sticks to traditional patterns done in the fabric and decoration of your choice, including silks; his finishing work is generally superior to that at Atlas, where cuff and hem facings are ignored and seams are not well finished. Ed-Dukkan, with its jewel-box of a shop hidden away in the Yamama Center and a branch at the Ramses Hilton Annex, has astonishingly beautiful things at high but well-justified prices. Citystars dedicates an entire floor to ethnic wear, carpets, jewelry, and knick-knacks.

EGYPTIAN FILMS AND ARAB MUSIC
Of course there is Virgin Records in Citystars, but also Oum el-Dounia, Downtown has Egyptian films with English and French subtitles, and both sell Arab music. Diwan has a good selection of both DVDs and music CDs.

JEWELRY
Cairo is home to hundreds, perhaps even thousands, of jewelry shops, and to some jewelers with international reputations. Work quality and design are generally good to excellent, and the government monitors the weight and purity of all gold and silver sold, so you are pretty safe as a consumer. Jewelry in gold and silver only is sold by gram weight, with work and age adding marginally to its cost. The current price for 18-carat gold is about LE60 per gram for Egyptian work and LE90 per gram for Italian work, with an extra LE15–25 per gram for Egyptian work, and LE20–40 per gram for Italian work. For sterling silver you pay LE2.50 per gram. The addition of precious stones sends the price spiraling upward, as none are native to Egypt, but semiprecious stones like onyx, amber, jade, and turquoise are very reasonable here.

Gold is available from 18 carats and up; very little under that is sold. Sterling silver is 95 percent pure. Shops selling the one usually do not sell the other. The three top gold jewelers are Sirghany, with a number of branches (including one in the Khan), Hassan Elaish (four branches), and Nassar

Brothers in the Khan. Others in the Khan include Mihran and Garbis Yazejian; Lalik, in Dokki and Heliopolis, are very good.

Silver jewelry, mostly in ethnic but some modern designs, is a bargain here. Saad of Egypt (many branches, including one in the Khan) is known for its design, quality, and high prices. Throughout town are many excellent shops; favorites are Qasr al-Shawq in Zamalek and Kafr al-Nada near the Shooting Club in Dokki; the young owner of the latter makes beautiful silver necklaces combined with semi-precious stones and beads at very reasonable prices. And more pricey, but unique is Azza Fahmy at First Mall, Mohandiseen, Maadi, and Heliopolis.

Shops selling beads and more beads, by piece and by weight, abound in the Khan. You choose and lay out, they string. Late in the evening, these places take on a comically mysterious air as people from all over the world sit on the floor to shuffle through the baskets, endlessly reconsidering their precious trinkets. Caveat emptor: ivory is on sale, too, along with ersatz camel-bone ivory. Most places will repair and restring your own heirlooms for very little in hopes of earning your good will. You can find unusual necklaces with muski glassware at Oum el Dounia. Try Mr. Beads at Turquoise for his friendly if well-practiced banter or the other shops listed in the Directory under **Khan al-Khalili.**

There are also a number of jewelry designers who work by word-of-mouth only and show by appointment only. Often members of the Women's Association can steer you to them, or they place notices in the *Maadi Messenger*, the *BCA Magazine*, or *Community Services Association Bulletin*, or *www.livingegypt.org*.

LITHOGRAPHS
L'Orientale in the Nile Hilton Mall has the biggest collection of original David Roberts lithographs in the world, as well as excellent

reproductions. Originals range from LE300 to LE5,000, depending on rarity, size, and condition, with reproductions a mere LE10 to LE50. Comparison shopping? At a well-known New York dealer, originals start at $1,600.

MARQUETRY (INLAID WOOD) AND MOTHER-OF-PEARL
These are very popular decorative touches on all sorts of furnishings, often in combination with mashrabiya (below). Zillions of small boxes displaying this work are hawked in every gift shop and all over Khan al-Khalili. Most are of poor quality on close inspection and very inexpensive; but beautifully done pieces—chests, mirrors, screens, tables in all sizes—can still be found in the Khan and elsewhere. Check the Old Shoppe to get an idea and ask the salespeople to educate you in what to look for.

MASHRABIYA
The best place to go to get a good overview of this lovely, painstakingly hand-lathed woodwork designed originally to hide the girls from the guys is at NADIM. The acronym NADIM stands for National Art Development Institute for Mashrabiya, but it is also really the name of the folklorist owner, Mr. Nadim, who preserves this craft along with his wife Dr. Nawal El Messiri, an anthropologist. They have greatly expanded their showroom, and it is a fascinating place to while away a few hours. The best mashrabiya is of beech, for its hard, tight, fine grain, but walnut, teak, and oak are also used. Prices are more or less fixed, and you can find nice things for less elsewhere if accompanied by a knowledgeable Egyptian friend, but you cannot beat NADIM's quality. They also do brass and copper work and have a large selection of wooden furniture.

On Road 9, Maadi, next to Café Greco, you can order mashrabiya screens, frames, and traditional furniture.

MUSICAL INSTRUMENTS
For authentic Egyptian and Middle Eastern instruments, head for Sharia Muhammad 'Ali downtown. Real musicians head directly to the source for these and Western instruments of all types as well: the Abdel Ghafar Group, which has moved to a new location in Sharia al-Bustan near Midan Falaki. You must make an appointment to see the manager, Mr. Hatem Abdel Ghafar. Check Maadi Music Centre for instruments and lessons. Oud in Zamalek has keyboards, violins, and is expert in ouds.

MUSKI GLASS
The vivid greens and blues, as well as the rarer reds and more common translucent whites of this handblown glassware make nice vases, pitchers, and casual drinking glasses. It is cheap, easily breakable, and available all over the Khan. Two places stand out: the Mosque Glass House for variety and volume, and Sayed Abd El-Raouf for the red Muski glass for your Christmas tree decorations. The glassblowers' district nearby is a treat for kids and grownups too. Oum el Dounia, Downtown, has a good selection as do several stores on Road 9 in Maadi.

NEWSSTANDS
International papers and magazines are found off Midan al-Tahrir just next to McDonald's, and on 26th July Street in Zamalek in front of Simonds. The major hotels all have adequate but more limited selections. Volume I in Maadi and El Shorouk Bookstore at First Mall both carry a good selection of magazines and newspapers.

PAINTING AND SCULPTURE
Egypt nurtures an enormous number of talented artists, whose work is regularly on display at the many fine arts galleries throughout Cairo. The gallery owners are highly knowledgeable, accessible, and often won-

derfully eccentric characters themselves. Check the listings in the *Community Times* and *Al-Ahram Weekly* or just browse using our by-neighborhood **Art Galleries** entries in the Directory. When you do go to a gallery, put your name on their mailing list.

PAPYRUS

You can buy papyrus all over the city, but one of the best places to go is Dr. Ragab's Papyrus Institute, a houseboat moored on the west bank of the Nile between the Cairo Sheraton and University Bridge beneath Golds Gym. Here you can learn about the papyrus-making process before you buy, and there are even make-your-own-papyrus kits for sale

PERFUMES

Create your own from essential oils diluted with alcohol or opt for perennial favorites like Cleopatra's Kiss. Among the (again) hundreds of perfume purveyors in the city, many of whom are in the Khan and around Midan al-Tahrir, you take pot luck, but one place to start educating yourself is at Abd al-Hady in the Khan. A well-dressed Egyptian woman would feel naked without her perfume, and after living here a while you may start to feel the same way. In no time, your dressing-table or bathroom counter could be full of the fragile perfume bottles that are nearly as numerous in Cairo shops as shoes are.

POTTERY

There are a few superb artist–potters, the late Nabil Darwish being one of our favorites. Fagnoon, who calls himself 'the Crazy Artist,' also does idiosyncratic and amusing pots (and metal and wood and whatever strikes his fancy at the moment) of all sorts in his atelier on the Saqqara road. Folksy figurines of dubious charm are widely available, especially at the Mud Factory in Mohandiseen, where large,

pretty Islamic–Persian-style vases are also made for lampshades and display, but prices for these are unduly high for the quality—LE300–500.

SHOES AND LEATHER GOODS

For those of us with the illness, Cairo at first glance would seem to be a shoe fetishist's dream. But alas, on closer examination, it is a nightmare! In a city with nearly as many shoe stores as feet (surely an understandable overreaction to the eleventh-century reign of the caliph al-Hakim, who banned the manufacture of women's shoes in order to keep the women inside, barefoot, and presumably pregnant), it is almost impossible to find decent shoes. Overall, poor manufacturing abounds, as do synthetics. And the heels! Either completely clunky and mismatched to the shoe or with a staggering proliferation of gold plastic curlicues, pyramids, and spikes that would fit right in on an S&M version of *Star Wars*. (Obviously, we are referring here primarily to women's footwear.) The only exceptions we have found after much footsore research are: the BTM department stores all around town, which sell Italian imports with prices to rival Italy's; Beymen at Four Seasons, Nile Plaza for the real thing: designer shoes; al-Baraem (two branches), which has good Italian shoes at reasonable prices; Santana (two branches), with some nice Egyptian-made shoes and boots; and perhaps the best, La Scarpa in Maadi, with excellent quality of work, soft leathers, and wearable styles, but limited stock and sizes.

The wives of oil emirs are luckier: they can go to Beymen in the Four Seasons, Nile Plaza and slap down a mere LE2,700 for a heaveny pair of crocodile pumps and designer shoes. It used to be possible to have shoes custom-made all over Cairo, but the old shoemakers are disappearing or selling out due to too much competition from the thousands of shoe stores. A few remain, including Abdel Moneim Abu Zeid (quality varies, mostly so-so) and El-Aziz (who makes cowboy boots) in Zamalek. Men fare far better in the shoe department, with Egyptian-made Bally shoes at around LE350 and up, available at Abbouda in Zamalek. For sports shoes, there are Nike and Adidas outlets in many of the major shopping malls.

Cairenes who can afford to do so bring shoes from abroad. We suggest you follow in their footsteps, and just buy your *shibshib* (slippers) from street kiosks or in Ataba market, or try the Moroccan-style ones from Khan al-Khalili.

Luckily, we can end our shoe diatribe on a high note as we consider other leather goods and clothing. Clothing of all sorts in leather and suede (chamois) of excellent quality and in a variety of styles, sizes, and colors can be bought off the rack or custom-made in many places throughout town. Prices are very reasonable—for example, men's bomber jackets in very fine suede for LE700 at the Leather Corner (two locations), a good shop with lots of choice and good service. Handbags, wallets, and briefcases are also well-styled, with good prices. At Choice and Seven K (numerous branches), with consistently superior styling and work, prices tend to be somewhat higher than elsewhere, but worth it.

TEXTILES, TOWELS, AND EGYPTIAN COTTON

These are generally good buys and make great gifts, given the worldwide cachet of Egyptian cotton. At all shopping malls, there are stores that specialize in Egyptian cotton products: towels, sheets, bedcovers, and bathmats. However, check each towel carefully as many qualify as 'seconds.' Halawa, Downtown, has quality Egyptian cotton products. Fitted sheets can be found at branches of Carpet City, Carrefour, and Spinneys.

Excellent-quality, ready-made men's all-cotton shirts are available at Mobaco. Custom-made shirts in a variety of fabrics, cuffs, and collars are available at Daly Dress Executive in the Nile Hilton Mall for LE130. The cheap place to go for fabric by the yard is the bowels of the Wikalat al-Balah (see above under **Major Suuqs**), where the occasional treasure amidst lots of sleaze can be found, and at Ouf in the Khan. There are excellent fabric shops of all kinds.

2 LEISURE AND LEARNING IN CAIRO

CAIRO FOR KIDS (OF ALL AGES)

First of all, get hold of a copy of *Cairo: The Family Guide* (AUC Press, 2006): If you find yourself in a Cairo hotel or apartment with lively offspring, you will have an escape route before you all start bouncing off the walls. Suburban children who have been used to a yard or local park may find the constraints of city living particularly hard to adjust to. At first glance, the busy streets might not seem welcoming, but there are spaces to roam and, unlike those in many cities, they are safe. In Cairo you can let your heirs out of your sight for a whole minute—hours, even—without becoming paranoid that they will be abducted by weirdoes. Do not underestimate the resulting peace of mind, and be grateful for it.

Your first and easiest option is to join a sporting club, or, simpler and cheaper, just go in on a daily fee basis. Indeed, if you live in town with small children this may be essential to your sanity. Tennis, swimming, gymnastics, karate, and just plain rolling around like puppies are only a few of the activities on offer, not to mention space for roller-blading and bike-riding. In Maadi, if you are fortunate enough to have access to the Cairo American College (CAC) facilities, your children can also explore the adventure playground there. Seven days a week at Victory College Field, there are all kinds of sports: soccer, rugby, cricket, softball, remote control auto racing, skate boarding, and a playground. There is a great family atmosphere around the ball games, and enthusiastic American-style support for the teams. Meanwhile, over on the Cairo Rugby field you will often find a game of cricket underway on Cairo's only public cricket pitch, where the thwack of leather on willow and the ripples of polite applause evoke quite a different world.

The Swiss Club in Imbaba near Kit Kat Square has a nice playground and grassy area in clean, quiet surroundings. Good for kids' parties. Al-Azhar Park is an excellent choice for space and green grass.

The Cairo Zoo, built in 1891, is one of the oldest in the world. Its maze of beautiful mosaic paths and many enclosures can be suitably exhausting for children. While the care of the animals does not perhaps reach the standard of world-class zoos, and the tendency of some parents to allow their kids to tease the animals may annoy, it is one of the few zoos where one can actually feed the animals. The keepers of hippopotami, giraffes, camels, and ostriches will sell you handfuls of the appropriate vegetation. (Political correctness aside, there is a great deal to be said for the velvety feel of a baby goat's lips on a child's hand.) In the reptile house, brave souls may even handle snakes. The zoo is crowded on Fridays and might, for the shy newcomer, be avoided on public holidays, when the plumage of obviously foreign visitors is likely to attract more attention than that of the animals.

If your family's interest in animals extends to wanting one in your own home, you can visit the Friday Pet Market. The easiest way to reach it is to take the Autostrade out of Maadi, and just near the turn to Muqattam (at the Esso petrol station) you will see two large concrete water towers on the left. Take the next left and then the next right to follow the railway tracks past brick-makers. It is no more than a kilometer from the main road. The Pet Market makes for an interesting outing, but it is definitely not for the squeamish or for animal rights activists, who will be upset by monkeys in cages far too small for them and endangered species of birds of prey offered for sale. Cairo's most popular pets, fish and birds, are in great abundance along with all their necessary equipment—and at prices far cheaper than can be found elsewhere.

The Fish Garden on Sharia Hasan Sabri in Zamalek was formerly a khedival garden and is great for hide-and-seek, walks, and jobs, as well as a good spot for fish-gazing. Al-Azhar Park has a children's playground. Arabica restaurant in Zamalek has paints and colors on separate tables. Fagnoon (Sabil Umm Hashim) on the Saqqara road offers activities for babies to adolescents: pottery-making, bread baking, painting, printing, woodwork, and a climbing wall spread out between palm trees. In Kid's Farm in 10th of Ramadan City on the Cairo-Ismaliya Highway, there is a garden where kids can feed animals. Also on the Cairo-Ismaliya road is Plein Air, a country club with swimming, cooking, farm animals, planting, tennis, horseback riding. And don't forget El Sawy Culture Wheel (El Sakia), which screens children's films.

Cairo National Circus was founded following Nasser's trip to the Soviet Union in the 1950s. Nightly performances take place under the faded big top on the Corniche in Agouza, except during the first half of Ramadan.

There is also the Puppet Theater in Midan Opera. The singing performances in Arabic attract a noisy crowd and are much loved by Egyptian children. Language is largely irrelevant in these lively Punch and Judy shows, and a good time is had by all. Command performances can even be arranged by contacting the French Cultural Center (**Organizations**). A charming group of multilingual puppeteers who go by the acronym ZASSY can be engaged at schools, nurseries, and orphanages to entertain both kids and grownups (**Children's Entertainment**), but note that prices from these AUC graduates are on the American, not Egyptian scale.

Dr. Ragab's Pharaonic Village on Jacob's Island, Giza, makes for a fascinating and educational day out. Definitely cut out the twenty-percent-off coupons frequently found in the Community Services Association bulletin. Take the floating guided tour past scenes from life in ancient Egypt and statues of gods and goddesses before alighting to visit a pharaonic temple and a replica of King Tutankhamun's tomb. Have your photo taken, if you must, in period costume—a very popular Christmas card idea for the folks back home—and then lunch in the restaurant. This is a good pre-Luxor outing. Some kids sneer at it, others love it.

For children at the upper end of that awkward post-diaper, pre-disco stage—eight to fifteen years' duration depending on precocity—the situation is bleak, as it is and has been throughout history, always and everywhere, in their eyes. Realistically though, Cairo offers a great deal to pre-teens and teens who eventually do decide to get off their butts after boring even themselves silly by whining, "There's nothing to do-oo-o!" For their health, and for their parents' sanity, there is a nearly infinite variety of sports, including some—such as horseback riding, rowing, tennis, squash, scuba diving, and gymnastics—that are far more affordable here than abroad, and generally of a high caliber in terms of facilities and instruction.

For some good, dirty (i.e., sweaty), family fun, escape the pollution and get out into the desert by joining the Hash House Harriers for their Friday afternoon jogs. The first Friday in the month is the family run, after which a refreshingly insincere effort is made to tone down the post-run dirty jokes. While getting winded, you will discover some great picnic locations. Visit *www.cairohash.com*.

In summer, many hotels have day rate entrances or seasonal family memberships, but limited space for kids to run and with unduly steep day rates in many cases—for example, the Marriott charges LE370 per day for a family of three. A better solution may be the Saqqara Palm Club or the Saqqara Country Club, both near Saqqara. Facilities vary but are generally good and include a wide range of sports. The Saqqara Country Club in particular has an excellent equestrian program. Facilities aside, teens will be inclined toward whichever place their friends go (**Sporting & Country Clubs**). Check out the Cairo American College for summer activities, as well as Fagnoon in Zamalek an Sakkara. Look in the *Mother & Child* magazine directory for listings.

The first water park in Cairo was Crazy Water on the road to 6th October City. It has slides for all ages, a wave pool, quasars, go-karts, and video games. Aquapark on the Ismailiya Road is safe, clean, and very crowded on Fridays.

Genena Mall in Nasr City has a large ice skating rink.

Wonderland, Nasr City is an outdoor amusement park and also has bowling, billiards, and a movie complex.

Media Production City at 6th of October the theme is Egyptian landmarks where everything is on a scale of the child's perspective, jungles, ice skating and dolphins too.

Dream Park in 6th of October, is a theme park with plenty of rides and restaurants.

Family Land at Osman Towers, Corniche al-Nil, billiards, bowling, ice skating, and laser storm for the adolescent and for the younger crowd, there are video games and miniature rides.

Fun Planet in Arkadia Mall, Corniche al-Nil, Downtown, has an outer-space theme.

Geroland in El Obour City has largest roller coaster in Middle East, water rides, ice skating, artificial lake with 5 different theme parks—European, Mexican, Western, Future and Children's island.

Magic Galaxy Park at Citystars Mall has a variety of rides and food court.

If all that is too much, The Beach at JW Marriott has a water park and sandy beaches.

Less strenuous alternatives: snooker and/or pool halls (known as '**Billiard Halls**') have recently sprung up all over the city. Few serve alcohol—sigh of relief—and most require no membership. You just pay and play for LE20 to LE30 a game. Ten-pin Bowling is popular, and some places have snooker and food outlets on site. Bandar Mall in Maadi, the Nile Bowling Center in Giza, and Maadi Grand Mall (MGM) are the main ones. There are plenty of cinemas to view the most recent Arabic and English language movie releases. Here are the newer theaters: Good News Cinema at Grand Hyatt Hotel; Al Sereg City Mall in Heliopolis; Genena Mall; Renaissance at Wonderland Mall; Stars Cinema at Citystars. Look in *Al Ahram Weekly* newspaper for all cinema listings and what is showing. Reasonably well-behaved teens can also work on their computer and social skills at cybercafés (**Computers**).

Expectant mothers and those with infants will be pleased by the level of care available in Cairo. The services of Katrina Shawky come especially recommended. She offers prenatal exercise and childbirth prep classes. Contact Katrina at 336-3930 for more details. In Heliopolis, there are pregnancy and childbirth classes in English and Arabic given by Maha el-Zokm at 2 67-2492. Call Ann Pittomvils for antenatal classes in English (380-3789/5357). International lactation consultant, Rania Hussni 012 742-7104 gives breastfeeding courses. Fitness for pregnant mothers is given at Samia Allouba Creative Dance and Fitness Center in Maadi and Mohandiseen.

HOBBIES, INTERESTS, PASTIMES, AND SELF-INDULGENCE

The array of things to see and do in Cairo is inexhaustible. Newcomers who tend to hit the ground running will be inspired to explore Islamic Cairo, improve their tennis game, sign up for Arabic lessons, and get their flats redone all at once. Shortly thereafter, they find themselves exhausted and overcommitted. A better strategy is to get selectively busy with just a few things at first. For non-Arabic speakers, one of them should certainly be learning some conversational Arabic in a group setting. It is a great way to meet other people in the same boat and to start learning the ropes from each other.

Because of what is wryly referred to as the E-factor (E for Egypt), it is hard for everyone, native Cairenes included, to pack in as much as one would like in the course of a day. Much of this has to do with the traffic. It can take ten minutes or over an hour to get from Dokki to Midan al-Tahrir; don't attempt it between 1:30 and 3 pm during school sessions or during the morning rush hours of 8 to 10 am if you can avoid it. Another element of the E-factor is time, a lot of which is spent waiting—for stores to open, plumbers to show up, classes to start, lines to get shorter, and so on. Take it easy and always have a good book at hand.

In addition to the gamut of activities in this and the next two sections (**Arts, Entertainment, & Night Life** and **Sports & Fitness**), up-to-date inspiration for what to do is available in *Egypt Today* (which carries excellent listings of everything from cultural centers to bars to art galleries), *Al-Ahram Weekly*, *The Croc*, and *Community Times* (for excellent cultural listings). The website directory lists addresses that provide more information. Note, though, that times, phone numbers, and programs are subject to change and that last-minute cancellations are not unheard of. Call ahead if you can, and have a back-up plan regardless, to keep frustration within manageable limits.

If your particular esoteric interest is not included here, the many community and social organizations invariably welcome anyone with the enthusiasm and expertise to organize something new.

ALTERNATIVE MEDICINE

Alternative Therapies are enjoying a resurgence in Cairo, mirroring a world trend. Herbs have been used to treat chronic ailments in Egypt for centuries, particularly by people too poor to see a doctor. At the Harraz Herb Shop in Bab al-Khalq, patients from all points on the social spectrum line up to discuss their ailments before picking up an individual herbal remedy. Business is booming, particularly among the better heeled, according to Ahmed Harraz.

The Lotus Room's Joanne Butler offers aromatherapy and reflexology as well as massage and reiki. CSA in Maadi also maintains a list of other alternative medical practitioners.

CSA offers many lectures and workshops on alternative medicine and each Wednesday is dedicated to health—Wellness Wednesday. Insight Inside is a group in Mohandiseen that also looks at the many sides of alternative medicine. More and more, you will find people working in this field, but do check their qualifications. *The Croc* and *Community Times* list people to contact for reiki, reflexology, yoga, and message.

Homeopathy, which first arrived in Egypt in 1864, at last seems to be gaining a foothold, while chi kung and reiki, the therapeutic placing of hands on one's chakra points, are less so, but all have their adherents and their recommended practitioners in Cairo.

Sand bathing is special to Egypt. The late Aga Khan visited Aswan every year to lie immersed in a shallow pit of sand as a cure for his aching bones and joints. It used to be very fashionable for the élite of cold, damp Europe to seek such cures, and the practice is back in vogue with hotels such as the Oberoi and the Amoun having special pits. Similar cures are offered at Siwa Oasis, where you can be buried up to your neck in sand at Gebel Dakrur, although the accommodations at the nearby hostelry are rather more basic than those at Aswan. Or there are the five-star hotels specializing in spa treatment in the Sinai area.

ARCHAEOLOGY

Could there be a richer place in all the world than Egypt for amateur and professional archaeologists? Anyone who thinks it is all dry bones and old stones has only to attend a lecture or go on a field trip with any of these organizations to be disabused of this notion: the American Research Center in Egypt (ARCE), the Egypt Exploration Society, or the Netherlands Institute (**Organizations**).

ARCHITECTURE

SPARE, the Society for the Preservation of the Architectural Resources of Egypt, organizes walks through the labyrinth of Cairo's history and is actively engaged in the preservation of many of the city's crumbling treasures in cooperation with ARCE (see Archaeology above).

ART CLASSES

Community Services Association (CSA) classes in pottery, painting, and drawing are given at The Workshop in Maadi and at al-Madyafa in Heliopolis. Studio 206 in Maadi offers classes in drawing, painting, sculpting, and pottery. Art and Design School in Heliopolis gives classes in pottery and clay, graphic and furniture design, and instruction in collage. The Francophone Art Academy in Cairo and Townhouse Gallery are great places to call for more information. Also check out *www.egy-art.com*, aimed in offering Egyptian artists a forum.

AVIATION

For about $15,000 inclusive, you can get your pilot's license through EgyptAir's Flight School at Imbaba Airport. It includes 135 hours of classwork and theory plus twenty-five hours of flight time. For those who already have licenses, the airport also has small planes for rent, but their maintenance is questionable. Experienced pilots should also note that much of Egypt's airspace is a carefully monitored military zone.

BACKGAMMON

Men can pick up a game at any of the cafés all over town. The one opposite the entrance to the Windsor Hotel is particularly lively and, due to its location, might even tolerate the presence of women who enjoy this popular pastime.

BEAUTY SALONS

There seem to be surprisingly few really top-notch salons in Cairo. Our evidence for this is that a large number of expatriate residents of long standing routinely have their hair, facials, manicures, massages, and so on, done by beauticians trained abroad who work out of their homes. Resistance to neighborhood salons seems to be based partly on language barriers, partly on concern about cleanliness and sterilization of equipment, and partly on a perceived lack of know-how. But by all means, check out a few for yourself, as a trip to a beauty salon is invariably a fascinating immersion into any country's feminine culture. At the upper end, three places are recommended: Mohamed Al Sagheer (branches throughout Cairo), Jacques Dessange, and Ahmed and Abdou in Heliopolis. Seasons Salon in Maadi has Color Me Beautiful products beauty services, plus clothes and accessories. Get recommendations from Egyptian friends, or ask for private practitioners at the WA.

BIRDWATCHING

Egypt's plethora of birds, native and migrant, such as bee-eaters, ibis, egrets, and hoopoes, make it a great place to take up birdwatching. The north coast and the oases are uncluttered viewing locations for birds, as is Lake Qarun closer by. Larger birds such as white storks and pelicans, which have to migrate over land because of their size, can be spotted in Sinai or on the Suez coast. In spring, the cliffs at 'Ayn Sukhna provide a perfect view of thousands of birds of prey, like eagles and vultures, which spiral on the thermals there before heading north. Read Richard Hoath's monthly "Nature Notes" in *Egypt Today*.

Individuals interested in birding can contact Mindy Baha El Din at 760-8160 or see the website about birdwatching in Egypt, *www.birdingegypt.com*.

BRIDGE

The Cairo bridge scene is hopping, if this can be said of such a sedentary pastime. The Annual International Bridge Tournament held in January in the Ramses Hilton is opened by Omar Sharif and attracts an impressive entry list. There are games at all the sporting clubs, and local groups advertise regularly. An excellent way to expand your social circle.

CAR AND MOTORCYCLE RALLIES AND MOTOCROSS

The annual Pharaoh's Rally held every October is a grueling 11 day, 4,800 km event for 4-wheel drives, trucks, and motorcycles through some of Egypt's toughest terrain. Motocross enthusiasts also have lots of organized company. The contacts given in the Directory, Rami Siag and Raed Baddar, can tell you all you need to know and more. Radio Auto Club at Egypt meet at Victory College Field twice a month—check *www.racegypt.org*.

CLASSIC CARS

Since it is illegal to export antique cars, there are some real gems in Cairo. Beautifully preserved and worth a fortune anywhere else, these vehicles can only be polished and admired here.

CHURCH ACTIVITIES

Finding kindred souls to worship and socialize with can ease the settling-in period for many newcomers. The most active Western Christian churches are All Saints Cathedral in Zamalek, Saint Andrew's downtown, and the Community Church in Maadi, but there are many others of most denominations represented in Cairo (**Churches**).

COMPUTER COURSES

AUC's CACE (Center for Adult and Continuing Education) offers classes on the most popular software programs. The British Council computer classes are reputedly the best on offer in Cairo. For more advanced or esoteric packages and programming courses, AUC's Computer Science Department, RITSEC, and Internet Egypt may be your best bets. Many of the computer companies (**Computers**) also offer group and private instruction. Look in the backpages of the *Community Times* and the advertisements of the *Maadi Messenger*. Community Services Association has a course about Internet services in Egypt.

COOKING CLASSES

The CSA in Maadi offers classes, mostly in Egyptian, Thai, and Indian cookery, depending on demand and the supply of teachers. The Marriott in Zamalek runs occasional

Teach and Taste sessions, as do some of the other hotels as part of their regular and advertised food promotions. For this kind of information, we have found it is best to contact the hotels' public relations officers, who invariably speak English and French at least, in addition to Arabic. Studio 206 in Maadi offers a variety of cooking classes.

COUNSELING

CSA has its own counseling unit offering a wide range of resources for psychotherapy, clinical and educational evaluation, and support groups of various kinds, including Alcoholics Anonymous. Befrienders offers non-judgmental, anonymous telephone support and referral for anyone at all who feels in need of a sympathetic ear or a lifeline in times of crises great and small. Both organizations often seek volunteer and professional additions to their staffs.

CREATIVE WRITING

If the muse strikes in Cairo, you can entice her continued company by taking a creative writing course along with other budding authors at CSA or at AUC. Classes at CSA are not offered regularly but can be arranged on demand. To learn more about classes at AUC contact the Department of English and Comparative Literature. AUC also has an excellent journalism program. Serafis Cultural Society (*www.serafis.net*) and Studio 206 have writing classes from time to time.

CULTURAL CENTERS

Egyptian and foreign cultural centers (**Organizations**) are listed in the back of *Egypt Today*, as well as in the Directory, and exist to show the best of their countries' cultures. Depending on their size and budget they offer films, plays, dance troupes, art exhibitions, libraries, and language classes. Specific programs are listed weekly in *Al-Ahram Weekly*. The Opera House is a frequent venue for visiting performers on goodwill tours. Its programs overall provide an accessible, inexpensive opportunity to douse oneself in cultural offerings that are too costly or crowded in other major capitals. Don't miss El Sawy Culture Wheel for a variety of programs.

DANCING

So far the Scots seem to have folk dancing all sewn up, as the American country–western or line dancing craze has not yet hit Cairo. There are two lively choices, the Cairo Scottish Country Dance Group and St. Andrews Church Scottish Country Dance Group. You do not have to be a Scot or own a kilt to join. Discotheques abound (see **Arts, Entertainment, & Nightlife**), and a few places have live music for slightly more staid dancing. A good spot for dancing under the stars: the top deck of Le Pacha 1901 in Zamalek. Arthur Murray has a studio in Maadi for ballroom dancing. Golds Gym and CSA offer Latin dance classes.

DIETING

Dieting is in vogue in Cairo. Exercise classes, hypnosis, herbs, slimming salons with vibrating tables and other exotic equipment, acupuncture, and liposuction; all can be—and are—utilized by foreigners and locals in pursuit of the perfect body or a reasonable approximation thereof. Beauty Essentials in Zamalek is a good source for the latest dieting information. You might consider fasting during Ramadan—but most people say that they add rather than subtract pounds then as a result of the lavish *ifTaar*s and *suHuur*s.

DRAMA GROUPS

Three groups are currently active: Maadi Community Players, Heliopolis Community

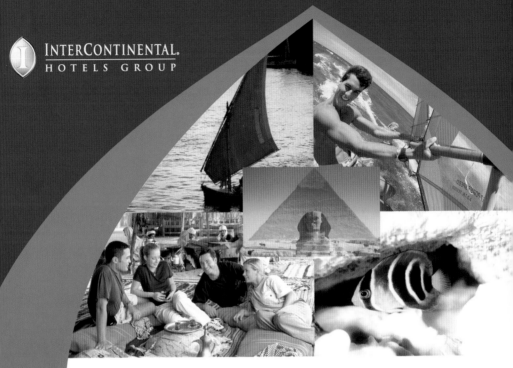

Egypt & Middle East Co. (EME)
Since 1975

Office Equipment:

- Copiers (Panasonic - Japan)
- Fax (Panasonic - Japan)
- Fax (Sagem & Philips - France)
- PABX (Samsung - Korea)
- Intercom (Aiphone - Japan / Hyundai - Korea)
- Air Condition (Carrier - Egypt)
- Office Furniture (Mobica - Egypt)

Central Installations

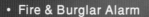

- Sound Systems (Tyco-BOUYER - France)
- Fire & Burglar Alarm (C-Tec - UK / Texecom - UK)
- Central Satellite Receivers
  (Blankom - Germany / Ankaro - Germany)
- CCTV (Videor - Germany / Hyundai - Korea)

Safety & Security

- Fire & Burglar Alarm (C-Tec - UK / Texecom - UK)
- CCTV (Videor - Germany / Hyundai - Korea)
- Air Purifiers (Trion - USA / Surroundair - USA)
- Reflective Sheets (Avery - USA)
- Traffic Safety (Code 3 - USA)
- Traffic Lights (Zelisko - Austrian)
- Radar Equipment (Kustom - USA)
- Shoplifting Prevention (National E.S.A - Canada)
- Rolls of P.V.C (Flag - Italy)

Egypt & Middle East Co. (EME)

www.eme-egypt.com

Dear Customer and Friend!

My sincere appreciation and gratitude for your trust and cooperation since 1975.

Thanks to your continuous confidence, we serve you always better in the fields of Office Equipment, Communications, Central Installations and Safety & Security.

We encourage you to contact us without any commitment.

All our team members are at your service .. to satisfy your needs in a professional, ethical and friendly atmosphere, as our ultimate goal is your success and satisfaction, and our motto:

Expertise, Magnitude, Endeavour

Cordially yours,

Odette Iskandar
President

Headquarters	Tel.: 2913133	Fax: 2910028	headquarters@eme-egypt.com
Down Town	Tel.: 5749205-8	Fax: 5776888	fax-sales@eme-egypt.com
Down Town	Tel.: 5749205-8	Fax: 5776888	communication@eme-egypt.com
Down Town	Tel.: 5749205-8	Fax: 5776888	fax-service@eme-egypt.com
Mohandeseen	Tel.: 3447990	Fax: 3444770	copiers-sales@eme-egypt.com
Mohandeseen	Tel.: 3447989	Fax: 3444770	copiers-service@eme-egypt.com
Heliopolis	Tel.: 2917820	Fax: 4171096	aircondition-safety@eme-egypt.com
Triumph	Tel.: 2905977	Fax: 4177978	firecontrol@eme-egypt.com
Triumph	Tel.: 6900257	Fax: 6900259	soundsystems@eme-egypt.com
Ramsis	Tel: 5907464	Fax: 5904978	ramsis@eme-egypt.com
Alexandria	Tel.: (03) 4865265	Fax: (03) 4874486	alexandria@eme-egypt.com
Tanta	Tel.: (040) 3303103	Fax: (040) 3319301	tanta@eme-egypt.com
Ismailia	Tel.: (064) 3330771	Fax: (064) 3329486	ismailia@eme-egypt.com
Zagazik	Tel.: (055) 2354493	Fax: (055) 2354495	zagazik@eme-egypt.com
Assiut	Tel.: (088) 2330570	Fax: (088) 2330571	assiut@eme-egypt.com
Luxor	Tel.: (095) 2370615	Fax: (095) 2370315	luxor@eme-egypt.com
Menia	Tel.: (086) 2346664	Fax: (086) 2346668	menia@eme-egypt.com

Lost at the newsstand?

GET NOTICED.

Activities Association (HCAA) Drama Group, and the Cairo Players. The Maadi group has been around for over twenty-five years. It is heavily American in its membership and productions—lots of Cairo American College faculty members—and does professional workshops, plus readings, in addition to the normal theatrical fare. Cairo Players and the HCAA group are more British in their orientation, with Cairo Players drawing much of its talent from the British International School. HCAA particularly encourages amateurs and is very community-oriented. Rasha Soliman Artist Workshop ofers classes in drama, puppetry, and animation.

FASHION SHOWS

Local and international designers hold shows throughout the year at the big hotels. Watch the press for details. Women's groups also frequently sponsor fashion shows; they are a good way to get a picture of the clothing and fashion scene in Cairo. If you are interested in modeling, check out ENVOGUE modeling school and agency.

FLOWER ARRANGING

The bounty of beautiful, cheap flowers in Cairo make this an ideal place to learn the art of arranging them well. Call the Japanese Embassy to find out about classes.

An annual flower and plant show is held each March at Orman Gardens in Giza, where you will see everything you could possibly need to create your own Hanging Gardens of Babylon.

LANGUAGE CLASSES

This cannot be overemphasized: you must learn some Arabic if a) you are living in Cairo, b) you are not a hermit, c) you disdain to live in an exclusively expatriate

world, and d) you certainly do not want to be taken for a tourist in Khan al-Khalili. Fortunately, opportunities abound. Berlitz, Community Services Association (CSA) in Maadi, Kalimat in Mohandiseen, and the International Language Institute (ILI) all have classes, both classical and colloquial. AUC has a year-long intensive program. Every foreign embassy has or arranges classes. Private tutors are plentiful and reasonable (LE40 per hour), and there are always ads in the English-language press for people seeking to barter Arabic-for-English lessons, so money is never a deterrent. Conversation usually precedes reading and writing in the learning process. Classes create a natural source for a social life, whereas semi-private or private tutoring works faster; most foreigners recommend starting with a class.

Because Cairo is such a cosmopolitan city, it is also the ideal place to learn or brush up on other languages as well. This is particularly true for French, which is widely spoken, but each country represented by an embassy can provide names of tutors or classes in its language.

LIBRARIES

Cairo has a glorious range of libraries esoteric and mundane. All those listed in the Directory are open to the public, and scholars can usually gain entrance easily to those that are not. For English readers, there are the British Council Library in Agouza and the American Studies Library at the US Embassy in Garden City. Both carry periodicals and provide audiovisual services, CD-ROM searches, and interlibrary loan facilities. CSA in Maadi also has a loan library available to the public for an annual fee of LE100. Two new libraries with wide selections in English have recently opened in renovated and palatial premises, namely the Great Cairo Library in Zamalek and the

Mubarak Library in Giza. The Music Library at the Opera House complex has listening rooms with tapes and CDs plus a wide range of musicology publications.

MUSIC AND SINGING

The Cairo Choral Society, the Maadi Community Chorus, and the Cairo Symphony Orchestra are just three of the groups that offer musicians an outlet for their talents. Voice and instrumental lessons are offered by a number of reputable teachers. For others, check with the groups above and in the Directory or contact the music departments of any of the larger schools.

MEDITATION

Serenity in Cairo is a rare commodity, but regardless of what is going on around you, it is possible to create your own internal island of calm and maybe even bliss through meditation. Sufi and yoga are the two most commonly practiced forms of it here. Groups start and stop, but the listings in the Directory will put you in contact with current ones. Insight Inside at *www.insight-inside.com* in Mohandiseen has a monthly schedule of activities.

NEEDLEWORK

The Heliopolis Tuesday Knitters meet weekly to knit for charity, the Women's Association has a sewing group, and Hetty, a woman in Heliopolis, organizes a weekly quilting group. As of 2006, the contacts are changing, but both groups still exist. Call Linn, who will help you get in touch with the right person.

PHOTOGRAPHY

For the past few years, there has been an annual photographic exhibition by the Jour-nalism and Mass Communication Darkroom Workshop at AUC. This would be the place to start finding out more about photography workshops and supplies. One place that comes well recommended for **Film Processing** with custom features is the Photo Center downtown. Studio 206 offers photography classes and has a dark room, as does Francophone Art Academy in Cairo.

POTTERY

Classes in pottery and many other arts and crafts are given at the Madyafa in Heliopolis (**Art Classes**). Modeling clay may be purchased from Samir al-Guindi at the Mud Factory on Sudan Street. The clay from Mar Girgis is not recommended, as it often contains impurities such as glass or wire. Studio 206 and Fagnoon on Saqqara Road are two good schools for pottery.

REFLEXOLOGY

Reflexology treats the whole body through the feet using a form of acupressure massage. Regardless of its therapeutic value, it feels wonderful. The Lotus Room is a good place to start. Check out *The Croc* and *Community Times* for listings.

WOMEN'S GROUPS

Not all are for women only, and they are the best places for newcomers to get firsthand information on life in Cairo (**Organizations**). Many of the groups have small weekly get-togethers as well as more formal monthly meetings with speakers or demonstrations. The groups vary in their purpose and composition, but all are very active, sponsoring a wealth of activities, a portion of which are invariably charitable. The Women's Association is the largest and has a very international composition including many Egyptians. The Maadi Women's Guild focuses heavily on Christian church-related charitable work. Cairo Petroleum Wives does not require either a petroleum connection or even a husband for membership. Middle East Wives is for non-Arab women married to Egyptians or Arabs. Many nationalities also have women's groups that give members a chance to socialize in their native language. Most groups and clubs tend to go into hibernation during the long hot summer, then go into full swing again in September. All cultural centers for information about specific nationalities or look in *Egypt Today*, *The Croc*, *Community Times*, and the CSA bulletin for listings.

VOLUNTEER WORK

Endless opportunities exist, some of which we review in Chapter 4.

ARTS, ENTERTAINMENT, AND NIGHTLIFE

From high-brow to low-life, Cairo's arts and cultural scene can keep even the most dedicated aesthete busy for a lifetime. And for those with energy to burn, New York cannot hold a candle to Cairo, which is the real 'city that never sleeps.' Foreigners may well wonder about the seemingly indefatigable Cairenes: how do they do it? The secret: nap time, either in the hot afternoon or in the early evening anywhere from 5 to 10 pm, before real life begins.

ART GALLERIES AND THE ARTS IN CAIRO

The astounding volume and perfection of ancient Egypt's monuments, sculpture, and painting are unmatched anywhere in the world. Modern Egyptian artists are fortunate indeed in their heritage, less so in their patronage since the days of the pharaohs, caliphs, sultans, and kings. Nevertheless,

Egypt does have a thriving arts community filled with people for whom creating is a passion. It is also home to, and inspiration for, a number of foreign artists.

If you are looking for a painting that will always remind you of Egypt, several painters portray the daily life in Cairo and the villages. Mansur Ahmad, who has a gallery in Maadi, captures the nuances of Egyptian life. Elhamy Naguib's works at Graffiti have a more mythical, dreamlike quality. The late Margo Veillon, a superb Swiss–Egyptian painter, spent much of her career capturing the verve of daily life in Egypt. Magdi Abd al-Aziz, who shows at Extra, reflects Egypt in abstract forms. For fresh new talents, you might try the Helwan University Faculty of Fine Arts in Zamalek, which exhibits the works of students and faculty, or the Hanager Arts Center in the Opera complex. In the Directory is a long list, by neighborhood, of many of the major galleries in Cairo. We have kept it largely to the fine arts, listing those that show artistic handicrafts under **Arts & Crafts**.

Those who appreciate the more abstract in art may be pleased to know what Mena Sarofim, the owner of Extra, passed on to us: most Egyptians, like most other people, prefer representational art and traditional subjects. This might not lower the price of that particularly exquisite piece of . . . what is it, anyway? . . . that you cannot live without, but at least it is unlikely that it will disappear immediately while you ponder the status of your bank account.

A good place to meet artists is the Townhouse Gallery, which is open to the public. Also visit the wonderful Museum of Egyptian Egyptian Art in the Opera complex in Zamalek.

BALLS

Ballroom dancing is not a big thing in Cairo, but there are annual institutions like the St. Andrews Ball in the fall, the Queen's (Elizabeth II, that is) Birthday Ball in spring, and the US Marine Ball. The ambassadors of the larger embassies usually also sponsor at least one big dance annually, as do many of the social clubs and some business organizations. Arthur Murray has a studio in Maadi for ballroom dance classes.

BARS

It was a dirty job, but someone had to do it. Our young researcher plumbed the depths and dives of bar life in Cairo for our readers' edification and came up with the observations, recommendations, and the few thumbs-downs found here. The coolness factor is highly fickle; what is really cool one night may become a wouldn't-be-caught-dead-there spot by the next. But some things never change, like the local 'cafeterias,' which look like every other café but also serve alcohol. Check a few of them out when you want your Stella served with no pretensions whatsoever. In the meantime, here are some of the hot and not-so-hot spots, Wednesdays and Thursdays being the hot nights:

Pub 28 is the closest thing we have found to a real neighborhood bar in Cairo. It is tiny, always busy but rarely packed, does not have music, attracts local and expatriate loyalists, treats women civilly, and is completely fad-resistant. What a relief!

Harry's Pub in the Marriott: your generic suburban New Jersey hotel bar right in the heart of Zamalek. It has it all—the ersatz pub atmosphere, the theme nights (Karaoke, Western, Ladies' Night), and Engelbert Humperdinck songs repeated ad nauseam. Everyone ends up there once in a while anyway. Just down the Saray al-Gezira in the bowels of Le Pacha 1901 is the far more appealing (quieter, cleaner, more comfortable) *Tycoons Bar*, a version of the same, with excellent imported beer on tap, but for

a pretty outrageous LE20 a pint. Go anyway and insist on Stella instead.

L'Aubergine offers relaxing dining downstairs, with a slew of vegetarian options, while its upstairs bar has been a student favorite for years. Tight, smoky, and loud, every city needs one of these! *Amsterdam* in Maadi offers a three-tiered lounge, restaurant, and wine bar. Run by the owner of *L'Aubergine*, it maintains the no-frills ambience he is famous for. The menu offers dishes from every corner of the globe. It may finally fill a vital niche for residents of Maadi tired of the endless trek to the bars in town.

Deals, behind Maison Thomas in Zamalek, is popular among the younger set. Also does the pub theme, but with a more contemporary twist, and inconsistently serves decent burgers. The tall tables and stools are designed to make adults feel like they are sitting in high chairs.

Abou El Sid just in front of Deals is the latest in a long line of restaurants and bars to occupy that location. The Arabic lounge atmosphere is very comfortable, and the food is good, but pricey.

The terrace bar on the roof of the *Odeon* Hotel downtown is, to devotees, the funkiest in Cairo. This is the place where dedicated barflies of all stripes—including head-scarved women having beers with their shisha—can be found at all hours: it is open all day, all night, every day. The view is fine, too. The bar at the Windsor Hotel is another local favorite, with its unpretentious environment and old-style British charm.

Flux is as cool as it gets; a sublime mix of modern art, lighting, and décor. It is a small and personable place with an attentive staff and innovative menu. A restaurant/bar that could hold its own in New York, Sydney, or London.

Le Tabasco is noted for both bar and food, with exactly the right fluid barrier between the two in a setting that somehow successfully mixes elements of a pharaonic tomb and the Flintstones' cave. The back is for dining, the front for seeing, being seen, and being democratically crushed by the chic and the great unwashed.

The Cairo Jazz Club performs admirably on all fronts, offering great music, food, and drink in a very hip atmosphere. Its interesting and varied entertainment program means it is the darling of the youthful bar crowd. See *www.cairojazzclub.com*.

La Bodega in Zamalek, with its outlandish trompe l'oeil decor is also a favorite. The dining room offers a good—albeit expensive—continental menu, while the bar is a bit more low key, providing a sophisticated atmosphere in which you can actually drink and talk at the same time.

Bar 10, across the landing, draws a younger, hipper, and LOUDER crowd,

Indigo in Dokki has been relaunched and boasts an impressive line-up of entertainment.

The *British Community Association* (BCA) bar in Mohandiseen requires membership in the BCA, but it is pretty cheap, has a nice outdoor garden, and is the best place in Cairo for the fish-and-chips and steak-and-kidney pie you occasionally pine for. Non-members can rent DVDs and videos.

For something completely different, try these places: *Da Baffo's* before 1 am, and *Borsalino* and *Africana* after. For something completely ordinary, all the hotels have their lugubrious clubby-type bars that attract mostly businessmen, but they are better than nothing when you don't want to watch the tube.

BELLY-DANCING

What you will see on the Nile cruise boats, which is all most tourists see, ranges from the sublime to the silly, mostly falling closer to the latter. It is definitely worth the loss of a night's sleep while in Cairo to see the nightclubs along the Pyramids and King Faisal roads, off 26th July Street downtown,

or at the Cave des Rois in Zamalek. Salima at the Casino al-Nahr is also a must-see.

CAFÉS AND SHIISHA

It is a man's world when it comes to cafés, and it is rare to see non-Egyptian men, let alone women, in any of them. The exceptions are to be found in Khan al-Khalili, on the terrace of the Nile Hilton, on the top deck of Le Pacha 1901, at the Odeon Bar, at the Hurriya in Bab al-Luq under the footbridge at Zahrat al-Bustan downtown, and at upscale cafes like Bint al-Sultan. Order apple tobacco *(tuffaaH)* in your shiisha—it is cool, delicious, heady in a harmless way, and smells divine.

CLASSICAL MUSIC— ARABIC AND WESTERN

Arabic and Western classical music is regularly performed at the Opera House complex, which is also home to the Cairo Opera and the Cairo Symphony. The Opera House's Main and Small Halls are terrific, by the way—comfortable, and aesthetically as well as acoustically delightful. Check out Makan for zaar, Sufi, and shaabi music every Tuesday and Wednesdy. Foreign cultural centers also regularly sponsor musical evenings, all to be found most reliably in the cultural listings of *Al-Ahram Weekly, The Croc, Community Times,* and El Sawy Culture Wheel: *www.culturewheel.com*.

CULTURAL CENTERS

The various Egyptian and foreign cultural centers (**Organizations**) enrich Cairo enormously. Lectures, films, performances, and exhibitions on a wide variety of topics, including political and economic, afford free or low-cost opportunities for everyone in Cairo to learn more about 'the other.' No excuses whatever for cultural illiteracy here.

DANCE PERFORMANCES (BALLET, CLASSICAL, MODERN, FOLK)

The Opera House is the main venue for international dance troupes. The various cultural centers also sponsor performances, as do the larger hotels now and then, usually in conjunction with international food promotions.

DISCOTHÈQUES

To a large extent, we have covered this already, but for dedicated disco dancers, there are a few other resources besides those under Balls, Bars, and Restaurants. Try al-Yotti in Mohandiseen, Jackies Joint at the Nile Hilton, Le Disco at the Gezirah Sheraton, Saddle Up at the Mena House, and Windows on the World at the Ramses Hilton. All late night, of course. Look in *The Croc* for the latest stomping grounds.

FELUCCA RIDES

The hourly price for feluccas now ranges from LE30 to LE50 depending on the size of the boat. It is worth it. The places near Sultana Boat in Maadi allow for more varied and longer rides as no bridges obstruct the feluccas' cruising, but the ones in town near the Shepheard and the Grand Hyatt are fine, even though after your tenth trip the basin feels like a bathtub. Feluccas are perfect for catching the breeze on a hot summer night and for brisker sails the rest of the year. They are ideal for an impromptu party after work, a romantic evening, and for soothing the tots on the weekends. Mosquito repellent is vital in the marshy waters near Maadi.

FILMS AND FILM FESTIVALS

Cairo in its glory days was considered the Hollywood of the Middle East, but the film industry declined sadly from the 1950s on.

However, in an attempt to reverse and recoup, a brand new mega-studio has been built on the outskirts of Cairo to produce films for distribution throughout the Arabic-speaking world. This is good news for the Egyptian film industry and its many internationally acclaimed professionals. In addition, the Cairo International Film Festival takes place in early December. It screens a good variety of films and has begun to accumulate favorable reviews. Appearances by some respected actors have helped its credibility. Sophia Loren and John Malkovich have been on hand in recent years. The Cairo International Film Festival for Children is usually held in March.

Quality foreign-language films are shown regularly, but for the briefest of runs, at the various cultural centers. They are often subtitled or dubbed in Arabic, not English, or neither. Check the listings.

Current American films are shown at many of the cinemas around town. A number of the movie houses downtown such as the Metro and the Radio are gorgeous old remnants of the 1930s and well worth the price of admission (LE15 to LE20). Egyptian movie audiences are a cigarette and cell phone addicted bunch so don't expect reverential silence when the lights go down, but do expect a smoke-break halfway through the film.

JAZZ AND LIVE MUSIC

The jazz scene in Cairo has always struggled to take hold, even though a handful of very talented musicians ply their trade here. It is a crying shame, but Cairo's many terrific musicians cannot support themselves except by going abroad or playing for the tourists in Sharm al-Sheikh and Hurghada. Main venues for Western and mixed-style jazz are the cultural centers, the Opera complex, Gumhuriya Theater, and the Wikalat al-Ghuri near the Khan, where Fathy Salama and his band, Sharkiat, have played. Catch this group whenever you can. It is idiosyncratic and inconsistent, but when they're on, they're really on. Yehia Khalil plays at After Eight, The Opera, and the Cairo Jazz Club, all downtown. The Cairo Jazz Club is making a bid to be the hub of the Cairo jazz scene and seems to be moving confidently in that direction. Heliopolis hotels may turn out to have the most interesting and mixed live music offerings, specifically Le 51 Bar at the Meridien Heliopolis, Pygmalion at the Concorde El-Salam, and the Terrace at the Baron Hotel. Note, though, that the live music scene is even more unpredictable than the bar scene.

MUSEUMS

A wonderful array of good, not so good, and deliciously odd museums graces Cairo. The ones devoted to the fine arts tend to be better maintained than the historical and natural history ones. Having reviewed the major museums (Egyptian, Islamic, and Coptic) plus a few minor ones (Post Office, Manyal Palace, Agricultural, and those in the Citadel complex) in Chapter 1, we give brief descriptions of a number of others here; all are listed together in the Directory.

The *Museum of Egyptian Modern Art* is superb, devoted to Egyptian art of this century. The *Mr. and Mrs. Muhammad Khalil Museum* houses a fantastic collection of French Impressionists. The *Mukhtar Museum* on the southern tip of Gezira shows the sculpture of Mahmoud Mukhtar, whose monument to modern Egypt rises at the entrance of the boulevard to Cairo University. *Dr. Ragab's Pharaonic Village* is a good place for kids because of the boat ride and the living pharaonic tableaus, and adults will enjoy its themed museums.

Close by Midan al-Tahrir are a number of interesting museums. The *Bayt al-Umma Museum* is more notable for its neo-Egyptian

architecture than for its contents devoted to the life of the nationalist hero Sa'd Zaghlul. The *Ethnological Museum* on Qasr al-'Aini displays artifacts of everyday life from all of Egypt. The *Entomological Museum* near the train station is devoted to bugs and to the eradication of the ones that destroy crops; the *Agricultural Museum* in Dokki has a better setting, broader exhibits, and is more fun for kids, even budding entomologists, as is the *Manyal Palace Museum*. The *Railway Museum* next to the train station also appeals to pint-sized and grown-up train buffs.

NILE DINNER CRUISES

If you are a tourist, this is obligatory. If you live here, you will have to take your mother and cousins when they visit. This is what the dinner cruise operators must count on at LE150–250 per head plus 22 percent service charges, as neither the bland buffet food nor the belly-dancing are up to snuff on any of them, even the Marriott's Nile Maxim, which is reputedly the best. The quality of the food does not change, but we suspect the entertainment is generally better on the late-night sailings, based on having seen an excellent belly-dancer and Sufi dancer one midnight on the Scheherezade. Another interesting option is the S.S. Nile Peking. Decorated in Boxer Rebellion fantasy style, it offers good Chinese food with set menus from LE55 to LE150. Entertainment is offered on its late-evening cruises.

OPERA

The very popular Cairo Opera season at the Opera House complex starts in October. This is one venue for which tickets do sell out, so reserve immediately if not sooner. The Cairo International Conference Center (CICC) in Nasr City also occasionally sponsors opera and other classical music productions. Some people put on the dog for these galas, and ties for men are always required at the Main Hall of the Opera House itself. The Ambassadors of Opera also show up annually and put on a potpourri of arias. Manasterly Palace is the venue to host superb international musicians.

THEATER

There are a number of lovely theaters scattered around Cairo, most of which primarily mount Arabic-language performances. A particular favorite is the elegant, intimate Gumhuriya Theater downtown, which also occasionally features foreign-language productions of excellent quality, as do the AUC's Falaki Theater and the Opera House. Not speaking Arabic need not deter one from at least attempting to get the gist of an Arabic-language performance, particularly comedies or politically-charged dramas. Being part of a theatrical audience and absorbing more through osmosis than language can be a revelation in itself. Try it if and when you see an interesting review in *Al-Ahram Weekly* that is published before rather than after the play's run is concluded, and when you can get an Egyptian friend to translate during and after. Your reactions, perceptions, and misperceptions are bound to enlighten and entertain both of you.

VIDEO

English-language videos are very popular in Cairo. The Video Rack, with locations around town, has a good selection. Libraries and cultural centers also rent videos in various languages, giving wider options to the non-fans of *Terminator VI*. The British Community Assocation in Mohandiseen rents videos and DVDs to non-members.

WALKING TOURS

Are these 'sports' or 'entertainment'? Both, but here they are. Most of the women's and cultural organizations regularly sponsor walking tours, except in summer, when no sane person would walk far. If you have reached the point where you are fussing and fuming about the Dust and Dirt and Disarray of Cairo, a walking tour with a knowledgeable guide and curious companions is the perfect antidote. It will awaken your imagination and refresh your eyes so that you can see the extraordinary beauty, history, and much intrigue that lie just under the surface of the three Ds.

Every spring, usually the second week in May, the Tree Lovers Association sponsors an annual tree walk in Maadi. It is a chance to enjoy the beauty of Maadi streets and learn about the diverse species of trees and plants. Watch for announcements in the *Maadi Messenger* and Community Services Association bulletin.

SPORTS AND FITNESS

Cairenes are addicted to both spectator and participant sports of every kind. For foreigners from cold and/or expensive climes, Cairo and Egypt are a godsend, especially—but by no means only—for equestrians and divers. For practically every sport, there is a sports federation to keep things bureaucratic; these are good sources of information on events related to your sport, but it helps if you speak Arabic when contacting them. *Sports & Fitness* magazine has especially good listings of dive centers in Cairo, Hurghada, and Sinai and keeps readers informed about the latest in sporting equipment, manufacturers, techniques, and personalities.

Contact information for each sport is listed alphabetically under **Sports** in the Directory. Sports supply sources are under **Sporting Equipment**. If your sport is not mentioned below, check **Sports Federations** in the Directory, where you will probably find it. If you find it difficult to get through to any places on the telephone, and you most definitely will, just go in person, but not on Fridays.

AEROBICS

CSA in Maadi has good classes, as does the Gezira Sporting Club, Samia Allouba's Creative Dance and Fitness Centers in Maadi and Dokki, Gold's Gym, STEP, and the Fitness and Dance Academy (**Sports—Exercise Classes**). Hotel health club classes tend to be irregular and not as good. Stretch, step, Callanetics, high and low impact, cardio-funk, street dancing: take your pick and rock out. Classes tend to be late mornings or early–late evenings. Create a groundswell of demand for early morning classes and someone good is bound to oblige. Note that many health clubs advertising classes directed to women, like aerobics, have limited women's hours; three examples are the American Fitness Hall in Dokki, the Sports Palace in Zamalek, and Gold's Gym in Giza.

BASEBALL

The Americans and anyone who wants to join them play serious league softball every Friday all day and every night from September to May, plus on Tuesday and Saturday evenings all summer at Victory College field in Maadi. They even send teams abroad for competitions. Just show up to see how to get involved.

BASKETBALL

Besides checking with the Basketball Federation, contact either Cairo American College's athletic department or Maadi House, both in Maadi, to find out how to pick up a game.

BELLY-DANCING

(Doing, not watching; for watching, see **Entertainment** above.) Egyptian belly-

dancers understandably subscribe to the position that foreigners cannot get the moves down. No reason not to try; you might surprise yourself and them. Besides, it is great exercise, surprisingly strenuous—albeit subtle—and lots of fun. Lessons are given at the Creative Dance & Fitness Centers in Maadi and Dokki, or you might eventually find your own personal belly-dancing guru or *ma'allima* to learn as the Egyptian women do.

BOATING (SAIL AND MOTOR)

The Cairo Yachting Club on the Nile in Giza accepts memberships from sail and motorboat owners. For Egyptians and permanent residents, there is a lifetime membership fee of between LE10,000 and LE20,000. For foreigners here temporarily, the annual fee is $1,200. Reciprocal privileges are extended to members of other yachting clubs. Rowing, water-skiing, and windsurfing are also available from the marina. The Maadi Yacht Club also has a marina and will rent sail or motor boats. Membership is $655 per year for a family of three and $340 for half-year memberships.

Swedish-designed motor boats and cabin cruisers called Ocean Classics are made and sold in Egypt. Might be a good thing to check into for the boat of your dreams.

BODYBUILDING AND WEIGHT TRAINING

These seem to be the preferred sports of gilded Egyptian youth, at least the males among them. Gyms and health clubs devoted to musculature exist all over town, sometimes advertised by wonderfully campy posters. A few of them have special women's hours. Not all have well-qualified trainers or state-of-the-art safety features, so check them out carefully and get recommendations. The required belts, harnesses, weights, and whatnot are available at the

Weider Fitness Centers or the Sports Mall (**Sports Equipment**). Elsewhere, unfortunately, steroids are freely available over the counter; while they may aid in producing that bulked up, Hulk-like look (ugh!), they are also linked to sterility. Make sure your fifteen-year-old 90-lb weakling aspiring to the Mr. Egypt title is aware of this.

CHESS

Contact the Arab Contractors Club and the Gezira Club to find out about chess-playing opportunities and competitions. Call the Russian Cultural Center for information about their classes.

CROQUET

There are lovely pitches at the Gezira, Shooting, and Maadi Clubs.

CYCLING

Cairo Cyclists ride Fridays and Saturdays starting at Cairo American College in Maadi and also sponsor occasional special events rides. According to the Cairo Cyclists, the best place in town for **Bicycle Repairs** is Ghoukho Trading & Supply near St. Mark's Church in al-Azbakiya; hard to find, but worth it. Five or six other good shops are nearby. Most cyclists advise bringing in spare parts when coming from abroad, as they are very hard to find here.

DARTS

Where else but at the British Community Association's clubhouses in Heliopolis and Mohandiseen? Contact them or drop in to any of the overabundant pubs or quasi-pubs in town. And, for your very own super-duper custom-made dartboard, contact Maher El-Sabagh in Shubra, surely one of Cairo's very best small businessmen (see

Cork Boards in Directory). He delivers quality work on time at reasonable prices in a most professional and courteous manner. A miracle!

DESERT

Approximately 96 percent of the land in Egypt is desert, providing many opportunities for exploration. The United Nations declared 2006 the International Year of Desert and Desertification, giving rise to new initiatives, programs, and events. The Cairo Desert Exploration Group meets every Tuesday to network about desert exploration and to plan trips For more information call 378-3748.

DIVING

The Red Sea is considered by many to be equal or superior to the Great Barrier Reef of Australia for diving and snorkeling. It is no wonder then that diving is big business in Egypt and that the social lives of its many devotees revolve around it. Through many of the diving schools and clubs in Cairo and at the resorts, one can get the PADI Open Water Diver certification in about a week, including a number of classroom sessions and in-pool practice held in the evenings, followed by four open-water dives at Sharm al-Sheikh or Hurghada on the weekend. Seascapes in Maadi also has an excellent reputation. Call Omar el-Naggar or visit *www.seascapesegypt.com.*

Various diving clubs like the British Sub-Aqua Club (highly recommended) and Cairo Divers Club sponsor exploration trips, underwater photography exhibits, and marine life lectures. Snorkelers are invariably welcome, and at Basata among other places they can just walk into a marine wonderland from the beach rather than having to take a boat. Serious divers rave about Marsa 'Alam; go only with a guide.

FISHING AND HUNTING

Lake, river, and deep-sea fishing are popular and accessible in Egypt. Hunting would seem to be confined to desert foxes and birds, with many areas like Lake Qarun thankfully now protected. There seems to be an alarmingly high number of ammunition and gun stores around Cairo. One of the best-stocked for both hunting and fishing gear is Abu Dief on Sharia al-Tahrir downtown. The owner and his family are knowledgeable on both sports. There is also the Anglers Federation downtown which even has a fax, but not a phone that works.

GOLF

The British Golf Society meets regularly at Mena House and sponsors local and international tournaments. It is open only to foreigners, apparently. Golf for women is organized by the Mena House Ladies. No fewer than fifteen eighteen-hole courses have sprung up in Egypt in recent years. In and around Cairo, Kattameya Heights, JW Marriott-Mirage City, Dreamland, and Soleimania all have good reputations. The Gezira Club and the Mena House have nine-hole courses. There are also courses in El Gouna and Soma Bay near Hurghada, Sharm al-Sheikh, Luxor, and Alexandria. The best equipment is available at the clubs' pro shops. *Golf in Egypt* magazine is the best way to keep track of the fast-paced developments.

HEALTH CLUBS

These are mushrooming everywhere, but Heliopolis probably has the highest concentration of them anywhere in the city. Facilities and prices vary from basic to lavish. As with many other things in Cairo, but this in particular as it affects motivation through convenience, the best may be the closest to home or work. Facilities tend to be sex-segregated and more time-limited for women than men. Most of the hotels have memberships for residents; shop and bargain on these. One of the clubs that seems to be popular with Cairo's movers and shakers is Gold's Gym, with branches in Giza, Maadi, and 6th of October City. You have to visit and inspect any club to see how it is run and whether it is right for you.

HORSEBACK RIDING

Don't miss out on the many and varied opportunities related to the equestrian art in Cairo. So what if you are pushing forty and still have not lived out your *National Velvet* fantasies? Now you can. Most of the stables-cum-schools are out by the Pyramids and Saqqara, but there is also one in Zamalek (al-Furusiya) and a famous one near Heliopolis, the al-Zahraa Stud Farm, where Arabian horses are bred and sold. If you play polo (or aspire to), you may run into Dr. Farouk Younes, whose lovely farm on the outskirts of Cairo boasts the only private polo field in Egypt. The Saqqara Country Club nearby has excellent stables.

The numerous stables located just south of the parking lot entrance to the Giza Pyramids vary in amenities and quality of horses, most of them being simple but adequate affairs. Each one develops a loyal following among its patrons, so just ask a few people for recommendations. Horses can be leased long-term everywhere as well as rented by the hour for LE25. It is LE100 for the five-hour round-trip between Giza and Saqqara. We understand that long-term leases are preferable to renting because the lessee has fuller control over the care and feeding of his or her horse for the duration; leasing is also preferable to buying because it is very difficult for foreigners in Egypt to recoup the horse's price when sold. Boarding one's own horse runs from about LE200 to LE500 per month depending on where you go and who you know.

Riding equipment, apparel, and horsefeed are available at Alfa Market in Giza and Zamalek (upstairs from the supermarket) and from Equicare in Zamalek, but prices are high. You can have boots custom-made at El-Aziz in Zamalek (see **Shoemakers**) for LE400–450.

GYMNASTICS

The Gezira Club has an excellent after-school and summer program in gymnastics for kids. STEP offers gymnastics classes.

MARTIAL ARTS

Boxing and the many Asian martial arts—judo, karate, kung fu, tae kwon do—are popular in Cairo. Each has its very own sports federation. Check the Sports Mall in Mohandiseen, which gives martial arts lessons (tae kwon do); they are very helpful and should be able to help you follow up on other types. Martial arts equipment is also well manufactured here by A-Sport, whose two owners, Amr Khairy and Nasser Shahata, are former tae kwon do champions; they may also be able to advise on competitions and teachers. Visit STEP for classes in gymnastics, karate, tackwando, and aerobics, *www.step-center.com.*

POOL AND SNOOKER

When the legendary Minnesota Fats went to heaven, it was probably to Cairo. There must be more pool halls here than there ever were in Chicago. Fats might be a bit disappointed, though, as many of them have a distinctly wholesome atmosphere, housed as they are in shopping malls and frequented by well-dressed teens. The BCA clubhouses in Mohandiseen and Heliopolis organize both British and American rules pool tournaments. The Ramses Hilton Billiard Hall is a particularly soignée venue straight out of a movie set, and it does serve alcohol.

ROWING

The Nile is a great spot for sculling, which is also a superb, soothing, strenuous form of exercise, as you can tell by the young gods working out in their shells early in the morning (women can do it, too). Start to explore the possibilities for learning or joining a crew by contacting the rowing people at the Rowing Club in Giza. The trick is getting the boats in the water; surprisingly, they are incredibly heavy. Get in touch with the Egyptian Rowing Club (Tel: 393-4350) for information on how to get involved.

RUGBY

The Cairo Rugby Club in Maadi has a very active rugby and social program, and its own clubhouse. Kids', women's, and men's divisions play lively matches on the Victory College fields. The Club is part of the Gulf Rugby Union, which conducts the second largest rugby tournament in the world. Cairo Rugby also has darts, pool, and cricket leagues and plays Gaelic football when enough Irishmen are in town.

RUNNING

Cairo's branch of the international Hash House Harriers, the drinking club for people with a running problem, has a long and cheerfully disreputable reputation reinforced by bizarre rites and rituals. Actually, they are a diverse, organized, and—dare we say it?—wholesome bunch. Runs are held every Friday afternoon two hours before sunset for runners (and even walkers) at every energy level. It is a very international and age-mixed group (from babies in backpacks up to octogenarians), occasional weekend-away running forays take place, and once in a blue moon it even deserves its accolade as one of the best places in Cairo to meet members of the opposite sex.

Independent-minded joggers run in Maadi's streets, at Merryland in Heliopolis, and at the Gezira Club's track. Very, very early in the morning before the traffic starts, it is also pleasant and perfectly safe to run the leafy streets of Zamalek, Dokki, and Mohandiseen. Just don't do it in shorts, girls.

SHOOTING

As in skeet shooting, not murder and mayhem, at the Shooting Club (known by all as Nadi al-Seid) they have a variety of shooting courses, including sheet and practice range.

SNORKELING AND SCUBA

See Diving above.

SOCCER AKA FOOTBALL

The national obsession. The two most important words in Cairo are Ahli and Zamalek, for the rival soccer teams. All semblance of work stops when they play, and the streets are jammed with their frenzied supporters careening by in cars and buses after a match. You can play yourself or just watch at the CAC fields in Maadi.

SQUASH

Not the national obsession, but since it is President Mubarak's game (yes, that's how this 76-year-old keeps in such good shape) it is starting to become one. Al-Ahram annually sponsors a lavish international tournament at the foot of the Giza Pyramids in portable plexiglass courts. Many sporting clubs have excellent courts, particularly the Gezira Club.

SWIMMING, DIVING, AND WATER-SKIING

Hardy souls can enjoy these year-round in Cairo. All the big hotels have good pools,

the Nile Hilton's and the Grand Hyatt's seeming to be the most popular. But note that fees at many of the five-star hotels are becoming exorbitant to the point of exclusion (LE250-plus per day), a good way to guarantee lost business from residents. Gezira has a stupendously high diving tower where national champions train, and a number of the international schools have excellent pools that are open on weekends and evenings for parents. Though one is not supposed to swim in the Nile, water-skiing in the middle of it must be okay, as plenty of people, some of whom are not crazy teenaged boys, do it. The theory seems to be that the critters that cause bilharzia and giardia don't swim or survive in moving water, so as long as you stay in the middle where the current is swift, you are all right. Still, the Nile is polluted, so think twice before getting into the water. Check with the Cairo Yachting Club Commodore on this and the arrangements that can be made for water-skiing.

TENNIS

Tennis is a good way for Egyptians and foreigners to meet as the sport is popular among both. We are told that at the sporting clubs you might have to sit around forlornly on the sidelines for quite a while before you are invited to join the regulars, but once asked, you are in, so be patient. Most courts in Cairo are clay. Many tennis sporting clubs have opened during the last three years, like Smash Tennis Academy near the airport. Also Wadi Degla Sporting Club in Maadi and Qattamiya Tennis Center have new tennis courts and facilities. Most charge LE50 per hour for a court and LE1–3 tip for the ball boys. In a five-star hotel, the fee is LE75 for an hour. The Maadi Ladies Tennis group meets weekly at the Maadi Club; all levels are welcome and lessons are available.

WALKING

If you are into power walking, don't feel weird even if you look weird. We have seen one Egyptian guy doing it.

WINDSURFING

It is impossible to get through to the Egyptian Windsurfers by phone, so just join them every second Monday of the month at 8 pm at the Cairo Yacht Club.

SPORTING AND COUNTRY CLUBS

Having touted the sporting clubs of Cairo in our discussion on sports, a few words devoted specifically to them are in order, particularly for ignorant foreigners. As near as we have been able to ascertain, the sporting clubs, with the sole exception of the Gezira Club, are not exactly foreigner-friendly unless one speaks Arabic or is married to an Egyptian member. The prices of new memberships at all the sporting clubs have skyrocketed recently: for Egyptians, it is now LE50,500 at the Gezira and the Shooting Club for lifetime (presumably family) memberships, plus small annual fees thereafter (LE200/year). For foreigners, a family of three will pay around $2,000 all-in for the first year, about $1,100 thereafter at Gezira; at the Shooting Club, which is not as pleasant, though more modern, it is also roughly $1,100 for the first year. The Heliopolis Sporting Club offers a July and August membership to Egyptian couples for LE2,000 and to foreigners for $1,500. One would have to do an awful lot of swimming in sixty days to make that worthwhile. And some clubs at least (Gezira for one) do not pro-rate membership fees depending on when one joins, so that if you join mid-year, you still pay for the whole year! You also pay additionally for every activity. The fees are not much, but it is a nuisance. These issues and oddities are raised in honor of our friend Caveat Emptor.

All the sporting clubs used to be very posh, particularly Gezira. But all are now government-owned, and it shows in the very spotty maintenance and extraordinarily poor service on the whole. Older Egyptian friends shake their heads in consternation and mourn the good old (grantedly elitist) days when locker rooms were clean, facilities were painted, grass was mowed, and waiters waited. The inflated membership fees seem to have a precisely inverse relationship to overall upkeep and management. Food, however, remains absurdly cheap, which, along with the range of activities available, partially offsets the fees in many members' eyes.

Anyone may enter most of the clubs for a LE20–50 fee without being a member, and use most of the facilities for small additional fees (swimming pools and tennis excepted at Gezira, although we are not sure how this is monitored). None of the clubs serves alcohol, and very few women feel comfortable in bathing suits except around the kiddie pools or very early in the morning. Nevertheless, families who can afford it join a sporting club for the sake of the children, tots through teens, for whom they provide quite superb sports facilities, playgrounds, and social centers.

An out-of-town alternative that is much more foreigner-friendly is the Saqqara Country Club—beer and bikinis allowed—with its particularly fine stables and setting. It is about a 45-minute drive from Cairo toward Saqqara and is privately owned. This is reflected in the generally superior upkeep and atmosphere, and in the considerably lower membership fees, at least short term. For Egyptians, they are LE8,000 one-time registration fee per family plus LE1,000 annually; for foreign residents, $400 one-time registration fee per family plus $1,000 annually. Horseback riding is LE25 per hour and horses can be boarded for LE300 per month. Non-members are admitted only as guests of members for LE10.50 per day for adults with children free.

Every hotel offers summer pool memberships and health club memberships, depend-ing on facilities. Check on them thoroughly regarding safety and sanitary conditions, especially with respect to children, and for hours and reliability of equipment and instructors before making any long-term commitment

3 LIVING IN CAIRO

BASIC DECISIONS

If you are lucky, you have made a positive choice about moving to Cairo. If not, pretend you have. Positive thinking exerts highly beneficial effects on energy levels, physical well-being, and social opportunities, all of which help anyone to make the transition to a new life in a new place. This decision—to anticipate your move with enthusiasm rather than dread—is the first choice you can make, and will simplify all the others.

In the first two chapters, we have done our best to demonstrate that Cairo is an exciting, amazing, multicultural, and highly livable city. That said, it is also huge, complex, crowded, and confusing, especially (but not only) to foreigners, and even more so to those who do not speak Arabic. If you have any form of institutional support from the organization you or a spouse work for, obviously take advantage of it. This chapter on living in Cairo is written largely on the assumption that you do not, either by choice or by destiny. In other words, we have assumed that you, the reader, are quite clueless and must rely basically on yourself and whatever hard-earned help we offer here to find a place to live, plan for children's schooling, make household purchases, and create a life. It is a challenge, it is exhausting, and as you may know if you have done it before, it is fun.

PRE-DEPARTURE CHORES AND CHOICES

Firstly, get the family's or your own medical basics taken care of the minute you know you are leaving. Cairo's medical care is generally excellent, but having to get rabies pre-exposure shots or find vaccination certificates or get that old root canal fixed is not what you will want to do first thing upon arrival. Secondly, if you are shipping household goods, find a good international mover. 'Good' is the operative word, and this chore is far easier said than done. Do not assume that the ones recommended or forced upon you by your government or company fit the bill. If you have a little time and any choice in the matter, contact people you know who have done international moves, preferably more than one, and get their advice and opinions on specific companies. Then interview a few places as to whom they have moved to Cairo and if possible, talk to, fax, or e-mail those references. (This is assuming the reader is a terribly organized person for whom information, good or bad, provides a modicum of control, however illusory.)

Once you have chosen a mover, buy a good-sized but portable notebook, on the first page of which should be all detailed contact information for everyone who is involved in your move, including the president of the moving company and all others involved, and the same for the shipping agent/receiver at the Egyptian end, both in Cairo and in Alexandria. Then begin making a polite but persistent nuisance of yourself to keep the move moving. This is obvious and standard to old pros, but not to novices. Other advice that may or may not be relevant follows.

Adopt a Zen-like attitude toward material possessions. In transit to anywhere, things can get lost, stolen, or damaged. Store or hand-carry rather than ship precious stuff. If you cannot conceive of life without Mother's heirloom silver, carry it. Bring one photo album but don't ship the five or ten that represent your family's history from time immemorial.

Get notarized copies of important documents (marriage license, birth certificates, divorce papers, passports, naturalization papers, insurance papers, wills), one set of which you leave at home in a safe but easily accessible place, the other you carry. You never know.

Back up computer files on CDs and carry them. Get and carry the software programs (including installation disks) that you use or might use. Also carry hardware manuals and documentation.

Use air freight rather than sea freight for most clothing. Use sea freight for big toys, carrying only the portable, absolutely-can't-live-without items that represent comfort, love, and security to little ones. Cairo has loads of inexpensive toys.

Do all the horrible, boring, picayune things necessary to secure your home and finances in your absence, writing down everything as you think of it in your notebook and checking off as you accomplish each task.

Update your address book, including the fax and e-mail numbers you never used at home but well might in Egypt.

Give or send close friends and family who will stay behind some little Egypt-related memento before you leave. They will be touched, you will feel virtuous. We used sphinx paperweights in plexiglass pyramids—tacky, but amusing and appreciated.

If you are paying your own airfare, make reservations at the earliest possible date. Choice and economy loom large the larger your family. (Sorry, but in the departure flurry, this item often gets shelved for too long.) If you do not have a company or embassy to help in relocation, there are professional consultants that specialize in relocation and repatriation. One such company is Global Relocation Consultants *www.grconsultants.biz.*

BRING AND DON'T-BRING LISTS

You really can find almost anything in Cairo—eventually. But it can be exhausting, even maddening, to do so, especially for new householders. Hence, the odd-lot array of items listed below, which are rarely available, expensive, of poor quality, or inconvenient to locate on short notice. So stash or ship whichever of them you deem essential, depending on how long you will be here. Instead of making two lists, one for visitors and one for householders, we have made a comprehensive alphabetical one from which you can pick and choose. People with embassy purchasing privileges can probably shorten the list considerably. If you will have some sort of deal that allows you to purchase regularly at a duty-free shop here, don't count on it for anything except booze (not wine) and cigarettes.

BRING:

Bath stoppers (the flat kind that fit most drains)

Bicycle spare parts, including lock and clincher-type tires

Books, books, books

Cat and dog repellent for furniture and/or outdoors

Computers, fax machines, modems, printers, all switchable to 220 volts or with correct transformers (but document everything and make sure you take it with you when you leave Egypt)

Cosmetics (imports cost a bomb; hypoallergenics rarely available)

Duct tape

Eye drops

Eyeglass and contact lens prescriptions

Flashlights in different sizes or a headlamp (handy for tombs, stairwells, nighttime taxis, power outages)

Gerber Multi-Pliers or Leatherman (compact all-in-one tools)

Insect repellent

Medications (only for unique medical conditions; all others are here)
Roach motels
Sports equipment and clothing
Stationery and cards (just an initial supply)
Sweaters (Cairo is cold in winter)
Tampons (only Tampax and Ria brands available here and expensive)
Telephones—cordless
Vitamins

For serious cooks: good knives and something to sharpen them on. For serious fashion plates: the clothes, clothes hangers, and most of all shoes you love.

Most flats come equipped with the basic—often very basic—large appliances. But if you will be here for years and you somehow know you will rent an unfurnished flat, and if you have a shipping allowance, consider buying and/or shipping your own 220-volt major appliances. Egyptian-made stoves (cookers) in gas and electric models are good and reasonable here, other appliances are not so by some European and American standards. You can buy 220-volt appliances in major cities in the United States, including at ABC Trading in New York (31 Canal St., New York, NY 10002, (212) 228 5080; fax (212) 529 5579; Rosetta knows all about shipping to the Middle East), which has better prices and a better selection than places around Washington recommended by shippers or the State Department. Carrefour has a good selection of appliances. The duty-free shop in Mohandiseen has imported appliances, but choice is limited.

DON'T BRING:
Basic toiletries (all easily obtainable)
Excess men's clothing; good quality, selection, and prices are here
Fitted American sheets unless you bring the mattresses they fit, too
Short shorts, skimpy tops, miniskirts; you'll look and feel like an idiot in them

Small appliances in 110 voltage; transformers in the kitchen especially are a nuisance
Pets, unless they're child or spouse equivalents; you can adopt pets easily here (many Muslims consider dogs unclean and may feel uncomfortable around them)

THE SHIPPING NEWS IN CAIRO

Sea shipments arrive at Alexandria in anywhere from two weeks to forever-never, a month being a good low, two months high-average, and three months not unheard of. Then the stuff must be trucked into Cairo after customs clearance in Alexandria. Customs clearance is a week- to a month-long affair, very much depending on the local expediter with whom you have been allied. You must have the originals of all shipping documents for the expediter. No substitutions whatever allowed. Egyptian friends swear that the right baksheesh to the right people can speed this process up, but we have not found anybody who has found anybody reliable in this category, so trust in your expediter. Express International in Dokki worked fine once; they seem generally competent, friendly, and reasonably accessible to the politely persistent. Cars are treated separately by us (see **Cars in Cairo**) and by the expediters.

Air shipments arrive and are cleared for customs at the Cairo Airport, which streamlines their processing somewhat. Some expediters advise their nervous clients to go to the port in Alexandria to help oversee the clearing of their sea shipment, but unless you have a lot of time on your hands—two or three days is not unusual—and a high tolerance for frustration, this undoubtedly educational experience might well be skipped. Large sea-shipped containers will arrive in Cairo at night, possibly very late at night, because trucks are not allowed in Cairo until after 10 pm. Therefore, get a good nap on moving day, and make sure to have plenty of LE10 and LE20 bills to tip each member of the moving army.

AS SOON AS YOU ARRIVE

Call the Community Services Association (CSA) in Maadi, and sign up for their two-day orientation program. It is a soup-to-nuts smattering on life in Cairo from a wide range of experts. You meet other newcomers in the same boat right away, and come out armed with good information and maybe a few potential buddies. It costs a little too much ($125) but some companies and embassies pay for it, and virtually everyone says it is well worth the price.

HOUSING DECISIONS

How much to spend . . . the kids' schools . . . the commute . . . security . . . proximity to shopping. The same factors that limit housing everywhere limit them in Cairo. Many new arrivals have no choice whatsoever, as their housing is preselected for them by families or employers. If you do have some leeway, you are lucky, but it also means you have to educate yourself quickly on the confusing Cairo real estate market. Here, then, is a primer, by no means exhaustive.

BUYING VS. RENTING AND WHAT YOU WILL PAY EACH WAY

A great many changes are occurring in the laws surrounding real estate. Foreigners can now buy flats in their own names. Rent control, the bane of Egyptian landlords and one of the reasons for the nonexistent maintenance in many buildings, is being phased out for Egyptians, with unforeseeable implications on the market for all. On one hand, there is a very serious housing crunch for middle-class Cairenes. On the other, one sees literally tens of thousands of empty or incomplete flats all over Dokki, Mohandiseen, and Giza. This is partly due to the parental obligation we mentioned earlier to provide male offspring with homes for marriage. Hence parents start acquiring flats as soon as they can, completing them in fits and starts as financing allows.

Property acquisition is no easy task, as mortgages per se do not exist. Either you pay the whole cost up front, or you pay at least 50 percent, with remaining payments stretched out over six months to three years. And what you get is a shell most of the time unless you buy a finished flat. In other words, it will have walls and flooring (usually raw), but no plumbing, electric wiring, tile, kitchen, or even windows. The owner installs everything.

If you are considering buying, consider having close to LE1 million in the bank for a raw, good-sized three–five bedroom flat in a good building in a good area, no Nile view. For really lavish, presumably finished, fancy flats and villas, we have heard quotes of between LE20 million and LE60 million. Alternatively, you could buy a raw three-bedroom, 115 square meter flat in downtown Abdin, which is not fashionable or foreigner-infested, but is very safe, convenient, and lively, for about LE150,000 and finish it to Western standards for an additional LE50,000. Add in another LE40,000 for appliances and nice but basic furnishings and include about LE10,000 for lawyer's and procedural fees, and you are talking about LE250,000 all-in. Legal establishment of ownership can be a tricky business best not left to novices. The purchase must be registered at a government office, but one may also go to court to have ownership legally established. And you must be certain that you are buying from the real owner, as a few hapless buyers have learned too late.

Most foreigners rent at least initially, usually through a broker/real estate agent.

Often the 'broker' is the *bawwaab* (door-keeper)! If you know exactly where you want to live, the bawwaab broker is the way to go. Just wander around with an Arabic-speaking friend and ask the bawwaabs in likely-prospect buildings if anything is available. Of course, if a bawwaab finds you your dream flat, a very generous tip is in order, perhaps not on the scale of a month's rent, but at least a hundred pounds. Discuss this with the landlord.

If you do not have any idea where you want to live, check out areas and flats or villas under the wing of a broker. Normally, the agent-broker receives a commission of one month's rent from the landlord, but the broker may want anywhere from a quarter to half a month's rent from you as well. Make this clear immediately before you start looking, to avoid uncomfortable misunderstandings later, and don't deal with anyone who hedges on this issue. Conserv, with offices in Zamalek and Maadi, is very good; you can look at good photos of what is available before going out to do some constructive eliminating, but it tends to have only high-end places available.

Here are some recent sample monthly rents for a range of properties, all rented to foreigners:

Simple, small two-bedroom flat in Abdin: LE750.

Cozy one-bedroom downtown flat, light and airy, great furniture and decor, LE1,000.

Decent two-bedroom, two-bathroom furnished flat in Maadi in an ugly building on a busy road: $375.

Funky, student-type digs on a quiet alley in a nice old Zamalek building, high ceilings, horrible bathroom: LE1,500.

Very nice smallish three-bedroom Zamalek flat, high floor, light, decent furniture, very iffy lift: LE4,000.

One floor of a reasonably well-maintained houseboat: LE3,000

Large, light three-bedroom furnished Mohandiseen flat, fourth-floor walk-up, big terrace, old kitchen and baths: LE4,500.

Top-notch Dokki duplex penthouse four-bedroom, three-bathroom, great kitchen, two big terraces, no furniture or appliances: $2,000.

Antique-filled three-bedroom flat overlooking US Embassy, high ceilings, great details, awful baths and kitchen: $3,000.

Huge three-story Maadi villa, big enclosed garden, furnished, undistinguished kitchen and baths: $4,500.

Lavish, large top-floor flat, elegant furnishings, the works, in Four Corners building, Zamalek: $7,000.

Seriously beautiful 1,000 square meter Maadi villa with pool: $8,000.

A few other miscellaneous price-related points: Rents in Maadi are skyrocketing because landlords think they can get the higher prices; a friend recently had to vacate her nice $1,500 flat because the landlady raised the rent to $2,300. Split-unit air conditioners cost landlords about $1,200 each, so their price is reflected in the rent; ditto reasonably state-of-the-art bathroom, which can cost $4,000. Buying all new furniture for a large flat can easily cost $20,000, which is one reason so many quote-unquote furnished flats seem to be warehouses for generations of cast-offs from the landlord's family. Flats on the Nile with views carry an asking price of $2,000–4,000. Landlords' initial asking prices are based largely on an uninformed what-the-market-will-bear notion and may have very little do with what they will ultimately take, but on the other hand, some seem quite willing to keep a flat unrented rather than lower the price. Heliopolis, Nasr City, Agouza, Abdin, and Giza Pyramids area rents are considerably lower than in others for reasons of proximity or fashion. And, at least until rent control really expires, some very wealthy Egyptians pay monthly rents of LE15 to LE50 for large, gorgeous, old flats that have been in the family for generations.

OLD VS. NEW, FURNISHED VS. UNFURNISHED

The stock of available old apartments is very small due to families hanging on to places because of rent control. If you have your heart set on one, the only places to look are in the heart of downtown, in Garden City, or along the Saray al-Gezira and the many beautiful older buildings in Zamalek. Dokki, Mohandiseen, and Giza Pyramids, being newer areas, have virtually none. Such flats, dating from the turn of the century through the 1940s, have enormous appeal—for their size, gorgeous architectural detail, and high ceilings. Kitchens, baths, plumbing, and wiring are usually pretty bad unless they have been redone.

Practically every place is rented to foreigners furnished, as unfurnished flats are at least theoretically subject to rent control. Except for a very few high-end flats, furnished—even 'furnished to Western tastes'—means crowded with odd assortments of stuff, often in what is affectionately referred to as the Louis Farouk style—lots of gilt, heavy patterned velvets, very ornate. Washing machines are almost always in the bathroom, clothes dryers are rare, and kitchens tend to be small and dark, as only servants used to enter them. Newer kitchens often have wonderful Egyptian granite countertops—a real luxury for many foreigners.

Large reception areas are rarely used by Egyptians except for entertaining; instead, a smaller television room is where the family normally spends time. Closets are custom-built cabinets often extending to the ceiling; all have keys rather than door knobs, and you will need a tall ladder to open, let alone reach into, the upper doors. Ideally, cupboard and closet doors have dust lips, which help somewhat to deter the dust. Leaking toilets, pipes, and faucets are the norm, even in new buildings. A shocking amount of water is wasted this way in this desert country, and a hue and cry is regularly raised about it in the newspapers, but little or nothing is done. Elevators are usually claustrophobically small and in most buildings it is forbidden to use them to transport anything but people and groceries. Hallways and stairwells are kept very dark, even in elegant buildings, so carry a small flashlight everywhere. On higher floors, an independent water pump (around LE700) may be a necessity to produce adequate water pressure; the landlord should pay for this.

All these fact-of-life points aside, foreign readers should know that with a little luck and a lot of persistence and flexibility, they will find a flat that well suits their needs and that the space they get will likely be far larger than what they could hope for in their home countries.

CHOOSING A NEIGHBORHOOD

"What choice?" as one friend said. "Where does he work? Where do the kids go to school? Yes, I guess we'll live here!" But if you do have some say in the matter, the brief descriptions of major neighborhoods below will help. You decide which elements of them are pros and which cons. One nice thing almost all have in common, except perhaps for the heart of the downtown commercial area, is a 'neighborhood' feel. Cairo is a city full of friendly street life, and as a resident you become part of it. Hence, all areas are wonderfully safe.

Agouza is cheaper than other neighborhoods, except along the Nile. It is fairly crowded, not too green, and generally lacks charm or atmosphere, but it is extremely convenient—you rarely need a car for errands. Rather few foreigners live here except in the high-rises along the river.

Downtown Cairo covers a lot of ground, and so is hard to characterize. While it is busy and noisy, there are many pockets of relative quiet to be found in the alleyways.

And a lot of charm—art nouveau balconies, mashrabiya screens, little markets tucked away. You just have to look under the dust. Lots of galleries and restaurants, and in Abdin, a great local atmosphere.

Dokki is perhaps the greenest part of Cairo after Zamalek, and fewer foreigners live there compared to Zamalek, so rents are lower. It is getting crowded, too, but less so than Mohandiseen. The Dokki market is fun, and the many small midans are lovely oases. Very few of the shopkeepers speak English and a car or taxi is required for shopping. A lot of hospitals are nearby. No Nile and rare Pyramid views.

Garden City is embassy country and a few of its streets are reminiscent of Paris. Lots of traffic, no parking, not convenient for shopping except for souvenirs. Quiet as a tomb at night, but very close to downtown nightlife. Not much of a neighborhood feel in comparison to others. Great old flats if you can find one.

Giza Pyramids area is booming. Lots of shopping, both Western and Egyptian. Quite a few mixed-marriage families live here, and there are a couple of excellent schools. It is a long way into town and not particularly green, edging the desert as it does. Good for avid horseback riders, convenient to the Cairo–Alexandria Desert Road. Much cheaper than more upscale areas, but maybe not for long, and you spend a lot on taxis.

Heliopolis (*maSr ig-gidiida*, 'New Egypt') was the first suburb, laid out by three French engineers. The president lives here, as do loads of foreigners. There is a strong French influence, and there are street signs—in Arabic and English. Convenient shopping, but spread out, so a car is necessary. Arduous commute into town, but close to the airport. Good restaurants, hotels, sports facilities, and schools.

Maadi is expat heaven, very suburban, very expensive, very American. Some people love it and never leave it; others would not be caught dead living there. Malls, ugly high-rises, and heavy traffic alternate with tree-lined streets and lovely villas. Excellent schools, good shopping, some decent restaurants, not much nightlife, very community- and family-oriented. Impossible street naming system involving the apparently random assignment of random numbers. The Metro into town is great.

Mohandiseen sort of overlaps with Dokki but is more fashionable and established, and hence in parts more expensive. There are lots of upscale shops, particularly around Sharia Shahab, and many good restaurants, as well as a number of pretty classy-looking new apartment buildings. No good schools, but convenient to those in Zamalek. A lot of nouveau-riche Cairenes live here, fewer foreigners.

Nasr City is a relatively new suburb-within-in-the-city composed almost exclusively of high-rises, and overlapping with Heliopolis. Rents are considerably cheaper here than elsewhere, and shopping is diverse and excellent. Foreigners may feel a bit isolated, as residents are largely middle- and upper-middle class Egyptians.

Qattamiya is a relatively new area with mostly villas and gardens and a definite suburban feel. Many schools and universities have moved up to the plateau for more spacious campuses. There are several golf courses and a beautiful country club. It is lacking in quality restaurants, but maybe in time, Cairenes will be driving to Qattamiya to dine out!

Zamalek is the in-town expat heaven, very cosmopolitan, lots of charm, the AUC dormitory, and completely walkable. For these attributes, you pay—a lot, in terms of both housing and shopping. It is also singles heaven for the well-heeled, with lots of bars and restaurants. And there is the Gezira Club, which is Cairo's rival to Central Park, but private. No parking to speak of, and very dense, but green.

6th of October City is 38 kilometers from downtown Cairo. Its draw for Egyptians is that it permits an escape from the city's congestion in favor of green gardens and villas. There are shopping malls, amusement parks, fitness facilities, and resorts so no need to come into Cairo. There are plans for an international airport in the future.

WHAT TO LOOK FOR
AND WHAT TO LOOK OUT FOR

Once you have chosen or been assigned to a neighborhood, start contacting agents and bawwaabs. A good agent will get a clear idea of your wants and needs after you have reacted to a few flats or villas. You can be relatively blunt about your feelings with a broker, and in fact it is far better than dealing directly with owners, which can be an awkward proposition. Much of life in Cairo is conducted on a word-of-mouth basis, including real estate, so tell everybody you know that you are looking. Agents often expect the client to provide transportation.

Having finally found a place or two that have potential, give them a thorough going-over. Some items to check carefully and note down are:

Leaks: These are standard, but should be fixed, however temporarily, before you move in.

Water pressure: See the comments on water pumps above, but also note that low pressure can be a simple matter of cleaning out faucet filters, which regularly get clogged with sand and debris.

Electrical outlets: In many places, these are few and far between. Outlet plates are usually poorly installed. Will landlord add outlets and repair existing ones?

Voltage current, circuit breakers, type of wiring (two- or- three-phase), and grounding: Depending on appliances, air-conditioners, etc., these may need upgrading. When you are getting down to the wire, make sure the landlord demonstrates and gives you a clear list or label for each circuit breaker, as it might be time-consuming later to figure out what goes to what. Outlets in Cairo are not generally grounded, but there is something that can be done to them to prevent electric shocks. Ask about this, particularly in relation to major appliances.

Telephones: Don't only pick up the phone to see if it is connected. Actually call someone in Cairo to see if and how well the phones work. Go armed with the number of a hotel or person in another city to see if the local long-distance feature actually works. International lines are becoming something of a moot point, thanks to calling cards and call-back services. It can take ages to get phone problems sorted out later, so make this a deal-breaker. Buy a mobile phone.

Elevators: Breakdowns are not an uncommon occurrence, regardless of the building, so if this would drive you nuts, get a ground-floor flat.

Electricity: Meters are inside the apartments. Once a month, a man from the electricity company comes to the house to read the meter. If you feel uncomfortable about this, ask the *bawwaab* or a neighbor to be present. About two weeks later, the bill collector from the electricity company will come to your door with the bill, which is to be paid on the spot. If you are not home, the bill is left with the *bawwaab* or returned to the electricity company where you will need to go to pay it.

Doors, windows, shutters, latches, drawers: Check and note down every little quirk of every single one, including the doors on closets. The year-round dust and the chill winds of winter, not to mention the badly hung door that screeches along the floor every single time you open and shut it, suggest that an ounce of prevention may ward off future insanity.

Water heaters: The size of these will definitely affect the length of your shower, especially in winter, and whether there is enough hot water to do a sinkful of dishes.

Fans: Ceiling fans are not common in Cairo homes, but they should be as they can keep air-conditioning bills way down. All-white Japanese models go for LE350–500; an elaborate wood-and-brass affair with Victorian light shades is about LE500. Negotiate these with the landlord, as standing and table fans are for some reason much more expensive and uglier.

Screens: These are not standard. Get as many installed as possible, as they keep out mosquitoes, flies, and some of the dust.

Bugs: These are not much of a problem in Cairo compared to, say, New York, but it might be wise to make sure the place is thoroughly fumigated before you move in.

Parking: At a premium everywhere in Cairo. Find out what, if any, provisions there are. A parking place in a garage is LE200–350 a month and well worth the money for the peace of mind it will bring.

LEASE NEGOTIATIONS

Just as one has to haggle over the price of tomatoes in the suuq, one has to negotiate several items in a lease contract and the price of the flat or villa. Good apartments go fast, so make offers on a few that fit the bill. The landlord or agent will likely have other prospective tenants bidding on desirable places.

There is a very standard, very simple one-page lease form to which the tenant makes addenda. These should be extremely precise in terms of dates, repairs, preexisting damages, and a penalty clause for lateness on agreed-upon repairs of LE100 per day. Do not make the mistake of moving in or paying rent before repairs are made. Make sure the lease or addendum specifies who pays the bawwaabs and security and trash men how much and when. Note that it is extremely easy to be taken in by the charm and friendliness of many agents and landlords, much to tenants' later dismay. Being friendly but firm and unsusceptible up front will save you both many hassles later on. Tenant and landlord both sign both lease and addendum, and for it to be worth the paper it is written on in a legal sense, the full document should be translated into Arabic and certified. In fact, the last thing you or the landlord wants to do is go anywhere near an Egyptian court, and so this formality is rarely observed.

The duration of the lease is negotiable. Rents can be paid either monthly or quarterly. Security deposits are flexible. Ten percent annual increases are common, but negotiable. Electrical, and if relevant, gas meter readings should be taken, noted, and signed on move-in day by tenant and landlord to avoid the tenant being billed for back utility charges.

FINDING A LOCAL MOVER

If, heaven forbid, you should have to move at some point while in Cairo, it is definitely worthwhile to explore options and get quotes from various sources. Official moving companies will charge foreigners an arm and a leg if they think it will fly, but labor is very cheap here, and a guy with a truck and a few helpers can do practically as good a job or better under careful supervision.

HOUSEBOAT LIVING

"The view is worth twice the rent —the Nile is my backyard." Some of the more fanciful among you might enjoy at least contemplating the notion of houseboat-living. Relics of a more exotic past, when they were scenes of passion and intrigue—especially during World War II—the twenty-five or so somewhat dilapidated houseboats moored at Kit-Kat near Imbaba still have a magic allure.

The atmosphere is an island of tranquillity far from the downtown bustle. The wooden,

A HUNDRED YEARS AGO, THIS *palace* PLAYED HOST
TO THE RICH AND FAMOUS FROM ACROSS THE WORLD.
THINGS HAVEN'T *changed* MUCH SINCE.

Once the home of the King of Egypt, Mena House Oberoi has welcomed royals, heads of state, celebrities and other distinguished guests since 1869. Set in the shadow of the Pyramid of Cheops and surrounded by 40 acres of jasmine-scented gardens, this magnificent hotel continues to be steeped in royal traditions. The décor is rich and luxurious, the service is impeccable and the tables are laden with an array of delicacies from around the world. The hotel's charm is further accentuated by spectacular views of the pyramids and leisure facilities like a 9-hole golf course, a casino, swimming pool, tennis courts and, of course, a stable of thoroughbred horses and camels. Rest assured Mena House Oberoi will give you memories of a grand lifestyle you will always treasure.

Mena House Oberoi
CAIRO, EGYPT

Luxury. Redefined.

Gateway To Egypt
Your Ultimate Corporate and Leisure Travel Consultant

creaking, frequently rocking houseboats are convivial international abodes of mostly young bohemians. Most boats are divided into three or so apartments. They are hooked up to electricity, telephone, and water, and all are supposed to have sewage tanks that are emptied daily, by law, by the boat bawwaabs, presumably into holding tanks whose contents are then disposed of *not* into the Nile. The boats used to be moored on the Zamalek side of the river but were moved after the Revolution and exist under sufferance. Owners must register regularly with countless authorities.

Houseboats appeal chiefly to diehard romantics. They are unbelievably cold in the winter, but delightful in the hot summer months, although mosquitoes can be a problem. To buy a houseboat will cost around LE500,000-plus, while a small, partly self-contained apartment will cost around LE2,000–4,000 a month to rent in a typical boat. Recently, however, houseboat-living has come back into vogue and some boats have been renovated and fitted with double glazing; obviously these come with a different price tag. Old-timers reckon that the bohemian atmosphere is changing as the boats' new inhabitants are better-heeled. Indeed, a couple have been turned into trendy restaurants. If you are curious, go talk to current residents.

SCHOOL DECISIONS

Cairo and environs offer a wide choice of schooling from preschool through the International Baccalaureate. Beyond that, there is the American University in Cairo (AUC) with its large international student body and American curriculum. We start with some general comments on education in Egypt, followed by a description of the schools that foreign and Egyptian parents recommend.

Egyptian parents and children take schooling very, very seriously. After-school and summer tutoring is a way of life, with public and private school teachers making far more money through tutoring than through classroom teaching. Tenured university professors may earn LE1,500 per month, and though moonlighting is technically illegal, many of them do it to supplement their incomes. Although public (state) school is free, books and uniforms are not, and the quality of education in the public system is regarded as abysmal by one and all. Hence, the deck is stacked against the poor, although poor bright children can be singled out and educated at the better schools, often producing enormous cultural gaps between parents and child.

The national curriculum controls Egyptian children's destinies very early on through a system of rigorous examinations. At the eighth-year level a major cutoff occurs: children who do not pass their exams with sufficiently high marks are relegated to a commercial–vocational track. At the end of secondary school, based on *thanawiya 'amma* exam scores, young people who are eligible for university are assigned to a particular faculty—science, arts, engineering, medicine, etc. Personal choice and parental control then are limited, a point that might help foreigners to sympathize with the great pressures that exist for Egyptian families regarding their kids' schooling.

One decision that couples in mixed Egyptian-foreign marriages and living in Egypt have to consider is their offsprings' cultural identity. The children will have a dual heritage regardless, but where they attend school affects whether they will identify more with Egyptian or with expatriate companions and the very different worlds represented by the two. Not all parents who can afford to make the choice of one of the large and very expensive international schools here opt for it. Their rationale makes sense: their Egypt-resident children deserve the security of feeling Egyptian, of using Arabic in school, of having friends who are Egyptian rather than often-transient foreigners. Others intentionally educate their children in schools with a foreign-language medium and exposure to foreign schoolmates with the goal of sending them abroad for university.

Depending on the age of your children and on how long you will be in Egypt, different factors carry different weights. For preschool-aged children, the nurturing environment of a nursery school close to home may supersede the vaunted rigor of the curriculum. One nursery school, for example, prides itself on having homework, exams, and competitive sports for three-year-olds, which may or may not be in keeping with the parents' child-rearing views. Others are excellent babysitting establishments, but may not address cognitive development at all. Most fall somewhere between these two extremes. For older children, the decision is largely based on how well the medium of instruction and the curriculum dovetail with the ones they will eventually return to. There are American schools, British schools, French lycées, German schools, and language schools that are based on the Egyptian system but taught in English or French. Part of your decision will hinge on where you live. The American schools are in or near Maadi and Heliopolis. There are British schools in Zamalek and Maadi. There is a good English- language private school near the Pyramids called El Alsson (*www.alsson.com*). If you are permanent residents of Cairo, a school with a strong Arabic program and with the curriculum leading to the Egyptian colleges is probably your best bet. Most English-language schools prefer children with at least one English-speaking parent.

Special education is becoming more available in Cairo, year by year. The Continental School of Cairo provides elementary to high school education for children with special needs and learning disabilities. The American International School and MISR Language School offer specialized classes in special needs. Dar el Mona is a school for children with Down's Syndrome. For diagnostic, educational, and therapeutic counseling, go to the Learning Resource Center in Maadi. *Silent No More: People with Special Needs in Egypt* (AUC Press 2002) includes current organizations working in the field. Also, *Mother & Child* magazine has a listing of schools for children with special needs.

Below, we describe the most-highly recommended 'international' elementary and secondary schools whose instructional medium is English. (There are two other excellent schools: the German School in Dokki and St. Joseph's Lycée Français, with instruction in German and French respectively.) They all have native-language, foreign-trained faculty. There are many others, some of which we have also listed in the Directory (**Schools**). Talk to your embassy, to Egyptian and foreign friends, and to the school directors to make a decision you are comfortable with. Most of these schools can be classified as expensive to outrageously expensive, for four reasons: 1) good teachers cost a lot to attract and retain, 2) good facilities cost a lot to build and maintain, 3) wealthy Egyptians will pay anything for their children's education, and 4) most expatriates do not pay for their children's schooling here, as it is provided as part of many employment packages, thus giving little or no leverage to those who pay out-of-pocket. For more information, also see:

www.schools-in-egypt.com

http://en.wikipedia.org/wiki/List_of_ schools_in_Egypt

http://en.wikipedia.org/wiki/List_of_ Egyptian_universities

ELEMENTARY AND SECONDARY SCHOOLS

American International School (AIS) in Nasr City has classes for children ages 3 to 18. It has a very good reputation. Tuition ranges per year: $4,200 for nursery, $5,000 for kindergarten, $6,100 for primary, $7,100 for grades 5–8, $7,400 for grades 9–12. Initiation fee: $1,500; bus: $800. AIS's *Learning Support Center* provides special curriculum to students with learning disabilities. Tuition starts at $12,500.

British International School Cairo (BISC) in Zamalek uses the British national curriculum and offers GCSE and IB programs. It has over 700 students aged 3–19 and a wide and creative curriculum, including sports and the arts, but no outdoor sports facilities on campus to speak of: the children use the nearby Gezira Club for these. The preschool is housed in a nearby villa. Annual tuition starts at £5,142 for grade P1, plus £850 for supplies, plus one-time primary admission fee of £1,714, plus £100 assessment fee, plus uniforms. Fees increase as the children progress through the school.

Cairo American College (CAC) in Maadi goes from kindergarten through twelfth grade and has an IB as well as AP high school curriculum. Currently there are 1,440 students enrolled, with 53 percent of the enrollment composed of American students, 14 percent Egyptian, and the rest a combination of over sixty-three other nationalities. In addition to a challenging curriculum, it has a good ESL program. Second-language study starts in third grade. All students are enrolled in Arab culture classes. Sports facilities are superb on the large suburban campus. Annual tuition plus bus (in Maadi only) plus fees comes to $17,350—even for kindergarten (includes $4500 one-time redistration fee).

El Alsson in Harraniya (out by the Pyramids). This school has a British curriculum and has programs for students from age 4 to 18. It has both the international track and the Egyptian government track for students going on to Egyptian universities. Most of the classes are taught in English, except for religion and of course Arabic or Arabic literature. Students in the upper grades can take either French or German. Tuition for primary starts at LE14,990 per year.

New Cairo British International School is for children from nursery school age to 17. It was established in 1978 and uses the British National Curriculum. Teachers are British-trained and -qualified. Fees are approximately £5,000 annually.

Maadi British International School in Wadi Digla is for ages 2–11 and has around one hundred pupils, hence small classes. It follows the British National Curriculum. It is a school with a lot of parental support and is growing.

Modern English School has a British curriculum. It is a popular school for those living in this part of the city and one advantage is that children can start at age 2 and go straight through until they are 18.

International School of Chouiefat near Heliopolis has been open since 1995. It is part of the worldwide SABIS system, which stresses frequent testing to detect gaps in students' learning. It is an NCA accredited institution and has an AP curriculum. It runs from KG1 through twelfth grade with a current enrollment of 1200 students. Its facilities rival those of CAC, with several tennis courts, two swimming pools, a large cafeteria, and auditorium. Tuition starts at $3,300 for KG1 and runs up to $5,500 for high school.

NURSERY SCHOOLS

Some of the schools listed above, including the British International Schools in Maadi and New Cairo have excellent preschool programs. Following is a list of others with English as the primary language. Virtually all the schools provide lunch and snacks, some have bus transport, and most are open year-round Sunday through Thursday from approximately 8 am to 4 pm, with a few having Saturday hours as well. Tuition ranges from about LE350 to LE800 per month.

Alf Leila Wa Leila Preschool is the nursery for AUC staff, faculty, alumni, and, if there is space, others. This school does not emphasize academics but believes in letting the "child be a child." Serves vegetarian meals.

American Wonderland caters to those who are particularly oriented toward sports and/or music. The owner, Maha Arram, hires professional sports and music coaches. The school is selective, it says, and evaluates both children and parents. There are also different sections (English, French, or German), all taught by native speakers.

Busy Bees in Heliopolis comes highly recommended.

Charlie Chaplin Nursery and Preschool is British-managed with qualified teachers and assistants. It has a special-needs class, videos, puppet theater, small zoo, bus service, and more. Children can start at 3 months.

The Irish School in Dokki provides immersion in a language (English, French, or German). Children stay with their core group so that they develop fluency in the language. Sixty percent of the children are Egyptian, the rest a mix of foreigners. All teachers are native speakers of the language they teach.

Reiltin Children start at age 2 and go through 6. It is academically oriented and children are taught reading readiness skills, some math and science, and art classes. One class is taught in German.

Schweizer Kinder Garten in Dokki. Children have a choice of three sections (English, French, or German). All teachers are university graduates who majored in one of the languages.

Sindbad al-Bashaer School in Maadi is a nursery, preschool, and primary school with programs in English, French, and German. A pediatric clinic is available.

Stepping Stones Nursery Schools (there are several in Cairo, all American-owned and -operated) offer Gymboree, music and dance classes, and monthly field trips.

Tom and Jerry Kids in Maadi accepts children from 6 months.

CARS IN CAIRO

Whether to buy a vehicle for use during your stay in Egypt is a decision that is best made prior to your arrival in the country. Different regulations for different folks allow diplomats and employees of certain companies with a government contract to bring in a vehicle duty-free during the first six months of their contract. Check your status with your employer.

A sliding scale of import duties depending on the options (power steering, central locking) and on the size of the engine can reach up to 200 percent of the purchase price, so this duty-free business is not one to be taken lightly. Duty free cars are 'temporarily' duty free, which means that they have to be driven out of Egypt every year, but company agents can make this relatively painless. To import a car, you will need an international tryptique. This should be issued in the country where the car is registered. The Automobile Club in Cairo (10 Sharia Qasr al-Nil, Downtown 754-3191/3348) is helpful and can assist with insurance and a driver's license.

If you prefer to buy your vehicle here (and save on shipping costs), and if you have duty-free privileges, you will be able to buy it much more cheaply than everyone else in Egypt. The locally produced Opel Vectra or Jeep Cherokee, for example, are assembled from an imported kit but have to have 40 percent local content to encourage local feeder industries. Thus you will not have to pay tax on the 60 percent imported parts of such a car.

When you leave Egypt, you must sell your duty-free car to someone else with the same status or else pay the duty. You can of course ship it out, but bear in mind that regulations in your next posting may require expensive alterations.

If you do not have duty-free privileges, the situation is not hopeless, but it can be very expensive. The past few years have seen a dramatic improvement in the quality of vehicles plying Cairene streets. Where previously a shiny new car was the exception, the growing number of cars produced here has made it quite unremarkable. There are even new taxi cabs! Suzuki, Jeep, Peugeot, General Motors, Citroën, Hyundai, and Mercedes are already manufacturing limited ranges here. Unfortunately, because of tax on their imported parts (see above) they are considerably more expensive than at home, but still cheaper than a fully imported duty-paid car.

WHERE TO BUY NEW CARS

Check the listings in the Yellow Pages for dealers and agents. Major distributors are located in Mohandiseen and on Sharia Huda Sha'rawi downtown but local dealers are springing up thick and fast. These guys will send your head into a spin with their patter, so take a notebook and don't be shy. A big drawback to buying a car is that there is no facility for a test drive. Reasons given by salesmen include lack of insurance and the fact that the public are wary of a car with more than a few kilometers on the odometer. *Al Waseet* is a weekly publication that lists all kinds of cars and models for sale.

USED CARS

There is no shortage of secondhand vehicles for sale. The Friday edition of *al-Ahram* carries a large classified section where private individuals advertise, and used-car

markets are held in Basatin and Nasr City every Friday and Sunday. Many showrooms have used cars on their books, but no one can offer any guarantee as to their quality or durability. Egyptian mechanics, however, can fix anything. Take one with you and drive the car to a gas station to test shock absorbers and suspension and chassis length to check for accident damage.

LONG-TERM RENTAL

Several companies, such as Europcar Leasing and Budget, offer long-term rental, ideal if you are not sure how long you will be here and wish to avoid all the hassle of registration, insurance, and maintenance. But this route is far from cheap. The spring 2006 price for a Toyota Corolla was $1,000 per month for a minimum of six months for a private individual, with limited mileage and full insurance coverage. And for unlimited mileage, the monthly rental begins at $1,500. A Mitsubishi Lancer is approximately $1,200 a month, a 2005 Jeep costs $2,000 a month, a Hyundai $1,000, and a Mercedes $2,000 plus LE50 for each kilometer after the first 100 kilometers.

REGISTRATION

Buying the car is the simplest part of the process. Ask someone from the showroom to lead you by the hand through the minefield of Egyptian bureaucracy surrounding registration of a new car. Cars must be registered in the traffic department in which you live. To obtain the car license you must produce ID (your passport) and proof of residential address in Egypt. Every vehicle must have a fire extinguisher and police insurance, which is third-party insurance; all can be purchased at the registration office. Police insurance costs LE27. An additional tax is levied from LE35 and up, depending on the size of the engine. The laminated computer printout license indicates when the car is next due for inspection (every three years) and when the document is due for renewal (normally after one year). In order to renew the license, any fines incurred in the interim must be paid. The total cost of license and plates is around LE25. Registering a used car in a new name involves a similar trip to the department. If the car was made in Egypt the fee is a small percentage of the price of the car. Registration of imported cars varies greatly and depends on the cubic centimeters of the engine and the model year, which starts at LE1,000–4,000.

INSURANCE

The Federal Insurance Association sets the tariffs, so all the insurance companies basically offer the same rates. The premium is calculated at 5 percent of the value of the car (assessed by the agent), a little more for Japanese and Korean cars. The companies compete by offering discounts based on no-claims bonuses. It is worth bringing your claims history with you as some companies will recognize it and it will significantly reduce your premium. The premium on a LE75,000 car with a five years no-claims bonus could be reduced from LE3,500 to LE1,250. Many Egyptian drivers do not bother with insurance—repairs are often cheaper than the premiums, and drivers are unfamiliar with the concept. In case of theft, insurance is essential, especially if your car is duty-free. If it is not insured and disappears, not only will you be car-less, but in a classic case of insult-added-to-injury, you will have to pay the duty when you leave.

LICENSES

You can drive on an international license issued outside Egypt for a year, or on your current foreign license for three months. An Egyptian license is obtained on production of a valid driver's license, a medical and an eye examination certificate, two photos, your passport showing proof of residence, and a nominal fee. You may have to take a test at the Traffic Department in your area of residence, which is usually quite simple; it involves driving around cones and identifying some international road signs.

FINES

Illegal parking will attract a sticker on the window indicative of a fine due. You pay this when you next re-register the car. Check that you were in the country and that you in fact owned the car when the alleged infringement took place; occasional inaccuracies have been known to occur. Serious illegal parking that obstructs the traffic will result in your vehicle being towed away. Wheel clamps have been introduced. Speeding is monitored by radar on most major roads out of Cairo. The joy of being able to finally put your foot down will usually keep the speed cops busy. They may take your license and give you a receipt; they will tell you where to collect it and how much the fine is. If you get three speeding tickets you can lose your license. However, leaving the scene of the accident may cause problems as well.

ACCIDENTS

A scrape between two cars, however slight, will often result in much gesticulation and shouting, and is likely to attract a large audience. Often the argument will be settled with no money changing hands, but face will have been restored. Foreigners should not generally get out of the vehicle, and only pay up if they were clearly in the wrong.

In the case of a serious accident when someone or an animal has been wounded or worse, foreigners are advised to drive straight to their embassy or company headquarters and then to report to the police, taking along details from the other driver's license and registration plate.

DRIVING A CAR

If you will or you must drive in Cairo, you should understand two basic rules: 1) the car in front has right of way even if it is only in front by a headlight rim, and 2) in the case of rear-ending, the fault lies with the rear driver. These rules underline most behavior patterns.

Cairene drivers often pay scant attention to their rear-view mirrors—they are more concerned about edging forward, with a carefree disregard for what is going on directly behind them. They may pay more attention to side mirrors, if present, to check the proximity of vehicles sidling up beside them. In order to attract the attention of the driver in front, they will sound the horn. This can start quite a tooting conversation as the driver behind says "Move over, will you, I'm trying to pass," the driver in front hoots "OK," and the first driver toots back "Shukran" and passes. This makes for a lot of noise, but it is mostly cheerful, friendly noise.

Lane markings are largely ignored by local drivers. To move across several disorderly lines of traffic requires nerves of steel, a feel for the horn, and confidence that the other vehicles will let you through. Amazingly, they usually do. Turn signals should not be afforded too much significance. Some drivers signal to the right when they wish to turn to the right, others when they want to inform you that the road ahead is clear, others again have forgotten to turn the thing off. If you want to make a turn by all means signal, but nothing beats a hand out of the window or a toot to drive the message home.

Beware of buses, the undisputed bullies of the road. Make sure they know you are there before you try to slip past them. Also watch for the driver of a battered vehicle:

what does another scrape matter anyway? Most of all, while ambulance and fire engine sirens are largely ignored, official motorcades should be shown the utmost respect. Never, ever, argue your turf or tarmac with ministerial police outriders or members of an embassy convoy.

Traffic lights are generally only observed if they are accompanied by a policeman, who has the authority to signal vehicles on—even when the light is red. Do not flout this authority: policemen on point duty carry little notebooks in which to record plate numbers and when you go to renew your registration, your fines will have to be paid.

While metropolitan Cairo positively buzzes at night, elsewhere the dark empty highways can be the scene of horrendous accidents. Many drivers do not believe in using their headlights until they realize that a vehicle is approaching, whereupon they flash on full beam. Also, since trucks are banned from the city during the day, at night they hurtle in from Suez and Alexandria in droves. Not the ideal fellow travelers, so avoid night-driving outside Cairo if you can.

You still want to do this? Well then, treat driving as the chance for a new adventure every day. It is full of surprises and unusual maneuvers that somehow, mostly, work. Generally drivers look out for each other and are remarkably tolerant. Mercedes and BMWs share crowded roadways with herds of sheep, bicycles, darting pedestrians, donkey carts, and a few brave wheelchair riders. Be tolerant too, and you will do fine with a little practice.

ALTERNATIVES TO DRIVING

For those who decide that driving is not for them, taxis are quite cheap and readily available. Their amenities vary widely, the ones with all handles and windows intact being the exception, not the rule. (Where do all those handles go, anyway? Is there a window-handle black market out there?) If you hit upon a good driver, get his number and call him regularly and he will be worth his weight in gold to you. Cairo taxis, by the way, do not know Maadi and vice versa, so always add at least twenty minutes to your schedule for getting lost either way.

If you do have a car and can afford the luxury, by all means consider hiring a driver for between LE600 and LE1,000 a month. He will run your errands, wash and maintain the car, deliver packages, take the kids to school, and generally simplify your life enormously. But take him for a few varied test runs and establish a clear trial period before hiring him permanently: if his road sense or twitches or lack of common sense alarm you, or if he seems even more clueless than you about directions, these characteristics will only get worse, not better, with time.

A last alternative is a bicycle. For short runs on quiet streets, they really work well here—much quicker than either driving or walking, good exercise, and non-polluting. Just exercise twice the caution you normally would, and you will be fine.

HOUSEHOLD HELP AND SERVICES

This is a complex and somewhat politically sensitive subject. The very high unemployment rates in Egypt do not translate into a large pool of willing and able domestic help. Nor do the inventive skills attributed to mechanics seem to extend to carpenters, painters, plumbers, electricians, and the like. Consequently, it is a constant battle to keep a home clean and in good repair. A very handy spouse with an excellent tool kit is the ideal solution to the latter, and doing it oneself is the horrible solution to the former. Handy spouses being in short supply and anything being better than cleaning in

most householders' eyes, getting help is the normal route.

MAINTENANCE AND REPAIRS

People would rather give you their first-born child than the names of their good, reliable maintenance people. They are in such short supply and little things go wrong so frequently that they must be hidden away on some sort of family retainer basis. Landlords are supposed to be good sources of these valuable folks. Some are, some are not: many are more concerned with the price rather than the quality of the maintenance people they employ, and many others are in exactly the same boat you are—they cannot find good people either. Once you have become friendly with your neighbors or a reliable taxi driver, they can be good sources for maintenance and repair people. Other avenues to explore: for plumbers, stores that sell and install plumbing fixtures; for carpenters and housepainters, home furnishings shops and places that make kitchen cabinets; for electricians, lighting stores. Every once in a blue moon, you will luck out. Foreigners who have lived here a long time and/or are married to Egyptians, ideally to Egyptians who are architects or have construction companies, are probably your best hope. Not speaking Arabic is a big drawback when dealing with repair people, so this in itself may be sufficient motivation to learn the language. Try Osman Group; they specialize in appliance repair and their engineers speak English.

Very close supervision of repair people is vital. It is far from certain that the plumber will have a wrench or the man who's come to install ceiling lights a ladder. Make sure you specify the time of day you want them to come, as it is not unheard of for a repairman's cheery "I'll be there at nine" to mean nine in the evening. Well-meaning as they may be, it all makes for a situation that will alternately make you want to cry, laugh, or have a nice old-fashioned temper tantrum.

DOMESTIC HELP

The domestic help situation is better by a hair. Well-off Egyptians and a lot of foreigners hire foreign domestic helpers if they can afford them, usually Filipinos, Sri Lankans, Indians, or Ethiopians, most of whom are here illegally unless they work for diplomats. Lacking papers, people who are here illegally may be very hard to track down should anything go wrong, but these foreigners are nevertheless perceived by many to be more reliable and trustworthy than their Egyptian competition, particularly in the cooking and childcare departments.

In the old days, a person would go to their family's village and find a young girl to work for them in Cairo. Today more village girls are getting the rudiments of an education and prefer to work in factories. Many do not want to be 'plate lickers,' a derogatory term they use to mean someone who eats the leftovers. Hence, many experienced housekeepers and cooks are very old. It is also a fact that many women say they do not want to work for Egyptians because salaries are low and abuse levels can be high. Working for foreigners is perceived as preferable, but that does not mean you will have droves of good people showing up at the door.

Before hiring a housekeeper, cook, or nanny, check references very carefully and take copies of identity papers. No matter how sad the stories you may hear, particularly if you are a foreigner who is unfamiliar with the culture, think at least twice before hiring someone who cannot provide references. It is practically impossible to verify tales of abuse proffered as a reason for leaving a previous employer; every potential new employer is in the dark here. Make sure to raise the honesty issue up front so that the person understands you will prosecute for stealing. Make very clear what he or she may use and not use, take and not take. Employers are understandably perceived by household helpers as being rich as Croesus, so keep temptation at bay in whatever ways seem comfortable and reasonable to you. If you are generous, kind, and firm, the last at least initially, you will most likely be paid back with great devotion and loyalty. And once in a great while you will get a kick in the teeth.

The question of living in or out depends on your and your employee's needs and wishes. Some people hate having live-in help, others love it. Fewer and fewer flats have rooms for this purpose, and if they do, they are usually pretty dreadful. Living out seems to be more common than living in.

FINDING AND PAYING
HOUSEHOLD HELP

An Egyptian housekeeper working full-time for a very generous Egyptian family makes LE500 per month; more often, it is closer to LE300 a month. An Egyptian housekeeper working for foreigners makes between LE800 and LE1,500—more than many professionals in Egypt earn. For this salary, you can expect them to work hard, to do heavy cleaning, babysitting, laundry, carrying groceries, and so on. They will also prove invaluable regarding the best prices and shops and service people. Normally they get their salary at the end of the month and bonuses—half a month's salary—at both Eid al-Adha and Ramadan, plus gifts of food and clothing then and throughout the year. Make sure to find out their birthdays and give a nice personal gift then, too. Usually a full-time worker gets at least a day off a week, often two, plus vacation time of two to three weeks annually. Do not get into the habit of giving loans for family problems unless you are willing to perpetuate further requests.

Foreign domestic workers, particularly Filipinos and Sri Lankans, get much higher salaries, usually between $500 and $600 per month, plus round-trip airfare home for a visit after two years at most.

Of course, it is also possible to find someone to come and clean your apartment on a part-time basis—say once or twice a week at LE30 to LE50 a time.

Part-time Egyptian cooks can be a real treat and a real bargain. A foreign couple we know and some Egyptian friends have women who come one day a week and do all the shopping and cooking for a week's worth of meals, which are then frozen. The foreign couple pays LE150 per week for this—including the groceries!—and the Egyptians pay LE50 excluding the groceries. Both say their cooks prepare delicious, nutritious meals. If this interests you, ask your Egyptian housekeeper or a friend's, who will undoubtedly find you an aunt or sister of theirs who will do the same for you.

The *Maadi Messenger* newsletter has big listings of people looking for work as housekeepers, houseboys, drivers, and cooks. At CSA in Maadi and at the Women's Association office in Dokki, there are bulletin boards for seekers and offerers of jobs. The Heliopolis Community Association has an English newsletter that carries ads for maids. But mainly, ask around. Everyone is happy to help find you a maid, and often word-of-mouth is the best way.

BUILDING SERVICES AND PERSONNEL

Most buildings still have *bawwaabs,* who may serve as concierge, mailman, guard, sweeper-upper, cigarette-runner, real-estate agent, and busybody all rolled into one. Often they or their wives wash the cars and keep the front of the building clean. They get paid between LE10 and LE20 a month by each tenant, plus tips for extra personal tasks. More and more of the fancier build-ings now have round-the-clock security guards, each of whom gets about LE10 per month from each tenant. You also give them food, money, and maybe clothing at the end of Ramadan and maybe on the Prophet's Birthday. Talk to Egyptian neighbors about all this so as to avoid ignorance and follow the customs of the building. Some buildings have an association to maintain the hall-ways, elevator, and guards. If you rent, settle with the landlord who is responsible for this yearly cost; if you own, you will be charged around LE500–2000 yearly, depending on the size and area of your building.

Since 2004, foreign garbage companies have been responsible for garbage collection; however, *zabbaliin,* people who were previously in control of garbage collection, are now hired to do this. In late 2005, the government added a garbage collection tax tact to the electrical bill. Still, you may have a man appear at your door wanting to be paid a monthly fee for collecting your trash. You have no obligation to pay, but may consider the LE5–10 as helping families less fortunate.

You will rarely see a mailman, but he does deliver to the building, so some sort of bak-shish is in order once or twice a year if you have mail delivered to your home rather than your place of work. If you plan on getting important mail at home regularly, it is a good idea to establish a friendly, personal, and remunerative relationship with your mailman.

OTHER SERVICES AND CHEAP THRILLS

Here are some other wonderful aspects of living in Cairo. They may not be on the same plane as the myriad cultural diver-sions, but they sure are nice. We will have more to say on psychological adjustments later on, but in the meantime, any of these can lift your spirits:

Men called *makwagis* come and iron your clothes and sheets for you or take them away to iron.

You can have fresh-squeezed orange juice every day all year long.

Veterinarians make house calls for LE100; so do some human doctors for more.

Many dry-cleaners pick up and deliver within a day or two.

The *bawwaab*'s wife or son will do your neighborhood grocery shopping for LE5.

Mangoes, delicious mangoes, are in season from early summer through late fall.

Maison Thomas in Zamalek is open twenty-four hours a day for pizzas and hot and cold sandwiches.

MAKING YOUR HOUSE A HOME

Even if you rent a furnished flat or have shipped furniture from abroad, there are many things you will have to or want to acquire while you are here. Following is a discussion in alphabetical order of what some of those things might be and on how to spend your money wisely. In the Directory you will find the source information under each heading. If you do not find what you are looking for here, look at the listings in the **Shopping** section in Chapter 1. February and August are sales times for household furnishings, so then is when to look for bargains. At the end of this chapter, you will find a practical, reasonably comprehensive series of Shopping and Other Lists for the compleat householder, in Arabic and English.

In the past five years, Cairo has seen an influx of hypermarkets. Carrefour has two branches (Ring Road and Alexandria–Desert Road) and in the summer of 2006, Spinneys will open a hypermarket at Citystars in Heliopolis. All these mega-outlets change show people shop. Small, family-owned shops and local supermarkets cannot compete with the discounted and often extensive range of products that cater to the middle-income Egyptian family. Furthermore, massive shopping malls have opened that house mega-names and mega-stores in themselves: Virgin

Records, Istikbal Furniture, Habitat, Adidas and Nike, Sony to name a few.

In 2005, Citystars mall opened with much fanfare and success, boasting everything from top brand name stores to restaurants to an amusement park. Other, higher-end malls are at the two Four Seasons hotels: First Mall in Giza and Beymen in Garden City; Grand Hyatt has a new shopping center. The older Ramses Hilton annex is still around but run-down and not as popular as Arkadia Mall on Corniche al-Nil, Genena Mall and Serag Mall in Nasr City, and Bahgat Stores and Hyper-one in 6th of October.

The government-owned department stores like Omar Effendi and Salon Vert have little left to offer in the way of product and price; both stores may soon be closed or bought out. Since the average Egyptian family favors warehouse shopping on account of the better prices and entertainment on offer, old-style small businesses may struggle and eventually disappear.

AIR CONDITIONERS

Split rather than window models are preferable—more powerful and somewhat quieter. Both types are dual purpose for heating in winter and cooling in summer. Carrier is the major brand as is Miraco. Try hard to get servicing documents in English from the vendor or your landlord and find out where to get filters, as they have to be changed frequently. Note that bills for heating with air-conditioners in the coldest months can reach LE800 per month for relatively modest use of four to five hours a day, one or two rooms at most. For big air-conditioning users, summer could be as bad or worse.

APPLIANCES

All major appliances made in Egypt are reasonably comparable to European models. Americans might find them somewhat below par, but they are serviceable—and they can be serviced (servicing may pose a problem with imports). Fresh is a good brand for stoves, National for other appliances. Their cost is comparable to middle-upper-middle-range American appliances. Imports are much more expensive. Refrigerators tend to be smaller than humongous American ones; many families have two to make up for this. Go to Carrefour stores, Spinneys, Hyper One in 6th of October, or FutureHome in Maadi. Avoid Chinese imported small appliances like phones; quality is poor. Also avoid Egyptian phones. Counter-top and under-sink water filters and purifiers are available here.

BATHROOMS

Bathrooms are a big deal, a major part of the marriage contract in Egypt. Whether to have a modern toilet and what kind of bath and water heaters to have can be major bones of contention in less affluent marriages. Whether to have imported or Egyptian marble and tile is the issue among the more affluent. Many older Egyptian flats have squat toilets, but flats for foreigners have the usual modern amenities. What they rarely have is a linen cupboard for storing toiletries and towels, or enough towel racks; ask your landlord to have these installed. Very often a supremely elegant all-marble bathroom with gold-plated fixtures will also house the clothes washer, except in the few places that have laundry rooms. Shower curtains can be found at major supermarkets such as Alpha or Carrefour, but the designs leave much to be desired. One unique item you should have in your bathrooms is a *jirkin,* a large closed plastic container with a cap to fill with water for the frequent water stoppages. Integrated Interiors in Agouza and Netline in

Mohandiseen are excellent places to look for state-of-the-art imported bathroom fixtures, but there are many others, less expensive, on Sharia al-Faggala off Midan Ramsis.

BEDS AND BEDDING

Good foam and spring mattresses in various firmnesses are available in all standard metric sizes, which is why Americans should not bring fitted sheets. Taki is the major brand; go to Carrefour or Spinneys. Pillow variety is limited to lumpy cotton or so-so dacron fills. If you are fussy, bring from abroad. All-cotton sheets, embroidered and plain, are a treat. White is hard to come by, as Egyptians prefer lots of color in their bedding. You can get sheets embroidered and monogrammed to your specifications at many places along Qasr al-Nil. Acrylic blankets in garish prints abound, but you can have cotton-filled comforters *(laHaaf)* made by the tentmakers or at department stores in your fabric selection. You have to specify that the filling should be thin or you will end up with a very heavy quilt. Down-filled comforters are not available here to our knowledge, and they are perfect for cold winter nights, so consider bringing them from abroad.

CARPENTRY AND CABINETS

There is a high demand for and rather low supply of genuinely good carpenters in Egypt. Wood is very expensive as it is all imported. Carpenters seem to charge on a basis of between LE500 and LE800, depending on the quality of the wood, per square meter for things like cupboards regardless of how simple or elaborate the work. Most furniture is custom-made; what you see in a showroom is not in stock but must be ordered, and it is usually an ordeal. Upholstered sofas and chairs rarely have canted backs, so they are rather uncomfortable, and having it done differently is not easy to explain or obtain. If you decide to embark on such a project, start with one piece and insist on seeing the piece at the frame stage, when changes can be made. Most carpenters want at least 50 percent of the item's cost up front to buy wood, but you can find ones who do not—they are better: they deliver faster to get their money. The more accurately you specify what you want with your carpenter, the better the results. And don't be afraid to send the piece back for adjustments until it is exactly as you like it.

CHRISTMAS TREES AND ORNAMENTS

Trees fill the sidewalks of Muslim Egypt just as they do in Christian counties; they are there for the foreigners and for the few Egyptians who like to have a tree at New Year (often confusingly referred to as *il-krismas*). They are a rather scruffy lot, and asking prices are high (LE100–300) for foreigners until down-to-the-wire Christmas Eve. The 'live' trees planted in pots often are not. It might be better to consider a large native plant strung with lights instead. Muski glass Christmas balls can be found in the Khan, and other decorations are sold at the many annual Christmas bazaars. Tinsel and such is available, as are white light strings. Bring giftwrap from abroad unless you are not remotely fussy about this.

CLOTHING

A bit of a problem for the fashion-conscious. A lot of foreign and Egyptian women say they have given up on buying clothes here. The very affluent will fly to Dubai or Beirut for a weekend spree. This is somewhat extreme, but you have to be resourceful if you care about style, work quality, and fit and do not want to spend a small fortune. At the very least, you can find fairly reasonable casual clothes, although check details closely.

Still, with all the new malls and megastores opening up in Cairo, the situation is improving. In the following categories, suggestions for each are limited but a starting point:

Alterations and Tailoring: Ask old-timers, particularly French-speaking Cairenes, for leads on dressmakers. Men's tailors seem to be more prevalent than women's. Recommended places for alterations are Chamade in Heliopolis and Melodies and Moods in Zamalek.

Bathing Suits: The selection in Cairo is limited, less so at the resorts. Energy in Zamalek is good place to try, or the Sports Mall. Also visit Carrefour and Alfa supermarkets. Women's suits are expensive, about LE150 up, for very so-so style, quality, choice, and size range.

Children's Clothes: Other than the places listed above, Bunny's, Bambi, and Gerard Darel have very cute kids' clothes, a bit pricey, but generally well made, with good fabrics, and not hopelessly frou-frou. Babycare in Zamalek is a small shop, also with some nice things on occasion. See *Mother & Child* magazine for suggestoins.

Designer/Sophisticated Women's Clothes: There are a number of good spots, some extremely expensive. Queeny is unique and has Paris designer originals and some Egyptian-made knockoffs of high quality and absurdly high prices—for example, LE800 for a simple silk T-shirt tunic. It is a beautiful shop, though. The oddly-named Up 16 in Zamalek has very sophisticated Italian imports. Luciano di Nardo is a good and welcome addition to the scene, with prices below the stratospheric level and excellent quality. Selective and Fashion both have some wild fun-sexy stuff in the high chic category as does Kookai, which is more teen-to-twenties oriented. Stephanie also has some amazing attire for men and women, custom- and ready-made. Beymen has haute couture designer clothes.

Discount Clothes: Very cheap, very good selection of casual wear made for export at New York in Heliopolis, and Fostok in Zamalek.

Evening Clothes: Belles of the ball who actually go to balls and have a lot of money to spend have their every need catered to in Cairo. Three places in the Dokki-Mohandiseen area very close to each other, Manelia, Boutique Viola, and Melodies, have exquisite stuff, as do Beymen and several stores in First Mall. Donna is a very strange shop— Madonna-type gear in the window, head-scarf-wearers' gear on the ground floor, and glamorous evening gear upstairs, some sexy, some mother-of-the-bridey.

Maternity Clothes: Good news for pregnant women: half the clothes for sale in Cairo look like maternity clothes even if they're not. They are long, loose, and have large-sized elastic waistbands. There are also some new specialty shops: see Motherhood in Mohandiseen, Our Kids in Dokki and Nasr City, stores in Citystars. See *Mother & Child* magazine for listings.

Men's Clothes: New Man is good for casual stuff, Executive Club irregularly has decent suits, BTM has expensive imports. Mobaco is good for shirts. Only Ties doesn't have only ties, but a full range of men's wear. A tiny place near the Shooting Club, Arrogant, has gorgeous Italian imported everything, very expensive and tempting. English House on Lebanon Street has the latest Hugo Boss fashions, also very expensive. Visit Beymen in Four Seasons hotel, Nile Plaza, for designer clothes.

Sweaters: Men get a much better choice than women, so women should consider looking in men's shops for their sweaters, unless they like a lot of gewgaws, pompoms, crocheted edges, and what-not on them. Rimy & Riry in Zamalek does good hand-knit wool sweaters.

Women's Clothes, Smart Casual: Clip has some, mostly black-gray, a bit unisex looking; it has men's clothes, too. Trendy is hit-or-miss, as is Elegante; both are worth a quick look when you are in their neighborhoods. One great shop for tailored, simple-but-sophisticated looks is Moods in Zamalek. The Marie Louis shops often have nice suits and dresses for office wear. Beymen has top fashion at top prices. Also try stores in Carrefour and Citystars.

COMPUTERS

Any hook-up gadgets you might need are available at the many Radio Shacks located throughout Cairo. As a private individual, it is somewhat difficult to get a competent engineer or technician to come to the house when something goes awry. The bigger companies have big-company clients to nurture. By hook or by crook, by eavesdropping, by begging, try to find a friendly nerd who will help you in your hour of need. AUC's computer science department and the cybercafé may harbor the one you are looking for. Supply shops for computers are popping up everywhere; see Multimedia Mega Store in Heliopolis and CompuCity in Mohandiseen. A few helpful hints: have all documentation on hand; bring or buy a name-brand machine rather than the one your genius brother-in-law built in the basement; have copies of all software installation disks.

DESIGNERS AND DECORATORS

These exist (**Interior Designers**), but not in the same formal sense as abroad. A number of wealthy women do this work for fun and profit. For opulent advice, try Nermine Mokhtar at Atrium. For highly original and artistically quirky advice and ideas, Alef is the place to go. There are also a number of excellent architects in Cairo who might lead you to a design consultant.

There are three interior-decorating books that specialize in Egyptian decorating needs and likes. These include all the best stores for furniture, fabrics, floor coverings kitchens, and bathrooms, as well as miscellaneous items such as hot tubs, glass fittings, and home accessories. Volume One carries all the books. They are produced yearly and cost between LE70–80. Here are four publications: *Image: The Ultimate Resource for Interiors* (www.image-interiors.com); *Selections Interiors 2006*; *Creation Interior Decorating Magazine*; and *Le Salon*.

FABRICS

The hardest thing about getting fabrics in Egypt is choosing what you want. There are exquisite upholstery fabrics in Cairo and good upholsterers *(munaggid)* are plentiful. Fabric shops will lead you to them. The same shops also carry lace panels, voile, and other curtain fabrics. They mostly carry the necessary hardware and will custom-make what you need.

There are many shops specializing in the up-scale fabric market. To name a few: Damask at Citystars and Shatex in Heliopolis, Maadi, and Mohandiseen; House of Fabric in Zamalek; Texmar in Heliopolis and Mohandiseen; Raytex Imported in Arkadia Mall and Raytex Local and Print Shop have branches throughout Cairo. Tanis in the First Mall has hand-block printed cottons. The shops in Wikalat al-Balah behind the World Trade Center have large selections of fabric at reasonable prices.

FLOOR COVERINGS (CARPETS)

Imagine rich Bedouin carpets (see **Carpets & Rugs**, Chapter 1) on beautiful marble floors, or fresh cotton rag rugs on bleached wood parquet. Both are easily obtainable in Cairo. Oriental designs made in Egypt are most reasonably available at Oriental Weavers. With luck you start with good floors such as parquet or marble, but if it is a flat that you are doing from scratch you will need to make these choices. Wood is warmer and slightly more resilient to stand on than marble or terrazzo, but it is a matter of preference. A carpenter can do the wood flooring. Ask to see samples of his work and to see the wood and different designs. For marble *(rukhaam)* you will need a stonemason *(banna)*, or if you want tiles *(balaaT siramiik)* you will need a tilesetter *(muballaT)* .

Doormats are a necessity here because of the grime in the streets. Carpet stores carry the fancy ones with watermelons or cute animals or 'Welcome' emblazoned on them. The rustic jute doormats found in cafes and village homes are called *mashshaaya* and have dark green, rose, or purple and yellow stripes on a light brown background. You need to soak them in water first to make them more compact, then dry them in the sun. They are sold in Ataba or the Muski. Expect to pay about LE10 for them.

FLOWERS

There is about any kind of cut flower you might want in Cairo, but, if shop-bought, there is a price to pay for them. In 2006, flower shops vie with international shops in terms of the variety of flowers, expert arrangement, and cost they offer. Most flowers come from greenhouses or are imported and though they are beautiful, they are expensive. Florists, throughout Cairo, are happy to deliver free of charge.

Still there are the seasonal fragrant red and pink *(baladi)* roses, still grown in the ground and which cost about LE15–20 for 12 to 15, still less if you buy them from street sellers, who can charge just LE10 for 20, but make sure the flowers are fresh! A wide range of freshly cut flowers are sold at reasonable prices on the street, just outside Alfa Market in Zamalek.

FURNITURE

Compared to the British, the French were only in Egypt a short time, but they made an enormous impact on the Egyptians as far as furniture goes. (Of course, ancient Egypt made a great impact on the tastes of the Napoleonic Empire, too.) The dream of most middle-class Egyptian brides is to have a salon in the French style with gold gilt chairs and sofas, tapestry upholstery featuring eighteenth-century ladies and their cavaliers cavorting, and heavy damask drapes. Comfy, contemporary, and casual are not the ideal.

In Cairo you can find some fine and beautiful furniture as well as a lot of schlock, the latter very often right in your own living room. If you like French reproductions, be aware that while they are somewhat cheaper than European reproductions, the quality is not as fine and the brass fittings are inferior. If you just want the look, a few pieces to add interest, shop carefully. Chairs are the best made of the French replicas. Also beware of authentic French 'antiques'; even in Paris there are Egyptian reproductions being passed off as French antiques to the unsuspecting. Good but very expensive places to look for antique European styling are Al Home, Gallery Mansour, Masterpiece, Mit Rehan, and Gallery Gaby.

More contemporary designs are gradually making progress against Louis Farouk. Furniture stores like the Design Centre in Heliopolis and the new Dimensione in Mohandiseen carry interesting contemporary pieces. Styler in Maadi is very contemporary and very reasonable (a glass-topped marble end table is about LE750). Al-Fostat, Animation, and Ultra also carry excellent modern pieces. Venezia in Roxy is another one. Istikbal Furniture has four branches. American Furniture and Ethan Allen are both in Heliopolis.

Oriental furniture with its inlaid mother-of-pearl and exotic woods, intricate carvings, and turned legs can be found in the Khan, at brass shops such as Ahmed Goma in Maadi, and in some galleries like al-Ain and Asila. The Mashrabiya Institute (NADIM) specializes in this sort of furniture and will custom-make pieces for you. If you want reproductions of ancient Egyptian furniture such as was found in King Tutankhamun's tomb, look in Khan al-Khalili or at Dr. Ragab's Pharaonic Village, but pickings are slim. Ironically, foreigners go for it far more than do the Egyptians.

Much of the office furniture is imported, particularly desk chairs with adjustable features, and so is expensive. A nice and less costly alternative for a home-office desk top might be a slab of marble or granite on a wrough-iron base or on pedestals. Animation does office design and sells good office furniture.

Simple, well-designed children's furniture is not abundant in Cairo. Much of it is fussy, brightly-colored, full of Western cartoon themes. Check *Mother & Child* magazine for up-to-date listings if where to go.

GARDENS—LARGE AND SMALL, INDOORS AND OUT

If you enjoy plants and gardening, Cairo is a delight, and the brilliant sunshine all year long is your ally. Although you can spend quite a lot of money on pots and plants if you go in for imports or shop at some of the Zamalek nurseries catering to foreigners, you do not have to. Everything you need to create your own personal oasis, whether on a handkerchief-sized balcony, in a corner of your living room, or on the larger canvas of a villa garden, is produced locally and reasonably.

Pots: Before buying plants, you will need pots to plant them in unless you have a real garden, in which case you will likely have a

EDGE

FASTEST DATA TRANSFER IN EGYPT EXCLUSIVELY ON MOBINIL'S NETWORK

Mobinil is the only operator in Egypt to launch EDGE technology. EDGE stands for Enhanced Data rates for Global Evolution. It is a radio technology that enables faster data transfer up to approximately 5 times the speed of the current GPRS (General Packet Radio Service).

Both GPRS and EDGE are data transfer technologies that enable mobile users to transfer data, in various formats like sound, images, etc., to or from other users or content providers.

EDGE has many advantages for mobile users, since it allows more and better applications in the following fields:

- Mobile office applications
- E-mail with its attachments
- Multimedia messaging with superb quality image and sound
- Video and audio streaming
- Interactive games

mobinil

gardener who can be your adviser. Terra-cotta and earthenware pots in all sizes can most easily and cheaply be found in the pottery fields along the main road in Old Cairo. If you plan on bargaining, and you should, avoid doing so in the heat of the day; the sun will sap your skill and patience much faster than it does the vendor's. Remember that you will also need a vehicle to transport the haul as the potters do not usually arrange for this. A pick-up truck, jeep, or van is best is if you plan on getting large pots, but a station wagon taxi also works, ideally one with a friendly driver who helps in the negotiations. Small pots are as little as LE2–5, medium–large LE10–20, and the largest, in which an agile adult could easily hide and good-sized trees can grow, can be had for as little as LE50. Outdoor candle-holders with pretty cut-out designs are also here; some have holes for the insertion of light bulbs and can be hung flat on walls.

If you want to go to the source for round water-jug–type pots, it is an ideal excuse for a morning in Fayoum, where a wide variety of baskets are also made and sold. To suspend clay pots from wrought-iron rings embedded in an outdoor wall, inquire of Madames Nahla or Mona at al-Ain Gallery on Sharia Husayn in Dokki (**Arts & Crafts**); their handyman–gardener, Osman, will be glad to oblige. And to preserve clay pots, we are told that coating the outside with a floor wax such as Flic works well.

If money is no object, the lightweight plastic imitation terra-cotta pots can be found too, but they are imported. You will also find rectangular planters in green or white plastic with hooks for hanging on balcony railings; they range from LE15 to LE30 each with hooks, depending on size and bargaining.

Soil: Next, dirt. For outdoor plants, the plain old soil from the ground is fine and available from wherever you buy plants, or from your *bawwaab*. For indoor plants, a cleaner potting soil mixture is required. This is rather expensive, as peat moss is imported. A less expensive alternative to pure peat moss is this home-made blend: 7 parts loam or plain soil, 3 parts peat moss, 2 parts washed, coarse sand. Remember the hauling problem: you may have to pay to have pots, soil, and plants carried up the stairs rather than by lift in your building. For sand and rocks, the place to go is where the sand trucks congregate in Ard al-Liwa across the railroad tracks in Mohandiseen.

Plants: And now for the fun part—buying the plants. For indoor plants, the very best, and wholesale, nurseries are in Mansuriya and Usim, about an hour northwest of Cairo on the Alexandria Desert Road. They include Egypt Green, Mahmoud Helmi, Nimos, and Forest Nurseries. For outdoor and indoor plants the many nurseries along the banks of the Nile on Roda Island and the Corniche toward Maadi and Helwan are fine, fun, and cool. The prices go down closer to Helwan, and in Giza along the road to Saqqara are also many less expensive nurseries. Closer in, another large one is Agami in Dokki, behind the small white mosque just west of Sharia Dokki off Sharia al-Tahrir. They have trees, dirt, cacti, and flowering plants. And an exception to high prices right in Zamalek can be found at Abu al-Ghayt inside the gate to the Furusiya horseback riding club just south of the Gezira Club. Every year in March, a weeks-long flower and garden show is held at the Orman Gardens in Giza. It will intoxicate anyone with a remotely green thumb.

Many of the most popular summer plants in temperate climates (nasturtium, pansies, impatiens, begonias, petunias, salvia) do well in Cairo in winter. Bougainvillea, jasmine, gardenias, clematis, geraniums, wisteria, and roses fill summer gardens with color and scent. For lots of showy color, geraniums are cheap and grow beautifully outdoors; pay 50 piasters to LE5.50 depending on size. In early spring, you will see great clumps of seneraria in blue, purple, white, fuchsia, and pink, for about LE5 per pot; these provide a quick and cheap jolt of intense color, but they are short-lived. Vinca with its small blue flowers and *sabbaar isra'iili*, a succulent with small red or pink flowers, are both good choices for hanging vine-like off balconies, as is the purple-leaved wandering Jew with its pale pink flowers. Another is morning glory, which self-seeds and produces clusters of deep royal purple flowers rather than the anemic-looking pale blues found in northern climes. For pale gray-green borders, ask for seneraria maritima, which comes in lacy and short-thick varieties.

If you have the room for larger bushes and trees, bougainvillea and hibiscus grow to gigantic proportions; the secret is to cut, cut, cut to keep them from getting spindly and forlorn-looking. The same is true of roses, both climbing and bush varieties, but neither do as well in the heat as the bougainvillea and hibiscus. Dracaena does well indoors and out, and you can sculpt its branches and nurture it to tree size by cutting regularly. Jacaranda and flamboyans, the fern-leaved trees that are carpeted with incandescent violet and red flowers respectively all spring and summer, can also be grown in large pots. Judicious watering and regular fertilizing keep the trees growing without the roots overgrowing the pot to seek water and food. A three- to four-meter jacaranda is only about LE50, but normally, the larger the plant, the more expensive, particularly in the case of cacti.

Some other advice on plant care: For indoor plants, water once weekly in winter and twice weekly in summer. Outdoor plants require two waterings a week in winter and once a day all summer. It is best to water outdoors in the early evening, as daytime temperatures in summer can literally boil the water on leaves. Although it is tempting, don't use manure as fertilizer; the flies it draws and the smell will prevent enjoyment of any garden. Instead, use slow-release chemical fertilizer, available from most nurseries and some supermarkets. Plants need rest, a period of dormancy, in order to grow, so don't fertilize from November through mid-February.

GARDEN SUPPLIES, SHADE, FURNITURE, AND DECOR

All sorts of gardening supplies are available from the Taht al-Rab'a market, which is in the street next to the big Security Police Administration building across from the Islamic Museum. Tools, fertilizers, garden hose, and Dutch and Egyptian flower and vegetable seeds are all here, but you should go with an Arabic speaker. You can also ask, but discreetly, for plants you see in pots at any of the municipal gardens in midans throughout Cairo, but especially in Dokki and Mohandiseen. Just point and say *Hilwa di . . . bikaam min faDlak?*—"This is pretty . . . how much, please?"

To enjoy a Cairo garden, some shade is a must. Balcony roofs provide it, but on larger open terraces, you need to think about awnings, trellises, umbrellas, or pergolas. One of the cheapest and most portable shade sources is a garden or beach umbrella. Large ones are made in the Wikalat al-Balah behind the World Trade Center off the Corniche for about LE100. In this crowded warren of alleys you will find all kinds of beautiful fabrics, often the same as in the posh shops, but for half the price. This is also the place to go for canvas (*'umaash khayyamiya*—the tentmakers' fabric) to cover outdoor or informal furniture; several stores carry it in bright stripes and rich solids, ranging from LE10 per meter. Remember that the sun, and, according to some, even more so the moon, will instantly fade whatever you choose. Prices at Wikalat al-Balah go lower as you go to the interior of the area where tourists rarely venture; therefore, dress modestly, be aware of crowds, and ideally, drag along an Arabic-speaking friend.

Outdoor furniture (**Furniture**) can be as simple as woven date palm chairs for LE50 each, available at a few roadside stands on the way to Saqqara; ask for *kursi*—'chair'— in the village after crossing the canal bridge at the police station and turning left (south) towards Saqqara. With a cushion, they are very comfortable, certainly cheap, and will last a few years at least—and they can be delivered. Wrought-iron tables, chairs, and pergolas can be ordered hand-made from the ironmongers along Sharia Ramsis. Egyptians who have chalets on the coast go to Sharia al-Gisri al-Suez in Heliopolis (near Roxy) to buy inexpensive pine furniture. Having garden furniture done in wood will be more expensive, but once you find a decent, reasonable carpenter, he can make trellises, slatted pergolas, and so on. NADIM on the Alexandria–Desert Road is another place to consider for more ornate carved and mashrabiya accents for your haven. Bamboo and cane, normally inexpensive and hence popular choices for outdoor furniture, are surprisingly expensive in Cairo because the raw material is imported, but you can check the many places along Sharia Ramsis past the train station and one on Sharia Ahmad al-Gindi near AUC.

For ornamental stoneware, columns, and fountains, look to your left along the Corniche heading south near the al-Salih Bridge. The craftsmen who display their wares there can often make anything you want from a picture or drawing if they do not already have what you want. Venus de Milo in bas-relief? No problem. An elaborate plaster medallion meant for a ceiling works well as a table when set on a column and topped with glass.

HARDWARE

Well-stocked all-in-one hardware stores were once hard to come buy in Cairo. You had to go to one for paint, another for wire, another for tools, and so on. Fortunately, one off-shoot of the Ataba market has a bunch of such places all in a row, and now Carrefour and Spinneys both have hardware supplies.

KITCHENS

Stocking up the kitchen and laying a nice table are pretty easy here. Supermarkets carry the basics, department stores much more, and arts and crafts galleries the interesting serving pieces and decorative tableware. For beautiful silver or copper serving pieces and trays, go to Khan al-Khalili. There you can find unique chafing dishes and bowls. Make sure anything that will carry food is tin-lined to avoid poisoning your guests. Wissa Wassef in Harraniya village has rustic glazed pottery. Tourists like the pottery camels with saddlebags that hold condiments. For everyday glassware like tumblers and pitchers, inexpensive Muski glass works well. Touch of Glass in Zamalek has very nice designs including wine glasses, beer stains, and the like, plus lovely vases. Carrefour has a large selection of glassware, pots, and pans.

Pots and Pans: Modern brides in Egypt like the same pans as foreigners, Teflon or stainless steel. You can find them at supermarkets, department stores, and houseware stores everywhere. To find the old-style conical aluminum pans used by their mothers means venturing into the markets at Ataba. They do not have handles, but they are great for slow even distribution of heat and make nice stews. Beautiful copper pots can be found in Khan al-Khalili for a fraction of what they cost in the States or Europe. There is also a very good Egyptian-made stainless steel line of cookware with brass fittings; good design and functionality at a pretty good price.

Kitchen Fittings: If you have to have kitchen cabinets and counters installed, there are many good places, but Contistahl, which has a high reputation and prices to match, is not one of them. You will get far more competent and professional service just about anywhere else. Amr Helmy kitchens in Maadi are beautiful and expensive.

LIGHTING

Good news for Americans: you can use your 110-volt lamps, even halogen ones, in Egypt—just have an electrician rewire them. If you need to buy new lamps and fixtures, there are a lot of beautiful ones on the market, more on the ornate than the modern end of the spectrum. Copper, brass, or ceramic vases can all be wired for use as lamps. Chandeliers, the bigger the better, are very popular; one place with an especially good selection is Asfour Crystal in Shubra. For modern lighting, two of the best places to go are Style Team and Pavillon right across the street from each other in the Zamalek Club alley off Sharia Gam'at al-Duwal al-'Arabiya in Mohandiseen.

MIRRORS AND WINDOWS

You only have to worry about windows if you are doing an apartment from scratch; then you would use a contractor such as Hassan Helmy and Company. Mirrors are very popular in Egypt. For mirrors try Golden Mirror, which has all kinds of decorative glass, including etched and stained, as well as mirrors. There are numerous other places listed in the directory. You can also go to Volume One in Maadi and buy a book about interior decorators in Egypt (see page 115), as these also have good listings.

HOUSEKEEPING

CLEANING

High on the list of good things about Cairo is that housekeepers are inexpensive. Yes, it is decadent, but yes, it is also delightful. Cairo is very, make that *very*, dusty. Especially if you like your windows open now and then, you have a constant battle against dirt. It is one you cannot win, but with help, it can be kept from reaching intolerable levels.

Egyptian cleaning techniques differ considerably from Western ones. Tools for cleaning are old-fashioned and generally back-breaking. Vacuum cleaners are not standard equipment, though good ones are available. Teach housekeepers to clean the way you want them to clean. Otherwise, they will throw buckets of sudsy water on your parquet floor, then sponge it up with a towel leaving puddles under the sofa. Dishwashing is likely to be done with cold water and minimal rinsing. Bleach cleansers like Clorox are either not used or way overused. Rugs get beaten with a wooden swatter over the balcony rather than vacuumed.

If none of these things bothers you, you are a paragon of mental health and much to be envied. If they do, be patient and appreciate fully that you, not your housekeeper, are the oddball here.

A few housekeeping hints from an Egyptian mother-in-law:

Relax about dirt. You will live longer.

Area rugs are more practical in Cairo than wall-to-wall carpet—easier to shake out or vacuum up the sand.

Parquet, tile, and marbled floors need daily sweeping with a soft broom or duster mop and weekly washing with water and a little vinegar (about two or three tablespoons to a pail of water).

Parquet is often heavily varnished and needs a good professional paste-waxing about every six months; hire outsiders with the machines to do the job.

Wood railing on balconies need weekly washings with Murphy's Oil Soap or warm water with a little dish detergent and a tablespoon of vegetable oil.

To wash windows, use equal parts vinegar and water.

Setting out a bowl of ammonia and water (two tablespoons to one cup water) will get rid of stale odors and cigarette smoke.

A cut onion will get rid of the smell of fresh paint if left in a dish overnight.

Baking soda sprinkled on carpet and left for thirty minutes, then vacuumed up, will freshen the smell of carpets and rooms.

Open all windows in the early morning to let out stale odors.

In bedrooms, take off all the bedclothes and allow the mattress to air out.

Take advantage of the disinfecting and deodorizing powers of the sun. Hang bed linens and used towels outside to freshen for a few hours in the morning.

To keep the heat out, draw shutters or drapes during the afternoon. Spray screens with water when windows are open.

To keep the house unfriendly to bugs, spray screens if you are lucky enough to have them. Use mosquito netting if not. Spray for bugs, especially mosquitoes, under beds and dining table, and use electrical vapor repellents. Plug up ant holes by rubbing them with a bar of soap and sprinkle black pepper in their haunts. For cockroaches, sprinkle boric acid. It is easier and much safer than fumigating, harmless to tots and pets, and works like a charm; you have to be persistent with your local pharmacist to get the boric acid in powder form, though. Lastly, flies are said to be deterred by the hanging of water-filled bags or balloons, but the cure seems almost worse than the disease in this case.

When you feel that dirt has reached epic proportions beyond the capacities of you and a housekeeper to manage, hire an outside **Cleaning Service** to give everything a real going-over. Makram Cleaning Service is reliable, and also look in CSA bulletin and *Maadi Messenger* for ads. You may have to watch the cleaners like a hawk, but it is worth it. After the *khamsiin* is over is a good time.

FOOD AND FOOD SHOPPING

EGYPTIAN HOME COOKING

In Chapter 1 we touched upon the Egyptian and Middle Eastern foods tourists and newcomers are likely to run into. For foreigners setting up their own homes here, a little elaboration and historical background may be of interest.

Egyptian cuisine seems to be almost the same today as it was in pharaonic times. Bread has always been a vital part of the diet. In ancient times it was made of barley, millet, and wheat, making hard, chewy loaves—perhaps like *'eesh shamsi*. Eventually, a new strain of wheat was developed which did not require heat to remove the husk for threshing; thus flour with the glutinous quality necessary for the production of a light loaf became available. Either by accident or design, the ancient Egyptians learned how to leaven their bread. Today, fully 60 percent of Egyptian caloric intake is from bread products (85 percent of which comes from wheat imported from the United States, and soon Australia).

Grilled fish, pigeons, and other fowl were also mentioned in the ancient papyrus texts and are still an important part of the cuisine. (Casino de Hammam on the Giza Corniche specializes in pigeons.). Other meats were less common and usually found only in the diets of the very rich or royal families. The peasants ate vegetables and bread and drank water from the Nile stored in porous clay jars, or milk. Their favorite drink was beer, which was invented in ancient Egypt.

The poor still eat vegetables, especially beans. *Ta'miyya* (fried bean croquettes) and *fuul midammis* (fava beans slowly simmered in a big pot until tender, then seasoned) are native Egyptian dishes. Dishes with lentils such as *kushari* and lentil soup are also traditional staples. Other vegetables common in particular to Egyptian cuisine are *'ul'aas* (taro root) and *mulukhiyya*. (*'ul'aas* becomes nearly as slimy as *mulukhiyya* if not prepared correctly.) Both are used in meat stews or soups. Okra and eggplant are also popular in Egypt.

Many of the most common dishes in Egypt are not originally Egyptian. The grilled kebabs are of Turkish origin, as are the stuffed vegetables and vine-leaves. The macaroni with béchamel is the Egyptian form of the *pastitsio* of the Greeks. *TaHiina* and *babaghannuug* come from the Lebanese. The difference in the Egyptian versions of many of these regional specialties is in the flavoring used. Egyptians use garlic, cumin, coriander, dried mint, and dill. Hot pepper is also popular, as is lots of salt. The extensive use of spices (cinnamon, cardamom, turmeric, cloves) as in the Gulf countries and the Levant is not common. Nor do Egyptians mix meats with fruit as the Iranians, Moroccans, and Iraqis do.

The Egyptians have many dishes that are connected with certain holidays. At Eid al-Adha they serve *fatta*, a soup of boiled lamb served over rice with pieces of bread in a piquant garlicky vinegar sauce. At Shamm al-Nisim they eat salty dried fish called *fisiikh* and spring onions. During Ramadan feasting, a special sweet is often served called *'aTaayif*, which is a filled sweet crepe deep-fried and then dipped in syrup.

OUTDOOR FOOD MARKETS
Most Egyptians do the majority of their food shopping at the outdoor markets. They are cheaper. Here you can find mounds of strawberries, carts full of eggplants, toma-toes, and zucchini, crates of live chickens and rabbits, and bundles of fresh herbs piled on mats. Fresh fish is sold in boxes of ice. Grains and pulses are sold from huge sacks. It all makes for a crowded, colorful scene.

All areas of Cairo have sections that cater to the local clientele. If you live close to a *suuq*, by all means try buying your fresh produce there at least a few times. In the *suuq* is where Egyptians haggle for their cucumbers and potatoes, where they choose a chicken for dinner and then have it slaughtered and plucked. To shop here, you need a basic command of Arabic, a knowledge of the prices and numbers in Arabic, and a will to bargain. Watch that the vendors do not slip in any rotten tomatoes or give you less than the whole kilo. Different prices among different vendors in the same *suuq* may have some valid reasons. All the vendors go to a special wholesale market outside of Cairo in the early hours of the morning to choose their produce. Some, depending upon their clientele, will buy B or C quality tomatoes or apples because they are cheaper and they know their customers are looking for price over quality. Others will look for the best because their customers are quality-conscious. The best time for produce in any market is very early in the morning, but not so early that no one is awake.

These markets have not changed in decades, even centuries. Ataba and Bab al-Luq are still the main ones. If you are going in order to save money, take your cost of transportation and time into consideration to see if it is really worth your while. If just for the sheer joy of the sights, smells, and social scene, do it!

SUPER- AND NOT-SO-SUPERMARKETS
Cairo now boasts several good supermarkets that stock everything from imported French Gruyere to chestnut paste. French mass retailer Carrefour has outlets in Maadi City Center and Alexandria, offering ample

parking, shopping convenience, and a wide assortment of products—both local and imported—under one roof, from fresh meat and groceries to books, music CDs, clothing, and home applicances. Alfa Market, with branches in Maadi, Giza, Zamalek, and Heliopolis, has a wide selection of American, European, and Egyptian foodstuffs, as well as appliances, glassware, and cookery. Its Maadi and Zamalek branches have an entire floor devoted to sporting goods. Metro Market offers an excellent selection and numerous outlets around town and will deliver. Seoudi Market in Mohandiseen, Zamalek, and Dokki is a good neighborhood grocer that delivers. For more budget-minded shoppers, there are a few small wholesale-like places, Abu Zakry in Dokki and Maadi, and 3S and al-Hawari in Mohandiseen. The government supermarkets called al-Ahram are scattered around town. Selection is limited, but prices are very good. The Goma Digla in Maadi are reliable and cater particularly to their many American customers. Imported foods are very expensive in Egypt, naturally; learn to live off the land. All markets deliver and will take orders by phone, but Arabic is a must for this.

BREADS AND BAKERIES

The major breads—'eesh shami and 'eesh baladi—plus a few sweet pastries like fiTiir—were touched on in Chapter 1. Bread bakeries are called furn; some also carry cumin- or sesame-flavored bread sticks called batusaleeh (French: batons salés). Another Egyptian bread is simiit, crusty wreaths of bread covered with sesame. In Upper Egypt, besides 'eesh shamsi, there is ru'aa', a crisp unleavened loaf made in huge rounds in a special oven. In addition you can get baguette-like breads, hamburger-buns called kayzar, small rolls, and even sliced bread for sandwiches at all the supermarkets and most of

the furns in better neighborhoods. Rich Bake is a commercial bakery that has good-quality Western-style breads and baked goods; their milk bread is good for American-type sandwiches. The City Baker in Maadi has good loaves and baguettes.

In addition to the furns, there is an abundance of pastry shops. Many of the old ones were owned by Greeks (Tseppas, for instance). Most have a variety of French-style pastries called bitifuur (petits fours) and gatooh (gateaux), plus the Oriental pastries like baqlaawa, kunaafa, and basbuusa. They also normally carry a variety of what the French call bouchés or little savory hors d'oeuvres. Alain Le Notre and Carnaval gets raves throughout Cairo as being among the best, but there are many others that have their specialties. Khoudier in Maadi and Zamalek has great kaHk (the traditional holiday cookies) and their European-style ice cream is made into beautiful layered desserts; especially delightful is their yogurt, ice-cream cake. The Marriott Bakery has good American-style cheesecake.

MILK AND DAIRY PRODUCTS

There are many safe dairy products to enjoy, including cottage cheese, heavy cream, milk, and yogurt. Make sure you buy your items in a reputable supermarket and that the packages are properly sealed. We have found Juhayna brand yogurts to be wonderful and the Subaniyah butter is great. Processed cheeses are available for hamburgers or quick sandwiches for the children.

Though the most popular cheeses are the ruumi (use as a cheaper substitute for expensive, imported parmesan cheese) and gibna beeDa, most delis carry cheddar (sheedar) and a selection of European cheeses such as Emmental, Gouda, or Brie. You can have them cut the cheese in slices (transhaat); this is especially great with the ruumi, which is a hard cheese. The feta-type buffalo cheeses called *gibna beeDa* come in a wide range of grades or types. Some are saltier, or more dry and pungent, some are creamy and mild. Try a variety until you find one that suits you. The creamy mild ones are good in quiches. These cheeses tend to spoil fast. Make sure you store them in a salty brine or rinse if they are too salty and put in a plastic container with olive oil and some oregano or basil.

BUTCHERS (MEAT, POULTRY, AND PORK)

Egyptian meat is very fresh: you can go to market and buy live chickens, ducks, lambs, occasionally cows (and, if you are inclined, pigs) and have them slaughtered. Many Egyptians prefer their meat never to touch a freezer or plastic wrap. But foreigners who are finicky about carnivorous realities can also go to a store where the meat is fresh but plastic wrapped. The butchers in the more affluent sections of Cairo are similar to the best butchers in Europe or the United States. They can cut you a crown rib roast or bone your chicken. It is normal to tip a pound for these special services. The veal is superb, but not milk-fed. Lamb is excellent. Chickens are flavorful and tender if you freeze them a few days prior to cooking. In fact, most of the meat benefits from a few days in the freezer, which tenderizes it. One acquaintance just in from four years in Paris avers that Egyptian meat is better than French.

For ground meat, it is best to have the butcher grind a piece of meat before your eyes to ascertain that you are not getting old scraps of who knows what. Remember that most ground meat dishes are more tender if there is a bit of fat in the meat, so ask the butcher to include some fat. Also tell the butcher how you want to cook the meat and he will suggest the best cuts. Poultry sellers, who also sell rabbits, are usually separate establishments from beef and lamb

butchers. Pork, of course, is separate from everything else. All meat in Egypt is slaughtered according to the *Halal* tradition. Good vendors of all meats are listed under **Butchers** in the Directory.

FISHMONGERS

The fish markets have a variety of fish and shrimp. It is safest, especially at restaurants, to eat fish and seafood in the cooler months, unless you are at the source in Alexandria. Follow the adage to eat fish only in months with an R in them. If the eyes are still glossy and there is no objectionable odor, the fish is fresh. One can find fish in the outdoor markets; there is one on the Corniche near the Nilometer that has fish piled high in boxes. One can also buy it cooked from a fish restaurant (such as Samak Mahmud downtown or Samak Hurriya in Maadi) very reasonably. Gumhuriya Fish on 26th of July Street in Zamalek, just east of the intersection with Kamel Mohamed Street, will prepare, to your specifications, the fresh fish you've just bought for only an additional LE2 per kilo! For the names of your favorite fish, look in the shopping vocabulary section at the end of this chapter.

Another unusual fish option (besides *baTTaarikh,* the pressed dry salmon roe), is the dried fish called *ringa.* Don't try eating it straight from the store. It is incredibly salty and some people get very ill from the salt concentration. Egyptian housewives wash it in cool running water to get rid of some of the salt, then they marinate it in a combination of olive oil and lemon and onions for a few days in the refrigerator.

FROZEN FOODS

Supermarkets carry an array of frozen foods that can save you a lot of time. Many of the prepared foods are Egyptian favorites such a ground beef *kufta* (little meat logs for grilling) or stuffed grape leaves, and they are delicious. Try *sambuusak* as a snack for the children and quick meals on the weekend. Frozen moussaka and the grape leaves are a good meal for those 'I don't want to cook' days. Hamburgers, hot dogs, and philo-and-egg roll wrappers are also available. Be vigilant about the freezers, as they are not set at high temperatures and break down frequently.

FRUITS AND VEGETABLES

Cairo's fresh-produce carts and shops, found everywhere in great profusion, are a feast for all the senses. Most local produce is safe if washed properly or peeled. Real fanatics or people with jumpy stomachs can sterilize produce by first washing it in a mild soapy solution, then rinsing thoroughly, then soaking for fifteen minutes in a gallon of water to which two tablespoons of bleach have been added, then rinsing again in purified water. Permanganate solution is available at the pharmacy. Soak the vegetables and fruit in a solution of 1 tablespoon permanganate to 2.5 liters of water. The whole prospect kills any appetite for the food along with the germs! A gentle quick wash with maybe a touch of dish detergent followed by a short soak in Cairo's already heavily-chlorinated water is what most philosophical types do with no ill effects.

Some fruits are the special delights of the Middle East: fabulous fresh figs, the fresh red dates that look like chili peppers and have a sort of nutty, astringent quality, and tamarind. Broccoli is considered a foreigner's vegetable, and though not much eaten by Egyptians, it is widely available. Organic produce is also available from Sekem. It is packaged under the name Isis and is available in high-end groceries. Here is a rough guide to what you will find when; many items, like oranges, are available more or less year-round, but we indicate their high and overlapping seasons, when they are at their finest.

Winter (Dec–Feb): apples, artichokes, broccoli, carrots, cauliflower, chili pepper, green pepper, lemons/limes, pears, peas, potatoes, sweet potatoes.

Spring (Mar–May): cantaloupe, chili pepper, garlic, ogen melon, onion, oranges, potatoes, strawberries, watermelon.

Summer (Jun–Sep): apricots (a few fleeting weeks in early June), avocado, cherries, corn, cucumber, grapes, guava, honeydew melon, mangoes, *mulukhiyya,* ogen melon, peaches (Sinai peaches are the best), prickly pears, plums (May–June), watermelon.

Fall (Oct–Nov): cabbage, dates, lemons/limes, pears, sweet potatoes.

SPICES AND HERBS

Fresh herbs are often sold at vegetable stands. Selection is limited because Egyptians generally use only fresh parsley, dill, mint, and coriander. Fresh basil, oregano, and thyme can be found in Metro Market. Or you can buy a large shrub-sized basil plant for LE10–15 from a nursery and grow it at home. The most popular spices are cumin and cinnamon. Liquid vanilla is impossible to find. To substitute with the local dried packets, use half a teaspoon of the dried for one teaspoon of the liquid in your recipe.

CATERING AND TAKE-AWAY

There are excellent private caterers, foreign and Egyptian, who work by word-of-mouth only and who are more flexible than the hotels, who also do catering, as do many restaurants. For professional and innovative solutions for catering and party menus, contact House 2 House. They offer a wide variety of cuisines and other party related services such as highly trained waiters. Check out *www.house2housecatering.com.* An excellent choice for solid professional catering with some superb Egyptian food is *Le Pacha 1901,* and Tandoori is also excellent. Bon Appetit in Mohandiseen and

Zamalek have an excellent reputation and do things on a less grand scale than some of the hotels, although they are also capable of a lot of panache with their ganache. These by no means exhaust the possibilities. Ask your favorite hosts how they do it and whom they use.

Everybody and his brother is scooting around town on motorcycles delivering every imaginable foodstuff to the hungry hordes of Cairo who cannot or will not cook. The demise of dishes in favor of tin pie plates and cardboard cartons is not far behind. Is this good? Well, it's modern, it's successful, it's fast and cheap: it's life in Cairo.

DINNER PARTIES

You can jump right in and host your first dinner party for a convivial crowd of foreigners and Cairenes as long as you keep a few things in mind: 1) have plenty of soft drinks as well as alcohol if you serve it; 2) worry more about the quantity than the originality of the food; 3) don't expect anyone to show up on time; and 4) figure out ahead of time what in the world you're going to do with all the pastry gifts!

The host and hostess are not supposed to leave their guests, so have the kitchen covered, perhaps with the help of a caterer or reliable assistant. Hire someone to do drinks if you have more than twelve people. Do a buffet so people, including you, can circulate until you get to know each other better. Westerners tend to forget how eclectic their palates are. Laden your table with several familiar, reasonably sure-fire casseroles, meats, and salads, and give guests something more than carrot sticks to nibble on before dinner. 'Salad,' by the way, is the term used in referring to dips like *TaHiina, labna,* and *babaghannuugh* as well as to Western salads. A reasonable compromise on when to serve dinner is 10 pm, not beyond the late pale for other foreigners, nor beyond the early one for Egyp-

tians, assuming you have invited people for 8 pm. Everyone but a few foreign die-hards will leave very shortly after dessert.

PARTIES FOR CHILDREN

Now that you have launched yourself socially, consider the kids. The Western rule of thumb is never to have more children than the age of your child. Not so in Egypt, where 'the more the merrier' prevails. Once your child is in school, he or she can end up being invited to a birthday party a week. For small children, it is the rule to invite the whole class to a birthday do, often held in a kids' restaurant, a hotel, a bowling alley, or maybe a pool. Quite a lot of parental vying for originality and excess can go on in the fancier schools. Which does not mean you have to join the fray or risk little Fauntleroy's becoming a social outcast at age six. Party hats and a french-fries-and ketchup birthday cake at McDonald's or some equivalent suit the kids just fine, and these places are professionals at their business. It is cheap, easy, and there is no mess to clean up afterwards.

PSYCHOLOGICAL ADJUSTMENTS

"People are rude. They can't drive. They don't stand in line. They smell bad. The pollution is awful and houses are filled with soot. The metro is disgustingly dirty." — Cairo? No, Paris! Paris from the perspective of an unsettled, disgruntled, and maybe scared American who found herself uprooted and unwillingly transplanted to the City of Light. (You knew it wasn't Cairo because the people and the Metro here are clean!)

Earlier on we suggested that even if you did not have a choice about moving to Cairo, you can pretend that you did—that is also a choice. Some newcomers immediately find Cairo fascinating: the haggling and joking in the streets, downtown pulsing with light and life at 2 am, the muezzin's mournful-joyous calls to prayer punctuating the silent dawn, the mystery and history lurking in the alleyways. Others find a filthy city with raucous people who yell rather than speak, honk their horns like maniacs, and cheat their customers at every turn. Cairo is both, and everything in between. Its 20-plus million people, the bulk of them very poor, endure a lot of pressures and frustrations, yet are for the most part astoundingly good-humored and gregarious in the face of it all.

For Westerners, differences regarding psychological space and privacy stand out between our cultures. Cairenes sit, stand, and talk together at closer range than Londoners, to make a broad contrast. You, the foreigner, are not being crowded; you are just—here. Yet no physical contact between the sexes in public is allowed (two men, however, are likely to walk holding hands, rest their heads on each other's shoulders, and even kiss, with no speculation as to sexual preference being warranted). Casual Westerners should note the sanctity of the private areas of the Egyptian home. The reception room—not the kitchen or closed doors or hallways—is the place for guests, period. The house is private, but finances, specifically yours, are not. You may feel a bit flustered when bluntly asked what you pay in rent; your Egyptian inquisitor may find this a little weird (we are a little weird this way, no?), but he or she certainly will not feel flustered. Related to privacy and space is the different perception of solitude. Most Egyptians prefer company to solitude and noise to silence. Westerners' apparent desire for the opposites at times must seem quite odd to the sociable, noise-tolerant Egyptians. Why would anyone want to take a ride in a taxi without the radio blaring? Or gaze at the Pyramids without being chatted up?

What can you do for yourself to aid and abet a smooth rather than a rocky transition

to Cairo? Work is the saving grace for those who have it. But if you have free time on your hands, first take that CSA Newcomers' Orientation as soon as possible if you can afford it. Then start something regular that involves other people, be it tennis, a book club, Arabic class, church, or hanging out at the neighborhood pub. Don't wait around like a wallflower to be invited. You will have to check out a few options before finding your niche. And don't spend all your socializing time with people who constantly bitch about Cairo; it is boring, catching, and extraordinarily rude and unattractive, as these insensitive idiots frequently do it within earshot of Cairenes. You will want to crawl under the table in mortification when you find yourself with them. Keep your kids away from them and make sure you do not become one of them for their sakes. In general, but with exceptions, children who are not adapting have parents who are not adapting.

The same old euphoria–crash–balance phases that accompany any move will accompany you in Cairo. The unlucky among us might skip the entire first step, but most people are at least somewhat susceptible to the excitement of change if they give it a chance (another choice). Euphoria lasts perhaps three months. Then you lose your doubles match or see a man with no legs begging or the shower head falls out of the wall again or your two-year-old has a tantrum and pees on the floor at the supermarket—Crrraaashh! So you mope around for a few days in total despair reciting the 'I-hate-this-place' mantra. Try to pull yourself out of it with whatever works best: a good book? a pedicure? giving the guy with no legs LE10? Occasional short forays out of town also work wonders. When you finally laugh again, at yourself, you know the worst is over. And life begins again, not way up, not way down, but balanced. If you are not going anywhere but down after the crash (staying alone, not eating or eating too much, overimbibing, sleeping too much, crying uncontrollably) for any more than two to three weeks maximum, get help. Having read this far, you know it is available. If you DO feel uprooted and transplanted, here is one final thought: Bloom where you're planted! Cairo is a rich and wonderful city in which to grow, no matter what your age.

4 WORK AND RESEARCH IN CAIRO

Work is the driving force behind the presence of almost all the foreigners in Egypt. For a small but considerable number of them, that was not the original intention at all, but for whatever reasons, they just 'fell into' Egypt, falling in love with the country or one of its citizens, with its history, with its tempo and/or its exoticism. Others, mostly (but not only) young people, come to study, either at al-Azhar or at AUC. A great many more foreigners are here living off the direct or indirect bounty of a foreign-assistance related job, trailing their reluctant or eager dependents behind them, and the whole international diplomatic community is a veritable industry in itself. Finally, there are the entrepreneurs, both individual and corporate, large and small, and yes, even legal and illegal, all banking on Egypt to put money in their pockets. Now add to these the incalculable number of Egyptians whose livelihood flows from this foreign presence—armies of bureaucrats high and low, a huge service-sector industry, and a good chunk of the business communities of Heliopolis, Maadi, and Zamalek at the very least. The sum total of connections and interdependencies is dizzying.

CHANGES IN THE ECONOMIC CLIMATE

The last few years have seen relatively dramatic changes in the Egyptian business climate as the country opened up to foreign investment and private companies challenged the state monopolies. Under Nasser the country was a socialist state, under Sadat the 'Open-Door' policy theoretically reversed its position, and under Mubarak the Investment Law 230 of 1989 has encouraged foreign direct investment.

On the street, evidence of these changes is glaring. The local Sport Cola has been pushed aside by giants Coca-Cola and Pepsi-Cola, and many of the fast-food franchises familiar abroad (McDonalds, Baskin Robbins) have opened up shop. Imported clothes are not as rare to find as in the past, and companies such as Mobaco and Concrete are producing Western-style clothing designed in Europe but manufactured in Egypt. As Egyptian produce entered the seasonal fruit and vegetable markets of cooler lands to the north, the local *suuqs* have been able to offer homegrown apples, sweet corn, and asparagus among other new varieties originally grown for export. Organic products by Isis are widely available at major grocery stores.

But as the marketplace has developed apace, it has become increasingly difficult to keep up with the latest rules and regulations governing business in Egypt. It is therefore essential to hire a consultant or expediter and to use the services of a reputable law firm to cut through the red tape of business as usual to accomplish anything here. Egyptian bureaucracy is still caught in a 1960s socialist time warp, with a welter of paperwork to slice through before licenses can be granted. Good advisors will know the right procedures and have friends in the right places.

In recognition of the time-consuming legal processes, temporary permits are often granted in the meantime that are quite valid until all the i's have been dotted, the papers prepared in triplicate and translated, and the whole lot stamped upside-down, inside-out, and back to front by any number of important officials.

Official hours for government offices are 8 am to 2 pm from Saturday through Wednesday, although a few government offices still open on Thursdays. Check times so as not to leave urgent business to the last minute only to find the office closed. It is always better to present yourself early in the day, yet not unduly early in view of the fact that these hours are, after all, official. Banks are open 8:30 am to 2 pm Sunday through Thursday. Many shops close on Sunday, some onn Friday, some not at all.

Doing business in Egypt is very much a matter of timing, as in taking enough of it to exchange the vital pleasantries and formal courtesies early on that will save hours later. Don't expect to rush people into doing as you demand; you will create a wall of hostility and leaden feet to do your bidding.

Thoughtful foreigners working here understand and appreciate that they are foreign, that their ways are different rather than necessarily better, and that they have more to learn than to teach.

WORK PERMITS AND OTHER PAPERWORK

As an employee coming to work in Cairo, your company will arrange for you to have a work permit, which happily allows you to avoid a personal visit to the Mugamma. Your company or the Mugamma will need your passport and seven photographs for a work permit; academics will likely need their academic qualifications notarized by their embassy. Work permits are valid for one year from date of issue, renewable for an additional year at a time. You must apply for a renewal one month prior to the expiry date. Issue of the permit depends on reciprocal treatment being granted to Egypt by your home country and the permit is issued in accordance with certain conditions laid down by the Ministry of Manpower and Training. These conditions are: the foreigner must not take work away from an Egyptian; consideration must be given to the economic needs of the country; the foreigner

must have the qualifications and experience required for the position; enterprises permitted to employ foreign experts and technicians are required to appoint an Egyptian assistant with the appropriate qualifications who is to be trained to replace the expatriate; and foreigners born in Egypt and who reside there permanently shall have priority over non–Egyptian-born and non–permanent-resident expatriates.

A work permit grants automatic residency for the duration of the permit, but you still have to apply for the residency stamp in your passport. Submit your request along with applications for your spouse and children as appropriate; they also have right of residence based on your work permit. Everyone needs to hand in two passport photos and a passport valid for at least two months longer than the residency period requested. Armed with a residency visa, you will not have to pay for a tourist visa (currently $15) at the airport when you enter the country and, far more significantly, you will reap the benefits of cheaper foreign-resident hotel rates and of internal airline tickets at a third of the tourist rate. These are not, by the way, economies that can easily be extended to your friends and relatives visiting from abroad, but discuss options with a travel agent or bargain with the hotel.

TAXATION FOR INDIVIDUALS AND BUSINESSES

TAX ON YOUR SHIPMENT

The government continues to amend laws regarding import and export of goods, so seek and take current advice. Normally individuals can import electrical and household goods as part of their shipment and not pay import duty if their company can submit a letter of guarantee. This means that if the objects in question do not leave the country with the individual who brought them in, then the company guarantees to pay the taxes due. Thus, even if your vacuum cleaner is irretrievably broken you must take it out with you, or you will be charged the full price for a new one, with duty.

However, import duty must be paid on air-freight shipments. This bill may be picked up by your company, but do get clarification, in writing, before you ship; the dues are very high, even on audio cassettes.

INDIVIDUAL TAXES

Depending on your company, you may be required to pay Egyptian taxes. Inquire at your payroll office. Check with your consulate about the tax requirements in your home country while you are working in Egypt.

Egyptian but not foreign employees are required to pay social insurance to provide for old age, injuries, sickness, unemployment, and retirement, and their employer must also contribute to this. If you own property, there is a nominal tax due each January at the local tax office in the area where the property is situated.

COMPANY TAXATION

The law governing corporate income tax is Law No. 157 of 1981 and is applied to joint stock companies, limited liability companies, and partnerships limited by shares. The tax rate is 40 percent except in the case of a) industrial enterprises in respect to their industrial and exporting activities, for which the rate is 32 percent; and b) oil exploration and production companies, for which the rate is 40.55 percent. The tax is paid on the net profits of the company in question as established by duly audited financial statements. Losses may be carried forward for a period of five years. There is no special tax treatment for capital gains.

However, since certain activities are exempted from this law, it is very important to seek expert legal advice.

ENTREPRENEURSHIP: STARTING YOUR OWN BUSINESS

Once again, since the laws, decrees, and regulations of Egypt are more complicated than those in Europe and North America, and often amended, it is essential to seek professional advice. This guide cannot hope to offer more than an outline. However, the **Law Firms** in the Directory are well recognized and established as the most reputable firms in the city. We have allowed more leeway with respect to individual **Lawyers**, as this is a more subjective question, but as far as law firms go, no quarter was given.

There are a number of forms of business organization in the Egyptian private sector. The usual vehicle for foreign investment is the joint stock company or the limited liability company. There are two regimes under which a foreign company may incorporate one of these companies: Law 230 of 1989 (the Investment Law) and Law 159 of 1981, known as the Companies' Law. Generally foreign companies prefer to form companies under the Investment Law to be eligible for the benefits and privileges available under that law.

JOINT STOCK COMPANY (JSC)

The joint stock company requires a minimum of three shareholders and a minimum issued share capital of LE250,000 if the shares are not offered to the public. If shares are offered to the public, the minimum of the share capital is LE500,000. The issued capital must be fully subscribed with 25 percent being paid up at the incorporation and the balance within the period of ten years as determined by the Board of Directors. Any capital contributed in kind must be fully paid at incorporation and the founder's valuation of such capital in kind must be ratified by a special committee set up within the Capital Markets Authority. At least 49 percent of the share capital must be offered to the Egyptian public via registration with the Stock Exchange. There is no restriction on transfer of shares and preference shares are permitted. The company is managed by a board of directors, the majority of which should be Egyptian nationals (unless the company is formed under the Investment Law). Employees must be allowed to participate in the management of the company and the law requires a share of the profits to be distributed to the employees, which must not be less than 10 percent of the net profits, and which must not exceed the total payroll.

LIMITED LIABILITY COMPANY (LLC)

A limited liability company may not carry out the activities of insurance, banking, savings, deposit-taking, or investment of funds on account of third parties. The minimum issued share capital is LE50,000, which must be fully paid up at incorporation. Capital contributed in kind does not require valuation by a committee as in the case of the JSC; an LLC may have this valuation done by an expert, but the shareholder in question may then be held liable for the excess if the capital contribution is overvalued. At least one of three managers of a limited liability company must be of Egyptian nationality. There is no requirement for employee participation in management as for the JSC nor for the distribution of profits to employees unless capital exceeds LE250,000. There is no public subscription, stock exchange registration, or preference share issue.

After you have come to grips with the laws governing the formation and activities permitted by your would-be company, you must familiarize yourself with the country's labor laws. A written employment contract must be drawn up, in Arabic, in triplicate, with a copy for the employee, the employer, and the Social Insurance Office. The Company Law 159 of 1981 provides that 90 percent of all employees must be Egyptian and that they must receive at least 80 percent of the wages paid. Similarly, at least 75 percent of technical and administrative staff of joint stock companies must be Egyptian and must receive 70 percent of the wages paid to employees in that category. An employee may be engaged for a definite (that is, limited) or an indefinite (that is, possibly interminable) period. Companies are bound by law to provide employment for the disabled—5 percent of staff must hold disabled status.

PREMISES

Companies investing directly in Egypt in the industrial sector are likely to need manufacturing premises—most probably in one of the new industrial cities such as 6th October City (southwest of the capital), 10th Ramadan City (northeast), or the Burg al-'Arab area west of Alexandria, complemented by an administrative office in Cairo. Foreign investors can also carry out projects in the Egyptian free zones, which are considered as being located offshore, and are free from the usual customs duties and from income tax obligations.

The areas most favored for corporate offices in Cairo are Garden City, Zamalek, Mohandiseen, and Heliopolis. Since luxury accommodation in downtown Cairo is expensive (smart apartments can be $2000-plus a month before utilities) and rooms at the top hotels complete with business centers can be around $100 a night, executives on a shorter stay may consider having a hotel address rather than taking up a lease on a property. There are a number of other **Business Service Centers**, whose rates and range and quality of services may compare favorably with those in hotels. For example, most of them can locate a more economical place to rest your weary head than on a hotel pillow while using their business address, services, and personnel.

PRIVATIZATION: THE CURRENT CLIMATE

In May 1991 Egypt agreed to sign an economic stabilization program supported by the IMF. As part of this program, trade has been freed up somewhat by selective tariff reductions and by the elimination or reduction of import and export quotas. Another important component has been the liberalization of the banking industry and the rejuvenation of Egypt's capital market. The most important part of the reform process has been the encouragement of private-sector development, activity, and investment in Egypt.

A first move in the major drive toward privatization in the public sector was simply to expose it to more competitive influences. The government created new organizational structures for public-sector companies aimed at allowing them to enjoy greater autonomy and to compete among themselves and with the private sector. Managers were also introduced to the concept of accountability for their results and made subject to the same financial disciplines as the managers of private-sector companies, including the risks of liquidation and bankruptcy. Banks were instructed to break with tradition and lend only on commercial terms. The sale of 125 public enterprises over a five-year period was planned along with the divestiture of the government's shares in over 250 public joint-venture companies and twenty-three public joint-venture banks. An independent advisory body, the Public Enterprise Office, was established in November 1991, funded by the government of Egypt and international agencies. Addi-

tionally, a series of holding companies assumed responsibility for the future sale of other state companies, which encompass almost every sector of the Egyptian economy except the public utilities.

The first wave of privatization included the sale of al-Nasr Bottling with assets of LE187 million and about 5,600 employees, which was sold by the Holding Company for Food Industries to a consortium made up of two local companies and Coca-Cola International for LE325 million. Under the deal, the investors were obliged to retain the company's workforce for at least three years and to invest LE500 million over a ten-year period—a reflection of government concern about the potential social upheaval that may accompany the privatization program.

However, the path to privatization has been far from smooth. What was to have been the opening of the flood gates has turned out to be a leaky faucet.

The leisurely pace of the 'Behemoths' Auction'—the sale of the large wholly state-owned public-sector units—has left room for the expression of much frustration on all sides of the issue. There is a perception that only the successful slices (tranches) of the unprofitable state monoliths are being offered for sale and that the whole process is going much too slowly. Meanwhile, a suit has been brought against the government challenging privatization on the grounds that it is unconstitutional. In another related corner, impassioned unionists raise their membership's consciousness with patriotic speeches about the threat privatization poses to its jobs and its very patrimony. Newspaper accounts of these issues make for instructive reading.

From potential investors comes a cry for a freer flow of financial information at all levels to increase confidence among local and international investors. The government has been slow to release reliable macro-economic data, nor do all companies publish full annual reports. However, the situation is improving: the Ministers' Cabinet Information Office in Zamalek and the Central Bank of Egypt now publish reports covering macro-economic issues, and companies quoted on the stock exchange must provide annual reports. Also on the positive side for those who support it is the fact that economic reform, specifically privatization, is now regarded as irreversible. Hopes are high that the large number of expatriate Egyptians who formed part of the massive brain drain during the Nasser years will now be willing to invest their considerable financial assets in their homeland, given the right economic climate and incentives—and that they may indeed return themselves, bringing with them other valuable assets for investment: their skills and expertise.

NETWORKING AND FINDING MORE INFORMATION

Before you go any further, make sure you have a good supply of suitably impressive business cards to hand. This essential tool is much used in Egypt and is quick and easy to acquire. It is a culturally sensitive touch to have these cards done up in English on one side and Arabic on the other.

Businesspeople will find the American Chamber of Commerce based in Mohandiseen a good source of information. The chamber issues occasional reports on specific aspects of the Egyptian economy and a magazine, *Business Monthly*. Their regular luncheon meeting is definitely a place to network and they have very interesting speakers.

The magazine *Business Today* carries not only business stories but also an invaluable mini-directory of government agencies, accountancy firms, aid agencies operating in Cairo, and so on.

There is a well-stocked commercial library at the USAID office in the Cairo Center Building near the Semiramis Intercontinental

Hotel, open to members of the public.

For laws, decrees and regulations in English contact the Middle East Library for Economic Services (MELES). They produce the *MELES List* and the *MELES Bulletin* covering Egyptian law to date with the latest amendments in English, at reasonable prices. The library can provide its subscribers with certain economic studies.

An invaluable source of information is the book *Egypt: Investment and Growth,* published by Euromoney Publications. It is revised every six months.

Finally, do not forget the commercial section of your embassy for advice and suggestions regarding useful connections.

SCHOLARLY RESEARCH

It is relatively easy to study in Cairo provided you have a letter of reference from your alma mater or current university back home. Many of the English-speaking students coming to do research for their doctorate of philosophy in, for example, ninth-century Arabic literature or archeology have been impressed by their welcome into local intellectual circles.

Take your introduction letter to the Office of Graduate Studies and Research. You can become a 'fellow without stipend,' which provides institutional affiliation with AUC and access to AUC's community and services, including the library. The research fee is equivalent to one graduate credit hour, which at writing is $750. If you already have your Ph.D., acceptance of a scholar as a 'fellow without stipend' is conditional upon the compatibility of your research interests with those of an AUC faculty member from a sponsoring department.

Access to AUC's library is restricted to individuals holding a valid AUC ID. Hopeful visitors off of the street will not be admitted. Eligibility information is available on the library's web site, *www.library.aucegypt.edu.*

Seek out public lectures in your subject (advertised in *Egypt Today*) and you will soon find a group of people with similar interests and knowledge to yours. There are weekly or monthly talks at ARCE (the American Research Center in Egypt), often on Egyptology but also on literature and the legal system, while the talks at the Netherlands Institute tend to focus on Classical Arabic and Egyptology. The French CEDEJ (Centre d'Études et de Documentation Éconmiques, Juridiques et Sociales) covers more modern subjects such as sociology and politics. The Townhouse Gallery holds weekly talks on modern poetry, art, and drama. There are frequent lectures at the British Council. The major institutes have resources you can use for a modest membership fee and your colleagues will pleased to help you with your research.

For more information from other **Organizations, Business & Scholarly**, check with the British Council and other cultural centers. For funding and alternative sources, contact:

Amideast, which provides information on all aspects of American education and training at post–secondary school level and material about graduate studies.

The Council for the International Exchange of Scholars, which has programs for senior scholars.

The European Commission, which provides some funding for research projects. You must apply on a form issued by the Cairo office by May for the following year. They have a documentation center and library on the premises open to the public.

The Ford Foundation, which sponsors projects rather than individuals.

The Fulbright Commission, which administers exchange of scholars between Egypt and the United States through a variety of programs. The core program oversees an exchange of post-doctoral professors for lectures or research in all fields. The com-

mission administers other educational and cultural exchange programs for Egyptians to study in the States. For Americans wishing to study in Egypt, Fulbright has two programs, the Senior and the Student Scholar.

The Hubert H. Humphrey North–South Fellowship Program, Eisenhower Fellowships, Fulbright-Hays Foreign Curriculum Consultant Program, Salzburg Seminar: Apply to the Fullbright Commission for more information on these.

The Institute of International Education, which organizes student scholar programs in the United States for Egyptians (contact the IIE in the United States.

Two others:

ICARDA (International Center for Agricultural Research in the Dry Areas) is the local branch of the main office situated in Aleppo, Syria, and supports applied agricultural research in the Nile valley. It aids Egyptian scientists and workers in planning and conducting research and produces reports in English that are available to the public.

IDRC (International Development Research Center, Canada) opened a regional office in 1977 to fund research projects of an applied nature. It accepts proposals from institutions only and publishes a quarterly newsletter in French and English and an annual journal in Arabic.

TEACHING

Professional teachers for schools in Cairo are generally hired direct from overseas. They may tutor in their spare time—the going rate is $20 an hour—although some contracts prohibit this practice. If you would like to tutor privately, register yourself with the CAC or BISC schools, or substitute teach until a suitable vacancy occurs. Salaries in local language schools can fall far short of those offered in the foreign schools; classes are bigger and less disciplined but the rewards from teaching may be greater. Local language schools are always keen to recruit native English speakers qualified overseas, as these fee-paying schools recognize their marketing potential to the parents. Teachers report that the administrative side of local schools can leave a lot to be desired; it is a question of going with the flow.

Teachers of English as a Foreign Language (EFL) are imported and home-grown, for there are a number of centers that offer the RSA CTEFLA certificate. This training program takes between four and five weeks and is very intensive. It costs around $900. There is an entry test to complete before acceptance into the course, which examines your command of the English language and your grammatical knowledge. The British Council runs its training course in the summer months and generally some employment opportunities for qualified teachers follow. Berlitz, too, has branches in Cairo and runs its own teacher training program.

The International Language Institute (ILI) is part of the International House group based in London. Some people come especially to Cairo to take the ILI course, as it is cheaper here than in Britain, as are living expenses. There are two ILIs, in Mohandiseen and in Heliopolis, which both run courses several times a year. AUC offers the course three times a year.

The advantage of these center-based courses is that you become familiar with their resource library and so do not have to reinvent the wheel every time you teach a new concept to your class. The possible disadvantage is that teaching hours are often in the late afternoon or evening, as that is when the regularly employed are free: you may prefer to devote such time to your family or socializing.

There is a considerable demand in Cairo for teachers of English. Everyone, it seems, wants to learn and practice English, as evi-

denced by the number of small boys whose opening line on the street is "What time is it?" or "What is your name?" Forward-looking businesses have approached the British Council to ask them to provide a series of classes to teach anything from technical English to how to answer the telephone in the language.

WORKING FOR EGYPTIAN COMPANIES

It is essential to know that if you are employed as a 'foreigner' from overseas, you will be paid the sort of salary you are used to. If, however, you accompany your spouse to Egypt with the idea that, with your professional qualifications, you will be able to find work and receive adequate payment for it, you will be sadly disappointed. 'Local hire' rates are very low by Western standards. A good salary here is LE5,000 a month. You can, however, get quite a bit more, depending on the perceived value of you and/or your qualifications to the given company.

A few observations from foreign friends working for Egyptian firms—schools, law firms, Egyptian NGOs (Non-Governmental Organizations): document every initiative you might ever want credit for; get an advance if you have been promised reimbursement for out-of-pocket money; make sure your employment contract is in a certified Arabic translation as well as in English; determine how best to assure receipt of your last paycheck particularly if you are working freelance; don't alienate yourself in the comfort and isolation of workaholism; and don't gossip, a most difficult rule to follow in Egypt's chatty and conspiracy-theory-prone corporate culture.

And now, a bouquet of comments and advice—and a few expressions of frustration—culled from a wide range of people in the world of work—an Egyptian woman who runs a large information technology

company, a foreign engineer managing a large Egyptian labor force, a few boutique owners foreign and Egyptian, temporary consultants, and so on. We have mixed them kaleidoscope-fashion, because this reflects well the range and diversity of their experiences:
"Egyptian laborers can make anything with their hands." . . . "It's very hard to delegate; you have to be on top of everything yourself." . . . "There's no management training here—people are given responsibility but no authority." . . . "Mine information like gold!" . . . "Where are the opportunities? Career development training, distribution franchises, technical education for adults, public relations/marketing/advertising, and entertainment for Egyptians and foreigners." . . . "Why do they want to cheat me instead of getting a good customer?" . . . "I got my job through the English Language Institute (AUC) bulletin board." . . . "They don't manage their time right. . . . It's constant phone calls and interruptions." . . . "A patchwork work background can work really well here." . . . "The good things about doing business as a woman here is that Egyptian women get a natural respect, plus sympathy, curiosity, and interest because they're a minority; the bad thing is that at the top, it's a real old boys' club." . . . "How to make life easy? Smile. How to make it difficult? Be the arrogant foreigner."

VOLUNTEER WORK

There are many opportunities to give of yourself in Cairo, depending on where your interests or talents lie and how much time you have. Below is a brief listing. If you have a particular skill or training, ask around—your help will be much appreciated.

Al-Nur wa-l-Amal ('light and hope') Association is founded and run entirely by volunteers and depends on donations to keep going. It is a boarding center for blind girls that educates and trains them to be self-sufficient, integrated members of society. By transcribing sheet music into Braille, the institute has taught the girls to master musical scores, and this professional orchestra is world famous.

Friends of Children with Cancer is a fundraising organization that helps children in Egypt to receive the best medical care possible. Eighty percent of children with leukemia in Europe are cured while only 30 or 40 percent of children in Egypt recover, mostly due to the high cost of the treatment required.

Awladi Orphanage in Digla looks after up to 220 boys and girls. (Remember, formal adoption is illegal in Egypt.) The girls can stay until they are married, the boys are transferred to another orphanage at age twelve. Volunteers are needed to supervise the children and it is better if they can be familiar faces: encouragement, love, and hope are essential to all children, and security is even more important to children in Egypt without a home. Telephone Shadia Salem at 358-5694.

The Thrift Shop under All Saints' Cathedral in Zamalek accepts used clothing and household goods, which it sells in order to raise money for a number of Egyptian charities. Recently, for example, they were able to buy braces for child victims of polio. The shop often welcomes help. Telephone 736-8391 for further information.

The Deaf School, run by the Episcopal Church in Egypt, needs volunteers to help deaf and hearing-impaired children with their afterschool activities. Contact 362-6022 or 340-9464.

'Ayn Shams Hospital's Clinic in Heliopolis welcomes volunteer staff with or without medical backgrounds.

Joint Relief Ministry needs people to teach English, basic computing skills and accounting, arts and crafts, and carpentry. Telephone 736-4836, 736-4837 for further information.

Shubra Evangelical Church needs native English speakers to teach adults. Telephone Maher al-Sabagh at 574-0023.

Befrienders Cairo, the local equivalent of the Samaritans, is a community service for the depressed and suicidal. Arabic speakers are particularly needed. Telephone 762-1602/3.

The following opportunities to help out are offered by the Maadi Women's Guild:

The Baby Wash program is part of the Caritas effort to help Egypt's poor. At its clinic near the Pyramids mothers are encouraged to bring their new-born babies for a bath and general medical check up. Volunteers do the bathing and bring anything unusual in the baby's appearance to the attention of the clinic staff.

The Home of Love and Compassion in Muqattam has babies and toddlers in need of a hug and old people whose families cannot care for them and need someone to talk with.

The National Cancer Institute needs volunteers to visit ninety children with cancer every week, and welcomes donations of crayons, coloring books, soap, and milk—indeed, anything to brighten these children's lives. Telephone 519-6076.

Hope Village Society cares for street children. *www.egyhopevillage.com*, 21 Sharia Ahmad al-Khashab (behind Egypt Air) Nasr City (272-4563, 272-4053).

Al-Gahd Cairo helps the child garbage collectors. They need volunteers to teach and prepare food. For more information contact the Community Service Association in Maadi.

The local free newsletter in Maadi, the *Maadi Messenger*, lists other opportunities to help as the need arises—and itself (because of the transient nature of most expatriates) is always looking for volunteers to take ads, type, or help distribute. Or you can visit the Community Service Assocation in Maadi.

Finally, you can always volunteer to help out at your local school and get to know other parents at the same time. There are opportunities to volunteer at sports events, for libraries, and indeed any organization. **Volunteering** is a well-know cure for many ills, and a tried-and-true avenue to successful networking as well.

5 CAIRO ARABIC: THE BASICS

"FROM THE ARABIC..."

Macabre (*maqaabir:* tombs), cipher (*Sifr:* zero), admiral (*amir al-baHr:* commander of the sea), camel *(gamal)*, algebra (*al-jabr:* reduction), assassin (*hashshashiin:* hashish-smokers), cotton *(quTn)*, coffee *(qahwa)*. These are just a few of the hundreds of words from the Arabic that color and enrich everyday English.

Short-term visitors limiting themselves to upscale hotels and tourist haunts can get by with no Arabic whatsoever in Cairo. But for foreign residents dealing with 'real life,' a minimal vocabulary is vital. Upper-class and professional Egyptians speak English, and often French as well, as do tourist-oriented shopkeepers, but the vast mass of Cairenes do not. So if you plan to travel independently, shop, and meet your neighbors, you can sally forth with this very brief introduction. We hope it will whet your appetite for more.

There are hundreds of Arabic classes and tutors in Cairo (see **Language Classes** in the Directory). You're bound to find one that suits your needs and interests. Learning Classical Arabic, the language of literature, newspapers, and formal discourse, requires a serious commitment. But picking up a useful vocabulary of colloquial, spoken Arabic, is relatively easy. The various guttural sounds may throw off native English speakers initially, but the pronunciation guide below will help demystify these. To expand upon the brief vocabulary given here, check the **Shopping and Other Lists** at the end of this chapter for all sorts of shopping and household terminology. Next, try Stevens and Salib's *A Pocket Dictionary of the Spoken Arabic of Cairo* (The American University in Cairo Press, 2004); if you are put off by phonetic transcription symbols, though, use *Say It In Arabic (Egyptian)* by Farouk al-Baz from Dover Publications.

So plunge in. Ask questions, make mistakes, and use this great tip from our Research Editor: label everything in the house as you learn its name, using whatever unique transcription works best for you. Then photocopy the lists at the end of this chapter and post them in the kitchen; using these words will earn you much kudos with your local shopkeepers.

PRONUNCIATION AND VERY LIMITED GRAMMAR

1) For gender variants, we use male version/female version
2) Alternatives and explanations are preceded by a semicolon

CONSONANTS

Distinctly lengthen any consonant that is doubled, e.g., pronounce "kk" as the "k" sound in bookcase, and don't ignore the oft-cited difference between *Hamaam* (pigeon) and *Hammaam* (toilet).

Capital letters anywhere in a word indicate a stronger emphasis on the sound than their lower-case counterparts; **D, S, T, Z, H** require a Heavier, Harder Hit than **d, s, t, z, h**.

g   is always pronounced hard, as in English 'go.'
j   is pronounced "zh," as in the English 'measure.'
kh   is equivalant to "ch" in the Scottish 'loch' or the German 'echt.'
gh   is similar to "kh," but with the vocal chords vibrating.
q   sounds like a softer English "k" uttered from further back in the mouth.
r   is a trilled r, as in Italian and Spanish.
s   is pronounced as in 'its,' never as in 'his' or 'hers.'
'   (apostrophe): glottal stop, like "tt" in American 'Manhattan' or Cockney 'matter'
'   (reversed apostrophe): the *'ain,* a forcing of the air through a constriction in the throat, a kind of backward gulp. If you find it impossible, substitute 'a' as in 'cat.'

VOWELS

a   as in 'back'
aa   as in 'car' if near an emphatic consonant (S, T, D, Z), otherwise as in 'care'
ee   as in 'cane'
i   as in 'win'
ii   as in 'clean'
oo   as in 'bowl'
u   as in 'put'
uu   as in 'cool'

MINIMALIST'S GRAMMAR

The Arabic verb 'to be' is rarely used in the present tense; instead, one uses the personal pronoun plus the adjective for statements which describe a condition, e.g., *ana 'ayyaan/a,* meaning 'I [am] sick.'

Nouns have gender, as in French and Spanish. Those ending in *-a* are usually feminine; the rest are masculine, with a few exceptions.

Sex further complicates matters as follows: In speaking to males, *-ak* is added to certain phrases; to females, *-ik* is added, e.g., *min faDlak* ('please') to a male, *min faDlik* to a female. We indicate this by showing *-ak/ik* where appropriate. Another version of this same general principal is the addition of -i to a verb, e.g., *law samaHt* ('if you please') to a male, but *law samaHti* to a female.

There are also linguistic differences between male and female speakers: in referring to themselves, men use the masculine (m) adjective form and women the feminine (f), e.g., *ana aasif* (m) and *ana asfa* (f) ('I [am] sorry'). We indicate this with a slash, with the masculine first, the feminine following.

Adjectives generally follow the noun thEey modify and agree in gender and number.

Verb conjugations are less irregular than in English; nevertheless, we're skipping the whole subject here.

Mish in front of a word negates it, e.g., *mish mumkin:* 'impossible.'

GENERAL VOCABULARY

COURTESY

hi/hello	ahlan; ahlan wa sahlan
goodbye	salaamu 'aleekum; ma'a-s-salaama; salaam
how are you?	izzayak/ik
fine, thanks	kwayyis/a il-Hamdulillaah
my name is ____	ismi ____
thank you	shukran
please	law samaHt/i; min faDlak/ik
excuse me, pardon me	'an iznak/ik
I'm sorry	ana aasif / asfa
I don't know Arabic	ana mish 'aarif / 'arfa 'arabi
I don't understand	mish faahim / fahma
I understand	faahim / fahma
to your health	fi SaHHitak/ik

QUESTIONS

what's your name?	ismak/ik eeh?
do you speak English?/French?	bititkallim/i ingiliizi / faransaawi?
who is that?	miin da / di?
what is this?	eeh da / di?
what are these / those?	eeh dool?
where (is) ——?	feen ——?
when?	imta?
how?	izzaay?
how much (money)?	bi kaam?
how many?	kaam?
why?	leeh?
which (one)?	anhi?
who knows?	miin 'aarif?

URGENCIES AND EMERGENCIES

where is the toilet?	feen il-Hammaam?
now	dilwa'ti
it's not working	'aTlaan/a; bayZ/a
help me! (emergency)	ilHa'uuni!
help me (less urgent)	saa'idni
emergency	Taari'
police	shurTa; buliis
fire	Harii'a
water	mayya
hospital	mustashfa

| call a doctor | 'ayziin duktuur ('we want a doctor') |
| help! thief! | ilHa'uuni! Haraami! |

COMMON EXPRESSIONS

Given in the approximate descending order in which you will hear them.

thanks be to God	il-Hamdulillaah
God willing	insha'allah
yes	aywa; aah
no	la'; la'a (more emphatic)
and	wa; u
don't worry; no problem	ma'lish
I mean	ya'ni
so / then	fa
again	kamaan
also	bardU
don't	balaash
okay, can do	maashi (lit. 'it goes')
sure, no problem	mish mushkila
can do, possible	mumkin
finished, done, okay	khalaaS
isn't it? n'est ce pas?	mish kida?
impossible	mish mumkin
not bad, okay, so-so	mish baTaal
okay, fine	Tayyib; Tab
connections, influence	wasTa; koosa
nonsense, empty talk	kalaam faaDi
exactly	miyya miyya, (lit. 'a hundred percent'); biZZabt
so-so, okay	nuSS u nuSS (lit. 'half and half')
only, quit it, enough	bass
bit by bit	shwaya shwaya
"in the time of apricots"	fil-mishmish (meaning 'almost never')

DIRECTIONS

Especially handy with taxi drivers.

straight ahead	'ala Tuul
right	yamiin
left	shimaal
next to	gamb
across from, in front of	'uddaam
facing	fil-wishsh
behind	wara
before	'abl
after	ba'd

near, close to	'urayyib min
far from	ba'iid 'an
corner (of a street)	naSya; this corner: in-naSya di
between — — and — —	been — — wa — —
at — —	fi — —
stop here	hina kwayyis
go slowly	bi-shweesh
go quickly	bi-sur'a
how many kilometers?	kaam kiilu? (better by far than 'How far?')

PLACES

Just say the word, and add *law samaHt/i* for 'please.'

airport	maTaar
bridge	kubri
cathedral	ik-katidra'iyya
church	kiniisa
embassy	sifaara
floating restaurant	resturan 'aayim
home	beet
hotel	fundu'
market	suu'
— — mosque	gaama' — —; masgid — —,
	e.g., gaama' SulTaan Hasan
museum	matHaf
office	maktab
post office	busta
school	madrasa
square	midaan
street	shaari'
train station	maHaTTit il-'atr
university	gam'a

For names of **Landmarks**, see the chart at the front of the book.

MONEY (AND POLITE BARGAINING)

pounds	gineeh
piasters	'irsh
and a half	nuSS, e.g., itneen gineeh u nuSS: two and a half pounds
and a quarter	rub', e.g., talaata gineeh u rub': three and a quarter pounds
small change	fakka
change (back from transaction)	baa'i (literally 'the rest')
do you have change?	ma'ak fakka?
no change	mafiish fakka

I'm broke	ana mifallis
how much?	bi kaam; kaam?
too much / unreasonable	kitiir; mish ma''uul
my last word / offer	aakhir kalaam
congratulations	mabruuk; response: allah yibaarik fiik/i; depending on tone of voice, this exchange concluding a bargaining session indicates genuine or sarcastic admiration of the opponent's bargaining skill

FAMILY, FRIENDS, AND OTHER PEOPLE

people	naas
(my) mother	umm(i); waldit(i) (formal)
(my) father	abu(ya); waalid (waldi) (formal)
(my) brother	akhu(ya)
(my) sister	ukht(i)
(my) son	ibn(i)
(my) daughter	bint(i)
(my) children	awlaad(i)
(my) husband	gooz(i)
(my) wife	maraat(i), il-madaam (formal)
man	raagil
woman	sitt
child	Tifl
children, kids	aTfaal; 'iyaal (slang)
baby	beebi; Tifl
boy	walad
girl	bint
my friend	SaHbi (m) / SaHbiti (f)
my sweetheart	Habiibi (m) / Habiibti (f)
my fiancé/e	khaTiibi (m) /khaTibti (f)
stranger	ghariib/a
foreigner	agnabi (m) / agnabiyya (f)
Westerner	khawaaga (m) / khawagaaya (f) (can be friendly, derogatory, or deferential)

TIME (WA'T)

now	dilwa'ti
later	ba'deen
today	innaharda
tonight	innaharda bil-leel
tomorrow	bukra
day after tomorrow	ba'da bukra
yesterday	imbaariH

morning	iS-Subh
afternoon / evening	ba'd iD-Duhr
evening / night	bil-leel
on time	fi-l-ma'aad
(five) o'clock	is-saa'a (khamsa)
half past five	khamsa u nuSS
five fifteen	khamsa u rub'
five forty-five (quarter to six)	sitta illa rub'
Sunday	il-Hadd
Monday	il-itneen
Tuesday	it-talaat
Wednesday	il-arba'
Thursday	il-khamiis
Friday	il-gum'a
Saturday	is-sabt

PERSONAL PRONOUNS AND DEMONSTRATIVE ADJECTIVES

I	ana
you (s)	inta (m) / inti (f)
he	huwwa
she	hiyya
we	iHna
you (pl)	intu
they	humma
this, that	da (m) / di (f)
those	dool

ADJECTIVES

To add emphasis indicating 'very' or 'too,' add *'awi* after the adjective; to negate, precede it with *mish*. Feminine endings are shown as /a; if not shown, the adjective is invariant.

big	kibiir/a
small	Sughayyar/a
more	aktar
less	a'all
nice / good / fine	kwayyis/a, Tayyib/a
beautiful / pretty	gamiil/a; Hilw/a (sweet)
ugly	wiHish/wiHsha
bad	wiHish/wiHsha; mish kwayyis/a
broken, not working	bayZ/a
interesting	kwayyis/a
boring	mumill/a
important	muhimm/a
crowded, busy	zaHma
tall	Tawiil/a

short	'uSayyar/a
fat	tikhiin/a
thin	rufayya'/a
funny	muDHik/a
generous	kariim/a
greedy	Tammaa'/a
happy	mabsuuT/a
honest	amiin/a; shariif/a
hot; cold	Harr; bard (for weather)
hot; cold	sukhn/a; saa'i' / sa''a (for temperature of things and food)
polite	mu'addab/a
sick	'ayaan/a
spicy	bi-shaTTa; Haami/Hamya
strange	ghariib/a
terrible	faaZii'/a
tired	ta'baan/a
wonderful	haayil/hayla

ADVERBS

slowly	bi-shweesh
quickly	bi-sur'a
immediately	Haalan
later / next	ba'deen
soon	'urayyib
often / a lot	kitiir
here	hina
there	hinaak

PREPOSITIONS

in	fi
inside	guwwa
outside	barra
up / on top of	foo'
down / under	taHt
around / about	ta'riiban; Hawaali
after	ba'd
before	'abl
with	ma'
without	bi-duun; min gheer

DETERRENTS

Women may experience unwanted attention from men in the street—from polite attempts at conversation to coarse language or gestures to physical assault. Talking to other foreign women about their experiences here and how they've dealt with them can be an enormous help and comfort. At first it is daunting and can even be frustrating and upsetting, but soon you will devise your own methods of dealing with street harassment. Carrying a shawl or light jacket to cover yourself, walking with purpose, looking like you know exactly where you're going, not making eye contact with men on the street, and avoiding conversation with taxi drivers (bring a book to read instead) are all helpful ways of deterring harassment. If you're someone who enjoys a walk or run through the streets at home, do it early in the morning (and cover up) or join a local gym.

If harassment does occur, depending on the situation, some of the following deterrents may be useful. And remember that if you raise your voice (in any language) you will immediately attract a crowd, who will probably deal swiftly and efficiently with your aggressor.

ana mitgawwiza	I'm married
'eeb	shame on you, for shame!
iHtirim nafsak	have respect! (lit. 'respect yourself')
inta magnuun?	are you crazy?
bass kifaaya	enough! leave me alone!

For situations in which you feel threatened, do not hesitate to say: hagiib al-buliis (I'll call the police). This works wonders, as the last thing any Egyptian male wants is to go near a police station.

Numbers: see the chart at the front of the book.
Colors: see **Shopping and Other Lists** below.

SHOPPING AND OTHER LISTS

FOOD

EGYPTIAN SPECIALTIES

babaghannuug	smoked mashed eggplant / oil / garlic dip
baTaarikh	semi-dry, pressed Egyptian salmon-roe caviar; an acquired taste
fuul	stewed broad beans; the Egyptian breakfast of champions
kufta	spiced, grilled meatball fingers
kushari	lentils, macaroni, and rice topped with dry-fried onion and spicy tomato sauce—delicious
'ul'aas	taro-like starchy root vegetable used alone or in soup
mazza	mixed appetizers

mulukhiyya	Jew's mallow, a slightly bitter, spinach-like green used in soup of the same name
Umm 'Ali	(lit. 'Mother of 'Ali') rich bread pudding with coconut, cream, nuts (for dessert or breakfast)
TaHiina	dip of ground sesame seed paste with mild spices
Ta'miyya	felafel: fried patties of ground chickpeas, onion, herbs, and (sometimes) egg
wara' 'inab	stuffed vine leaves

BREADS AND PASTRIES

'eesh	bread in general
'eesh baladi	wholewheat pita-like bread
'eesh shaami	white-flour version of *'eesh baladi*
'eesh shamsi	Egypt's answer to *pain poilane*; superb, but so far available only in Upper Egypt
[pastries]	all sweeter than sweet; try *kunaafa* (thread-like cake), *ba'laawa*
fiTiir	a versatile puff-pastry; great for home-made pizza crust, or top with sweet fruit topping
[baguettes, croissants, etc.]	use the same words for these and other khawaaga (foreigner) foods

DAIRY PRODUCTS

butter	zibda
eggs	beeD
ghee	samna
milk	laban; Haliib
sour cream	ishTa fallaaHi; ishTa miziz
whipping cream/heavy cream	krem labbaani
yogurt	zabaadi
yogurt, Middle Eastern	labna (used to make dips with lemon and olive oil)
clotted cream	ishTa

CHEESE (gibna)

Egyptian cheeses are listed by their very approximate English equivalents.

cheddar	sheedar; much less sharp than foreign brands; a good all-purpose cheese
feta	gibna beeDa; available hard or soft, spiced or plain, dry or runny
mozzarella	mutsarilla; look for wet plastic bags marked "for pizza"
parmesan	barmizaan (old gibna ruumi will do)
ricotta	rikutta; sold in plastic bags

| romano | gibna ruumi |
| Swiss | gibna swisri; usually imported |

FRUIT (fakha)

For ripe fruit, say *mistiwi;* for juice, ask for *'aSiir* ('juice') followed by the fruit's name; for dried fruit, add *naashif* ('dried') after the fruit.

apples	tuffaaH
apricots	mishmish; dried in sheets: 'amar id-diin
avocado	abukaadu
bananas	mooz
cantaloupe	kantalubb
cherries	kireez
coconut	gooz il-hind ('India nut')
dates	balaH
figs	tiin
gooseberries	Harankash
grapefruit	gribfruut
grapes	'inab
guavas	gawaafa
kiwi	kiiwi
limes, lemons	lamuun
mango	manga
mulberries	tuut
olives, black	zatun iswid
olives, green	zatun akhDar
oranges	burtu'aan
peaches	khookh
pears	kummitra
persimmon	kaaka
pineapple	ananaas
pomegranates	rummaan
prickly pear	tiin shooki
raisins	zibiib
strawberries	farawla
sweet melons	shammaam
tamarind	tamr hindi
tangerines	yustafandi
watermelon	baTTiikh

VEGETABLES (khuDaar)

artichoke	kharshuuf
asparagus	kishkalmaaz
aubergine	bidingaan
beets (beetroot)	bangar
broad beans	fuul
broccoli	brakli

carrots	gazar
cauliflower	'arnabiiT
celery	karafs ifrangi
corn (maize)	dura
courgettes	koosa
cucumber	khiyaar
eggplant	bidingaan
fennel	shamar
fenugreek	Hilba
french beans	lubya
green beens	fuSuulya beeDa
Jew's mallow	mulukhiyya
leeks	kurraaT
lentils, brown	'ads bi-gibba
lentils, yellow	'ads aSfar
lettuce	khass; salata (greens in general)
lupine	tirmis
mushrooms	'ish ghuraab; shampinyoon
okra	bamya
onions	baSal
onions, pearl	'awirma
peas	bisilla
peas, sweet	bisillit iz-zuhuur
peas, black-eyed	lubya
peppers, sweet	filfil ruumi
potatoes, sweet	baTaaTa
potatoes, white	baTaaTis
pumpkin	'ar' 'asali
radish, red	figl ruumi
radish, white	figl abyaD
scallions	baSal akhDar
spinach	sabaanikh
taro	'ul'aas
tomatoes	'uuTa; TamaaTim
turnips	lift
zucchini	koosa

POULTRY (Tuyuur)

breast	Sidr
chicken	firaakh
duck	baTT
gizzards	'awaaniS
goose	wizz
leg	wirk
pigeon	Hamaam
quail	simmaan

rabbit	arnab
turkey	diik ruumi

MEAT (laHma)

bacon	beekan
beef	kanduuz
brains	mukhkh
chitterlings	mumbaar
feet	ruguul
filet	filittu
ham	jamboon
heart	'alb
kidney	kalaawi
lamb	Daani; 'uuzi
liver	kibda
pastrami	bastirma (not always beef)
pork	khanziir
roast beef	ruzbiif
roast	rustu
sausage	sugu'
scallops	iskalubb
shanks	kawaari'
steak	bufteek
tongue	lisaan
tripe	kirsha
veal	bitillu

FISH (samak) AND SEAFOOD

anchovies	anshuuga
calamari; squid	kalamari; subeeT
clams	gandufli
crabs	kaburya
grouper (sea bass)	wa'aar
mullet, grey	buuri
mullet, red	barbuuni; murgaan
mussels	balaH il-baHr
herring	ringa
lobster	istakooza
salmon	salamun
sardines	sardiin
shrimp / prawns	gambari
sole	muusa
tuna	tuuna

NUTS, SEEDS, AND GRAINS

almonds	looz

barley	shi'iir
bulghur	burghul
carob	kharruub
chickpeas	Hummus
couscous	kuskusi
filberts (hazelnuts)	bundu'
lentils	'ads
peanuts	fuul sudaani
pecans	bikaan
pinenuts	sineebar
pistachios	fuzdu'
popcorn	fishaar
pumpkin seeds	libb abyaD
sunflower seeds	libb suuri
walnuts	'een gamal

HERBS (a'shaab) AND SPICES (tawaabil; buharaat)

ground	maTHuun
whole	SiHiiH
allspice	buharaat
anise seed	yansuun
basil	riHaan
bayleaf	wara' lawra
capers	abu khangar
caraway	karawya
cardamom	Habbahaan
cayenne	shaTTa
celery seeds	bizr karafs
chard (leaves)	sal'
chicory	shikurya
chili powder	filfil aHmar amrikaani
spring onion	baSal akhDar
cinnamon	'irfa
cloves	'urunfil
coriander	kuzbara
coriander, fresh	kuzbara khaDra
cumin	kammuun
curry powder	kaari
dill	shabat
fennel	shamar
fennel seeds	Habbit il-baraka
fenugreek	Hilba
garlic	toom
ginger	ganzabiil
green mixed spices	khuDra (dill, parsley, coriander, and/or chard)

horseradish	figl baladi
mace	bisbaasa
mint	na'naa'
mixed spices	buharaat (nutmeg, cinnamon, sweet pepper)
nutmeg	guzt it-tiib
oregano	za'tar
paprika	paprika; filfil ruumi
parsley	ba'duunis
pepper	filfil
pepper, black	filfil iswid
pepper, hot	shaTTa
pepper, white	filfil abyaD
peppercorns	'arn filfil
rosemary	HaSa libaan
saffron	'uSfur; za'faraan (usually not genuine)
sage	maryamiyya
salt	malH
savory	stoorya
sesame seeds	simsim
tarragon	Tarkhuun
thyme	za'tar
turmeric	kurkum
vanilla	vanilya

FOOD STAPLES

baking powder	bakinbawdar
baking soda	bikarbunaat
candy	bunboon
chocolate	shukalaaTa
cookies (biscuits)	baskoot
cornstarch	nisha
flour	di'ii'
gelatin	jelatiin
honey	'asal abyaD
hot sauce	hut soos; shaTTa
ketchup	katshab
mayonnaise	mayuneez
molasses	'asal iswid
mustard	mustarda
oil	zeet
oil, corn	zeet dura
oil, olive	zeet zatuun
oil, safflower	zeet 'uSfur
oil, sunflower	zeet suuri
pasta	makaroona
rice	ruzz

salt	malH
sugar	sukkar
sugar, icing	sukkar budra
vinegar	khall
wine vinegar	khall 'inab
Worcestershire sauce	lii an birinz
yeast	khamiira

BEVERAGES

alcohol	kuHuul; khamra
alcoholic beverages	khumuur
beer	biira
cocoa	kakaw
coffee	'awha
hibiscus tea	karkadeeh
juice	'aSiir
soft drinks	[use brand name]; haaga sa''a
tea	shayy
water	mayya
water, mineral	mayya ma'daniyya
wine	nibiit

CLOTHING (huduum)

do you have — —?	'andak/ik — —?
my size	ma'aasi
I need size — —	'ayz/a ma'aas — —
medium	mutawassiT
large, larger	kibiir/a, akbar
small, smaller	Sughayyar/a, aSghar
same style, different color	nafs il-stayl bass loon taani
bathing suit	mayooh
bathrobe	burnuus
blouse	biluuza
brassiere	sutyaan
cardigan	biluuvar maftuuH
coat	balTu
dress	fustaan
jacket	jaakit
nightgown	'amiiS noom
pajamas	bijaama
panties	kilutt
pantihose	kuloon
pants (trousers)	bantaloon
scarf	isharb

scarf, wool	kufiyya
shawl	shaal
shirt	'amiiS
shoes	gazma
shoelaces	rubaaT
skirt	jiiba; juup
slip / underskirt	'amiiS taHtaani
slippers	shibshib
socks	shuraab
suit	badla
suit jacket	jakitta
suit, women's	tayiir
sweater	swiitar; biluuvar
undershirt	fanilla
underwear, men's	slibb

COLORS

light	faatiH/a
dark	ghaami'/a
plain	saada
patterned	man'uush/a
striped	mi'allim/a
beige	beej
black	iswid / suda
blue	azra' / zar'a
blue, pale	labani
blue, navy	kuHli
brown	bunni
gray	rumaadi
gold	dahabi
green	akhDar / khaDra
maroon	nibiiti
orange	burtu'aani
pink	bamba
purple	moov
purple, violet	banafsigi
purple, royal	bidingaani
red	aHmar / Hamra
white	abyaD / beeDa
silver	faDDi
violet	banafsigi
yellow	aSfar / Safra

FABRICS ('umaash)

canvas	kheesh; 'umaash khiyam
cotton	'uTn
corduroy	'aTiifa
flannel	kastuur
leather	gild
linen	tiil; kittaan
silk	Hariir
suede	shamwaa
velvet	'atiifa
wool	Suuf

VERY IMPORTANT PEOPLE

I need a/an — — who is excellent, honest, and reasonably priced

'ayz/a — — mumtaaz, amiin, wa mish ghaali

barber	hallaa'
cabinetmaker	naggaar
carpenter	naggaar
doorkeeper	bawwaab
dressmaker	khayaaT/a
driver	sawwaa'
drycleaner	tanturleeh
dyer	maSbagha
electrician	kahrabaa'i
exterminator	raagil yurushsh il-beet
gardener	gineeni
hairdresser	kwafeer
ironer	makwagi
maid	shaghghaala
mailman	bustagi
nanny	naani
painter	na''aash; mibayyaD
plumber	sabbaak
servant	sufragi
tailor (men's)	tarzi rigaali
tailor (women's)	tarzi Hariimi
translator	mutargim

FURNISHINGS (farsh) AND FURNITURE (mubiliya)

used furniture	mubliliya musta'mal
awning	tanda
bed	siriir
blanket	baTTaniyya

bookcase	maktaba
chair	kursi
crib / cradle	mahd
cupboard	dulaab
curtain	sitaara
desk	maktab
file cabinet	shaanun
lamp	abajuura
lampshade	burneetit abajuura
mirror	miraaya
picture frame	birwaaz
pillow (bed)	makhadda
pillow (floor)	shalta
pillow (sofa)	khudadiyya
sheet	milaaya
shelf	raff
sofa	kanaba
shutters	shiish
table	tarabeeza
table, dining	sufra
tent	khiima
tentmaker	khayyaam
towel	fuuTa
towel, large	bashkiir
toys	li'b aTfal

HANDY HOUSEHOLD TERMS AND ITEMS

this — — doesn't work / is broken	il- — — da / di bayZ/a
this chair is broken	il-kursi da bayZ
this table is broken	il-tarabeeza di bayZa
clean (adj.)	niDiif/a
dirty	mish niDiif/a
air conditioner	mukayyif
air filter	filtar hawa
bathroom	Hammaam
bathtub	banyu
batteries	Higaara
bedroom	oodit noom
bucket	gardal
butagaz tank	anbuuba
candles	sham'
dining room	oodit sufra
door	baab
drawer	durg
drill	shanyuur

electrical switch	muftaaH nuur
electrical outlet	bariiza
elevator (lift)	asanseer
extension cord	waSla; silk
faucet (tap)	Hanafiyya
flashlight (torch)	baTTariyya
floor	arD
flowerpot	'asriyya
flowers	ward
freezer	friizar
garden hose	kharTuum gineena
hammer	shakuush
heater	daffaaya
ice	talg
key	muftaaH
kitchen	maTbakh
living room	oodit saloon
lock	kaloon
mop	mamsaHa
multiplug socket	mushtarak
newspaper	gurnaal
oven	furn
padlock	'ifl
rat(s)	faar (firaan)
receipt	faTuura
recipe	waSfa
refrigerator	tallaaga
roaches	SaraSiir
scissors	ma'aSS
screwdriver	mifakk
shower	dushsh
sink	HooD
sponge	safinga
stairs	sillim
stove / cooker (butane)	butagaaz
subscription	ishtiraak
toilet	twalitt
towel rack	fawwaaTa
transformer	tarans
voltage stabilizer	stibilayzar
washing machine	ghassaala
water heater	sakhkhaan
water pressure	DaghT il-mayya
window	shibbaak
window screen	silk shibbaak

CARS AND CAR TROUBLE

fill it up	fawwilha
I'm having trouble with my car	fii mushkila ma' 'arabiiti
I think it's the — —	aftikir hiyya fi-l-— —
battery	baTTariyya
car	'arabiyya
carburetor	karbiriteer
engine	mutoor
fuel line	sikkit il-banziin
gas (petrol)	banziin
gas (petrol) station	maHattit banziin
gasket	juwaan
headlight	fanuus
ignition	marsh / kuntakt
oil	zeet
shock absorber	musaa'id
spark plugs	bujihaat
steering	diriksyoon
tire	kawitsh
wheel	'agala

DIRECTORY

Note: Entries are largely recommendation-based, except for categories such as Airlines, Banks, Embassies, Theaters, etc. The Arabic for 'street,' *shaari'* (sharia), is not included; use it in front of the street name when giving addresses.

ABBREVIATIONS

AG: Agouza
CA: Cairo International Airport
DT: Downtown Cairo
DK: Dokki
GC: Garden City
GA: Gazira
GZ: Giza
HE: Heliopolis
KK: Khan al-Khalili
MA: Maadi
MN: Manyal
MO: Mohandiseen
NC: Nasr City
PY: Pyramids
WTC: World Trade Center
ZA: Zamalek

EMERGENCY AND OTHER IMPORTANT NUMBERS

Ambulance	123
Bill inquiry	177
Cairo governorate	13
Complaints	160
Directory inquiry	140
Directory inquiry	141
Directory inquiry	142
Electricity information	121
Fire brigade	180
International inquiry	144
International operator	120
Petrogas	129
Police help	122
Emergency Road Service	
012 111-0000	
Water 575 7416	

DOCTORS

Central beeper dispatch telephones: 577-7474 and 575-1851. Dial and give dispatcher your doctor's beeper number in English, French, or Arabic.

With real touch-tone phone only: Dial 010, then doctor's beeper number. Wait for tone, then enter your own telephone number followed by two hash signs (# #).

HOSPITAL EMERGENCY AND AMBULANCE

Arab Contractors Hospital, Nasr City, 342-6000

Misr International Hospital, Dokki, 760-8261, 335-3658

As-Salam Int'l Hospital, Corniche al-Nil, 524-0077

Nil Badrawi Hospital, Corniche al-Nil, 524-0212, 524-0022

Al-Salam, Mohandiseen, 302-9970, 302-9091–5

'Ain Shams Specialized, 'Abbassiya 260-7589

DIRECTORY INFORMATION

140 or 141, www.140online.com

TELEPHONE CENTRALE NUMBERS (FOR SERVICE, REPAIRS, COMPLAINTS)

Bab al-Luq, 796-1717
Dokki, 337-4259
Garden City, 794-8390
Giza, 570-0701
Heliopolis, 638-9013
Maadi 1, 358-9805
Maadi 2, 702-1695
Mohandiseen, 346-4466
Zamalek, 736-1519

LOCAL NUMBERS FOR INTERNATIONAL LONG-DISTANCE SERVICE

AT&T, 510-0200
MCI, 795-5770
Sprint, 796-4777

LOST/STOLEN CREDIT CARDS

American Express, 570-3411/2–9, 569-3299 (24 hr.), fax 570-3147

Diners Club, 578-3355, 736-8778, fax 579-4936

Mastercard, 797-1179, 796-2844, 796-2966, fax 393-1504/1415.

Visa, 796-2877, 797-1149

IMPORTANT NUMBERS

Alcoholics Anonymous (AA), Meetings in HE, GC, MA, contact CSA below

Al-Anon: contact AA or CSA (below)

Befrienders Cairo, 762-1602/3, e-mail: befriending@befrienderscairo.org.eg

British Community Association (BCA), 2 'Abd al-Rahman al-Rifa'i, MO

Community Services Association (CSA), 4 Rd. 21, MA, 358-0754, 358-5284

Fire Department, 125 or 391-0115

Nadim Center for Victims of Violence (abuse, torture), director Dr. Suzanne Fayad

Tourist Police, 126 or 391-0115

Western Union Money Transfer, Cairo Hotline, 797-1374/5/85/86 (9 am–10 pm); fax 797-1386.

Federal Express 797-1300

Cairo International Airport (new airport), 267-5882/42/22
Cairo International Airport (old airport), 265-5000
TWA, 574-9904/5/6/7/8, 574-9913/4/5/6
EgyptAir, 390-0999, 390-2444, 265-7055; call center: 0900-7000, mobile, 1717
Flight Information, 0900-77777; mobile, 2777. Information Desk at Terminal 1, 265-5000/1/2/3; Terminal 2 Departures, 265-2222; Arrivals, 265-2077
Ramsis Train Station, 579-0767, 575-3555/1

ACCOUNTING FIRMS

Allied Accountants (Arthur Andersen), Mobica Tower, 37 al-Ahrar, MO, 336-2000, fax 760-0813
BDO Saleh Barsoum, 'Abd al-Aziz & Co., 95C al-Mirghani, HE, 290-3278, fax 290-4038
Farid S. Mansour (Coopers & Lybrand), Tiba 2000 Center, Rabi'a al-'Adawiya, NC, 260-8500, fax 261-3204
KPMG Hazem Hassan, 72 Muhi al-Din Abu al-'Izz, MO, 336-9094/8, fax 749-7224/748-7819
Nawar & Co., International Chartered Accountants, 21 Tal'at Harb, DT, 391-6987, fax 392-1615
Price Waterhouse P.W., 4 Rd. 261, MA, 516-8169, fax 703-0915
Shawki & Co., Deloitte Touche, Tohmatsu International, Banque Misr Tower, 153 Muhammad

Farid, 19th-20th fl., DT, 392-6000/6111/6400, 391-7299, fax 393-9430
Youssef Nabih & Co., 22 Qasr al-Nil, DT, 393-7801/2/3, fax 393-7804

AEROBICS

See Sports

AIR CONDITIONERS & REPAIR

Adel Serour, 16 'Abd al-Hamid Adel Serour, 16 'Abd al-Hamid Lutfi, MO, 335-2965, fax 335-2781 (also heating, ventilators)
Al Tawheed Co., 7th Area 15/13 al-'Uruba, MA, 703-6242
Seven Engineers, 1 El Obour Building, Salah Salim, 401-5694
Spring Air Co., 90-92 Musaddaq, DK, 335-0362, 335-52071, fax 336-0728

AIRLINES

Aeroflot, 18 al-Bustan, Bab al-Luq, DT, 390-0429/393-7409, fax 390-0407; CA, 291-4602
Air Algeria, 13 Qasr al-Nil, DT, 574-0688, 575-0688, fax 574-0686; CA, 291-0409
Air Canada, c/o Imperial Travel, 26 Mahmud Basyuni, 575-8939/8402, 578-4658, 578-4634, fax 574-3322; CA, 417-1979
Air France, 2 Midan Tal'at Harb, DT, 770-6262, fax 577-1744; CA, 417-5306/07
Air India, 1 Tal'at Harb, DT, 392-2592, 393-4873/75, fax 393-4875
Air Malta, Trade Center, Nile

Hilton Hotel, DT, 575-6022, fax 574-4184
Air Sinai, Nile Hilton Hotel, Midan al-Tahrir, DT, 577-2949, 576-0750
Alitalia, Nile Hilton Hotel, Midan al-Tahrir, DT, 576-7109, fax; CA, 418-8168/9
American Airlines, 20 al-Gihad, Midan Libnan, MO, 345-5707, 347-0033; c/o Emeco Travel, 2 Tal'at Harb, DT, 574-9360, 390-7045, 578-5901/2, fax 574-4212
Austrian Airlines, 4D al-Gazira, ZA, 735-2777, fax 738-2815
Aviation Int'l Scorpio (charters only), 17 Midan Aswan, MO, 346-3709, fax 346-1287
British Airways, 1 'Abd al-Salam 'Arif, off Midan al-Tahrir, 578-0742/3/4/5/6, fax 574-7674; MA, 358-2264/65; CA, 690-1690
Bulgarian Airlines, 17 Qasr al-Nil, DT, 393-1152, fax 393-9199
Cathay Pacific, 20 al-Gihad, Midan Libnan, MO, 302-9627/8, fax 302-9627
Continental Airlines, c/o Imperial Travel, 26 Mahmud Basyuni, DT, 575-8402, 578-4634/58, fax 574-9129
Cyprus Airways, 10 Tal'at Harb, Evergreen Tower, 579-7400
Czech Airlines (CSA), 9 Tal'at Harb, DT, 393-0395, 392-0463; CA, 265-4766
Delta Airlines, c/o Five Continents, Jeddah Tower, 17 Isma'il Muhammad, ZA, 737-0861, fax 736-2696

EgyptAir, 9 Tal'at Harb, DT, 393-0381, call center: 0900-70000, fax 392-7664; Nile Hilton Hotel, 577-2410, 579-3049; Mövenpick Hotel, 418-3720; Cairo Sheraton, 748-9122, fax 748-8630; 26th July, MO, 347-5193; 22 Ibrahim al-Laqqani, HE, 290-4528; CA, 634-1460

El Al Airlines, 5 Maqrizi, ZA, 736-1795, 736-1620, fax 736-1620; CA, x3821 or 268-2931

Emirates Airlines, 18 Wizerit al-Zira'a, MO, 336-1555, fax 748-4202, CA, 418-0305, fax 291-9039

Ethiopian Airlines, Nile Hilton Hotel, Midan al-Tahrir, DT, 574-0911/0785/0852, fax 574-0189; CA, 265- 4398

Finnair, 15 Midan al-Tahrir, 1st floor, DT, 579-8602, fax 578-0979

Gulf Air, 64 Gam'at al-Duwal al-'Arabiya, MO, 748-7781/83 fax 749-0955; 21 Mahmud Basyuni, 575-0852, 575-8391, fax 574-9129

Iberia Airlines, 15 Midan al-Tahrir, 2nd floor, 579-5600; 97 al-Muntazah, HE, 575-1514; 62 al-Nasr, MA, 516-7195, fax 516-7177; Nile Street, Nasr Building, GZ, 748-2989/5452, fax 760-8959; CA, 417-7297, fax 290-5190

KLM, 11 Qasr al-Nil, DT,580-5757, 580-5747, 580-5700, fax 580-5707; 44 al-'Uruba, HE, 418-2388/9, fax 418-2389; freight: 291-2509, 290-6043, fax 574-7330; CA, 418-2386/7

Kenya Airlines, 11 Qasr al-Nil, DT, 574-7004, 580-5757,

580-5747, 580-5761/2, fax 579-8530; CA, 265-2246, 291-4386, fax 265-2249

Korean Airlines, c/o Emeco Travel, 2 Tal'at Harb, DT, 578-5902, 574-9360

Kuwait Airlines, 10 Tal'at Harb, DT, 574-2447, fax 574-5157; CA, 291-9591

Lufthansa, 6 al-Sheikh al-Marsafi, ZA, 739-8339, fax 737-0475; CA, 417-6419, fax 418-5210

Malaysian Airlines, Nile Hilton 579-9714/5, fax 579-971; CA 266-3146, fax 266-3144

Malev-Hungarian Airlines, 25 Mansour, ZA, 735-2196, fax 575-3111; CA, 265-3783

Middle East Airlines (MEA), 12 Qasr al-Nil, DT, 575-0736, 575-0888, fax 574-2157; CA, 415-3670/5396

Olympic Airways, 23 Qasr al-Nil, DT, 393-1318, 392-0919, fax 391-0574; CA, 290-5878

Pakistan International Airlines (PIA), 22 Qasr al-Nil, 393-1868, 737-2940

Portugal Airlines, c/o Emeco Travel, 2 Tal'at Harb, DT, 578-5901/2, fax 574-4184

Qatar Airlines, 13 Midan al-Tahrir, DT, 575-3208/0343, fax 575-0057

Royal Air Maroc, 9 Tal'at Harb, DT, 392-2956, fax 393-4574; CA, 290-8698

Royal Brunei, 44 Muhammad Mazhar, ZA, 739-2940, fax 737-2464

Royal Jordanian, 6 Qasr al-Nil, DT, 575-0875/905, CA, 418-9536

SAS, 2 Champollion, DT, 575-3955/627/546/718, fax 576-1005

Saudia Arabian Airlines, 5 Qasr al-Nil, DT, 574-1200, fax 577-4909

Singapore Airlines, Nile Hilton Hotel, Midan al-Tahrir, DT, 575-0276, 578-8777, fax 574-7084; CA, 291-5144

Sudan Airways, 1 'Abd al-Salam 'Arif, DT, 578-7299/398, fax 575-9946; CA, 418-4181, 415-0049

Swiss, 4 Behler Passage, Qasr al-Nil DT, reservations 396-1737, information 396-1733/4, fax 391-6080; CA, 291-0283/9

Syrian Arab Airlines, 25 Tal'at Harb, DT, 392-8284/5, fax 391-0805; CA, 392-8284/5

Tunis Air, 14 Tal'at Harb, DT, 575-3476, 575-3420, fax 574-0677; CA, 268-0188

Turkish Airlines, Nile Hilton Hotel, Midan al-Tahrir, DT, 574-9009, 574-9600

United Airlines, 6 al-Sheikh al-Marsafi, ZA, 739-8339

Varig (Brazilian Airways), 97 Muntaza, HE, 632-0993, 633-5230/6713, fax 635-7299

Yemenia Airways, 7 Zamalek Club, 26th July, MO, 346-6799, fax 303-4552; 10 Tal'at Harb, Evergreen Building, 2nd fl., 574-0711; CA, 636-6499

AIRPORTS

Cairo International, 244-1460, 245-9332 or switchboard 291-4255/66/77

Alexandria, (03) 459-1485/6/7

Aswan, (097) 480-320/33

Luxor, (095) 374-655, 383-294

Hurghada, (065) 442-831/3976

Sharm al-Sheikh, (069) 601-140/1/2/3/4

AIRPORT MEET & ASSIST

American Express, CA; GZ,
570-3411; DT, 574-7991/6;
HE, 418-2144/7; fax
569-3310

ALTERNATIVE THERAPIES

ACUPUNCTURE

Dr. Amgad al-Zoghbi, 11 Latif
Mansur, al-Qiyada al-
Mushtaraka, HE, 290-1624;
59A 'Abd al-Mun'im Riyad,
MO, 345-3064
Contact Mira 010 180-9501

AROMATHERAPIST

Ashling Badrawi, 735-0813

AROMATHERAPIST AND REFLEXOLOGIST

Joanne Butler, 012 370-5061,
521-0561, by appointment
only
Chi Kung practitioners:
Lotus Room, 012 370-5061
Tony Wang, 012 766-6872
Chanmin Yang, contact CSA,
376-8232; 358-5284

CHIROPRACTOR

Shamil Fahmy, 358-4470; 358-
1685

FELDENKRAIS MOVEMENT METHOD

Carol Ann Clouston, 736-1769

HERBS

Harraz Herb Shop, Bab al-Khalq

MASSAGE

Contact Mira 010 180-9501
Pam Rizk, 736-2927
Tony Wang, 012 766-6872
See Muhammad Saghir under
Beauty Salons

REIKI PRACTICTIONER

Contact Mira 010 180-9501
Women Healers Group
736-2979, Leslie Zehr

YOGA

See Yoga

AMUSEMENT PARKS

Aqua Park, Ismailiya Road, 32
km out of Cairo after al-
'Ubur market, 477-0088/99
The Beach, JW Marriott Hotel,
Mirage City, 411-5588
Cooky Park, behind Mövenpick
Jolie Ville near Pyramids
Dreamland, 6th of October
City, 840-0564/5
Dream Park, 6th of October
City, 855-3191
Fun Planet, Arkadia Mall,
Corniche al-Nil, 579-2246
Geroland, Cairo-Ismailiya
Desert Road, after al-'Ubur
market, 477-1084
Kid's Farm, 10th of Ramadan
City, Cairo-Ismailiya
Highway, next to Abu al-
Azayem Psychiatric Hospital,
Magic Galaxy, Citystars, HE
Magic Land, 6th of October,
855-5064
Magic Planet, Maadi City
Center, Exit 8 on Cairo Ring
Road
Merryland, Roxy, al-Higaz,
HE, 451-7439
Plein Air, Ahmed Orabi
Association, Land Piece 662,
Km28 Cairo–Ismailiya Road,
010 188-2315, 012
322-9462
Sindbad Amusement Park,
Ismailiya Road, near Airport
Wonderland, end of 'Abbas al-
'Aqqad, NC

ANTIQUES & ANTIQUE REPRODUCTIONS

DOWNTOWN

Ahmed Zeinhoum, Huda
Sha'rawi

Gallery Baha, 28 Bustan,
393-0344
Gallery Hamada, 44 Qasr al-
Nil
Hassan & Ali, Huda Sha'rawi
Louvre Meuble, 14 Huda
Sha'rawi
Mahrous, Huda Sha'rawi
Philippe Devlay, 9 'Urabi,
574-6349

HELIOPOLIS

Ashraf & Khalid, Midan (brass
beds) al-Gami', 241-8417,
mobile 012 211-6193
Hamdi Fayek, 49 Hurriya,
241-8417
Poupi Interiors, 5 Siti (off
Baghdad), 419-9991
Sadek Gayed and Sons, 7
Talkha (at Midan al-Gami'),
241-8417
Sucash, 12 'Abd al-Mun'im
Hafiz, 390-2695

KHAN AL-KHALILI

Old Shoppe, 7 Khan al-Khalili

MAADI

Bric-a-Brac, 43 Misr-Helwan
Rd. near Bukhara Restaurant
Morgana, 57 Rd. 9, 380-2370
Nelly Essawy, 703-35599
Patu Antiques, El Karnak
Tower behind Military
Hospital, 364-8835
El Safa, 41 Rd. 7, 358-7948

MISCELLANEOUS

Khatun, 3 Zuqaq al-'Ain, off
Sheikh Muhammad 'Abdu,
behind al-Azhar next to Bayt
al-Harawi, 514-7164, 012
226-5329

MOHANDISEEN

Clarine, 11 Suliman Abaza,
760-8393
Samia Imports, 42 'Abd al-
Halim Husayn, MO

ZAMALEK

Atrium, 4 Muhammad Mazhar, 735-6869; owner: :Nermine Mokhtar

Avenue 30, 30 al-Gazira al-Wusta, 735-6058

Caravanserai, 16 Muhammad al-Mar'ashli

Galerie Odeon, 110 26th July

Nostalgia, 6 Zakaria Rizq, 737-0880; contact: Mr. Marwan

Noubi Antiquaire, 157 26th July, 735-1385, 345-2331

ANTIQUES, RESTORATION & REPAIR

Ahmed Seif, Samia Imports, 42 'Abd al-Halim Husayn, MO

Ayman El-Azabawi, Morgana, 57 Rd. 9, MA, 380-2370

Guido Leone, 5 Suliman al-Halabi (off Ramsis), DT, 574-2771

APPLIANCES

Electric House, 3 Wahib Dos, MA, 358-7029 (local & imported, also satellite dishes); contact: Nasr

FutureHome, 23 al-Nahda at Rd. 6, MA, 380-8555; fax 380-8444

Genedy, 51 Ahmad 'Urabi, MO, 347-0095-6 and 52 Shahab, MO, 303-3001, 344-1018 (large appliances)

Helwagi Electric, 60 Suliman Guhar, DK, 749-3242

Maison Khedr, 14 Baghdad, HE, 290-7314 (small appliances)

Ogeil, 134 26th July, ZA, 735-4368

APPLIANCE REPAIRS

Abraham, 298-7756

Magdi Mahmud, 2 Mi'mar Fahmi, off Muhammad Mahmud, DT, 794-1604

Mohsen Gomaa, GZ, office 561-6755, home 561-3741, mob. 012 216-0025

Osman Group, 4 & 23 Rd. 205, Digla, MA, 754-3575/7787, 520-1669, 519-6152

ARCHAEOLOGY

American Research Center in Egypt (ARCE), 2 Midan Qasr al-Dubara, GC, 794-8239, 795-8683, fax 795-3052; e-mail: arce@internetegypt.com

Egyptian Antiquities Project, 2 Midan Qasr al-Dubara, GC, phone/fax 796-4681; e-mail: arceeap@internetegypt.com

Egypt Exploration Society, at the British Council, 192 al-Nil, AG, 303-1514, 347-6118, fax 344-3076; 4 El Minya, off Nazih Khalifa, HE, 452-3395/7, fax 258-3660; e-mail: british.council@britishcouncil.org.eg, contact: Rosalind Phipps

Netherlands Institute, Dr. Mahmud Azmi, ZA, 735-0076

ARCHITECTS

Dr. 'Abd al-Halim Ibrahim, 391-1656, 760-2858

Gamal Amer, 012 315-1132, e-mail: GamalAmer@hotmail.com

Ibrahim Nagi, 335-6576

Markus El-Katcha, 301-5402

Dr. Mona Zakaria, 760-3191

Rami El Dehan and Soheir Farid Assoc., 344-2481

ARCHITECTURE

SPARE (Society for the Preservation of the Architectural Resources of Egypt); contact ARCE, 2 Midan Qasr al-Dubara, GC, 794-8239, 795-8683, fax 795-3052; e-mail: arce@internetegypt.com

ART CLASSES

DOKKI

Francophone Art Academy in Cairo (AFCA), 37 Iran, 338-0205/3199, 012 467-3435, e-mail: afca.infos@gmail.com

HELIOPOLIS

Art and Design School, 7 Baghdad, al-Kurba, HE, 415-9752

Art Room, 27A Baghdad, Kurba Center, al-Kurba, HE, 291-7231, 290-7616, fax 291-3878

Fagnoon Sabil Om Hashim, Saqqara Rd., 12.5 km from al-Haram Rd., 815-1014

El Madyafa, 34 Nabil al-Waqqad, Ard al-Gulf next to Bon Appetit, 418-7809; 419-8111, Shaheera Fawzi

MAADI

Community Services Association (CSA), 4 Rd. 21, 376-8232, 358-5284, fax 376-8319

Studio 206, 18 Rd. 200, Digla, MA, 519-5713

The Workshop, 38 Rd. 6 (next to Conserv by the flyover)

ART GALLERIES

DOKKI

Atelier 87, Marwat al-Zahraa, 337-2553

Atelier Palette, 25 Rifaa, Midan al-Misaha

Bashayer, 58 Musaddaq (upstairs), 337-3233

Horizon One Gallery, 1 Kafur, DK, 748-2156

Orman Gallery, 48 al-Giza, 749-8627

DOWNTOWN, GARDEN CITY, AND OTHER

The American University in Cairo, Midan al-Tahrir, Falaki Art Gallery, 797-6376; Ewart Gallery, 797-5022; Sony Gallery at Adham Center, AUC, Midan al-Tahrir, 797-5422

Arabesque, 6 Qasr al-Nil, 794-8677

Atelier du Caire, 2 Karim al-Dawla, DT, 574-6730

British Council, 192 al-Nil, AG, 300-1666

Contemporary Image Collective (CIC), 20 Safiya Zaghlul, Munira, 794-1686, 012 115-8700

Duroub Gallery, 4 Amrika al-Latiniya, 794-7951

Espace Karim Francis, 1 al-Sharifein (off Qasr al-Nil), 736-2183

Gallery Salama, 36A Ahmad 'Urabi, MO, 346-3242, 344-8109, e-mail: salamagallery@hotmail.com

Mashrabia, 8 Champollion, Midan al-Tahrir (Stephania Angarano), 578-4494

Orient Express the apARTment, 21 'Abd al-Mun'im Riyad, MO., 749-7808

Townhouse Gallery, 10 Nabrawi, off Champollion, 576-8086

HELIOPOLIS

Hend Shalabi, 38 Sheikh 'Ali Mahmud, 635-8234

Kharamana, 32 Ishaq Ya'qub, 290-4644

Mesteka Art Gallery, 83 al-Hurriya, 290-1143

Noun Gallery, 4 Mahmud Abu al-'Uyun (off Hegaz), 638-0082

Al Nuqta (calligraphy), 415-7038

MAADI

Gamila Gallery, 23 Rd. 233, Digla, 521-2294

Graffiti, 28d Rd. 232, Nerco Complex, Digla, 521-2044

Haddouta Amir, New Maadi, 702-4352

Mansour, 116 Rd. 9, 358-3707

Le Touche, Midan al-Ittihad and Rd. 106

Al-Shomou Art Gallery, 12 Rd. 150, Midan al-Hurriya, 358-3142

World of Art Gallery and Framing, 6 Rd. 77C, 359-4363

ZAMALEK

Akhnaton Gallery V (Center of Arts), 1 al-Ma'had al-Swisri, 735-8211

Alef, 14 Muhammad Anis, 735-3690

Anas al-Wagoud, 23B Isma'il Muhammad, 6th fl., flat 40, 736-8189

Egyptian Center for Cultural Cooperation, 11 Shagarit al-Durr, 736-5419

Extra, 3 al-Nasim, 735-6293

Faculty of Fine Arts, 4 Muhammad Ibn Thaqib, 735-7570

Fine Arts Gallery, 173 26th July, 737-0904

Four Seasons, 11 Hasan Sabri, 736-3601

Gezira Art Center, 1 al-Sheikh al-Marsafi, 737-3298

Hanager Arts Center, Opera House Complex, 735-6861

Khan al-Maghraby, 18 Mansur Muhammad, 735-3349

La Bodega & Karim Francis Contemporary Art Gallery, Baehler's Mansion, 3rd fl., 156 26th July, 738-1525

Mervat Masoud Gallery, 6 Gazira, 736-2493

Museum of Egyptian Modern Art, Opera Complex, 736-6665

El Mustardia, 1 Mahmud Mukhtar, 736-8005

El Nil, Gezira Exhibition Grounds, 736-8796

Nostalgia, 6 Zakaria Rizq, 737-0880

Picasso, 30 Hasan 'Asim, 736-7544

Riyash, 6 al-Gazira al-Wusta, 735-9994

Safar Khan, 6 Brazil, 735-3314

Sheba Gallery, 6 Sri Lanka, 735-9192

Zamalek Art Gallery, 11 Brazil, 735-1240, 012 224-1062

ARTS & CRAFTS

DOKKI

Al Ain Gallery, 73 Husayn, 338-1342-, 749-3940

Bashayer, 58 Musaddaq

Shahira Mehrez & Companions, 12 Abi Imam (left-hand entrance between Omar Effendi and Cairo Sheraton), 3rd fl., 748-7814

HELIOPOLIS

Association for the Protection of the Environment, 7 Suliman Basha Sayyid, 341-2723

Oasis, 3 Mahmud Nashid (off Harun al-Rashid)

Sahara-El Souk, 34 Nabil al-Waqqad next to Bon Appetit, 418-7809

MAADI

Bedouin Market 15 Rd. 231,
Digla
Catacomb, Building 3, Rd 231,
Basement, 518-6321
El Patio, 4 Rd. 77, Ard al-Gulf,
359-6654
Morgana, 57 Rd. 9, 380-2370
Per Nefer, Maadi Grand Mall,
703-8261
The Workshop, 38 Rd. 6
World of Art Gallery and
Framing, 6 Rd. 77C, 359-4363

MISCELLANEOUS

Bayt al-Sinnari Workshop,
Haret Monge (off Port Said
toward Sayyida Zeinab)
Khatun, 3 Zuqaq al-'Ain, off
Sheikh Muhammad 'Abdu,
behind al-Azhar next to Bayt
al-Harawi, 514-7164, 012
226-5329
Marisa & Ismail, 17 Ahmad
Tulun, opp. Ibn Tulun
Mosque, 257-9422
Nabil Darwish Studio, Saqqara
Road, Harraniya 385-5894
(Pottery)
Nagada, 8 Dar al-Shifa', GC,
792-3249
Oum el Dounia, 3 Tal'at Harb,
1st floor, 393-8273
Senouhi, 54 'Abd al-Khaliq
Sarwat, 5th fl., DT, 391-0955.
Wikalat al-Ghuri Workshop,
near al-Azhar
Wissa Wassef Studios, Saqqara
Road, Harraniya, 385-0746;
contact: Suzanne Wissa
Wassef

MOHANDISEEN

Samir El Guindi (The Mud
Factory), 261 Sudan, 347-
3445/7032 (Pottery)

ZAMALEK

Bayt Sherif, 3A Bahgat 'Ali,
736-5689

Egypt Crafts Center, 27 Yahya
Ibrahim, Apt. 8, 736-5123,
fax 735-0387;
www.egyptcrafts.com
Nomad, Cairo Marriott,
736-2132; 14 Saray al-
Gazira, 1st fl., 736-1917;
owner: Carol Sidky
Sami Amin, 15 Mansur
Muhammad, 736-1424

AUCTIONS

Catsoros, 22 Gawwad Hosni,
DT, 392-6123
Osiris, 17 Sharif, DT, 392-6609

BABY SUPPLIES

Baby Admiral, 749-4195, cloth
diapers made in Egypt
La Leche League, contact CSA,
358-5284
Our Kids, Mustafa al-Nahhas
(beside Pizza Hut), NC,
274-8741; 5 Midan al-
Misaha, DK, 336-3602
Taki, 685-4422, bedding,
furniture, etc.
Zero 2 Five, Carrefour, City
Center, MA, 520-4412; 13
al-Kurum, 749-7034

BAKERIES

DOKKI

Abu Higazi, 1 Wizarat al-
Zira'a (for fiTiir)
La Parisienne, al-Husayn and
al-Tahrir Streets.

DOWNTOWN

Etman, 17 Muhammad
Mahmud past AUC Library,
794-9160 (croissants)
La Chesa, 21 'Adli, 393-
9360/5768

HELIOPOLIS

La Palma, 3 al-Qubba, Roxy,
258-3998/2743 (24 hr.)

MAADI

The City Baker, 7 Rd. 261,
New Maadi, 520-3511; 82
Rd. 9, 380-6841
Mirabelle, 71 Rd. 9
Swiss Gourmet Bakery, 516
Rd. 231, 516-5783

MISCELLANEOUS

Bon Appetit, 21 Wadi al-Nil,
MO, 346-4937/303-5815; 2
Isma'il Muhammad, ZA,
735-4382; HE, 632
4734/4736/4754
La Poire, DK 749-6931; GC
795-1509; MO 346-2766;
GZ 752-3497; PY 584-2803;
NC 275-3771; MA 358-
7179; ZA 736-2388
Le Bec Sucré, Midan Sheikh
Yusuf, GC, 795-6792; 105
al-Mirghani, HE, 290-4165;
14 Rd. 218, MA, 702-5908;
22 Taha Husayn, ZA, 735-
0652/0718
Marriott Bakery, Marriot Hotel,
ZA, 735-8888; 10 'Abbas al-
'Aqqad, NC, 401-6610;
26/27 Gam'at al-Duwal al-
'Arabiya, MO 304-2527; 1
Rd. 151, MA, 526-4515; 7
al-Nasr, New Maadi, MA,
516-8873; 2 Hashim al-
Ashkar, New Nuzha, HE,
295-9261
Rigoletto, Yamama Ctr., 3
Taha Husayn, ZA, 735-
8684; MA 380-9318; MN
702-2665

MOHANDISEEN

La Brioche, 7 'Abd al-Mun'im
Riyad, 760-6121
Trianon, 17/18 Zamalek Club
Gate, Gam'at al-Duwal al-
'Arabiya, 345-2012,
347-0838

ZAMALEK

Postres, 2 al-Gazira al-Wusta, Abu al-Fida, 735-0815 x422

Soufflé, Hasan Sabri, 735-2833/5133

BALLS

Marine Ball, US embassy, DT, 795-7371, (annual, Nov.)

Queen's birthday, British embassy, DT, 794-0850, (annual, June)

BANKS

African Arab Egyptian Bank, 5 Midan al-Saray al-Kubra, GC, 794-5094, 761-6623, fax 795-6239

American Express, head office 4 Syria, MO, 760-1564, 760-5258, 760-5256, fax 760-8227; 72 'Umar Ibn al-Khattab, HE, 290-9528, fax 290-9527; 6 Gezira, ZA, 738-2118; 7 Lazoughly, GC, 791-0003, fax 792-4919

Arab American International Bank, 5 Midan al-Saray al-Kubra, GC, 792-1505, 794-3193, fax 795-8493

Arab Bank PLC, 50 Gazirit al-'Arab, MO, 301-2135, 302-9069/70, fax 302-9068

Arab International Bank, 35 'Abd al-Khaliq Sarwat, DT, 391-6391/8021, fax 391-6233

Arab Investment Bank, 8 'Abd al-Khaliq Sarwat, DT, 575-9249, 576-0031, 577-0376, fax 576-6916

Bank al-Mashriq (formerly Bank of Oman Ltd.), 21 Giza, Nile Tower, GZ, 571-0418, fax 571-0423

Bank of Alexandria, 49 Qasr al-Nil, DT, 574-8226, fax 391-9805

Bank of Commerce & Development (al-Tegaryoon) 13 26th July, Midan Sphinx, MO, 347-5584, 344-0585, international div. 344-7537, fax 305-0043

Bank of Nova Scotia, 3 Ahmad Nasim, GZ, 336-5731/4/5, fax 336-5730

Banque du Caire, 22 'Adli, DT, 393-5428, 390-9575, fax 393-1317; 30 Rushdy, DT, 390-6414, 390-8386

Banque du Caire et de Paris, 43 Musaddaq, DK, 345-9356/7, 795-1585, 761-2038

Banque Francaise du Commerce Exterieur, Representative Office, 48/50 'Abd al-Khaliq Sarwat, 3rd floor, DT, 390-4667/5173, fax 391-5705

Banque Misr, 151 Muhammad Farid, DT, 391-2150/2106, fax 391-9779

Banque Nationale de Paris, Representative Office, Nile Hilton Commercial Center, Midan al-Tahrir, DT, 579-1534/1, fax 579-1536

Banque Paribas, 6A Ghandi, GC, 794-7323,795-7278, fax 795-5082

Barclays International S.A.E., 12 Midan al-Sheikh Yusuf, GC, 366-2600, fax 366-2810/11

BNP Paribas Le Caire, 3 Amrika al-Latiniya, GC, 794-8321/4/5, fax 795-8156, 794-0619

Central Bank of Egypt, 31 Qasr al-Nil, DT, 392-7717, 393-1514, fax 392-5045

Chase Manhattan Bank, 3 Ahmad Nasim, GZ, 761-0393, fax 761-0498

Citibank, 4 Ahmad Pasha, GC, 795-1873/4/5/6/7, 794-9523/7246, fax 792-2776; branches in Cairo, address all inquiries to 796-4646, fax 792-3886

Commerzbank AG, Banque Misr Tower, 22nd fl., 153 Muhammad Farid, DT, 393-1661, 390-7242, fax 392-3718, e-mail: repcairo@commerzbank.com

Commercial International Bank (CIB), Nile Tower, 21–23 Giza, GZ, 570-1951/7/8, fax 570-2691/3172;

Credit Commercial De France, representative office, 26 Mahmud Basyuni, 4th fl., DT, 578-8020, fax 577-7603

Credit Suisse First Boston, 21 Charles de Gaulle, GZ, 567-7600, fax 567-7680

Delta International, 1113 Corniche al-Nil, 575-3492, fax 576-2851

Deutsche Bank Bankers Trust, 5 al-Zuhur, MO, 336-9102/3/4, fax 336-8641

Dresdner Bank AG, Nile Tower, 12th fl., 21/23 Giza, GZ, 572-3451, 572-8168, fax 572-3782

Egyptian American Bank, 4–6 Hasan Sabri, ZA, 735-0063, 738-2661, 739-1575, fax 737-0265, 735-9430

Egyptian Commercial Bank (formerly Alexandria Kuwait International Bank), Evergreen Tower, 10 Tal'at Harb, DT, 577-9766, 579-4819, fax 579-9862

Egyptian Gulf Bank, al-Urman Plaza Bldg., 8–10 Ahmad Nasim, GZ, 419-1559, fax 760-6512

Egyptian Saudi Finance Bank
(former Pyramids Bank), 8
Ibrahim Nagib, GC,
795-0673, 794-7112

Egyptian Workers Bank, 10
Muhammad Hilmi Ibrahim,
574-6254, fax 576-8973,
579-9243

Export Development Bank of
Egypt, Evergreen Building,
10 Tal'at Harb, DT, 570-
1185, 577-2537, 577-7003,
fax 577-4553, 579-0394

Housing & Development Bank,
10 Kamil Muhammad, ZA,
735-4549, 749-2013

HSBC, 3 Abu al-Fida, ZA,
519-5462/3735-9186/286,
fax 736-4010

Industrial Development Bank
of Egypt, 110 Gala', DT,
577-9087, 574-5735, fax
579-0002, 578-7245

MIBank (Misr International
Bank), 54 al-Batal Ahmad
'Abd al-'Aziz, MO, 749-
4424/7091, fax 748-9796,
749-8072

Misr Exterior Bank, Cairo Plaza
Bldg, 1187 Corniche al-Nil,
579-6571, fax 574-8161

Misr Iran Development Bank,
Nile Tower, 21 Giza, GZ,
572-7311, fax 570-1185

Mohandes Bank, 30 Ramsis,
DT, 575-1973; 3, 5
Musaddaq DK, 748-5399,
fax 336-2741

National Bank for Development,
5A Bursa al-Gadida, DT,
392-3245, 392-1529, fax 395-
2905, 390-5540

National Bank of Abu Dhabi,
21 Giza, GZ, 573-5342, fax
571-7584

National Bank of Egypt, 24
Sharif, DT, 392-4057, fax
393-6481

National Bank of Greece, 2 'Aziz
'Usman, ZA, fax 736-8530

National Bank of Pakistan, 64
Gam'at al-Duwal al-
'Arabiya, 3rd fl., MO,
749-8307, fax 749-8955

National Bank of Sudan,
1 Behler Passage (off Qasr
al-Nil), DT, 392-1945,
fax 393-4526

National Societe Generale
Bank SAE, Evergreen
Building, 10 Tal'at Harb,
DT, 574-9376, 579-9761,
fax 577-6249

Nile Bank, 35 Ramsis, Midan
'Abd al-Mun'im Riyad,
574-1417/3502, fax
575-6296, 574-5577

Societe Arabe International De
Banque, 56 Gam'at al-
Duwal al-'Arabiya, MO,
574-9376, fax 760-3497,
748-9733

Societe Generale, 10 Tal'at
Harb, DT, 580-3800

Suez Canal Bank, 11 Sabri Abu
'Alam, DT, 393-1010/66/33,
fax 391-3522

Sumitomo Bank Ltd., 21/23
Giza, GZ, 570-3644,
fax 570-3655

Swiss Bank Corporation, 3
Ahmad Nasim, GZ

Union de Banques Arabes et
Francaises, 4 Behler Passage
(off Qasr al-Nil), DT,
393-3678, 392-4654,
fax 392-4654

Al-Watany Bank of Egypt,
Head Office, 13 Thimar,
Midan Muhi al-Din (off
Gam'at al-Duwal al-
'Arabiya), MO, 338-
8816/17, fax 337-9302

BARS

Africana, al-Haram, GZ

After Eight, 6 Qasr al-Nil, DT,
574-0855, 012 354-8877

Amsterdam, 17 Rd. 9B, MA,
012 383-0453, 010 540-1417

Bam-Bu, Casino al-Shagara,
Corniche al-Nil, 579-6511,
579-9701

Beer Corner, Nile Hilton Mall,
DT, 578-0321

Bull's Eye Pub, 32 Jeddah, MO
761-6888

Cairo Cellar, President Hotel,
22 Taha Husayn, ZA,
735-0718/0652

Cairo Jazz Club, 197 26th July,
MO, 345-9939

Da Baffo, 15 al-Batal Ahmad
'Abd al-'Aziz, MO,
344-8468, 346-7490

Deals, 2 al-Sayyid al-Bakri,
ZA, 736-0502

Deals 2, 2 Gul Gamal, MO,
305-7255

Deals 3, 40 Baghdad, HE,
291-0406

Duke's, Grand Hyatt Hotel,
Corniche al-Nil, GC,
365-1234

Flux, 2 Gama'iyat al-Nisr, MO,
338-6601

Hard Rock Café, Grand Hyatt
Hotel, Corniche al-Nil, GC,
532-1277/81

Harry's Pub, Cairo Marriott,
ZA, 735-8888

Indigo, 8 'Abd al-Rahman al-
Rifa'i, DK, 335-3330

Johnny's Pub, Le Pacha 1901
boat, ZA, 735-6730

L'Aubergine/Café Curnonsky
5 al-Sayyid al-Bakri, ZA,
788-0080

La Bodega, 157 26th July, ZA,
735-0543/6761

Latex, Cairo Nile Hilton Hotel,
Midan al-Tahrir,
578-0444/0666

Le 51 Bar, Meridien
Heliopolis, HE, 290-5055
x8151, 290-1819

Le Tabasco, 8 Midan 'Amman,
DK, 336-5583; 45 Rd. 7,
MA, 359-1222

Longchamps, 21 Isma'il
Muhammad, ZA

Mint, 30 Gazirit al-'Arab, MO,
302-3870/1

Nomad, King Hotel, 20 'Abd
al-Rahim Sabri, DK,
335-0869/0939

Odeon, Odeon Hotel, 6 Dr.
'Abd al-Hamid Sa'id, DT,
577-6637, 576-7971

Oxygen, Atlas Hotel, 2
Muhammad Rushdi, DT,
391-8127

Pub 28, 28 Shagarit al-Durr,
ZA, 735-9200

Red Onion, 27 Rd. 276, MA,
520-0240

Sangria, Casino El Shagara,
Corniche al-Nil, Maspero,
579-6511

Sequoia, end of Abu al-Fida,
ZA, 735-0014

Sevilla, Flamenco Hotel, 2 al-
Gazira al-Wusta, ZA,
735-0815/16

Taverne, Nile Hilton Hotel,
Midan al-Tahrir, 578-0444

TGI Friday's, Americana Boat,
26 al-Nil, GZ, 570-9690

Tycoons, Le Pacha 1901, Saray
al-Gazira, ZA, 735-6730

Versailles Palace, Cave des
Rois, 10 Muhammad Ibn
Thaqib, ZA, 736-8980

Windsor Hotel Bar, 19 Alfi
Bey, DT, 591-5277/5180

Whiskies Pub, Atlas Zamalek
Hotel, 20 Gam'at al-Duwal
al-'Arabiya, MO, 346-4175/
6569/7230

White, 25 Hasan 'Asim, ZA,
012 230-4404

BASEBALL / BASKETBALL

See Sports

BATH ACCESSORIES

Abu Nil, 41 Suliman Pasha, DT
(next to Group Americain)

Sidi, 159 26th July, ZA,
735-9142, fax 737-2059

BATHROOM FIXTURES

Faggala, near Midan Ramsis,
many shops

Integrated Interiors, 134 al-Nil,
AG, 749-0479 (Kohler,
Gaggenau)

BEAUTY SALONS

Ahmed and Abdou, 15 al-
Sheikh 'Ali 'Abd al-Raziq,
HE, 624-2697; 11 Nadi al-
Seid, MO, 760-9937, 338-
9176; Citystars, 480-2220,
010 5197-431.

Beauty Essentials, 14 Ahmad
Hishmat, ZA, 736-2927

Carinna Beauty Center, 27
Muhammad Yusif al-Kadi,
HE, 415-6502

Centre Carita, Sonesta Hotel, 4
al-Tayaran, NC, 262-8111;
261-7100 x261, Madame
Veronique.

Color Me Beautiful, 8 al-
Sharifa Dina, MA, 380-1830

Figaro, 11A Hasan Sabri, Digla
Center, ZA, 735-2690

Gharib (men & women),
Meridien Heliopolis,
290-6617 or 290-5055
x8075; 15 Qasr al-Nil, DT,
575-0950

Jacques Dessange, 70 Gam'at
al-Duwal al-'Arabiya, MO,
336-4810

Jacqui Beauty Center, 86 Rd. 9,
MA, 358-2430

Lily Beauty Recreation Center,
23 Surya, MO, 345-0432,
347-3160/4, Dr. Nagwa
Mustafa

Mohamed Al Sagheer, 20 al-
Sawra, MO, 761-4046/0369;
Semiramis Hotel, 795-5920;
16 Salah al-Din, ZA, 736-
3501; www.alsagheer-co.com

Santé Sport Beauté, 67 'Abd al-
'Aziz al-Sa'ud, MN, 365-
2300, Sharon Rooney

BEAUTY SUPPLIES

Digla Center, Benetton bldg.,
ZA

Faces, 30 Gazrit al-'Arab, MO,
344-4206/7

La Beauté, 13 Suliman Abaza,
MO, 335-9961

Morgana, Taha Husayn, al-Nil
Towers, ZA, 736-7904;
Yamama Center, 3rd fl., ZA,
579-7787

Sephora Beauty, 3 Abd al-
Hamid Lutfi, MO, 336-7136,
762-3927, 344-4418

BEER DELIVERY

Al-Ahram Beverages, GZ 331-
2444; MA 359-2315, 380-
3297; ZA 738-1694; HE 010
177-7230; all areas 0800-
100-100-1

Bazaar al-Ashwal, 200 Sudan,
MO, 346-1011, 010 146-2932

Drinkie's, 157 26th July, ZA,
738-1694, 735-3194,
0800-100-1001

King Soliman, 3 Midan
Suliman Guhar, DK,
335-9942

Maison Thomas, 157 26th July,
ZA, 735-7057, 7350415

BICYCLES

See also Sports
Ayad Kamal, 79 Rd 9, MA,
358-3498
Azkalany Bicycle Shop, 12 Rd.
15 and 54 Rd. 77, MA
Ghouko Trading & Supply Co.,
99 Gumhuriya, al-Azbakiya
near St. Mark's Church, 593-
5880 (repairs)

BILLIARDS

Alamein Recreation Products
Co., 13 Muhammad al-
Mar'ashli, ZA, 735-9987
El-Alamein, WTC, 578-0383
Billiard Room, Nile Hilton
Mall, DT, 578-0325
Bustan Commercial Center, 18
Yusif al-Gindi, DT, 395-
0100, 390-1086
Cairoland, 1 Salah Salim, HE,
366-1097
Cheers, 22 Gam'at al-Duwal
al-'Arabiya, MO, 347-6292
Planet, Arkadia Mall, 5th floor,
Corniche al-Nil, 579-2083
Ramsis Hilton Annex Mall, top
floor
Rules, 16 Muhammad Kamil
Mursi, MO, 337-9079

BOATS & BOATING

Cairo Yachting Club, al-Nil,
Giza, 338-3548, Commodore
Nabil Sirghany
Maadi Yacht Club, Corniche,
Maadi, 380-2066
Ocean Classics, 582-0766; fax
582-0632

BOOKBINDING

Muhammad 'Abd al-Zaher, 31
Sheikh Muhammad 'Abdu,

behind al-Azhar, 511-8041;
e-mail:
abdelzaher_binding@hotmail.com
al-Rawwaq al-Misri, 16 Safiya
Zaghlul, Munira, 794-7487

BOOKSTORES

DOKKI

Academic Bookshop, 121 al-
Tahrir, 336-8288, 748-5282

DOWNTOWN

Al-Ahram Bookshop, Nile
Hilton front courtyard;
Semiramis Intercontinental
lobby, 578-0666
Anglo-Egyptian Bookshop, 165
Muhammad Farid, 391-4337
(academic/medical/psy-
chology, literature)
AUC Bookstore, Main
Campus, Midan al-Tahrir,
797-5370
Dar al-Bustani, 29 Faqqala,
590-802
General Egyptian Book
Organization, 18 26th July
Lehnert & Landrock, 44 Sharif,
393-5324, 392-7606
Livres de France, 36 Qasr al-
Nil, 393-5512
L'Orientale, Nile Hilton
Shopping Mall, 576-2440
(also fax); e-mail:
kamy@intouch.com
(rare/used)
Madbouli, 6 Midan Tal'at
Harb, 575-6421
Reader's Corner, 33 'Abd al-
Khaliq Sarwat, 392-8801
(rare/new/used)
Rose al-Yousef, 89 Qasr al-
'Aini, Munira, 792-0536/7
El Shorouk, 1 Midan Tal'at
Harb, 393-0643

HELIOPOLIS

Baron Bookshop, Le Meridien
Heliopolis hotel, 290-5055
x8040
Everyman's Bookstore, 12
Baghdad, 417-6064 (good
children's section)
Horus Stationery, 72B
Granada, Roxy
International Language
Bookshop, 2 Muhammad
Bayumi (off al-Mirghani),
419-0420
Oxford Books, 5 Ibrahim al-
Laqqani, 259-6771
Palace, 1 Baghdad, al-Kurba

KHAN AL KHALILI

Seif El Nasr Megahed

MAADI

Book Mark, 2A Rd. 209, Digla,
754-5212, e-mail:
bookmarkdegla@hotmail.com
The Bookspot & Café, 71 Rd. 9,
378-1006
D & S Bookshop, Maadi Grand
Mall, basement, 518-2112
International Publications, 95
Rd. 9, 359-6244
Isis, 88 Rd. 9, 358-6034
Al Kotob Khan Bookshop, 3/1
al-Lasilki, New Maadi, 519-
4807, www.kotobkhan.com
Volume I, 17 Rd. 216, 519-8831

MOHANDISEEN

Book Galaxy, 23 al-Batal
Ahmad 'Abd al-'Aziz,
346-3868
Dar al-Nashr Hatier, 20 al-
Sawra, 761-5835
International Language
Bookshop, 3 Mahmud 'Azmi
(off Ahmad 'Urabi),
Sahafiyin, 344-0996
Madbuli, 45 al-Batal Ahmad
'Abd al-'Aziz, 347-7410,
344-2250

Volume 1, 3 'Abd al-Halim
  Husayn (off al-Sawra),
  338-0168

NASR CITY

Al-Saeed for Trading, 25
  Makram 'Ibeid, phone/fax
  274-2685; bargain books

ZAMALEK

Aly Masoud, 159 26th July
  (entrance from Behler)
AUC Bookstore, 16
  Muhammad Ibn Thaqib,
  739-7045
Dar al-Shark, Brazil
Diwan, 159 26th July,
  736-2598/78/82
Maktabit Hishmat, Ahmad
  Hishmat
Romansia Bookshop, 32
  Shagarit al-Durr, 735-0492
Shady, 26th July
Zamalek Bookstore, 19
  Shagarit al-Durr, 736-9197

BOWLING

Bandar Mall (Chili's), MA,
  520-3144
Bowling Kingly, Maadi Grand
  Mall, 5th fl., 518-1468/1614
Bustan Bowling Center, Bustan
  Commercial Center, 9th fl.,
  Bab al-Luq, DT, 395-0100
Cairoland, 1 Salah Salim, HE,
  366-1097
Maadi Family Land (behind
  Osman Towers), Corniche
  al-Nil, MA, 524-3300
Nile Bowling, al-Nil, AG

BRASS

See also Khan al-Khalili
Essam Brass & Copper, 5 Rab'
  al-Silahdar, upstairs, KK,
  591-8774, engraving

BREASTFEEDING

La Leche League, contact
  Community Services Assoc.,
  358-5284 or 358-0754.

BRICKS

The Arab Brick Co., 3 Ahmad
  'Urabi, MO, 346-0762

BRIDGE

Heliopolis Sporting Club
Maadi Duplicate Bridge Group,
  Tues 6:45 Sofitel Maadi;
  contacts: Mrs. Cressaty, 380-
  3304; Mrs. Issa, 358-3526
Ramses Hilton, Sun. afternoons

BROKERAGE HOUSES

Arab Investment Bank
  (Financial Securities), 8
  'Abd al-Khaliq Sarwat, DT,
  575-9249, fax 766-916
Cairo Stock Exchange, 4A al-
  Sharifein, 392-1402/1447,
  fax 392-8526
Capital Market Authority, 20
  'Imad al-Din, 6th fl., DT,
  777-774, 772-626, fax
  579-4176
EFG Hermes Financial, 65
  Gam'at al-Duwal al-'Arabiya,
  MO, 336-5960, fax 336-
  0104/5589, 55 Charles De
  Gaulle, Giza, GZ, 571-7846/8,
  fax 571-6121, 3 Ahmad
  Nasim, 336-1566, 749-1162,
  fax 336-1536, 58 Tahrir DK,
  338-3626/8, fax 338-3629, e-
  mail: rsamir@efmg.efg-
  hermes.com
Egyptians Abroad Investment,
  21 Giza, GZ, 572-9106
El-Eman Co. for Brokerage and
  Dealing in Securities (SAE),
  105 'Umar Ibn al-Khattab,
  HE, 417-8910/2/417-2294/7/
  8, fax 417-2295

Hussein Shukri & Co., WTC,
  13th fl., 1191 Corniche al-
  Nil, 577-9723
Investment & Securities Group
  (ISG), Nile Tower, 21 Giza,
  19th fl., GZ, 571-0844/1845,
  fax 570-3100
Misr Financial Investment Co.,
  56 Gam'at al-Duwal al-
  'Arabiya, MO, 749-8537/8,
  fax 749-3394
Mondial Expatriate Services
  Ltd., 5A Rd. 208, Digla,
  MA, 703-0626, 517-0090/1,
  fax 517-1115
Okaz, 35 'Imad al-Din, 591-
  8955/4741, 589-5321,
  fax 589-1499, e-mail:
  okaz@mst1.mist.com.eg
Omnia International, 8 Rd. 258,
  MA, 702-9526

BUSINESS SERVICES CENTERS

CBC (Computer & Business
  Center) NC, Midan al-
  Tahrir, HE, 417-8425/1167
  and 290-8234
IBA (International Business
  Associates), 1079 Corniche
  al-Nil, GC, 797-1300 and
  794-7475; 21 Muhammad
  Ghunaym Hilali, HE, 291-
  3410; 24 Surya, MO, 331-
  3500 and 760-1276; 31 Gulf,
  MA, 359-6070; 19 Rd. 151,
  MA, 358-7172
ISS (Int'l. Service Systems, 19
  al-Shahid Hilmi al-Misri,
  Almaza, HE, 291-2218, fax
  418-7273
Markenz Services, 81 'Abd al-
  Hamid Badawi, HE, 638-
  7216; fax 634-0115
Premier Recruitment, 35B
  Corniche al-Nil, MA,
  795-0776

El-Rashad, al-Bustan Trade
Center, 393-7580, fax 393-
7586, e-mail:
elrashad@ritsec2.com.eg

BUSINESS EQUIPMENT

See also Computers
Systel, 2A Shafiq Mansur, ZA,
736-1800, 737-7333/5700,
fax 736-3800; al-Sheikh
Gadd al-Haqq, NC, 272-
4855 fax 274-2793; Maadi
Grand Mall, MA, 517-1218,
fax /1219
(mobiles/pagers/beepers)
Xerox, 2 Lebnan, MO, 344-
4918; for servicing,
347-7735

BUTCHERS

Australian Meat Boutique, 29
Mustafa Kamil, Midan
Mahatta, MA, 359-3398;
barbecue cookbooks, sauces,
spices, grills, and accessories
B&P German Butchery, 35 Rd.
232 (near CAC), MA, (pork)
Boucherie de la Republique
Bolbol, 122 26th July, ZA,
735-2330; 736-1940; 735-
1844
Maison Thomas, 157 26th July,
ZA, 735-7057 (pork)
Miro Protein Market, 84 Rd. 9,
MA (pork)
Morcos, Ataba Market Grand
Bazaar, DT, 390-5477 (pork)
Omarah, 13 al-Shirbini at
Suliman Guhar, DK 337-
4068
Sobkey Protein (larger), al-
Tahrir at Dokki, DK, 748-
3522/3, 335-3259, 386-0500
Viennoise Meat Market, 3
Midan Tal'at Harb (across
from Sednaoui), DT, 393-
6294 (pork)

CAFÉS

See also Cybercafés
Alain Le Notre, 29 Gam'at al-
Duwal al-'Arabiya, MO,
335-8172, Nile City, Saray
al-Gazira, ZA, 737-8300
Arabica, 20 Muhammad al-
Mar'ashli, 735-7982, ZA
Badaweia, 33 Nasr Ahmad
Zaki, NC
Beano's, Lufthansa Sq., ZA,
736-2388; Muhammad
Mahmud, DT, 795-5300
Bint al-Sultan, Midan al-
Thawra, MO, 760-6633
Café Au Lait, Nile Hilton,
Corniche al-Nil, Midan al-
Tahrir, DT, 578-0325
Café Coutbis, 13 Brazil, ZA,
738-1652, 736-4601
Café Greco, 64 Rd. 9, MA,
380-9326
Café Riche, 17 Tal'at Harb,
DT, 391-8873, 392-9793
Café Tabasco, 7 Musaddaq,
DK, 762-2060; 18b
Mar'ashli, ZA, 735-8465
Cilantro, 159 26th July, ZA,
736-1115, 735-6761; WTC
3rd fl. Annex, 580-4181;
AUC gate, DT, 792-4571/2;
4 Ibrahim, al-Kurba, HE,
415-0167/8
Coffee Roastery, 3 Makka (off
Suliman Abaza), MO, 761-
0995; 46 Nadi al-Seid, DK,
749-8882; 140 26th July,
ZA, 738-0936; 5 Samir
Mukhtar, HE, 291-8070
Costa Coffee, Muhammad
Mahmud, DT; Rd. 250 (in
front of Maadi Grand Mall);
15 Muhammad al-Mar'ashli,
ZA; 16 al-Mirghani, HE;
Citystars, HE.
Green Mill, 32 Rd. 231, MA,
521-0120

Harris Café, 6 Baghdad, HE,
417-6796
Insomnia, 110 26th July, ZA,
735-4242
Maison Thomas, 157 26th July,
ZA, 735-7057
Monalisa's Home Made
Goodies, 15 Isma'il
Muhammad, Jeddah Tower,
ZA, 737-1035; 7 Qattamiya,
City Center, MA, 520-4392
No Big Deal, al-Sayyid al-
Bakri (next to Deals), ZA,
736-0052/0502
Retro, 2 Suliman Abaza, MO,
760-8274
Sidi Mansour, 22 Muhammad
Mahmud Sha'ban (formerly
al-Kurum), MO, 336-1859
Simonds, 112 26th July, ZA,
735-9436
Spectra, 14 'Abd al-Hamid
Lutfi, MO, 748-5831
Trianon, 17/18 Zamalek Club
Gate, Gam'at al-Duwal al-
'Arabiya, MO, 345-2012,
347-0838
Xpresso, 17 Shahab, MO,
303-5248

CALL-BACK SERVICES

Kallback (USA) 206-684-8600;
fax 206-682-6666; e-mail:
care@kallback.com
Magic Service, 9A Abou al-
Feda, ZA, 738-3214/15
New World
Telecommunications (USA)
201-996-1670; fax 201-996-
1870; e-mail newworld@
newworldtele.com

CALLIGRAPHY

Ibrahim Badr, 19 Muhammad
Farid, DT, 393-5490

CAR & MOTORCYCLE RAILLES

Motocross, contact Raed Baddar, 290-0989

Pharoah's Rally, contact Rami Siag at Siag Travel, 385-2626, fax 384-0874

CAR RENTAL

Alex Limousine, 33 al-Tawfiq, NC, 401-7350

Avis, 16A Ma'mal al-Sukkar, GC, 794-7400/7081/8698, fax 796-2464; Meridian368-9400, Nile Hilton 579-2400; e-mail: ruavis@rusys.eg.net

Bita Car Rental, 34 Abu Bakr al-Siddiq, HE, 454-2620

Budget Rent-A-Car, Km 28 Cairo-Alexandria Desert Road, 539-1501/2/3/4, fax 539-1506

Egytrav, (24 hr.), Nile Hilton Hotel, DT, 576-7444/ 5666, fax 577-8861

Elite Rent-A-Car, 2 Tehran (off Musaddaq), DK, 337-6050, fax 337-6050

Europcar/InterRent, Egypt, Max Bldg., 27 Libnan, MO, 304-8307, 304-2510, 303-5125/5630, fax 303-6123

Fast Car Rental, 7 Yanbu', DK, 761-3743/6183, 748-3037 fax 748-3937

Hepton Limousine (buses only), al-Nuzha, HE, 417-7800/7900

Hertz Rent-A-Car, 195, 26th July, AG, 347-4172/2238, 303-4241, fax 344-6627; Intercontinental Pyramids Park, 383-8666 ext:2428; Le Meridien Pyramids 383-0383 ext: 4089; Ramses Hilton 574-4400, 575-8000; CA 265-2430; e-mail: hertz@internetegypt.com

Iveco (bus & coach), 22 Mahmud Basyuni, DT, 575-9061, 574-7006/7377

Limousine Misr Touristic Company, Misr Travel Tower, 13th fl., Midan al-'Abbasiya, DT, 685-6721/5, fax 685-6124

Muhammad Hafez Co. (car & limousine), 4A Harun, DK, 760-0542, 748-6652, fax 748-1105, e-mail: mhafez@intouch.com

Rawas Car & Limousine Rental, 4 Tahran (off Musaddaq), DK, 749-9831, 335-0477, 749-5313; Gezirah Sheraton 736-1333/1555 x8341/2; Ramses Hilton 554-4400; CA 291-4255/77/88/99 x2207/8

Smart Limo, 151 Corniche al-Nil, MA, 524-3006, fax 524-3009

Sunshine Car & Bus Rentals, 106 Muhammad Farid, DT

Top Car, 11 al-Misaha, DK

CARPENTERS

Ehab, 298-7524, 012 210-7032

CARPET CLEANING & REPAIR

Ali Kazrouni, 14 Sarwat (across from Cairo University Faculty of Commerce), DK, 749-3011

El-Assiouty, 118 26th July, ZA, 736-6732, 737-1609

El Kabbany, 11 Khan al-Khalili, KK, 591-4236

Muhammad Rahmy, 5 Rab' al-Silahdar, 907-873, 591-2282

Nasr Ahmed Muhammad, 7 Isma'il Muhammad, ZA, 737-0852

CARPETS

El-Assiouty, 7 al-Batal Ahmad 'Abd al-'Aziz, MO, 345-1499; 118 26th July, ZA, 736-6732, 737-1609

Classic Carpet, 10 al-'Ubur Bldgs., Salah Salim, HE, 263-3097

Egypt for Oriental Carpets, Saqqara Road, GZ, 802-2203/802-2208/802-2228; 012 213-0288; www.egypt4 orientalcarpets.com

Mamdouh El-Assiouty, Sofitel, MA, 359-6777

Medhat El-Assiouty, 31 Muhi al-Din Abu al-'Izz, MO, 336-0305, 337-4975

Oriental Weavers, Airport Rd, HE, and off Gam'at al-Duwal al-'Arabiya, MO, 304-3642

CARS, CLASSIC–REPAIRS

Automobile Club in Cairo, 10 Qasr al-Nil, DT, 754-3191/3348

Club Muhammad Aly (pre-1950 car club); contact: Maged Farag, Max Group, 636-5233

Safwat Saleh, 3 Yusif al-Digawi, MN, 364-4014 (mechanical)

Samayo Car & Part Co., 25 al-Lasilki (behind satellite station), MA, 702-1384

CARS, NEW

Artoc Auto, 144 26th July, AG, 304-0193, 347-3685 (Skoda)

Daewoo Motor, 195 26th July, AG, 303-1583/1595

Ezz el-Arab, 13 Dr. Shahin, AG, 749-7100 (BMW, Citroen, Chrysler, Dodge, Jeep)

Giza National Automotive, 1
Tahrir, DK, 336-3806, 336-
8207/8/9 (Mercedes-Benz)
KIA Motors, 69 al-Nasr, New
Maadi, MA, 518-1782/ 5/fax
518-1786 (Duty-free
available)
Al-Mansour, 54 Gam'at al-
Duwal al-'Arabiya, 344-
4177, 345-7030, 346-0087
(Opel)
Modern Free Zone, 11 'Uqba,
DK, 748-8500/1; 749-2930
(Suzuki & Nissan)

CATERING

Amelia's Kitchen, 585-2301
(Brazilian specialities)
Bon Appetit, 21 Wadi al-Nil,
MO, 346-0393; 2 Isma'il
Muhammad, ZA, 735-4382
CARE Service, 339-7109
House 2 House, 010 668-2144
Le Pacha 1901, 15 Mahmud
Basyuni, DT, 575-3130,
574-6169
Samy, 10 Bahr al-Ghazal (off
Ahmad 'Urabi), Sahafiyin,
MO, 346-6393 (ice cream,
dairy products, etc.)

CHEMICALS, AGRICULTURAL

Ismail Ahmed al-Hadidi and
Co., 17 al-Higaz, MO, 346-
0521, fax 346-4930

CHILDREN'S ENTERTAINMENT

See also Amusement Parks
Arabica, 20 Muhammad al-
Mar'ashli, ZA, 735-7982
Young Star Club, Le Meridien,
Cairo–Alexandria Desert
Road, Pyramids, 383-0383/
0772
ZASSY Puppets, 346-8705

CHOCOLATES

Choco Chocola, 106 Muhi al-
Din Abu al-'Izz, MO, 762-
0738; 11 Hasan Sabri, Digla
Center, 2nd fl., ZA, 738-1540
Chocofolie, Midan 'Amman,
DK, 761-3389,
www.chocofolie.com
Fauchon, 4 al-Gazira, ZA,
735-0636
Neuhaus, Nile Hilton Mall, DT,
394-5747; al-Shahid 'Abd
al-Mun'im Riyad, MO,
748-7579

CHURCHES

DOKKI
German Evangelical Church
Community (Lutheran), 6
Gaber Ibn Hayyan, 761-4398

DOWNTOWN
Christian Science Society, 3
Midan Mustafa Kamil, 392-
9032, 525-3781, 525-0670
Church of God: St Andrew's
United Church Hall, 38 26th
July (between Ramsis and
Gala') 575-9451
Eglise Evangelique du Caire,
services in MA and DT;
contact: Pasteur Martin,
392-8199
Friends Meeting (Quaker).
Meetings move from home
to home; contact: Ray
Langsten at 797-6969 or
337-0181
German Speaking Catholic
St.Markus Community
Church, German School, 8
Muhammad Mahmud, 795-
7516, e-mail:
kathkairo@gmx.net
St. Andrew's United Church,
38 26th July (between Galaa
& Ramsis) 575-9451

St. Joseph's Roman Catholic
Church, Muhammad Farid;
contact: Father Mamdouh
Shehab Bassilios, 393-6677

HELIOPOLIS
Heliopolis Community Church,
10 Seti, (at St. Michael's,
below), 414-2409,
www.hcccairo.co; e-mail:
hcc_cairo@link.net
St. Anthony's Coptic Orthodox
Church, 'Ali 'Abd al-Razik
(off al-Higaz); contact:
Father Antonius, 636-4962
St. Clare's Convent, Corner of
Isna and al-Sawra, 415-
2769, 425-9027
St. Michael's Episcopal Church,
10 Siti (off Baghdad), al-
Kurba, 418-6828

MAADI
Church of Christ Fellowship,
Rd. 11, Bldg 18, Apt 38
Church of Jesus Christ of
Latter Day Saints, 21 Rd. 17,
359-2571/6137
The Church of St. John the
Baptist (Episcopal/Anglican),
Rd. 17 & Port Said, 358-3085
German Evangelical Church (at
St. John's, below); contact:
Rev. Selbach
German Speaking Catholic St.
Markus Community Church,
Borromean Sisters' Convent,
Rd. 75, 795-7516, e-mail:
kathkairo@gmx.net
Holy Family Church (Roman
Catholic), 55 Rd. 15;
contact: Father Abel,
358-2004.
Korean Church (at St. John's,
below); contact: Rev. Joon-
Kyo Lee, 358-4620.
Maadi Community Church (at
St. John's, below); contact:
Dave Petrescue, Senior
Pastor, 359-2755

ZAMALEK

All Saints' Cathedral (Episcopal/Anglican), 5 Mishil Lutfallah, 736-8391. Father Doust, provost & chaplain

St. Joseph's Roman Catholic Church, 4 Ahmad Sabri; 738-4178.

CINEMAS

Cairo, Saray al-Azbakiya, DT, 574-5350

Cairo Sheraton, Midan al-Gala', DK, 760-6081

City Centre, 3 Makram 'Ibeid, NC, 010 667-5096

Cosmos 1 and 2, 12 'Imad al-Din, DT, 574-2177

Diana, 17 Alfi, DT, 592-4727

Drive-In, Entrance of Shuruq City, Cairo-Ismailiya Desert Road, 012 219-0831, 687-1400

Faten Hamama, MN, 364-9767

Galaxy Cinema, 68 'Abd al-'Aziz al-Sa'ud, MN, 532-5745

Genena, Genena Building, Batrawi, NC, 263-0744/5

Good News, Grand Hyatt, Corniche al-Nil, GC, 365-4448, 368-1515

Al Haram, al-Haram, GZ, 385-8358

Al Horreya 1 and 2, al-Ahram, HE, 479-8025

Karim 1 and 2, 15 'Imad al-Din, DT, 592-4830

Lido, 23 'Imad al-Din, DT, 593-4284

Maadi Cinema, Bandar 2000 Entertainment Complex, MA, 519-0770, 519-0455

Maadi Grand Mall, Midan Kulliyit al-Nasr, MA, 519-5388

Metro, 35 Tal'at Harb, DT, 393-7566, 735-7061

Miami, 38 Tal'at Harb, DT, 574-5656

Normandy, 31 al-Ahram, HE, 258-0254

Odeon, 4 'Abd al-Hamid Sa'id, DT, 575-8797

Qasr al-Nil, Qasr al-Nil, DT, 575-0761

Radio, 24 Tal'at Harb, DT, 575-6562

Ramses Hilton 1 & 2, top floor of Annex, 574-7436/5

Renaissance, Nile City, Corniche al-Nil, 461-9101

Renaissance, WTC Annex, 578-4915, 580-4039

Renaissance 2, Wonderland Mall, end of 'Abbas al-'Aqqad, NC, 401-2326

Rivoli 1 and 2, 26th July, DT, 575-5053/95

Roxy, Midan Roxy, HE, 258-0344

Stars, Citystars, 'Umar Ibn al-Khattab, NC, 480-2014/3

Swissôtel Cairo al-Salam Hotel, 65 'Abd al-Hamid Badawi, HE, 296-1419

Al Tahrir, 112 al-Tahrir, DK, 335-4726

Tiba, 74 al-Nasr, NC, 262-1084

CLEANING SERVICES

First Inter-City, 390-9103

Makram Cleaning Service, Digla, MA, 519-9955, 521-0035, 010 143-2266, 754-3575

CLINICS

MAADI

Cairo Cancer Clinic, 33 Corniche al-Nil, 378-3774

Family Healthcare Clinic, 71 Rd. 9 (above Baskin Robbins), 380-6766; 010 602-3118

Dr. Mahmud Shirbini and Jaqueline Shirbini, RN; family medicine, general and critical care, anesthesiology and cardiology

MOHANDISEEN

Cairo Breast Clinic, 2 al-Fakawih (above Chili's), 336-6645

Cairo Medical Tower, 55 'Abd al-Mun'im Riyad, 344-5717

Shaalan Clinic, 11 al-'Anab, 760-3920, 010 105-0571

Shaalan Surgicenter, 11 'Abd al-Hamid Lutfi, 760-3920/5180; fax 760-3124

CLOCK & WATCH REPAIR (ANTIQUE)

Francis Papazian, Midan Ataba, 390-5616

Tewfik Goma, near Flower Market, Muski

Tewfik Goma, near Flower Market, Muski

CLOTHING

ACCESSORIES

Tumuh, 63 al-Sayyid al-Bakri, ZA, 736-5243 (scarves)

ALTERATIONS

Chamade, 96 al-Mirghani, HE,

CASUAL & SPORTSWEAR

Beymen, Four Seasons Hotel, GC, 792-6679

Concrete, branches everywhere (HE, NC, DT, ZA, GC, MA, MO, GZ), 569-6254, 531-0425, 575-3755

Elegante, 1A al-Sayyid al-Bakri, ZA, 736-6130 (women's)

Lois Jeans, branches everywhere (HE, GZ, MA, MO, NC, DT), 263-0018

Mexx, branches everywhere (DT, GZ, HE, MA, MO, NC), 519-3100

Mix and Match, branches everywhere (WTC, Ramses and Nile Hiltons, DT, MA, HE, ZA), 303-6157, 749-6167, 736-4640

Mobaco, branches everywhere (HE, DT, GZ, MA, MO, NC, ZA), 347-3791, 575-4276

Naf Naf, branches everywhere (MO, GZ, NC, HE, DT, MA, WTC, ZA), 346-3426

On Safari, branches everywhere (Citystars, HE, 415-6680; 20 Sharifa Dina, MA, 380-9194; 10 Mishil Lutfallah, ZA, 735-1909; Nile Hilton, 579-0845; Marriott, ZA, 735-1125

Rimy & Riry, 8 Brazil, ZA, 735-9633 (handmade sweaters)

Timberland, branches everywhere (MA, DT, GZ, MO, NC, ZA), 520-2170

CHILDREN'S

Babycare, 17 Hasan Sabri, ZA, 735-4661 and al-Batal Ahmad 'Abd al-'Aziz, MO

Bambi, Qambiz, DK, 337-8325

Bunny's, 12 Suliman Abaza, MO, 761-0156; call for other new locations (MA, Nile Hilton)

Confetti, branches everywhere (HE, DT, MA, MO, ZA), 415-1662, 736-3173

Dream Baby, 14 al-Kawsar, MO, 762-3275

Gerard Darel Kids, 6 'Abd al-Hamid Lutfi, MO

DISCOUNT

New York, 48 Salim al-Awwal, Zeitun, and 44 Ramsis, Roxy, HE, 259-1769

ETHNIC

Ed-Dukkan, Ramses Hilton Annex Mall

Halawa, 'Abd al-Khaliq Sarwat, DT, 391-5272/2733/2013

Hazem Hafez, 35 Nazih Khalifa, HE, 258-1376

LINGERIE

Bloom Lingerie, 3 'Abd al-Hamid Lutfi, MO, 762-5346/7

Elle, Fayrouz Center, 140 26th July, ZA

Frivole, 38 al-Kawsar, MO, 760-4868

Jolie Jolie (Valisere) 33 'Amman, DK, 760-3819

La Beauté, 13 Suliman Abaza, MO

Women's Secret, Citystars, NC, 012 555-9387

MATERNITY

Mom & Me, 20a al-Mansur Muhammad, ZA, 736-5751

Motherhood, 24 al-Fawakih, MO, 760-6983

Our Kids, Midan al-Misaha, DK, 336-3602; Mustafa al-Nahhas, NC, 374-8741

MEN'S

Armani, 35b Gazirit al-'Arab, MO, 303-0077

Arrogant, Midan Ibn al-Walid near Nadi al-Seid

Beymen, Four Seasons hotel, Nile Plaza. GC

Borsalino (suits, tailoring), 33 al-Batal Ahmad 'Abd al-'Aziz, MO, 345-2199

Only Ties, 2nd fl., WTC, 580-4274; 41 al-Batal Ahmad 'Abd al-'Aziz, MO, 012 474-3550

MISCELLANEOUS

Sharia Shawarbi, DT, for every kind of clothing

WOMEN'S DESIGNER & HIGH FASHION

Beymen, Four Seasons hotel, Nile Plaza. GC

Borsalino, 33 al-Batal Ahmad 'Abd al-'Aziz, MO, 345-2199

Boutique Up 16, 114 26th July St, ZA, 736-8459

De Luca, 4 al-Gazira, ZA, 735-4434

Fashion, 39 'Abd al-Mun'im Riyad, MO, 748-3373; 760-7774

Guess, several branches (MA, MO, GZ, HE), 520-4415

Kookai, 15 Surya, MO, 345-5197; 102b al-Mirghani, HE, 419-9703

Luciano di Nardo, 215 Sudan, MO, 344-8375 and 1 Brazil, ZA, 736-2428

Moods, 27 Abu al-Fida, ZA, 736-3634

Morgan, 122 Muhi al-Din Abu al-'Izz, MO, 335-3417

Pandora's Box, WTC, 578-8729

Queeny, 17 Suliman Abaza, MO, 749-6638

Selective, 42 Musaddaq, DK, 335-2893

Stephanie, 10 Mahmud 'Azmi, ZA, 736-3926; 49 Dr. Hasan Aflatun, Nuzha, HE, 257-2903

Tia, 17 Hasan Sabri, ZA, 736-2567

WOMEN'S—EVENING

Bekhita, Cairo Marriott, ZA, 735-1094

Boutique Viola, 20 al-Sawra, MO, 761-4405

Cocktails, 2 Bahgat 'Ali, ZA, 736-8043

Donna, 25 Makka at Muhi al-Din Abu al-'Izz, MO, 337-0928

Fantastic, 5 Brazil, ZA,
735-9930
Manelia, 18 al-Quds al-Sharif,
MO, 344-8488 (also dressy
sportswear)
Melodies, 24 al-Sawra, MO,
336-7424 (also dressy
sportswear)
Nagada, 8 Dar al-Shifa, GC,
792-3249

COFFEE

'Azmi Shahata, 24 Mushtuhar,
'Abdin, DT, 393-4022
(espresso)
Brazilian and Yemen Coffee
Store, Midan Bab al-Luq,
794-2532
Café do Brasil, 1 al-Qadi Abu
Seif, DK, 749-7375
Café Greco, 64 Rd. 9, MA,
380-9326
Coffee Roastery, 3 Makka (off
Suliman Abaza), MO, 761-
0995; DK, 749-8883; 140
26th July, ZA, 738-0936
Green Mill, 32 Rd. 231, MA,
521-0120
El Oruba, 103 al-Tahrir, DK

COFFEE SHOPS

See Cafés

COMPACT DISKS

Cinderella, Arkadia Mall
Diwan, 159 26th July, 736-
2598/82/78
Fono, 60 Musaddaq, DK,
335-9208
Mirage Megastore, 71 Gam'at
al-Duwal al-'Arabiya, MO,
760-9793
Musicana, 15 Baghdad, Kurba,
HE, 406-0290
Up 2 Date, 13 al-Ahram, Roxy,
HE, 414-6062
Vibe (next to Deals), al-Sayyid
al-Bakri, ZA, 736-0502

Video Rack, 17 Dr. al-Mahruqi
(off Midan Aswan), MO,
304-5311/12; 23 al-Ma'had
al-Ishtiraki (Merryland), HE,
453-5503/4; 41 'Abd al-
Hamid Badawi (Nadi al-
Shams), HE, 240-4108; 15
Abu al-Atahia (International
Garden), NC, 273-6810; 1/5
Lasilki, MA, 754-3619
Virgin Megastore, Citystars,
Star Centre, 'Umar Ibn al-
Khattab, NC, 480-2244

COMPUTER CLASSES

The American Univeristy in
Cairo, Center for Adult and
Continuing Education,
Greek Campus, 28 al-Falaki,
Bab al-Luq, 797-6874/7,
fax 797-6858
The British Council, 192 al-Nil,
AG, 300-1666, fax 344-
3076; 4 El Minya, off Nazih
Khalifa, HE, 452-3395/7, fax
258-3660, e-mail:
british.council@britishcounc
il.org.eg

COMPUTERS

Sales, Repairs, Maintenance,
Supplies, Training
Note: All recommended by
users and/or computer
professionals
Alpha Omega Group, 102A al-
Nil, DK, 749-2652
American Maintenance and
Computer Co., 38 Hasan al-
Sharif, NC (near club al-
Ahly), 012 212-3519,
313-0784, e-mail:
marco_eg@usa.net
Amr Aboul Dahab, Midan Fini,
DK, 761-4189, 336-0217,
e-mail:
dahabmcs@intouch.com

AppleLine Computer, 75 Qasr
al-'Aini, GC, 795-1200/1356
(IBM & Apple, new &
used), e-mail: appline@ie-
eg.com
Aptec Egypt, 3 Mahmud
Nashid, HE, 635-5634, fax
637-5255,
www.aptec.com.eg (Epson,
Microsoft, Fujitsu, Borland)
CBC (Computer & Business
Center), HE, 280-8234
(hard/software for IBM,
Microsoft, Apple, Xerox, HP)
CITE, Suite 77, 7th fl., 68 Qasr
al-'Aini, GC, 794-5626,
796-0531 (indiv. & instit.,
mainly Apple), fax 795-1034
Compu City, 49 Nubar, DT,
792-3724 ext 115; 26
Gam'at al-Duwal al-
'Arabiya, MO, 346-8196
Computek, 23 'Amr, DK,
760-2234; 154 al-'Uruba,
HE, 418-2264, 417-4297,
fax 761-4576
Computer City, 2 Isma'il
Muhammad, ZA, 738-1361
Diamond, 126 al-Nil, DK,
760-0857 (Parts)
Egyptian Advanced
Technologies, 3 'Usman Ibn
'Affan, MO, 344-3001
ETS, 193 Sudan, MO, 303-
7512/9151; Maadi Town
Center, Rd. 151, MA,
380-3457
Gateway 2000/Blue Max, 10A
'Umar Tusun (off Ahmad
'Urabi at Midan Sphinx),
MO, 303-5473; contacts:
Mustafa Abu Bakr and Selim
Gamal (Gateway, Fountain),
fax 303-5478
Giza Systems Engineering, 2
Midan al-Misaha, DK,
749-0140, fax
749-9253/760-9932

Kolaly Engineering, 15 Nadi al-Seid, MO, 335-6499, fax 748-2732 (IBM, institutional)

Logitek, 336 al-Haram, GZ, 868-888.

Marco International, 22 Atiya al-Sawalhi, NC, 272-2256, e-mail: marco_eg@usa.net

Micom, 7 Dr. Hussein Kamel, Nuzha, HE, 634-0466

El Nekhely Bros., 176 al-Tahrir, Bab al-Luq, DT, 392-7529; 393-6301, fax 392-8612; contacts: Emad or Wagid

Odec, 414-5994, 012 212-7546 (IBM, Compaq, Hewlett Packard)

Ofis, Badr al-Din, MO, 303-1221, 305-7858; contact: Engineer Muhammad

Pyramids Computer Center, 54 'Abbas al-'Aqqad, NC, 260-6004

Triangle (Sun Microsystems), 54 Libnan, MO, 336-0353, 304-6689/6703, fax 795-2388

CONFERENCE CENTER

Cairo International Conference Center (CICC), NC, 263-4631/2

CONSULTANTS

Abt Enterprises LLC, 9 'Abd al-Qadir Hamza, GC, 792-3085, fax 792-3087

Center for Quality Assurance, 21 Yusif al-Gindi, 3rd fl., Bab al-Luq, 393-2996, fax 395-0954

International Executive Services Corporation, Bustan Commercial Center, Suite 1, 390-3232, fax 390-2929

TerraConsult, 32 'Abd al-Khaliq Sarwat, 392-6497/33, fax 390-8600

CONTACT LENSES

See Opticians

COOKWARE

See Kitchenware

COOPER

See Khan al-Khalili

CORK BOARDS & DART BOARDS

Maher El Sabagh, Gazirit Badran, Shubra, 576-2531

COSMETICS

See Beauty Supplies

COUNTRY CLUBS

See Sporting & Country Clubs

COURIERS

Aramex, 31 Musaddaq, DK, 338-8466; 4 al-Mustashar Tayil al-Ahwal, HE, 635-6369

DHL, 34 'Abd al-Khaliq Sarwat, DT, 393-5322; 20 Gamal al-Din Abu al-Mahasin, GC, 795-7118/7301; 35 Isma'il Ramzi, HE, 636-0324/3751; 43 Rd. 6, MA, 380-8900; 16 Libnan, MO, 302-9801, fax 302-981

Express Mail Service, Midan al-'Ataba, 390-5874/69 and most post offices

Federal Express, 19 Khalid Ibn al-Walid, Masakin Sheraton, HE, 268-7888/999 (head office); 15 Shahab, MO, 760-7922; 17 Wadi al-Nil, MA, 358-3284; 67 Higaz, HE, 636-4197

IML Air Couriers, 2 Mustafa Kamil, MA, 358-1160/1240/1, fax 358-1240

Middle East Couriers, 1 Mahmud Hafiz, Midan Safir, HE, 635-9281, 633-6328

Overseas Courier Service, 9 Darih Sa'd, Munira, 793-3337

SOS Sky International, 45 Sahab, MO, 346-0028/ 2503

TNT Skypak, 33 Dokki, DK, 749-9851, fax 346-0028

UPS, 7 Hussein Zohdy, Ard al-Gulf, NC, 414-1456

CRANE RENTAL

Target, 2 Suliman Abaza, MO, 760-3052

Triangle, 30 Nadi al-Seid, MO

CREDIT CARDS, LOST

See Emergency and Other Important Numbers

CRUISES

See also Travel Agents

Christina motor yacht, moored at the Cairo Sheraton, DK, 336-9700 (ask for captain Leonardo Patsalis)

CULTURAL CENTERS

See Organizations

CURTAINS

See Fabrics

CUSTOMS CLEANING AGENTS

See Movers (international)

CYBERCAFÉS

See also Cafés

4U Internet Cafe, 8 Midan Tal'at Harb, 1st fl., DT

Cafe de Paris, Bustan Commercial Center, DT, 391-0151 x117

CyberCafé, Nile Hilton Mall, Food Court, Corniche al-Nil, DT, 578-0444/666, x758

IEC CyberCafé, 11 Abu al-Mahasin al-Shazli, MO, e-mail: postmaster@iec.egnet.net

Internet Café, 58 Libnan, MO, 347-4024

Internet Club, 120 al-Mirghani, HE, 419-5666, 417-5908

Internet Egypt CyberCafé, 2 Midan Qasr al-Dubara, 6th fl., GC, 796-2882, fax 794-9611, e-mail: info@internetegypt.com; Zamalek Club Passage, off Gam'at al-Duwal al-'Arabiya, MO, 305-0493

NileNet, 5 Sharq Nadi al-Tersana, MO, 302-4270

Rd. 9 Cafe, Rd. 9, MA, 378-4514

Style Internet Cafe, 65 Isma'il al-Qabbani, NC, 403-2818

The Way Out, 18 al-Shahid Muhammad 'Abd al-Hadi, Ard al-Gulf, NC, 418-0995

The Way Out 2, 41 Rd. 218, MA, 519-8403

Way Out Sushi, 18 al-Shahid Muhammad 'Abd al-Hadi, HE, 417-8999

DANCE CLASSES

EGYPTIAN DANCE

Contact Fatiha, 012 328-2807, or e-mail: fatiha@arabist.net

FLAMENCO

Enquire about lessons at the Cervantes Institute. *See* Organizations

SALSA

Nile Hilton Hotel. *See* Hotels

DANCE GROUPS

Cairo Scottish Country Dance Group, Meets Mondays at 8pm; contact: Nelle Evenhouse, 259-0141 or Gillian Lee, 794-0842

DAYCARE

See Schools

DENTISTS

See Doctors

DEPARTMENT STORES

Sednaoui, 17 Qasr al-Nil, DT, 393-7990

DESERT AND/OR DIVING SAFARIS

Abercrombie & Kent (Trailmasters), Bustan Commercial Center, 10th fl., Bab al-Luq, DT, 393-6272/5179, fax 391-6255, www.abercrombiekent.com

Adventures Safari, 14 al-Naser, HE, 634-5147, fax 240-6992; contact: Diaa Shawki

Atlantis for Scuba Diving Mobile 010 108-8090/010 885-1439

Hany Amr Desert Adventure, 010 190-5999 or e-mail: desertadventures@gmail.com

Isis Travel, 48 Giza, GZ, 748-7761/5592, fax 748-4821, e-mail: itcs@isis.ie-eg.com

Maadi Divers, 18 Rd. 218, Digla, MA, 703-7144, e-mail: mdivers@intouch.com; contact: Magdy el-Araby

Max Travel, 27 Libnan, MO, 347-4713

Red Sea Yacht Safari, 202-4924, fax 575-7864

Mr. Saad Ali El Badawiya 575-8076, www.badawiya.com

Seascapes, al-Lasilki (Satellite Area), MA, 519-4930, fax 519-4927, www.seascapesegypt.com

Siag Travel, Siag Pyramids Hotel, Saqqara Road., PY, 385-1444/2626

DIRECTORIES

American Chamber of Commerce Membership Directory, 33 Suliman Abaza, MO, 338-1050, fax 338-1060

Egypt Trade, ABC Business Service Ltd. Head Office: 6 al-Ma'had al-Sahari, HE. 417-8427/8, fax 417-8428

Egypt Yellow Pages, 19345, www.egyptyellowpages. com.eg

MobiNil Directory, 8000

Vodafone Directory, 2121

DISCOTHÈQUES

See also Bars

Castle Discothèque, Shepheard Hotel, Corniche al-Nil, GC, 792-1000

Hard Rock Cafe, Grand Hyatt Hotel, Corniche al-Nil, GC, 532-1277/81

Jackie's, Nile Hilton Hotel, Midan al-Tahrir, DT, 578-0444/0666 x214, fax 578-0475

Latex, Cairo Nile Hilton Hotel, Midan al-Tahrir, DT, 578-0444/0666

Le Disco, el-Gezirah Sheraton, ZA, 736-1555

El Morocco, Blue Nile boat, 9a Saray al-Gazira, ZA, 735-3114, 012 390 0256

Oxygen, Atlas Hotel, 2 Muhammad Rushdi, DT, 391-8127, 391-1022

Saddle, Mena House, GZ, 383-3222

Sangria, Casino al-Shagara, Corniche al-Nil, DT, 579-6511/2

TGI Friday's, Americana Boat, 26 Corniche al-Nil, GZ, 570-9690

DOCTORS

HOSPITAL/CLINIC CONTACT TELEPHONE NUMBERS

Anglo-American Hospital, ZA, 735-6162/3/4/5

Cairo Tower Hospital, Cairo Medical Tower, CairoScan, MO, 303-0810/0815

Nil Badrawi Hospital, MA, 524-0022

Al-Salam Hospital, MO, 302-9091/2/3

As-Salam Hospital, MA, 524-0250/0077; outpatient clinic, 362-0644

Shaalan Surgicenters, MO, 760-5180, 760-3920, 748-8578, 337-6672

ALLERGISTS

Dr. Hisham Taraf, Nil Badrawi Hospital (524-0022) and Cairo Tower Hospital lab cancer specialists

Dr. Reda Hamza, National Cancer Institute, 363-2665, 362-6774; also contact Director of Nursing: Dr. Nagwa El-Khasib, 362-8199.

CARDIOLOGISTS

Dr. Abd al-Hakim Mahmud, 2 Sherif, DT, 392-1576

Dr. Abdel Moneim al-Rifai, 2 Sherif, DT, 392-1501

Dr. Ayman 'Abd al-Meguid, Al-Salam and Shalaan Surgicenter (760-3920/5180)

Dr. Emad Awad, Anglo-American Hospital, ZA, 735-6162/3/4/5

Dr. Galal el Sayid, 121 Muhammad Farid, Bab al-Luq, DT, 391-1333, Al-Salam Hospital, & home 358-1807

Dr. Magdy Gomaa, 42 al-Dukki, DK, 760-7099

Dr. Midhat al-Rifai, 761-0979

CHILD PSYCHOLOGY/PSYCHIATRY

Dr. Emad Ismail, HE, h: 291-4006

DENTISTS

Dr. Aida Bastawi (General & Cosmetic), 183 al-Tahrir (Strand Building), DT, 794-7554

Dr. Ibrahim Hanna, 89 al-Mirghani, HE, 291-5668

Dr. Ihab Korra, 60 Libnan, 1st fl., 346-8004, 303-9070

Dr. Muhammad A. Farag, 7 al-Batal Ahmad 'Abd al-'Aziz, DT (not MO), 393-9161, Home, 336-1718/1719

Dr. Nadia Metwalli (orthodontics and pediatric), #2, 1st fl., 22 al-Tahrir., DK, 338-2144/5, 012 210-2334

Dr. Sabri Karnouk, 34 Tal'at Harb, DT, 575-8392

Dr. Raouf Abbassy, 9 al-Gabalaya, Tonsi Bldg., ZA, 735-1133/1144

Dr. Rawy Barsoum, 1 Rd. 217, Digla, MA, 519-8733

Dr. Wafik Mahrous, 87 Rd. 9, MA, 359-4067/358-2323, h: 359-1158/358-3660

DERMATOLOGISTS

Dr. Medhat el Mufti, Al-Salam Hospital

Dr. Ramzi Onsy, Anglo-American Hospital

EAR NOSE THROAT

Dr. Abu Bakr Shannon, 73 Rd. 9, MA, 359-5631

Dr. Ayman Daoud, Anglo-American Hospital

GENERAL PRACTITIONERS

Dr. Ahmed Ismail, 146 al-Gumhuriya, DT, 391-5815

Dr. Sherif Zakher, Anglo-American Hospital and 735-9836, h: 417-9396, 012 211-0144, 010 555-1000

INTERNAL MEDICINE

Dr. Akil Youssef, Anglo-American Hospital, ZA, 736-8630 (direct), 735-6162/3/4/5 x315

MAMMOGRAPHY

Dr. Hanan Gweifel, CairoScan, MO

Mammoscan, The Mammography Center, 6B Midan Aswan, MO, 345-8575

NEUROLOGISTS

Dr. Akil Youssef, Anglo-American Hospital, 736-8630 (direct)

Dr. Hassan Hosny, Shaalan Surgicenter and Cairo Medical Tower

NEUROSURGEONS

Dr. Ahmed Naguib, As-Salam Hospital and 47 'Abd al-'Aziz al-Sa'ud, MN, 364-0615, h: 380-1315

Dr. Ahmed Zokhdi, Anglo-American Hospital

OBSTETRICS/GYNECOLOGY

Dr. Ahmed el-Menaoui, 2 Tal'at Harb, DT, 587-5575

Dr. Claude Mehreb, HE, 634-0848

Dr. Khaled Zaki, Shaalan Surgicenter and Family Health Care Clinic, MA, 380-6766

Dr. Hossam Badrawi, h: 344-2260 & Nil Badrawi Hospital

Dr. Mahmud al-Sherbini, Family Health Care Clinic, MA, 380-6766, emergency only: 012 212-3665

Dr. Mostafa M. El Sadek, Cairo Medical Tower, MO, 302-0167, 012 214-1511 (specialist in IVF and assisted conception)

Dr. Nevine Hafnawi, Cairo Motherhood Center, 760-1605

Dr. Salah Zaki, above Aberdeen Steak, Rd. 9, MA, 359-2844 (infertility specialist)

Dr. Sameh Zaki, 66 al-Manyal, MN, and Al-Salam Hospital outpatient, 362-0644

Dr. Salah Bassili, Anglo American Hospitals

Dr. Sherif Hamza, 53 al-Zahraa, MO, 748-737-4 and al-Fayrouz & Damascus Hospitals

OPTHAMOLOGISTS

Dr. 'Adel Hassouna, Anglo-American Hospital

Dr. Samia Sabry, 3 Rd. 79, Delta Bank Building, MA, 358-8008

ORAL, DENTAL, AND MAXILLOFACIAL SURGEONS

Dr. Hatem 'Abdel Rahman, 17 Gam'at al-Duwal al-'Arabiya, MO, 347-8282

Dr. Mahmud Hosny, 40 Tal'at Harb, Apt. 31, 575-7910, phone/fax 575-6276; e-mail: dsmc@ritsec1.com.eg.

ORTHOPEDISTS

Dr. Ashraf Muharram, 92 al-Tahrir, DK, 762-0560, 010 142-0049

Dr. Atef Hanna, Anglo-American Hospital

Dr. Samir Fanous, Shaalan Surgicenter (760-3920) and 18 Mahmud Basyuni, 575-4623

Dr. Sherif Zaghloul, 6 Rd. 162A, MA, 378-7208, 359-5806

PLASTIC & RECONSTRUCTIVE SURGEONS

Dr. Fathi Khodeir, Cairo Tower, 338-1868, h: 572-6372

Dr. Ibrahim Naguib, Shaalan Surgicenters

Dr. Karim Massaoud, Anglo-American and 'Ain Shams

Dr. Nabil Elsahy, Cairo Tower Hospital

PEDIATRICIANS

Dr. Adel Reyad, 10 Abu Bakr al-Siddiq, HE, 639-6373, 633-0842

Prof Elhamy Rifky, 8 Rd. 78, MA, 359-5347

Dr. Fawzan Shaltout, 87 Rd. 9, MA, 359-5323

Dr. Ibrahim Shoukry, Cairo Tower and h: 359-1737, 392-2585, 358-4207, evenings, 302-4577

Dr. Lamas Ragab, Shaalan Surgicenter

Dr. Nasr Gamal, 344-8055 and h: 302-2255

Dr. Sandra (aka Hayat) Tabbara, Shaalan Surgicenter

Dr. Sherif Ibaa Faltaous, 43 Rd. 9, MA, 358-5196, 012 218-5563

PSYCHOLOGISTS/ PSYCHIATRISTS

Dr. Isis Badrawi, Community Services Association, 735-5284, 376-8283

Maadi Psychology Center, 16 'Urabi, Old Maadi, 359-2278, 010 657-0691;

Emergency on–call Behman Hospital, 555-7551

Dr. Nasser Loza, Behman Hospital, Helwan, 358-0711, 229-2821, 591-9340 (clinic)

SURGEONS, GENERAL

Dr. Adel Hosny, 3 Rd. 79, Delta Bank Blg, MA, 378-7525

Dr. Galil Greis, Anglo-American, As-Salam, and 31 Wizarat al-Zira'a, DK, 335-9334

Dr. Samir Massaoud, Anglo-American

UROLOGISTS

Dr. Hossam Mustafa, Al-Salam and Shaalan Surgicenter

DOOR KNOBS

Modern Metals, 1 Qattawi, Ataba

DRAMA GROUPS

Cairo Players, contact CSA on 358-0754

HCAA Drama Group, 632-3615, 290-9885

Maadi Community Players, 358-5577, www.angelfire.com/ca/maadiplayers

DRAPERIES

See Fabrics

DRESSMAKERS/DESIGNERS

Dafna Edwards, DK, 337-9597

Nagada, 8 Dar al-Shifa, GC, 792-3249

Women's Association (for referrals), 760-3475

DRYCLEANERS

Nile Hilton Drycleaning, Nile Hilton, DT, 578-0666

Ramsis Drycleaning, 161, 26th July, ZA, 735-3058

Select, 50 Ahmad Hishmat, ZA
(specialist in leather)

EDUCATIONAL EVALUATIONS

Dawna Peterson, CSA, 358-
5284

ELECTRONIC SUPPLIES

CompuMall, 7 al-Sakhawi, off
al-Khalifa Ma'mun, HE

Multimedia Mega Stores,
Midan Sphinx, MO

El-Nekhely Brothers and Co.
Ltd., electronic and scientific
equipment components, 176
Tahrir, DT, 392-7592, 393-
6301, 390-9916, fax 392-
8612, 20 Yusif al-Gindi, DT,
392-3500

Radio Shack, 42 Shahab, MO,
303-4799; NC, 403-7430;
MA, 520-3386; Beirut, HE,
414-9153; Merryland, HE,
454-6858; ZA, 737-1506;
GZ, 762-63137; Ataba, 391-
1633; Ramsis Hilton,
575-5717

EMBASSIES & CONSULATES

Afghanistan, 59 'Uruba, HE,
417-7236, fax 417-7238

Albania, 18, Salah al-Din, ZA,
fax 736-9130

Algeria, 14 Brazil, ZA, 736-
8527, 736-1520, fax
736-4158

Angola, 12 Muhi al-Din Abu
al-'Izz, MO, 337-7602,
749-8259, fax 337-8683

Argentina, 8 al-Salih Ayyub,
Apt. 2, ZA, 735-1501,
736-0652, fax 736-4355

Armenia, 20 Muhammad
Mazhar, ZA, 737-4157/9,
fax 737-4158

Australia, World Trade Center,
WTC, 12th floor, 575-0444,
fax 578-1638, visa 1636,
trade 579-2022

Austria, 5 Wisa Wasif, Riyad
Tower, 5th fl., GZ,
570-2975, fax 570-2979

Azerbaijan, 22 Hasan 'Asim,
ZA, 735-1230, 736-1228
(both also fax)

Bahrain, 15 Brazil, ZA,
735-6605, fax 736-6609

Bangladesh, 20 Gazirit al-
'Arab, MO, 346-2003/9, fax
336-2008

Belgium, 20 Kamil al-
Shinnawi, GC, 794-
7494/95/96, fax 794-3147

Bolivia, 5 Dar al-Shifa, GC,
762-4361

Bosnia/Herzogovinia, 42 al-
Sawra, DK, 749-9191, fax
749-9190

Brazil, 1125 Corniche al-Nil,
Maspero, 577-3013, fax
576-1040

Brunei, 24 Hasan 'Asim, ZA,
736-6355/65, fax 736-6375

Bulgaria, 6 al-Malek al-Afdal,
ZA, 736-3025, fax 736-3826

Burkina Faso, 22 Wadi al-Nil,
MA, 380-8956/63, fax
380-6974

Burundi, 27 Riyad, MO, 302-
4301/2, fax 344-1997

Cameroon, 15 Muhammad
Subki, MO, 344-1114, 344-
1101, fax 345-9208 (No
diplomatic representation)

Canada, 26 Kamil al-Shinnawi,
GC, 794-3110, fax 796-3548

Central African Republic, 46
Muhi al-Din Abu al-'Izz,
MO, 762-9481/2, fax 760-
6595

Chad, 12 Midan al-Rifa'i, DK,
337-3379, 749-4461, fax
337-3232

Chile, 1 al-Salih Ayyub, 7th fl.,
ZA, 735-8446, fax 735-3716

China, 14 Bahgat 'Ali, ZA,
935-9728, fax 735-9459

Colombia, 6 al-Gazira, ZA,
736-4203, fax 735-7429

Commission of the European
Community, 37 Gam'at al-
Duwal al-'Arabiya, MO,
749-4680, fax 735-0385

Comoros, 13 /Arafat, DK,
phone/fax 760-9876

Congo (Brazzaville), 4 Ibn
Umayya, NC, 345-9431

Croatia, 3 Abu al-Fida, 10th fl.,
ZA, 735-5815, fax 735-5812

Cuba, 10 al-Kamil Muhammad,
ZA, 736-0651, fax 736-0656

Cyprus, 23A Isma'il
Muhammad, ZA, 736-
1288/0327, fax 736-5299

Czech Republic, 4 al-Dukki,
GZ, 748-5531/6550, fax
748-5892

Democratic Republic of Congo,
5 al-Mansur Muhammad,
ZA, 736-1069, 735-7954,
fax 735-4342

Denmark, 12 Hasan Sabri, ZA,
735-6500, fax 736-1780

Djibouti, 15 Muhammad 'Abd
al-Sa'id, DK, 336-6434/5,
fax 336-6437

Ecuador, 4/6 Ibn Kasir, Suez
Canal Bldg., 11th fl., GZ,
736-1839, fax 760-9327

Eritrea, 6 Salah, MO,
phone/fax 335-5958

Ethiopia, 11 Midan al-Misaha,
MO, 335-3693/6, 335-3937,
fax 335-3699

Finland, 3 Abu al-Fida, 13th fl.,
ZA, 736-1487/3722/7786,
735-2801, fax 737-1376

France, 29 al-Murad , GZ, 570-
3916/17-20, fax 571-0276

Gabon, 59 Surya, MO,
304-3972/3, fax 303-4249

Georgia, 28 al-Sadd al-'Ali, DK, 335-9024/34, fax 336-6129

Germany, 2 Berlin, ZA, 739-9600, fax 736-0530

Ghana, 1 26th July, Midan Libnan, MO, 303-2294, 344-4000/455, fax 303-2292

Greece, 18 'Aysha al-Taymuriya, GC, 795-5915/1074/0443, fax 796-3903

Guatemala, 17 Port Said, 5th fl., MA, 380-2914, fax 380-2915

Guinea, 46 Muhammad Mazhar, ZA, 735-8408, 735-8109, fax 736-1446

Honduras, 21 Ahmad Hishmat, ZA, 344-1377/8, fax 736-3835

Hungary, 29 Muhammad Mazhar, ZA, 735-0659/8634/8659, fax 735-8648

India, 5 'Aziz Abaza, ZA, 736-3051/0052, 735-6053, fax 736-4038

Indonesia, 13 'Aysha al-Taymuriya, GC, 794-7209/7200/7356, fax 796-2495

Iran interests section, 12 Rifa'a al-Tahtawi, Midan al-Misaha, DK, 762-2731/2, fax 749-6821

Iraq, 9 Muhammad Mazhar, ZA, 735-9205/8087/8735, fax 736-5075

Ireland, 3 Abu al-Fida, 7th fl., ZA, 735-8547/8264, 736-4653, fax 736-2863

Israel, 6 Ibn Malik, GZ, 761-0380, fax 761-0414

Italy, 15 'Abd al-Rahman Fahmi, GC, 794-0658/3195, fax 794-0657

Ivory Coast, 9 Ibrahim Suliman, MO, 303-6374/4373, fax 305-0148

Japan, Cairo Center Bldg., 2nd fl., 106 Qasr al-'Aini, DT, 795-7553/3962, fax 796-3540

Jordan, 6 al-Guhayni, DK, 748-5566/6169/7543, 749-9912, fax 760-1027

Kazakhistan, 4 Rd. 256, al-Ma'adi al-Gadida, MA, 358-6445 (fax and phone)

Kenya, 29 al-Quds al-Sharif, MO, 345-3628, 345-3907, fax 302-6979

Kuwait, 12 Nabil al-Waqqad, DK, 760-2661/2, fax 760-2656/7

Lebanon, 22 Mansur Muhammad, ZA, 738-2823/4/5, fax 738-2818

Lesotho, 21B 'Uman, DK, 749-3211, fax 748-9543

Liberia, 40A Muhammad Mazhar, ZA, 336-7046, fax 735-6094

Libya, 7 al-Salih Ayyub, ZA, 736-7862, fax 735-0072

Malaysia, 21 al-A'nab, MO, 761-0013/19/68/73, fax 761-0216

Mali, 3 al-Kawsar, DK, 337-1895, fax 337-1841

Malta, 25, Rd. 12, MA, 736-2368/9, fax 380-4452

Marshall Islands, 8 Muhammad Bayumi, Ard al-Gulf, HE, 417-4246, fax 291-8828

Mauritania, 114 Muhi al-Din Abu al-'Izz, DK, 749-0671, 749-1046, 749-0699, fax 748-9060

Mauritius, 156 Sudan, MO, 761-8102/3, fax 761-8101

Mexico, 17 Port Sa'id, 5th fl., MA, 358-0256/7/8/9, fax 359-1887

Mongolia, 14 Rd. 152, MA, 358-6012, fax 359-6074

Morocco, 10 Salah al-Din, ZA, 736-4718, fax 736-1937

Mozambique, 2 Tehran, DK, 748-6389, fax 748-6378

Myanmar (Burma), 24 Muhammad Mazhar, ZA, 735-4176, 736-2644, fax 736-6793

Nepal, 23 al-Hasan, MO, 760-3426, 761-6590, fax 337-4447

Netherlands, 18 Hasan Sabri, ZA, 739-5500, 739-5599, fax 736-5249

New Zealand, for visas and emergencies call the British embassy

Niger, 101 al-Haram, GZ, 386-5607, 386-5617, fax 386-5690

Nigeria, 13 al-Gabalaya, ZA, 735-6042, 736-7894, 735-3907, fax 735-7359

North Korea, 6 al-Salih Ayyub, ZA, 736-9532, fax 735-8219

Norway, 8 al-Gazira, ZA, 735-3340, fax 737-0709

Oman, 52 al-Higaz, MO, 303-6011, 303-5942, fax 303-6464

Pakistan, 8 al-Saluli, DK, 748-7806/7677, fax 748-0310

Palestine, 33 al-Nahda, DK, 338-4761/2/3, fax 338-4760

Panama, 4A Ibn Zinki, ZA, 736-1093/94, 735-0784, fax 736-1092

Paraguay, 9 Shagarit al-Durr, ZA, 735-1708, fax 735-1708

Peru, 8 Kamil al-Shinnawi, GC, 356-2973, fax 795-7642

Philippines, 14 Muhammad Salih, DK, 748-0396/0398, fax 748-0393

Poland, 5 'Aziz 'Usman, ZA,
735-5416, 735-9583,
736-7456, fax 735-5427

Portugal, 1 al-Salih Ayyub,
ZA, 735-0781, 735-0823,
fax 735-0799

Qatar, 10 al-Simar, MO,
760-4693/4, fax 760-3618

Romania, 6 al-Kamil
Muhammad, ZA, 736-0107,
fax 736-0851

Russia, 95 al-Giza, GZ, 748-
9353/4/5/6, fax 760-9074

Rwanda, 21B 'Uman, DK,
337-9947/8, fax 335-3364

San Marino, 5 Ramiz, MO,
760-2718, fax 393-9362

Saudi Arabia, 2 Ahmad Nasim,
GZ, 749-0797, 749-0775,
fax 749-3495

Senegal, 46 'Abd al-Mun'im
Riyad, MO, 346-0946,
346-0896, fax 346-1039

Serbia-Montenegro, 33 al-
Mansur Muhammad, ZA,
735-4473, 735-4061,
fax 735-3913

Singapore, 40 'Adnan 'Umar
Sidqi (formerly Babel), DK,
749-5045/0468,
fax 748-1682

Slovakia, 3 'Adil Husayn
Rustum, DK, 335-8240,
335-7544, 337-6901,
fax 335-5810

Slovenia, 21 Suliman Abaza,
6th fl., MO, 749-1771,
749-9878 fax 749-7141

Somalia, 27 Iran, DK, 337-
4577/4038, fax 337-4577

South Africa, 55 Rd. 18., MA,
359-4975, 359-4952,
359-4365, fax 359-5015

South Korea, 3 Bulus Hanna
Basha, DK, 761-1234/5/6/7,
fax 761-1238

Spain, 41 Isma'il Muhammad,
ZA, 735-6437, 735-5813,
fax 735-2132

Sri Lanka, 8 Sri Lanka, ZA,
735-4966, 735-0047,
fax 736-7138

Sudan, 3 al-Ibrahim, GC,
794-9661, fax 794-2693

Sweden, 13 Muhammad
Mazhar, ZA, 736-
1484/4132, fax 735-4357

Switzerland, 10 'Abd al-Khaliq
Sarwat, DT, 575-8133/ 8284,
fax 574-5236

Syria, 18 'Abd al-Rahim Sabri,
DK, 335-8806/8320, 337-
7020, fax 335-8232

Tanzania, 11 Abu al-Karamat,
AG, 345-7559, fax 345-7559

Thailand, 2 al-Malik al-Afdal,
ZA, 735-8356/0299, fax
736-0094, e-mail:
thaiemb@idsc.gov.eg

Tunisia, 26 al-Gazira, ZA,
735-4940, 736-8962,
fax 736-2479

Turkey, 25 al-Falaki, Bab al-
Luq, 794-8364, 796-3318,
fax 795-4600

Uganda, 9 Midan al-Misaha,
DK, 748-6070, fax 748-5980

Ukraine, 50 Rd. 83, MA,
378-6871/2, fax 378-6873

United Arab Emirates, 4 Ibn
Sina, GZ, 776-6102,
fax 570-0844

United Kingdom, 7 Ahmad
Raghib, GC, 794-0850/52-
58, fax 794-0859

United States of America, 5
Tawfiq Diyab (Amrika al-
Latiniya), GC, 797-3300,
fax 797-3200

Uruguay, 6 Lutfallah, ZA, 735-
3589, 736-5137, fax 736-
8123, e-mail:
urugemb@idsc.gov.eg

Uzbekistan, 18 al-Sadd al-'Ali,
DK, 336-1723/4516,
fax 336-1722

Vatican, 5 Muhammad Mazhar,
ZA, 735-2250, fax 735-6152

Venezuela, 15A Mansur
Muhammad, ZA, 736-4332,
736-4343/3517,
fax 736-7373

Vietnam, 39 Jeddah, MO,
335-1189, fax 336-8612

Yemen, 28 Amin al-Rifa'i,
Midan al-Misaha, DK,
761-4224/5/6, fax 760-4815

Zaire: see Democratic Republic
of Congo

Zambia, 21 al-Sheikh
Muhammad al-Ghazali, DK,
761-0281/82, fax 761-0833

Zimbabwe, 40 Ghazza, MO,
305-9743, 303-0404,
fax 305-9741

EMBROIDERY

See Sewing Supplies & Notions

ENVIRONMENTALISM

Arab Office for Youth and
Environment (AOYE), 302-
8391/2/4/5, fax 304-1635,
e-mail: aoye@ritsec1.com.eg

Association for the Protection
of Services in Zamalek, 1 al-
Kamil Muhammad, ZA,
735-6256, fax 337-6001;
contact: Ennas Omar

Association for the Protection
of the Environment, PO Box
32, al-Qal'a, Cairo, 341-
2723, fax 341-7149, e-mail:
ape1@idsc.gov.eg

Egyptian Environmental
Affairs Agency, 735-2665

Tree Lovers Association;
contact: Nour al-Daly, 380-
6868 or Dr. Abdel al-Wahab
al-Morsy, 358-0229

EXERCISE CLASSES

See Sports

EXTERMINATORS

Bestox, 16 Huda Sha'rawi, DT,
392-0021, 395-6606,
fax 392-4019

Sayonara Cleaning Service, 4
Bahgat Sharara, Shubra, DT,
203-5592

Soteico, 2 al-Shahid Sayyid
Zakariya, HE, 266-1274/6,
fax 266-1342

EYE GLASSES

See Opticians

FABRICS

CLOTHING

Ahmed & Mahmud, Qasr al-
Nil, DT

Chalons, Qasr al-Nil, DT,
393-1026

Champs Elysées, 32 Qasr al-
Nil, DT

Chez Elle, 32 Makka, MO,
365-7605

House of Fabric, 6 Isma'il
Muhammad, ZA, 736-0486

Lamour, Qasr al-Nil, DT

Madame, Qasr al-Nil, DT

Miss Paris, 21 Qasr al-Nil, DT,
393-8818/1492

Nagada, 8 Dar al-Shifa', GC
792-3249

Raytex, 38 al-Hurriya, HE,
290-1734; Arkadia Mall,
Corniche al-Nil, 574-8747;
28 Tal'at Harb DT, Maadi
Grand Mall, MA, Citystars,
NC, 480-2017; 15 Nadi al-
Seid, DK, 335-0715

Salem, 18 al-Quds al-Sharif,
MO, 302-8357/8356

Sayyidati al-Gamila, Qasr al-
Nil, DT

Shatex, 26 Ibrahim al-Laqqani,
al-Kurba, HE, 417-6937; 72
al-Nasr, New Maadi,
754-6783; 27 Libnan, MO,
305-3813

TexMar, 73 'Umar Ibn al-
Khattab, DK, 418-4212

HOME FURNISHING

Bayan Palace, 9 al-Sawra, HE,
634-3177; also Ramses
Hilton 5th fl.

Carpet City, branches
everywhere

Etoile Mardini, 33 'Amman,
DK, 760-0936 & 761-0695;
13 al-Khalifa al-Ma'mun,
HE, 291-5199/2126; WTC

Everon, 19 Abu al-Fida, ZA,
735-9575/3488; 19 Rd. 231,
Digla, MA, 702-6652

La Part du Sable, 4 Ahmad
Hishmat, Flat 9, ZA, 738-
3345; contact: Christine
Roussillon

Ouf, al-Azhar, KK

Tanis, 577-7972; First Mall, 35
Giza, GZ, 573-0609

FAX MACHINES

See Business Equipment

FILM PROCESSING

Alfa Market, Riyadh Tower, al-
Nil, GZ, 572-6203

Antar Photo Stores, 180, al-
Tahrir, DT, 794-0786,
795-4449

Kodak, 20 'Adli, DT,
394-2200, fax 393-1199

Kodak, 19 Isma'il Muhammad,
ZA 735-9517, 737-0583

Philippe Photo Trade, 1A Midan
al-Misaha, DK, 748-5181

Photo Center, 3 al-Mahrani, off
al-Sharifein between Qasr
al-Nil and Sabri Abu 'Alam
DT, 392-0031 (professional
quality)

FLAGS AND BANNERS

El Banna, 53 al-Gumhuriya,
DT, 593-4951

Seif Nasr Flags, 22 Qasr al-Nil,
DT, 392-1581

FLORISTS

AGOUZA

Fessel A. Shaib, next to British
Council, 192 al-Nil,
347-8800, 303-1114

DOKKI

Dina Flor, 143 al-Tahrir,
748-4417 (wholesale)

Rika, 1 Midan Ibn Affan and
Gamal Salem (near Feyrouz
Hospital), 760-0769

GIZA

Fleurtations, 3 Ibn Kasir, GZ,
761-9470

MAADI

Flower Center, 6 Rd. 205,
Digla

Orchide Flower, 85 Rd. 9,
359-3446

Pharonic Flowers, 70 Rd. 9
(across from Pizza Hut)

ZAMALEK

Gardenia Flowers, 5 al-Sayyid
al-Bakri, 735-9586,
738-0692

Touch Flowers, 14 Taha
Husayn (at Muhammad al-
Mar'ashli), ZA, 736-9007

FLOWER ARRANGING CLASSES

Japanese Embassy, 795-7553

FOOTBALL

See Sports

FRAMING

Amgad Naguib, 392-1054

Espace Karim Francis, Cairo

City Center, 1 Sharifein, 2nd fl. off Midan Tal'at Harb, DT, 736-2183

Framco, 26th July (near High Court), DT, 575-2456; contact: Mrs. Iman

Reader's Corner, 33 'Abd al-Khaliq Sarwat, DT, 392-8801

World of Art Gallery and Framing, 6 Rd. 77C, MA, 359-4363

FREIGHT FORWARDERS

See Movers

FUNERAL SERVICES (CHRISTIAN)

Antoine George Tawaf, 127 Ramsis, DT, 591-3275

FURNITURE

DOKKI

Al Home, 38 Michael Bakhoum, 762-9526 (all types furniture & furnishings)

Asala, 8 Midan Ibn al-Walid, 761-4418 (all furnishings including custom kitchens)

Bon Bon, 34 Michael Bakhoum (children's), 335-2663

Collection, 87 Musaddaq, 749-4157 (traditional); contact: Said Moharam

Jadis, 38 Qambis (off Nadi al-Seid) (excellent traditional); contact: May Rehim

HELIOPOLIS

Belmondo, 3A Salah Salim, HE, fax 749-1266 (rustic)

Design Center Cairo, 7 Baghdad, 415-9752 (modern Italian and Egyptian copies)

Sucash, 12 'Abd al-Mun'im Hafiz, Almaza, 290-3695 (interior design, antiques, reproductions)

MAADI

Ahmed Gomaa, 73 Rd. 9, 380-4870 (Islamic-style inlaid furniture & antique metal work)

Artex Decorating and Contracting, 21A Rd. 275

Benzaion, Rd. 153, 358-4573 (furniture and housewares)

Carpet City, 151 al-Hurriya Sq., 525-5617 (all household needs); also branches everywhere

Styler, 3 Wahib Dos, 378-3198 (high fashion contemporary furniture)

MISCELLANEOUS

Alfostat, WTC, 580-4542, 577-6531 (high-style wrought-iron furniture); owner: Nadim Ayoub, www.alfostat.com

Cane, bamboo, rattan: Ramsis past railroad station

Fagnoon, WTC, 1st fl., 577-6180 (metal garden & other furnishings)

Gallery Mansour, Arkadia Mall, Corniche al-Nil, DT, 575-9045; 15 el Obour Bldgs, Salah Salim, HE, 260-1598; 64 al-Maryutiya, PY, 383-5349 (very expensive, high quality)

Khatun, 3 Zuqaq al-'Ain, behind al-Azhar and next to Bayt al-Harawi, 514-7164, 012 226-5329

Manasra District, 1 km down Sharia Muhammad 'Ali: many shops, prices a third of showrooms; also upholstering

Moroccan Konooz, 26 Rd. 233, 521-2548, www.moroccankonooz.com (furniture and home accessories)

Nadim, Industiral Zone, Abu Rawash, 28 Km Cairo–Alexandria Desert Road, (202) 539-1601-8

Rustic, 91A al-Mirghani, GC, 401-1282, 402-1282 (solid ·country-style furniture)

Taki, Idara Bldg., al-Firdus, 'Abbasiya (main outlet)

MOHANDISEEN

Animation, 28 Libnan, 344-0958; contact: Walid Gohar (modern & traditional home/office furniture; design service)

Arkadia, 7 'Abd al-Mun'im Riyad, 748-7579

Dimensione, 17 al-Higaz, 346-1237/0198, 347-0737; showroom, 2 al-Fawakih, 336-4326

Le Style de Paris, 13 'Abd al-Mun'im Riyad, 364-4136

Masterpiece, 17 Gazirit al-'Arab, 303-3196 (French and English style)

Mffco, 3 Libnan, 345-3071 (lots of bedroom suites)

Wood Mark, 32 'Abd al-Mun'im Riyad, 337-4100 (modern & traditional)

ZAMALEK

Alef, 14 Muhammad Anis, 737-0848, fax 737-0849 (eclectic; the best)

Bayt Sherif, 3A Bahgat 'Ali, 736-5689

Bizarre Bazaar, 10 Zakariya Rizq, 735-9509 (antique reproductions, modern)

Caravanserai, 12 Muhammad al-Mar'ashli

Ebony, 27 Abu al-Fida, 735-1823, 736-3634 (traditional)

Mit Rehan, 13 Muhammad al-Mar'ashli, fax 735-4378

Moroccan Konooz, 2 Isma'il
Muhammad, 735-3775,
www.moroccankonooz.com
(furniture and home
accessories)

Philosophy, 40B Muhammad
Mazhar, 738-0163
(European and Japanese
designers)

Ultra, 3 Mishil Lutfallah, 736-
4907 (modern high-style
furniture; branch in WTC)

USED/SECONDHAND

Noshiner, 14 Gawad Husni,
DT, 392-4371

Osman Furniture, 213 Ramsis,
DT, 592-4223

Sandy Trading, 1165 Corniche
al-Nil, Bulaq, 576-2402

GALLABIYAS

See also Clothing, Ethnic;
Khan al-Khalili, Gallabiyas

GALLERIES

See Art Galleries

GAMBLING CASINOS

Note: Foreign passport required
for entry; foreign currency
only

Cairo Sheraton Casino, Cairo
Sheraton Hotel, GZ,
336-9700/800

Casino Las Vegas, Shepheard
Hotel, GC, 795-3800

Casino Libnan, al-Salam
Swissôtel Cairo,
297-4000/297-6000

Casino Ramses Hilton, Ramses
Hilton Hotel, DT, 574-4400/
575-8000

Casino Semiramis, Semiramis
Intercontinental Hotel, GC,
795-7171

Le Casino, al-Gezirah Sheraton
Hotel, ZA, 736-1333

Mövenpick Casino, Cairo
Heliopolis Mövenpick Hotel,
HE, 291-9400/637-0077

Nile Hilton Casino, Nile Hilton
Hotel, Midan al-Tahrir, DT,
578-0444/666

Omar Khayyam Casino, Cairo
Marriott Hotel, ZA,
735-8888

Sheherazade, Mena House
Oberoi Hotel, Pyramids
Road, GZ, 383-3222/444

GARDENING SUPPLIES

See also Plant Nurseries

Taht al-Rab' market next to
Security Police Adminis-
tration Building opposite
Islamic Museum, DT

GIFTS

See Arts & Crafts

GLASS

El Nasr Glass & Crystal Co.,
11 al-Sharifein, DT, 392-
1675, 393-1711

National Company for Glass &
Crystal, 16 'Abd al-Khaliq
Sarwat, DT, 392-6615

Stained Glass, 95 al-Mirghani,
HE, 418-3235, 263-9376,
Hazem Shoukry

GLASS BLOCKS

Buildmore Installation
Services, 17 'Ali Shalabi,
HE, 636-7821, 632-9609

Nassib Torcom, 15 'Imad al-
Din, DT, 591-1800/1102

GLASSWARE

See Khan al-Khalili

A Touch of Glass, 8 al-Sheikh
Marsafi, ZA, 736-2392

GOLF

See Sports

GREETING CARDS

See Stationery

GROCERIES

See Supermarkets

GUNS

See Hunting & Fishing

HAIRDRESSERS

See Beauty Salons

HANDICRAFTS

See Arts & Crafts

HARDWARE

Dary (*see* Home Repairs)

Khatib Co., 45 al-Azhar (near
Bur Sa'id), Ataba

HEALTH CLUBS

DOKKI

American Fitness Hall, 17 al-
Mathaf al-Zira'i, 335-5598

New Silhouette Figure Shapers,
10 Midan al-Misaha, 749-
7958

DOWNTOWN

Nile Hilton Health Club, 578-
0444, 578-0666 ext. 207

SheriNile Health Club, Ramses
Hilton, 577-7113

SheriNile Health Club, WTC,
576-8030

WTC Health Club, WTC,
764-425

GIZA

Nile Gold's Gym, 121
Corniche al-Nil, 748-5565

STEP, Villa 13, Hadayik al-
Ahram, off Cairo–
Alexandria Desert Road,
behind Movenpick Hotel
Pyramids, GZ, 383-2571,
742-2980, 010 606-6181,
www.step-center.com

HELIOPOLIS

Royal Health Club, 4A al-
Khalifa al-Ma'mun, Roxy,
454-6700, 455-0001/11
SheriNile Health Club,
Meridien Heliopolis,
290-5055
The Studio, 26 Muhammad
'Abd al-Hadi, Ard al-Gulf,
417-0445
Valentines, 70 al-Mirghani,
417-738-1 (women only)
World Gym, 13 al-Ma'had al-
Ishtiraki (Merryland),
450-9212/3/4

MAADI

Community Services
Association, 4 Rd. 21, 358-
5284, 768-8232, 358-0754
Gold's Gym, 1 Midan al-
Mahatta, Maadi Palace Mall,
8th fl., 380-3601
Maadi Health Club, Maadi
Hotel, 358-5050 x333

MOHANDISEEN

Creative Dance and Fitness
Center, 6 'Amr, off Surya,
302-0572, fax 302-0571
Al Nabila Hotel Health Club, 4
Gam'at al-Duwal al-
'Arabiya, 346-1131,
347-3384, fax 347-5661

ZAMALEK

Fitness and Dance Academy,
Yamama Center, 8th fl., 3
Taha Husayn, 737-7500
Silhouette, 4B Muhammad
Mazhar, 735-5039

HEARING AIDS

El Nahar Commercial Co., 6A
Gawad Husni, DT, 393-
0247, fax 392-5839

HEATERS

See Appliances

HENNA

Sattuna, 012 210-1428 (for
parties, weddings, and
individuals)

HERBS

Harraz Herb Shop, Ahmad
Mahir, Bab al-Khalq

HOBBIES

See also Bridge, Needlework,
etc., and Sports
Hobby Shop, 9 Mukhtar al-
Misri, Ard al-Gulf, HE,
419-9258

HOME REPAIR

Dary, 330 al-Haram at Midan
Madkur, GZ, 578-8086/7

HORSES & HORSEBACK RIDING

See Sports

HOSES

See Gardening Supplies

HOSPITALS

DOKKI

El Fayrouz Hospital, 25 Gamal
Salim
Misr International Hospital, 12
al-Saraya, Midan Fini, 335-
6555, 760-1624

DOWNTOWN

Italian Hospital in Cairo, 17
Bayn al-Sarayat, 'Abbasiya,
682-1581/1582/ 2397

GARDEN CITY AND SOUTH

El Nada Hospital (Obstetric
and Gynecology), 54
Manyal, Roda, 531-1616
National Cancer Institute, 33
Qasr al-'Aini, 368-0106

Qasr al-'Aini Teaching
Hospital, Corniche al-Nil,
365-4060/1/9

HELIOPOLIS

Arab Contractors Medical
Center, Autostrade, NC
342-6000
Cleopatra Hospital, 39
Cleopatra, Midan Salah al-
Din, 414-3931/25
Hayatt Medical Center, 6
Minis, 290-7017/7027,
fax 417-5832
Nozha Int'l Hospital, behind
Sheraton buildings,
266-0555

MAADI

As-Salam International
Hospital, Corniche al-Nil,
524-0250/0077
Nil Badrawi Hospital, Corniche
al-Nil, 524-0022

MOHANDISEEN

Damascus Hospital, 1 Dimishq,
347-0194
El Safa Hospital, 40 al-'Iraq off
Shahab, 336-1010,
fax 749-8750
As-Salam Hospital, 3 Surya,
302-9091–5
Shalaan SurgiCenter, 10 'Abd
al-Hamid Lutfi, 760-
3920/5180; inpatient
748-8578; clinic 748-5479,
010 105-0576

ZAMALEK

Anglo-American Hospital, al-
Burg (just west of Cairo
Tower), 735-6162/6165, fax
735-4304

HOTELS IN CAIRO

DOKKI

Cairo Sheraton, Midan al-Gala',
336-9700, fax 336-4601

193

Pyramisa, 60 Giza,
336-7000/8000/9000,
fax 760-5347

DOWNTOWN AND GARDEN CITY

Conrad International, 1191
Corniche al-Nil, next to
WTC, 580-8000,
fax 580-8080

Cosmopolitan, 1 Ibn Tha'lab,
DT, 392-3845/3663/3956,
fax 393-3531

Four Seasons, 1089 Corniche
al-Nil, GC, 573-1212

Garden City House, 23 Kamal
al-Din Salah, GC, 794-
4969/8400, fax 794-4126

Grand Hyatt Cairo, Corniche
al-Nil, GC, 365-1234,
fax 362-1927

Nile Hilton, Midan al-Tahrir,
578-0666/444, fax 578-0475

Pension Roma, 169
Muhammad Farid, 4th fl.,
DT, 391-1340/1088, fax
(reservations only) 579-6243

Ramses Hilton, 1115 Corniche
al-Nil, 577-7444, 574-4400,
fax 575-7152/578-2221

Semiramis Intercontinental,
Corniche al-Nil, GC,
795-7171, fax 796-3020

Shepheard, 5 Corniche al-Nil,
GC, 792-1000, fax 792-1010

Sun Hotel, 2 Tal'at Harb,
Midan Tahrir, 773-0087,
578-1786

Talisman, 39 Tal'at Harb, 393-
9431, 010 125-6212

Windsor, 19 al-Alfi, DT, 591-
5277/810, fax 592-1621

HELIOPOLIS

Baron, 8 Ma'had al-Sahari, off
al-'Uruba, 291-5757, fax
290-7077

Intercontinental Heliopolis
Cairo, 'Umar Ibn al-Khattab,
480-0100

Le Meridien Heliopolis, 51 al-
'Uruba, 290-5055/1819, fax
291-8591

Mövenpick Heliopolis, Airport
Road, 637-0077; 291-9400,
fax 418-0761

Novotel, Cairo Airport, 291-
8577/20, fax 291-4794

Sheraton Heliopolis, al-'Uruba,
267-7730, fax 267-7600

Swissôtel as-Salam, 69 'Abd
al-Hamid Badawi, 622-
4000/6000, fax 622-6037

MAADI

Sofitel, Corniche al-Nil, Maadi
Towers, 526-0601/2, fax
526-1133

MOHANDISEEN

Atlas Zamalek, 20 Gam'at al-
Duwal al-'Arabiya, 346-
6569/4175, fax 347-6958

Jasmin, 29 Gazirit al-'Arab,
346-3621, 347-2278, fax
344-5906

Al Nabila, 4 Gam'at al-Duwal
al-'Arabiya, 303-0302, fax
347-5661

PYRAMIDS

Four Seasons, 35 Giza, 573-1212,
fax 568-1616

Jolie Ville, Cairo–Alexandria
Desert Road, 385-2555,
fax 383-5006

Le Meridien Pyramids,
Cairo–Alexandria Desert
Road, 377-3388/7070,
fax 383-1730

Le Sphinx Sofitel,
Cairo–Alexandria Desert
Road, 383-7444/555, fax
383-4930

Mena House Oberoi, al-Haram,
383-3222/444, fax 383-7777

Sheraton Royal Gardens,
Hilmiyit al-Ahram,
781-2211

Siag Pyramids Hotel, al-
Haram, Saqqara Road,
385-6022, fax 385-7413

SIXTH OF OCTOBER

Hilton Pyramids Golf Resort
Dreamland, al-Wahat, 6th of
October City, 855-3333

Movenpick Cairo Media City,
6th of October, 840-1001

ZAMALEK

Cairo Marriott, Saray al-
Gazira, 735-8888,
fax 735-6667

Flamenco, 2 al-Gazira al-
Wusta, 735-0815/6,
fax 735-0819

Gezirah Sheraton, 737-3737,
fax 736-3640, 735-5056

Horus House, 21 Isma'il
Muhammad, 735-3634,
fax 735-3182

Mayfair Hotel, 9 al-'Aziz
'Usman, 735-7315,
fax 735-0424

Pension Zamalek, 6 Salah al-
Din, 735-9318

President, 22 Taha Husayn,
735-0652/0718,
fax 736-1752

Safir Zamalek, 21 Muhammad
Mazhar, 737-0055/1203, fax
737-1202

HOTELS OUT OF CAIRO

Mövenpick: central
reservations 291-9400; fax
292-9684; locations: Sirena
Beach(Qusir), Crocodile
Island (Luxor), Giza
Pyramids, Heliopolis,
Fortune 1 Diving Ship

ALEXANDRIA

Cecil Hotel, Midan Sa'd
Zaghlul, Raml Station, (03)
480-7224

Helnan Palestine Hotel,
Montazah Palace Grounds,
(03) 547-4033
Marriott Renaissance Hotel,
544 al-Geish, Sidi Bishr,
(03) 549-0935
Montazah Sheraton, al-
Corniche, (03) 548-0550
El-Salamlek Palace Hotel and
Casino, Montazah Gardens,
(03) 547-7999

ASWAN
Amoun Club Med,
(097) 313-800, 313-850
Basma Swiss Inn,
(097) 310-901
Kalabsha, (097) 322-666
Old Cataract, (097) 316-000

DAHAB
Helnan Dahab Hotel, (069)
640-425/6, fax (069) 640-
428
Hilton Dahab Resort, (069)
640-310, fax (069) 640-424

GOUNA
Movenpick Resort,
(065) 544-501
Sheraton Miramar, (065) 545-
684, fax (065) 549-065
Three Corners Rihana Resort,
(065) 58-0025

HURGHADA
Intercontinental Resort and
Casino, (065) 446-911,
fax (065) 446-910
Marriott Beach Resort (065)
446-950
Sofitel, (065) 442-266, fax
(065) 442-270

LUXOR
Club Med Bella Donna,
(095) 384-000/4 (in Cairo:
Club Med, 48 Musaddaq,
DK, 761-4441, 748-2783)
Gaddis, (095) 382-838, fax
382-837

Mina Palace, (095) 382-194,
372-074
Al Moudira (West Bank), 012
325-1307,
www.almoudirahotel.com
Movenpick, (095) 374-855
Pharaoh's (West Bank) (095)
310-702
Winter Palace, (095) 371-191,
371-196

NUWEIBA
Domina Nuweiba Hotel,
(06) 950-0401
Helnan Nuweiba Village,
(069) 500-401/2-4, fax
(069) 500-407
Nuweiba Hilton Coral Resort,
(069) 520-320/1-6, fax
(069) 520-327
Shams Safaga Hotel,
(06) 525-1781

SHARM AL-SHEIKH
Camel Dive Hotel,
(069) 6000-700
Coral Bay Hotel, Sheikh Coast,
(069) 601-610/40, fax (069)
600-843
Hilton Fayrouz, Na'ama Bay,
(069) 600-272, 600-137
Marriot Beach Resort, Na'ama
Bay, (069) 600-190, fax
(069) 600-188
Novotel, Na'ama Bay, (069)
600-173/74-82, fax (069)
600-177/93
Ritz-Carlton, Ras Umm al-Sid,
(069) 661-919, fax (069)
661-920
Sanafir, Na'ama Bay, (069)
600-197
Sharm Movenpick Jolie Ville,
Na'ama Bay, (069) 600-
100/1-5, fax (069) 600-111
Sharm al-Sheikh Hilton
Fayrouz Resort, Na'ama
Bay, (069) 660-136/37-43,
fax (069) 661-040

Sofitel, Na'ama Bay, (069)
600-081/2-4, fax (069)
600-085
Sonesta Beach Resort, Na'ama
Bay, (069) 600-725/26-32,
fax (069) 600-733

HOUSING AGENTS
See Real Estate Agents

HUNTING & FISHING EQUIPMENT
Abu Dief, 168 al-Tahrir, DT,
392-5244
Alfa Market (upstairs)
Corniche al-Nil, Maadi,
525-6400/30; 4 al-Malik al-
Afdal, ZA, 737-0801/02

HYPNOSIS
See Alternative Therapies

IMPORT-EXPORT
See Directories

INSURANCE, MEDICAL
Anglo-American Hospital,
736-8630 or 735-6162/3/4/5
x315

INTERIOR DESIGNERS
Dibaj, 54 al-Zahraa, MO,
336-3219
Dimensione, 2 Simar, MO,
336-4326/6864; contact:
Muhammad Hafez
Mona Hussein, 403-9237/9284
Nermine Moktar, Atrium, 4
Muhammad Mazhar, ZA
Zachy Sherif, 393-7485

INTERNET SERVICE PROVIDERS
Datum, 51 Beirut, HE, 290-
3501, fax 290-3527, e-mail:
help@mailer.datum.com.eg
Egypt Online (Accessme), 52
al-Sawra, HE, 413-6800

Internet Egypt, 2 Midan Qasr al-Dubara, 6th fl., GC, 796-2882, fax 794-9611, e-mail: info@internetegypt.com

LINKdotNET, 3 Musaddaq, DK, 336-7711, e-mail: info@link.net, www.link.com.eg

Menanet, 51 Beirut, HE, 416-6200, fax 416-6204

Menatel (for DSL), 19004

RITE, 10 al-Kamil Muhammad, ZA, 736-4345/6, fax 736-4347, e-mail: info@rite.com

Soficom, 30 Bahgat 'Ali, ZA, 737-1952

St@rNet, 23 al-Nahda, MA, 331-9993, faz 768-0601, www.starnet.com.eg

TE Data (Gega Net), 55 al-Nakhil & al-'Anab, MO, 749-4025, 749-9312, 749-9301, www.tedata.com

INTERPRETERS

See Business Services Centers

INVESTMENT BANKING SERVICES

Cairo Capital Group, 4 Amrika al-Latiniya, GC, 794-8301/8018, fax 795-7479; Managing Director: Dr. Khalil Nougaim

JAZZ & LIVE BARS

See also Bars

After Eight, 6 Qasr al-Nil (off Midan al-Tahrir), 574-0855

Bull's Eye Pub, 32 Jeddah, MO, 761-6888

Cairo Jazz Club, 26th July (before Midan Sphinx) MO, 345-9939

Fathy Salama & Sharkiat—whenever and wherever advertised; for information, call 403-8289

Le 51 Bar, Meridien Heliopolis Hotel, 15 'Uruba, HE, 290-1819/5055

Lebanon Corner, Gezirah Sheraton, 736-1333 (Arabic)

Pygmalion, Swissôtel al-Salam Hotel, 'Abd al-Hamid Badawi, HE, 297-4000/6000

Starlight Bar Restaurant and Terrace Restaurant, Baron Hotel, 8 Ma'had al-Sahari, HE, 291-2467/5757

JEWELRY

See also Khan al-Khalili

Hassan Elaish: WTC, 577-3920; 3 Sur Nadi al-Zamalek, MO, 302-4440, 303-4767; 28 Gam'at al-Duwal al-'Arabiya, MO, 302-2938, 303-4997; 10 Harun al-Rashid, HE, 258-1845, 258-0227

Lalik, 49 'Amman (corner of Qambis), DK, 760-5295, 335-0807; 2 Maspero, HE, 257-9535

Qasr El Shouk, 11 Brazil, ZA, 737-2111/2666 (silver)

Saad of Egypt (I. A. Ibrahim), KK, 589-3992/3; Ramses Hilton, 574-6980; al-Mirghani, al-Hurriya, HE, 290-9466 (silver)

Sami Amin Gallery, 15A Mansur Muhammad, ZA, 738-1837; 24 'Usman Ibn 'Affan, HE, 636-3243; www.sami-amin.com

Sirgany, many branches including: KK; 'Abd al-Khaliq Sarwat, DT, 391-7780; Suliman Abaza, MO

Song for Silver, 1 Ahmad Hishmat, ZA, 735-8714

JEWELRY, ETHNIC

See also Khan al-Khalili

Al Ain Gallery, 73 al-Husayn, 749-3940, 335-7133

Azza Fahmy, First Mall, GZ, 573-7687; 73 al-Husayn, MO, 338-1342; 8 Rd. 262, New MA; 25 Hasan Sadiq, HE, 4198058

Bashayer, 58 Musaddaq, DK, 335-3233

Katr El Nada, 18 Ibn al-Walid (off main entrance to Nadi al-Seid), DK, 760-0290

Marie Louise Ibrahim, 337-1655

Nomad, 14 Saray al-Gazira, 1st fl., ZA, 736-1917 and Cairo Marriott, 736-2132

Shahira Fawzi, 3 Nabil al-Waqqad, HE

Shahira Mehrez & Companions, 3rd fl., 12 Abi Emama (left-hand entrance between Omar Effendi and Cairo Sheraton), 748-7814

Sheba Gallery, 6 Sri Lanka (Yahya Ibrahim), behind Marriott, ZA, 735-9192

Suzanne al-Masri, at Khatun, 3 Zuqaq al-'Ain, behind al-Azhar next to Bayt al-Hawari, 514-7164

JUDO

See Sports (Martial Arts)

KARATE

See Sports (Martial Arts)

KHAN AL-KHALILI

(all recommended)

ALABASTER

Ali Hassan Ali, 8 Wikalat al-Makwa, 593-3463

ANTIQUES

Handy El Dab', 5 Sikkat al-Badistan, 590-7823

BEADS & BEDOUIN JEWELRY

Bedouin Shop, 7 Khan al-Khalili, 589-6155

Emeil Sif Falamon, near Naguib Mahfouz Café, 419-8372

Turquoise, 19 Khan al-Khalili (see Emad, "Mr. Beads"), 593-2843

Saad Artisans, 8 Wikalat al-Makwa (upstairs), 591-7466

COPPER & BRASS

Adel M. Aly, 5 Rab' al-Silahdar (upstairs), 591-2282

Ahmad Goma, 5 Rab' al-Silahdar (upstairs)

Essam Copper & Engraving, 5 Rab' al-Silahdar (upstairs)

Muhammad al-Mostafa, al-Mu'izz li-Din Allah (al-Sagha) Noppein Copper, 6 Khan al-Khalili

Noppein Copper, 6 Khan al-Khalili

Said Ali Abu Tahoun, 8 Wikalat al-Makwa, 589-3635

Sayyid Hearrche or Ashraf, 5 Rab' al-Silahdar (upstairs), 589-6423

Sayyid Mustafa, 8 Wikalat al-Makwa, 588-0552

GALLABIYAS

Abbas Higazi, 592-4730;

Atlas Silks, 10 Khan al-Khalili, 590-6139

JEWELRY

Gouzlan, 6, 8 Khan al-Khalili, 590-4721, 593-1064, www.gouzlan.com (gold)

Mihran & Garbis Yazejian, near Naguib Mahfouz Café, 591-2321 (gold, cartouches)

Nassar Bros., 12 Khan al-Khalili, 590-7210 (gold)

Saad of Egypt, 10 Shuwikar Bldg., 589-3993 (Mr. I.A. Ibrahim; silver)

LEATHER

Lutfi Rashid Co., 591-2748, 592-0023 (upstairs, has toilet)

Sayed Abbas Said, 2.5 Sikkat Khan al-Khalili, 590-6718

MUSKI GLASS

Mosque Glass House, 8 Wikalat al-Makwa (upstairs; Said Masheest)

Sayyid 'Abd El-Raouf, 8 Khan al-Khalili, 593-3463 (red glass)

PAPYRUS

Old Papyrus House, 8 Wikalat al-Makwa (upstairs; Mohsen Saad), 589-7077

PERFUMES

'Abd al-Hady, 73 Gawhar al-Qa'id, 590-9223

RESTAURANTS

Hotel al-Hussein top fl.; Naguib Mahfouz Café, 5 al-Badistan, 590-3788, 593-2262

T-SHIRTS

El Safa Bazaar, 12 Khan al-Khalili, 593-6934 (made to order)

KINDERGARDENS

See Schools

KITCHENWARE (POTS & PANS)

See also Khan al-Khalili

Amr Helmy, 34 'Urabi, MA, 359-0540

Bazaar Zamalek, 107 26th July, ZA, 736-0346 (crockery & good oven-proof casseroles)

Carrefour, MA

Zahran, 5 'Abd al-Rahman al-Rifa'i (behind Makka), MO, 748-5828, 749-7460 (good brand also sold elsewhere)

KNITTING

See Sewing Supplies

LABORATORIES, MEDICAL

Cairo Institute of Radiology, 23 Wadi al-Nil, MO, 347-3274, 344-4763

Cairo Tower Hospital Laboratory, 358-9781

Technolab, 75 Muhi al-Din Abu-'Izz, MO, 760-0965

LAMPS

See Lighting

LANDSCAPE DESIGN

Ennas Omar, Forest Nurseries, 29 'Abd al-Mun'im Riyad, MO, 335-3875; h: 735-6256

Fiorissima, 7 Ahmad 'Urabi, MO, 346-0416/4811

Hydroscapes Egypt (Fatma & Adel Niazi), 380-2817, 358-5968

LANGUAGE CLASSES

Community Services Association, 4 Rd. 21, 358-5284, 358-0754 (Arabic, English, French)

ARABIC

Arabic Language Institute (AUC), 28 al-Falaki, DT, 797-5055, fax 795-7565

Berlitz, DK, 338-1350/1/2 (fax)

Egyptian American Center, 749-6934

Egyptian Center for Cultural Cooperation, 11 Shagarit al-Durr, ZA, 736-5419

International British Institute
(IBI), 47 Misr-Helwan Rd.,
MA, 358-6272, 359-2646

International Language
Institute (ILI), 2 Muhammad
Bayumi (off al-Mirghani),
HE, 418-9212, 291-9295,
fax 415-1082; 3 Mahmud
'Azmi, Sahafiyin, MO,
346-3087/8597

International Living Language
Institute (ILLl), Arabic
Language Department, 34
Tal'at Harb, DT, 574-8355,
392-7244, 794-8964

Kalimat Language and Cultural
Center, 22 Muhammad
Mahmud Sha'ban (formerly
al-Kurum), MO, 761-8136,
fax 760-3528,
www.kalimategypt.com,
e-mail:
info@kalimategypt.com

Maadi/Mohandiseen School for
Teaching Arabic (MSTA),
MA, 358-2671 (private or
group classes year-round)

ENGLISH

The American University in
Cairo (AUC), 28 al-Falaki,
DT, 794-2964, fax 795-7565

The British Council, 192 al-Nil,
AG, 300-1666, fax 344-
3076; 4 al-Minya, off Nazih
Khalifa, HE, 452-3395/7, fax
258-3660; Alexandria: 9 al-
Batalsa, Bab Sharki, (03)
482-0199/9890, fax (03)
484-6630, e-mail:
british.council@britishcounc
il.org.eg

International Language
Institute (ILI), 2 Muhammad
Bayumi (off al-Mirghani),
HE, 418-9212, 291-9295,
fax 415-1082; 3 Mahmud
'Azmi, Sahafiyin, MO,
346-3087/8597

FRENCH

French Cultural Center, 1
Madrasat al-Huquq al-
Faransiya, Munira, 795-
3725, 794-7679, fax 794-
1012; 5 Shafi al-Dib, Ard al-
Golf, behind Centrale al-
Maza, 419-3857

Lycée Francais, 10 Rd. 14,
MA, 358-3574,
fax 359-9514

GERMAN

Goethe Institute, 5 Midan al-
Misaha, DK, 748-4500/1

ITALIAN

Italian Cultural Institute, 3 al-
Sheikh al-Marsafi, ZA,
735-8791, fax 736-5723

JAPANESE

Japanese Cultural Center, 106
Qasr al-'Aini, DT, 795-3962,
fax 796-3540

SPANISH

Spanish Cultural Center, 20
Bulus Hanna Basha, DK,
760-1746/43, fax 760-1743

LAW FIRMS

Baker & McKenzie, in assoc.
with Helmy, Hamza &
Partners, WTC, 18th fl., 579-
1801–6, fax 579-1808;
partners: Samir M. Hamza,
M. Taher Helmy

Denton Wilde Sapte in
association with al-Oteifi
Law Office, 9 Shagarit al-
Durr, ZA, 735-0574, fax
736-7717; contact: resident
partner, Bridget McKinney

Hassouna & Abou Ali, Cairo
Center, 5th fl., 2 'Abd al-
Qadir Hamza, GC, 795-
7188, 796-0852, fax 795-
6140; contacts: Muhammad
A.K. Hassouna, Ahmad G.
Abou Ali

Kamel Law Office, 4 al-Shahid
Ahmad Yahya Ibrahim, MO,
fax 345-2009; contact: Dr.
Muhammad Kamel

Shalakany Law Office, 12
Muhammad al-Mar'ashli,
ZA, 739-9454, fax 737-
0661; e-mail:
shalakan@intouch. com;
Partners: Ali El-Shalakany,
Salah Morsi; Mona Zulficar,
Saleh Hafez, Khaled El-
Shalakany

Sherif Saad Law Office, Maadi
Palace Tower, MA,
378-6201/2/3

Veil Armfelt Jourde, 4 Gaber
Ibn Hayyan, DK, 749-
2217/2498/8678; Partners:
Andrew P. Armfelt, Nigel
Hartridge

LAWYERS

Ahmed El-Shabini, 3 Rd. 159,
Midan al-Ittihad, MA, 525-
8561, 525-9452,
fax 525-2848

Medhat Abu El Fadl, 8 Nakhla
al-Muti'i, HE, 632-0934,
fax 634-0742

LEATHER GOODS

Choice, 7 'Ubur Buidlings,
Salah Salim, HE, 263-5148;
61 Canal, MA, 380-6455;
'Abd al-Hamid Lutfi and al-
'Anab, MO, 748-0760;
Ramses Hilton, 575-2752
x622; WTC, 575-5087

Leather Corner, 171 26th July,
ZA, 736-2110 and 10 Midan
al-Misaha, DK, 337-6989;
contact: Khaled 'Abd al-
Wahed

Montagna, Nile Hilton Mall,
DT, 735-9987, 737-3375,
578-0325 x736

Sami Amin, 15 Mansur
Muhammad, ZA, 736-1424
Seven K, 46 Syria, MO, 761-
4743; 3 Wahib Doss, MA
Vero Chic, 19 Tal'at Harb, DT,
393-1895

LIBRARIES

All Saints Cathedral Library, 5
Mishil Lutfallah, ZA,
736-8391
American Research Center in
Egypt (ARCE) Library, 2
Qasr al-Dubara, GC, 794-
8239, 795-8683, 796-4681,
797-2429, 792-2023, e-mail:
arce@internetegypt.com; head
librarian: Mr. Hammam Fawzi
American Studies Library, US
Embassy, 5 Amrika al-
Latiniya, DT, 797-3133,
797-3295
The American University in
Cairo Library, 113 Qasr al-
'Aini, DT, 797-6903,
www.lib.aucegypt.edu
The American University in
Cairo Rare Books and Special
Collections Library, 22 al-
Sheikh Rihan, DT, 797-5060
AMIDEAST Educational
Research Center, 23
Mussaddaq, DK, 337-8265
British Council Library, 192 al-
Nil, AG, 300-1666, (book
renewal) 301-8738-, fax
344-3076
Cairo American College
Library, Rd. 253, Digla,
MA, 702-9393
Community Services
Association, 4 Rd. 21, MA,
358-5284, 768-8232,
358-0754
Egyptian Museum Library,
Midan al-Tahrir, DT, 575-
7035; head librarian: Dr.
Adel Farid

Egyptian National Library (Dar
al-Kutub), Corniche al-Nil,
DT, 575-3254
Geographic Society of Egypt
Library, 109 Qasr al-'Aini,
GC, 794-5450
Goethe Institute, 5 al-Bustan,
DT, 575-9877
Greater Cairo Public Library,
15 Muhammad Mazhar, ZA,
736-2278/2271
Le Prince, WTC, 576-9489
(traditional); Ultra, 576-4424
(modern), Temple of Light,
403-923
Maadi Public Library—
Integrated Care Society, al-
Nasr, New Maadi, 145-8457.
245-8457, 345-8457
Mubarak Public Library, 15
Tahawiya, Corniche al-Nil,
336-0291
Music Library, Opera House
Complex, ZA, 739-9131
Mubarak Library, 4 al-
Tahawiya, GZ, 336-0291-4
National Library and Archives
(Dar al-Kutub), Corniche al-
Nil, 575-1078, 575-0886.
Netherlands Institute of
Archaeology & Arabic
Studies, 1 Dr. Mahmud
'Azmi, ZA, 735-4376
Pro Helvetica, 10 'Abd al-
Khaliq Sarwat, DT,
575-8733
Sohair Osman Library, Opera
House Complex, ZA,
736-8796/7628
Spanish Cultural Center
Library, 20 Bulus Hanna,
DK, 760-1746
UNESCO Library, 8 'Abd al-
Rahman Fahmi, GC,
794-3066/5599
US Agency for International
Development Information
Center, Cairo Center, 5

Amrika al-Latiniya., GC,
797-3225/738-5/3357; head
librarian: Soad Saada

LIGHTING

Asfour Crystal, Shubra al-
Khima, Cairo, 220-
3859/7198, fax 220-2561
(lamps, chandeliers)
Atelier, 18 Jeddah, MO,
761-3668
International, 19 Shagarit al-
Durr, ZA, 736-4307; 14
Ibrahim Salem, HE
Khatun, 3 Zuqaq al-'Ain,
behind al-Azhar next to Bayt
al-Harawi, 514-7164, 012
226-5329
Pavillon, Sur Nadi Zamalek
(off Gam'at al-Duwal al-
'Arabiya), MO, 303-2766
(modern high style); contact:
Mr. Sadoon El Rawy
Philosophy, 40B Muhammad
Mazhar, ZA, 738-0163
(European and Japanese
designers)
Style Team, Sur Nadi Zamalek
(off Gam'at al-Duwal al-
'Arabiya), MO, 303-2721,
335-7258, 414-4562,
760-3175 (modern &
traditional)
Ultra, 3 Mishil Lutfallah, ZA,
736-4907 (modern high-
style)

LINGERIE

See also Clothing

LINENS

See also Fabrics
Caresse, Yamama Center, 3
Taha Husayn, ZA
Gallerie Hathout, 114
Muhammad Farid, DT,
393-6782

Menders

LOCKS & SECURITY SYSTEMS

Sidi, 159 26th July, ZA, 735-9142

LUMBER

G.T.S., 6 Brazil, ZA, 735-6364
W.S., 206 Sudan, MO, 345-7679

MAGAZINES

British Community Association (BCA) Monthly Magazine; editor: Janice Roberts-Currie, 267-5417, 010 524-6520, fax, 271-5929, e-mail: magazine@bcaegypt.com
Business Monthly, American Chamber of Commerce in Egypt, 33 Suliman Abaza, MO, 338-1050, fax 338-1060
Business Today, 3A Rd. 199, Digla MA, 755-5000, fax 755-5050, e-mail: letters@businesstoday-eg.com
Egyptian Reporter, 99A Helwan Agricultural Road, Karnak Tower, MA, 525-4115/43/45, 526-5854, fax 525-4118, e-mail: egyptianreporter@hotmail.com
Egypt Today, 3A Rd. 199, Digla, MA, 755-5000, fax 755-5050, editor-in-chief: Mursi Saad al-Din; managing editor: Patrick M. Fitzpatrick
Insight Magazine, 11 Midan Aswan, MO, 304-9127/1174, 525-4115/4143/4154, e-mail: insight@thewayout.net
KidMix, Egress Int'l, 6 Rd. 9B, MA; editor-in-chief: Guinar Esmat; free parents' magazine; English/Arabic

Medina, 2 Faruq Sarwat, Ard al-Golf, HE, 414-9835, fax 419-6243, e-mail: medina@intouch.com
Mother-to-Be, Link Int'l, 71 Rd. 9, Apt. 11, MA, 359-5029; free; editor-in-chief: Rania Badr al-Din.
Pharaohs, 15 Giza, GZ, e-mail: pharaohs@rite.com
RA: Residents Abroad, Financial Times, London. PO Box 461 Bromley, BR2 9WP, United Kingdom. Fax 44-181-402-8490.
Sports and Fitness, 3 'Abd al-Hamid Lutfi, MO 336-9256, fax 336-4157

MAPS

Cairo: The Practical Guide Maps and many others available at AUC Bookstores, Main Campus, Midan al-Tahrir, DT, 797-5377/6895; 16 Muhammad Ibn Thaqib, ZA, 739-7045
Lehnert & Landrock, 44 Sharif, DT, 393-5324, 392-7606, 393-4421; director Dr. Edward Lambelet

MARBLE & GRANITE

Sharia Ahmad Maher, Bab al-Khalq (numerous dealers)
MARBLeye (Marble & granite contractors), 85 'Abd al-Aziz al-Sa'ud, MN, 362-0095

MARKET RESEARCH

AMER, 9 al-Shahid Hilmi al-Misri, HE, 418-7273/5, fax 414-7905, e-mail: amereg2@link.com.eg
Artoc Suez Trading Co., 15 Giza, GZ, fax 570-1780/1803

Financial and Management Consultants, the Office for Studies & Finance—OSAF, 13 al-Khalifa al-Ma'mun, HE, 291-2733; e-mail: osaf@ritsec1.com.eg, fax 291-3878
Kompass Egypt, Fiani & Partners, 143 al-Tahrir, DK, 748-7353, fax 748-5204
Middle East Marketing Research Bureau, 21 Dr. Muhammad Gum'a, HE, 240-1799, 632-1685, fax 639-7099, e-mail: memrbeg@intouch.com
RAC, Dr. Samy 'Abd al-Aziz, 39 Gam'at al-Duwal al-'Arabiya, MO, 760-8439, fax 760-4851
Rada Research & Public Relations, 1 Mustafa al-Wakil, HE, 291-2077/7956, fax 291-7563
Wafai & Associates, 6 Dimishq, MO, fax 347-0118

MASSAGE

See Beauty Salons, Health Clubs

MEDIATION

Lynda Clausel, Virginia Supreme Court-Certified Mediator, ZA, 736-4035

MEDITATION

See also Yoga
Sufi: 'Abdel Hayy, AUC, 797-5106

MENDERS

Nabil, Hasan Sabri, ZA
Sayyid al-Hariri, 76 Bustan, DT, 390-3851

MINISTRIES

Ministries and Governmental Departments Information, 131

Prime Minister, 1 Maglis al-Sha'b, Midan Lazughli, 795-8014/35/36, 794-7370/76/77, fax 795-8016

Council of Ministers, 1 Maglis al-Sha'b, Midan Lazughli, 795-0164/8020, 794-7370/76/77, fax 795-8048

Agriculture & Land Reclamation, Wizarat al-Zira'a, DK, 761-5967/72, fax 749-8128

Awqaf (Waqfs), 5 Sabri Abu 'Alam, DT, 392-6022/6163

Communications and Information Technology, al-Sheikh al-Hussari (off Ahmad 'Urabi), MO, 534-1300

Culture, 2 Shagarit al-Durr, ZA, 735-2195/6469, 737-0359, 748-6957, fax 735-644

Defense & Military Production, 23 al-Khalifa al-Ma'mun, Kubri al-Qubba, 260-2566, fax 291-6227

Economy & Foreign Trade, 8 'Adli, DT, 390-6796/6804, 391-9661/9278, fax 390-3029

Education, 12 al-Falaki, DT, 578-7643/4, fax 796-2952

Electricity & Energy, Extension of Ramsis, 'Abbasiya, 401-7845, fax 261-6302

Environment, 30 Misr-Helwan Rd., behind Sofitel, MA, 525-6452, fax 525-6490

Finance, 1 Maglis al-Sha'b, 2nd fl., Midan Lazughli, 686-1200/300/600, fax 794-5433

Foreign Affairs, Corniche al-Nil, Maspero, 574-6861/62/71/72/84, 574-6903/04/41, 574-9820, fax 574-9533

Health, 1 Maglis al-Sha'b, Midan Lazughli, 794-1076/1277/0426/1507, 795-7445, fax 794-0526

Higher Education, 4 Ibrahim Nagib, GC, 795-3437, 794-8210

Housing & Utilities, 1 Isma'il Abaza, DT, 795-3468/7014, 794-4867, fax 795-7836

Industry, 2 Amrika al-Latiniya, GC, 794-3600, 795-7048, 794-4261, fax 795-7507

Information, Television Bldg., Corniche al-Nil, Maspero, 574-6927, fax 577-9782

Interior, al-Sheikh Rihan, DT, 794-5897/8307/8, 795-7500, fax 795-7792

International Cooperation (Ministry of State), 8 'Adli, DT, 574-6862, 390-2945, fax 390-9707

Irrigation & Water Resources, 3 al-Sheikh Rihan, DT, 544-9446, fax 795-8008

Justice, Midan Lazughli, 792-2263/5, fax 795-8103

Local Government, al-Islah al-Zira'i Bldg., 10th fl., 4 Nadi al-Seid, DK, 749-7470/7656, fax 749-7788

Manpower, 3 Yusuf 'Abbas, NC, 260-9890, fax 260-9356

New Urban Communities (Ministry of State), 1 Isma'il Abaza, off Qasr al-'Aini, DT, 795-6835/3468/7836, fax 795-7836

Parliamentary Affairs, Press Office, Maglis al-Sha'b, Midan Lazughli, 794-8930

Petroleum & Mineral Resources, 16 al-Mukhayyam al-Da'im, NC, 263-1000, 670-6401, fax 263-6060

Planning, Salah Salim, NC, 401-4530, fax 263-44747

Population & Family Welfare, Corniche al-Nil, (next to As-Salam International Hospital), MA, 363-8137/8786/8093/9818/8207, fax 363-8207/9818

Public Enterprises Sector & Administrative Development (Ministry of State), 2 Amrika al-Latiniya, GC, 795-9288 fax 795-3606/9233

Public Works and Water Resources, 1 Gamal 'Abd al-Nasser, Corniche al-Nil, al-Warraq, 312-3315/3248, 544-9446/7, fax 312-7083

Scientific Research, 101 Qasr al-'Aini, DT, 794-5205/6/9, 794-7642/0804, fax 795-8609

Social Affairs & Insurance, Social Affairs: al-Sheikh Rihan, DT, 794-2900/3873; Social Insurance: 3 al-Alfi, DT, 592-2717, 337-8573

Supply & Internal Trade, 99 Qasr al-'Aini, DT, 795-7613, 794-7832, fax 794-4973

Tourism, Misr Travel Tower, Midan al-'Abbasiya, 685-9371, 682-8435, fax 685-9551

Transport, Communications & Civil Aviation, 104 Qasr al-'Aini, DT, 794-3623, 795-5566/5567/5568, fax 795-5564

MIRRORS

Golden Mirror, 7 Abu al-Mahasin al-Shazli, AG, 347-1330, 760-5394 (mirrors & stained glass)

Misr El Gedida for Glass and
Mirrors, 14 Aswan, HE
Stained Glass Designs, 95 al-
Mirghani, HE, 418-3235,
263-9376

MOBILE PHONE RENTAL

Systel, 2A Shafiq Mansur, ZA,
736-0420, 736-8247

MOBILE PHONES

Badawi (Nadi Shams), HE;
customer service: 529-8888,
www.vodafone.com.eg
Click Vodafone, 1B Rd. 257
(behind Maadi Grand Mall),
MA; 19 26th July (Midan
Sphinx), MO; Abdel Hamid
MobiNil, 80 'Abbas al-'Aqqad,
NC; 110 al-Mirghani, HE;
49 al-Lasilki, MA; 39
Shahab, MO; WTC;
customer service: 760-9090,
012 320-2110

MOTHERS' GROUPS

Ante and Post-Natal Meetings,
Ki Studio, 17 al-Fawakih
(behind Mustafa Mahmud
Mosque), MO, 336-3930;
contact: Katrina Shawky
Mom's Morning Out, Maadi
Community Church, MA,
358-7376 or 359-2755
Mother and Baby Support
Group, 31 Rd. 254, Digla,
MA, meetings Wed.
mornings

MOVERS

Danzas, 760-1710, fax 336-5598
(local & international)
Express International, 60 al-
Tahrir, DK, 749-0521,
761-6850
Four Winds, 11A Corniche al-
Nil, MA, 358-0113/3608
(local & int'l)

Global Movers, 258-7509,
256-2317 (local & int'l)
GR Consultants (International
Relocation Associates), 19
Rd. 151, MA, 525-
5755/5618, fax: 525-5616
T.G. General Services, 22 Rd.
205, Digla, MA, 703-1353
(local & misc. services)
Trans-Express Worldwide Inc.,
15 Khurshid, New Maadi,
MA, 703-4915, e-mail:
texp@wtca.geis.com (local
& int'l)

MOVIE THEATERS

See Cinemas

MUSEUMS

Abdin Palace, Midan 'Abdin,
DT, 391-0042/6906
Agricultural and Cotton
Museums, al-Islah al-Zira'i,
DK, 337-2933
Ahmad Shawqi Museum,
Corniche al-Nil, GZ,
572-9479
Coptic Museum, Old Cairo,
Mar Girgis Metro station,
362-8766, 363-9742
Egyptian Antiquities Museum,
Midan al-Tahrir, DT,
579-6948/4596
Entomylogical Museum, 14
Ramsis, DT
Ethnological Museum, 109
Qasr al-'Aini, GC, 794-5450
Folklore Museum, 18 al-Bursa,
DT, 575-2460
Gayer Anderson House, 4
Midan Ahmad Ibn Tulun,
364-7822
Mahmud Mukhtar Museum, al-
Tahrir, Gazira, 340-2519
Manyal Museum, Gazirit al-
Roda, Roda
Military Museum, Citadel,
592-7094

Mr. and Mrs. Muhammad
Mahmud Khalil Museum,
1 Kafur al-Ikhshidi, DK,
336-2358/76
Muhammad Nagi Museum, 9
Mahmud al-Gindi, GZ,
383-3484
Museum of Islamic Art, Bur
Sa'id, Bab al-Khalq,
390-9930
Museum of Egyptian Modern
Art, Opera Complex, Gezira,
736-6665
Pottery Museum, 1 al-Sheikh
al-Marsafi, ZA, 736-8672,
737-3298
Dr. Ragab's Pharaonic Village,
Jacob's Island, GZ, 571-
8675/6/7; Papyrus Institute,
Corniche al-Nil (near Cairo
Sheraton), GZ, 748-8177
Railway Museum, Midan
Ramsis, DT, 576-3793
Solar Boat Museum, Pyramids
Taha Husayn Museum,
Madkour, PY, 585-2518

MUSIC AND SINGING, GROUPS & LESSONS

Cairo Choral Society, director
Larry Catlin, 735-4197
Cairo Music Center, HE;
contact: Mr Tobgy,
266-7544/8649
Carol Ann Clouston, voice,
speech, drama, &
Feldenkrais method,
736-1769
Maadi Community Choir,
director Barbara Comar;
contact Cairo American
College, 702-9393

INSTRUMENT LESSONS

Contact BISC (760-6674, 736-
5959) or CAC (519-
6665/6825) for the
following: Woodwinds: Mr.
Samir Oboe: Mr. Ivan

Violin: Mr. Osman Piano:
Greig Martin, Jane Hassan,
Brian Kelly
Cello, Mr. Evgeni, 735-7730
Guitar, Hesham Abdo Shedy,
516-3278, 010860264;
Michael, 735-7730;
Mr. Valerie, 735-2915
Latin Jazz Combo, Trumpetist
Mitko, 735-7730, bassist
Ahmed, 368-7394, for
private parties or
performance schedule
Maadi Music Center, 36A Rd.
206, Digla, MA, 521-1692
Trumpet, Mr. Mitko, Principle
Trumpetist, Cairo Symphony
Orchestra, 735-7730
Violin, Krasen Penev, Concert
Master, 338-7153; Maria
Sinbel, 741-0932, 012
326-5762

MUSIC, RECORDING STUDIOS

CAC Community Orchestra,
378-3421, 010 626-0684
Double Vision, 30b Ahmed
Mokhtar Higazi, near al-
Manyal Museum, MN,
362-8276, 363-6896

MUSICAL INSTRUMENTS

The 'Abdel Ghafar Group, 39
al-Bustan, 1st fl., 794-4948,
792-2070; manager Mr.
Hatem 'Abdel Ghafar; by
appt. only
Meter, Garden City, close to
hospital
'Oud, Abu al-Fida and 26th
July (beside British
Commercial Bank), ZA,
736-7386
Piano Marzouk, DT, 393-7242
Yamaha, Heliopolis

MUSKI GLASS

See also Khan al-Khalili
Maryse and Ismail Borhan, 17
Midan Ahmad Ibn Tulun
(opposite Ibn Tulun
Mosque), 598-2863,
257-9422

NATURAL FOODS

Sekem Healthy Foods, 69 Rd.
206, MA, 519-6882; 10
Salah Magdi, HE, 290-023;
8 Ahmad Sabri, ZA, 738-
2724; also available in Alfa
and Metro supermarkets

NEEDLEWORK

Wednesday Coffee Morning;
contact Linn, 290-8256
Women's Association,
760-3475

NEWS AGENCIES

AFP, 748-1236
AP, 578-4091/4092/4093,
fax 578-4094
Bloomberg (business news),
794-2284
Bridge (business news),
736-1844, 012 216-0901
MENA (Middle East News
Agency), 17 Huda Sha'rawi,
DT, 393-3000; chairman
Mustafa Naguib, 392-8888
Reuters, 153 Muhammad Farid,
21st fl., DT, 578-3290/1,
777-150, fax 574-7078;
bureau chief Rawhi Abeidoh

NEWSPAPERS & NEWSLETTERS

Al-Ahram, Al-Ahram Weekly,
www.ahramorg.eg/weekly,
and Al-Ahram Hebdo,
www.ahram.org.eg/hebdo/,
al-Gala', 578-6100/200/
300/400/500.

Community Times (free), 7 Al
Madfaleya Bldg., Ard al-
Golf, HE, 419-570,
www.community-times.com
Egyptian Gazette (daily) and
Egyptian Mail (Sat), 24
Zakaria Ahmad, DT, 578-
3333/1515, fax 578-1110;
ads: 578-1290/1010
International Herald Tribune
and Egypt Daily Star, 14
Muhammad Anis, ZA, 735-
0802; Fax 735-5863; e-mail:
subscriptions@dailystaregyp
t.com
Maadi Messenger (Maadi
Community Church), 378-
4882; editor Jan Learmonth
(good classifieds)
Middle East Times,
http://metimes.com
The Niler, U.S. Embassy, 797-
2737 (embassy-related
personnel only; classifieds)

NIGHTCLUBS

See Bars, Jazz & Live Music

NOTIONS & BRIDAL

La Poupée, 21 Qasr al-Nil, DT,
393-3734 (bows, veils,
barrettes)

NURSE-MIDWIVES & OBSTETRICAL NURSES

Karen Betts (Brit. reg.
midwife), 634-6943

NURSERY SCHOOLS

See Schools

NURSES

Arylis Milligan, RN, Shaalan
Surgicenter, 760-3920
International Nurses Group;
contact Lorea Ytterberg, RN,
359-0385
Jaqueline Sutton Shirbini, RN,
380-6766

OPERA

Cairo Opera House, P.O. Box 11567, al-Dokki, GA, box off. 737-0602, 339-8114, info. 737-0589

OPTICIANS

Baraka Optics, WTC, 574-8989; 159 26th July, ZA, 737-0343; 10 Baghdad, HE, 418-4679; Sofitel, MA, 526-0607; First Mall, GZ, 573-4009; 19 'Abd al-Hamid Badawi (Nadi Shams), HE, 242-2776; 5 'Abbas al-'Aqqad, NC, 403-4571; 14 Wadi al-Nil, MO, 305-5728

Instant Center for Contact Lenses, 25 al-Bustan, DT, 795-6566 and 180 Tahrir, DT, 796-2686

Jean Greish, 33 Tal'at Harb, DT, 392-7897

Maghrabi Optical, 112 Muhi al-Din Abu al-'Izz, DK, 761-8047; 157 26th July, ZA, 735-7929; 22 Baghdad, HE, 291-5532; Grand Mall, MA, 519-5309; 3 Midan Sphinx, MO, 304-1836; 13 'Abd al-Khaliq Sarwat, DT, 576-3053

ORGANIZATIONS, BUSINESS & SCHOLARLY

Alliance for Arab Women, 28 'Adli, Apt. 74–5, DT, 393-9899, fax 393-6820

American Chamber of Commerce in Egypt, 33 Suliman Abaza, MO, 338-1050, fax 338-1060

American Research Center in Egypt (ARCE), 2 Midan Qasr al-Dubara, GC, 794-8239, 795-8683, fax 795-3052, e-mail: arce@internetegypt.com

Amideast, 23 Musaddaq, DK, 337-8265; country director Elizabeth Khalifa

British Egyptian Business Association, 124 al-Nil, AG, 749-1401

Cairo Chamber of Commerce, 4 Midan al-Falaki, DT, 792-5963/7

CEDEJ, 5 Sikkit al-Fadl, DT, 392-8711/16/39, fax 392-8791

Central Agency for Public Mobilization and Statistics (CAPMAS), Salah Salem, NC, 402-4110, 402-3191

Cervantes Institute, 20 Bulus Hanna, DK, 760-1746, 337-1962; 20 'Adli, Kodak Passage, DT, 395-2326/7, 335-5097

Club d'Affaires Franco-Egyptien (CAFÉ), 5 Shagarit al-Durr, 2nd fl., ZA, 346-9417/8

Council for the International Exchange of Scholars, 3007 Tilden NW, Suite 5M, Washington, DC 20008-3009, USA, 202-686-4019, fax 202-362-3442

Egyptian-American Businessmen's Association, Nile Tower, 21 al-Giza, GZ, 573-7258, 573-6030, 573-3020

Egyptian Antiquities Project, 2 Midan Qasr al-Dubara, GC, 344-8622 (also fax), e-mail: arceeap@internetegypt.com; director Robert K. Vincent

Egyptian Businessmen's Association, Nile Tower, 16th fl., 21 al-Giza, GZ, 573-6030, fax 573-7258

Egyptian Center for Economic Studies, 1191 Corniche al-Nil, 14th fl., WTC, 578-

1202, fax 578-1205, e-mail: eces@eces.org.eg

Egypt Exploration Society, British Council, 192 al-Nil, AG, 301-0319; contact: Rosalind Phipps

Egyptian Financial Group (Euromoney Publications), 55 al-Giza, GZ, 568-8455/7764, 571-7846/8; fax 571-6121; contact: Ahmad Marwan

Egyptian Organization for Human Rights (EOHR), 8-10 Mathaf al-Manyal, MN, 363-6811, 362-0467

European Commission, 6 Ibn Zanki, ZA, 735-8388, 736-9393, fax 735-0385; director Michael McGeever

Federation of Egyptian Chambers of Commerce, 4 Midan al-Falaki, DT, 347-2000, fax 795-7940

Federation of Egyptian Industries, Immobilia Bldg., 26A Sharif, DT, 579-6590/2, fax 392-8075

Ford Foundation, 1 Uziris, 7th fl., GC, 794-9635/4450, 795-2121/4521, fax 795-4018; e-mail: hdavies@fordfound.org; representative Humphrey Davies

French Commercial Section, 10 'Aziz 'Usman, ZA, 736-5694, 736-5694/6, e-mail: teecaire@sosicom.com.eg

Fulbright Commission, 20 Gamal al-Din Abu al-Mahasin, GC, 794-4799/8679, 797-2216/2258; fax 795-7893; e-mail: aradwan@bfce.eun.eg; executive director Dr. Ann B. Radwan

German-Arab Chamber of Commerce in Egypt, 3 Abu al-Fida, ZA, 336-8185, fax 736-3663

Greek-Arab Chamber of Commerce in Egypt, 17 Suliman al-Halabi, DT, 574-1190, fax 575-4970

ICARDA (International Center for Agricultural Research in the Dry Areas) 15G Radwan Ibn al-Tabib, 11th fl., PO Box 2416 GZ, 572-5785/4358, 573-5829, fax 572-8099; director general Dr. Adel El Beltagy (Aleppo); regional coordinator Dr. Mahmud Sohl (Cairo)

Information and Decision Support Center (IDSC), Cabinet Bldg., Maglis al-Sha'b, DT, 796-1600, fax 794-1222

IDRC (International Development Research Center, Canada), 3 Midan 'Amman, 5th fl., DK, 336-7051/2/3/4, fax 336-7056, e-mail: fkishk@ idrc.ca; director: Dr. Fawzi Kishk.

International Executive Service Corporation, Commercial Center, Bustan Street, Suite 1, 390-3232, fax 390-2929

Institute of International Education (IIE), 809 UN Plaza NY, NY 10017-3580, 212-984-5329, fax 212-984-5325

Italian-Arab Chamber of Commerce in Egypt, 33 'Abd al-Khaliq Sarwat, DT, 393-7944, fax 391-2503

Japanese Foreign Trade Organization, WTC, 7th fl., 574-1111, fax 575-6966

Makan, 1 Sa'd Zaghlul, Munira, 792-0878

Manasterly Palace International Music Center, Roda Island, 363-1467

Middle East Library for Economic Services, (MELES), 6 Suliman 'Abd al-'Aziz (off Duktur Shahin), AG, 335-1141, 760-6804, fax 760-6804; director Mr. Nabil Foda

Netherlands Institute for Archaeology and Arabic Studies, 1 Dr. Mahmud 'Azmi, ZA, 738-2522

El Sawy Culture Wheel, 26th July, ZA, 736-8881, 012 440-0100, www.culturewheel.com

Serafis Cultural Society, 34 Rd. 218, Digla, MA, 521 2104, e-mail: serafis@gmail.com

Sixth of October Investors Union, 6th October, fax 833-8327, 011 231-1593

Tenth of Ramadan Investors Union, 10th Ramadan City, 015-364-570-2586/11, fax 570-2565

ORGANIZATIONS, CULTURAL

Food and Agricultural Organization (FAO), 11 al-Islah al-Zira'i, DK, 337-5182/2789/2229/3412/5029, fax 749-5981

International Civil Aviation Organization (ICAO), 9 Shagarit al-Durr, ZA, 267-4840, 735-1463/735-1532, fax 735-5344

International Finance Corporation (IFC), WTC, 12th fl., 579-9900/5353/6565, fax 579-2211

International Labor Organization (ILO Egypt), 9 Taha Husayn, ZA, 736-9290, 735-0123, fax 736-0889

International Monetary Fund (IMF), 31 Qasr al-Nil, DT, 392-4257, fax 359-7137

Red Cross, DK, 335-7724, 337-9282

UN Children's Fund (UNICEF), 87 Misr-Helwan Rd., MA, 526-5083/4-7, fax 526-4218

UN Development Program (UNDP), WTC, 578-4840-6, fax 578-4847

UN Educational, Scientific and Cultural Organization (UNESCO), 8 'Abd al-Rahman Fahmi, GC, 794-5599, fax 794-5296

UN High Commissioner for Refugees (UNHCR), 13 al-Falah (off Shahab), MO, 346-0618, fax 303-1753

UN Information Center and Library, 790-0022, 794-5153, 795-3705, fax 795-0682, 795-3705

UN Population Fund, WTC, 578-4840-6, fax 578-4847

UN Relief & Work Agency for Palestinian Refugees (UNRWA), 2 Dar al-Shifa, GC, 794-8504, fax 794-8504

UN Truce Supervision Organization (UNTSO), Observer Group Egypt (OGE) Headquarters, 41511 Box 247, Ismailiya, (064) 329-305, fax (064) 329-250

Universal Postal Union, Postal Center, Midan Ramsis, 574-9196

World Bank (Resident Cairo Mission), WTC, 574-1670, 574-1671, fax 574-1676

World Food Program, WTC, 527-1575, fax 578-4847

World Health Organization (WHO), Sultan 'Abd al-'Aziz, Alexandria, (03) 483-0090/6/7/9, fax (03) 483-8916; Cairo, 13 Ahmad Sabri, ZA, 670-2448/52, fax 737-3300

ORGANIZATIONS, SOCIAL AND MISCELLANEOUS

British Community Association, HE, 418-5133

British Community Association, MA, 519-7018; contact: Rosemary

British Community Association, MO, 748-1358

Cairo 41 Club; contact Bill Hunter, 291-3979

Community Services Association (CSA), 4 Rd. 21, MA, 358-5284, 358-0754, www.csa-egypt.com

Egyptian Chef's Association, 260-1137

Heliopolis Community Activities Association; contact: Hamida, 012 120-9122

Hungarian Women's Club, Hungarian Cultural Center, 13 Gawad Husni, DT, 392-6692

Latin American Circle in Egypt; contact Argentina Yassin, 346-2977, 010 123-5753

Maadi Women's Guild, Maadi Community Church office, 359-2755

New Middle East Wives; contact: Sue, 415-5136, Helen, 633-8878, Besty 415-0186

Republicans Abroad Egypt, c/o Semiramis Business Center, PO Box 60, Corniche al-Nil,

Cairo, 796-3020; or contact Priscilla del Bosque, 735-5490 (evenings)

Rotary and Inner Wheel Heliopolis; contact Hussein Hashad, 291-8822

Spanish-Speaking Ladies Club; contacts: Monica, 261-8113; Sandra, 736-1224

The Swiss Club, Villa Pax, al-Salam, Kit Kat, 315-1455

Tree Lovers Association; contact Dr. Abdel al-Wahab al-Morsy, 358-0229

Women's Association of Cairo, 21 Bulus Hanna Basha, DK, 736-4187

ORGANIZATIONS, SPORTS

See Sporting & Country Clubs, Sports Federations

PAPYRUS

Dr. Ragab Papyrus Institute, Corniche al-Nil between the Sheraton and University Bridge, 748-8177

PARQUET FLOORING

Eng. Tarek Fouad, 3 al-Batal Ahmad 'Abd al-'Aziz, MO, 303-4019

El Tawfik Parquet, 23 al-Qal'a, DT, 512-9108

PARTY PLANNERS

Modern Touch, 2 Taha Husayn, 8th fl., Apt. 81, ZA, 738-2692, 010 109-0940, www.moderntouch-ent.com

Suzi Damati, AG, 344-16500

PERFUMES & ESSENTIAL OILS

See also Khan al-Khalili

G. Fleur Essential Oils, 53 al-Zahra 5th fl., apt. 23, DK, 749-0902/3049, Mme. Nagat

International Perfumes & Cosmetics, 5 al-Zahra (at Musaddaq), DK, 761-1624

PEST CONTROL

See Exterminators

PET ADOPTION

Brooke Hospital for Animals, 2 Bayram al-Tunsi, Sayyida Zeinab, 364-9312

Egyptian Society of Animal Friends, 30 Rd. 301, MA, 702-1142, www.animalfriends.info

People's Dispensary for Sick Animals (PDSA), 60 al-Sikka al-Bayda, 'Abbasiya, 482-2294, Dr. Farouk, Dr. Osama Safar, Dr. Ahmed Obeida

PET BOARDING

Dr. Berj Ya'qub, 40 al-Fallah, off Midan Libnan, MO, 305-4806; 44 al-Ahram, HE, 415-0821

People's Dispensary for Sick Animals (PDSA), 60 al-Sikka al-Bayda, 'Abbasiya, 482-2294, Dr. Farouk

Dr. Rafik Nashed, Sharif Mansur at Sri Lanka, ZA, 736-2402

PET SHOPS & SUPPLIES

Mr. Amr's Pets, Heliopolis Flower Shop, Meniz (behind Baghdad), HE, 291-7812

Anton Aziz, 229 & 191 Ramsis, DT, 591-2833

Karim Pets, 18 Rd. 82, MA, 359-6881

Momen Azam's Pet Shop, corner of Rds. 9 & 82

Sami's Farm, 134 26th July, ZA, 735-5173, George Girgis

PETROLEUM COMPANIES

See Directories, esp. Maadi
   Women's Guild Directory

PHARMACIES

DOKKI
Amman Pharmacy, 'Amman
   and Qambis, 749-2889/1529
Sherif Pharmacy, 16 Qambis
   (off Musaddaq), 749-9122

DOWNTOWN
Anglo-Eastern Pharmacy,
   corner of 'Abd al-Khaliq
   Sarwat and al-Sharif
Atallah Pharmacy, 13 al-Sharif,
   393-8917, 393-9029
   (24hr. and delivery)
Gezira Pharmacy, 157 26th
   July, 735-0809
Isaaf, Ramsis and 26th July,
   743-369 (24hr.)
Seif, 76 Qasr al-'Aini,
   794-2678 (24hr.)

HELIOPOLIS
Al Ezaby, 1 Ahmad Taysir,
   Kulliyat al-Banat, 418-0838,
   415-3409 (24hr.)
Maqsoud, 29 Mahmud Shafiq,
   635-3918 (24hr.)
El Marwa, 82B 'Abd al-'Aziz
   Fahmi, 637-7293 (24hr.)
Roxy Pharmacy, Subki,
   290-5946

MAADI
Essam, 101 Rd. 9, 375-1611
   (24hr.)
Hindam, Rd. 9, Midan al-
   Mahatta, 359-3846 (24hr.)
El Rahma, 35 Rd. 276, New
   Maadi, 702-1568, 703-4733
   (24hr.)

MOHANDISEEN
Aly & Aly Pharmacy, 37
   Suliman Abaza (9am-12pm)

El Ezaby Pharmacy, 11 Surya,
   304-1647/1847
Khater Pharmacy, 14 Surya,
   760-1135, 336-4202 (24hr.,
   delivery available)

ZAMALEK
Myra Pharmacy, 3 al-Gazira al-
   Wusta (opp. Flamenco
   Hotel), 737-0645
New Universal Pharmacy, 12
   Brazil, 735-4896
Pharmacy Zamalek, 3 Shagarit
   al-Durr, 736-6424 (24hr.)

PHILATELISTS
Cafe Muktallat, 14 'Ataba
   Khadra, 'Ataba, DT
Egyptian Association for
   Stamp Collectors, 16 'Abd
   al-Khaliq Sarwat, 1st fl., DT
Post Office Museum, off Midan
   Ataba
World of Stamps, 16 'Abd al-
   Khaliq Sarwat, 1st fl., DT,
   392-7556

PHOTOGRAPHERS (FASHION, COMMERCIAL, PORTRAITS)
Ahmed Mokhtar, 735-4526
Al Arise, Midan al-Tahrir,
   578-9751
Arman, 12 Tal'at Harb, DT,
   575-3369
Studio Garo, 40 Qasr al-Nil,
   393-8575

PHOTOGRAPHIC SUPPLIES
See also Film Processing
Antar Photo Stores, 180, al-
   Tahrir, DT, 794-0786,
   795-4449
Kodak, 20 'Adli, DT, 394-
   2200, fax 393-1199
Kodak, 19 Isma'il Muhammad,
   ZA, 735-9517, 737-0583

PHYSICIANS
See Doctors

PHYSIOTHERAPISTS
Katrina Shawky, 336-3930
Mira Tesar, 347-0039,
   010 526-5515

PIANO LESSONS
See Music and Singing

PIANO RENTAL
Essam, 233-9282
Mustafa the Piano Man, 266-
   5029, 267-8987, 259-3138

PLANT NURSERIES (WHOLESALE)
See also Gardening Supplies
Egypt Green, 6 Zakariya Rizq,
   ZA, 737-0374/5
Egypt Green Land, 27 Tal'at
   Harb, DT, 392-9987, 393-
   0975; contact: Nabil 'Abdel
   Razik
Fiorissima, 7 Ahmad 'Urabi,
   MO, 346-0416/4811; owner:
   Piero Donato
Forest, 29 'Abd al-Mun'im
   Riyad, MO, 335-3875;
   contact: Inas Omar
Mahmud Helmi, (018) 400-
   346, 401-221
Nimos farm, 128 Immobilia
   Bldg., al-Sharif, DT, 392-
   5714/5822, fax 393-1101;
   contact: Nadia Niazi

PLANTS
See Gardening Supplies, Plant
   Nurseries

POTTERY
See also Arts & Crafts
Samir El Guindi (The Mud
   Factory) 261 Sudan, DK,
   347-3445
Suzanne Wissa Wassef, Wissa
   Wassef Studios, Saqqara,
   Harraniya, 385-0746

POTTERY CLASSES

See Art Classes

PREGNANCY CLASSES

Ki Studio, 17 Fawaki (behind
Muhammad Mahmud
Mosque), MO, 336-3930
Samia Allouba, Creative Dance
and Fitness Center, MA
519-6575; MO 302-0572
Rania Hussni 012 742-7104
Ann Pittomvils 380-3789/5357
Maha el-Zokm, 267-2492

PRINTSHOPS

AUC Printshop, 113 Qasr al-
'Aini, 797-6936
Concorde Press, 52 Ratib,
Shubra, DT, 205-7902/3, fax
205-7901
Elias Modern Publishing
House, 1 Kanisat al-Rum
al-Kathulik, PO Box 954,
al-Daher, 590-3756,
fax 588-0091
International Press, 5 Gamal al-
Shahid, Sahafiyin, MO,
345-8412
Masters Press, near Coptic
Hospital in Daher (off
Ramsis), 920-189, fax same;
contact: Fouad Lobbos
(business cards & stationery)
Modern Egyptian Press,
75 'Amman (off Mustafa
Haf'z), 'Ain Shams East,
298-1735/5715, fax 298-
0736; contact: Manal
Nubar, Madrasat al-
Mu'allimin, Shubra, 432-
8316 (good basic workhorse
printers)

COLOR SEPARATION

Intergraph, DK, 337-6300
JC Center, HE, 635-8797,
633-7124

Moody Graphics International,
1 Amrika al-Latiniya, GC,
794-1800, 794-6002,
fax 794-9335
Peak Image, 104 Gam'at al-
Duwal al-'Arabiya, MO,
749-8117 (tel and fax)
Style, 3 Abu Saber (off Ahmad
'Ismat), 'Ain Shams,
250-1580
Virgin Graphics, MO 760-3565

PUBLICATIONS

See Newspapers & Newsletters,
Magazines

PUBLISHERS

See also Newspapers &
Newsletters, Magazines
A. A. Gaddis & Sons, Khalid
Ibn Walid, Luxor, (095) 382-
838, fax (095) 382-837
The American University in
Cairo Press, 113 Qasr al-
'Aini, 797-6926,
fax 794-1440, e-mail:
aucpress@aucegypt.edu
Egyptian International
Publishing Co. – Longman,
10A Husayn Wasif, Midan
al-Misaha, DK, 749-7946/7
Hoopoe Books, 13 Rashdan,
748-0050, fax: 347-7383
Kassem Press, 14 Saraya al-
Kubra, GC, 794-3396, fax
794-3396
Lehnert & Landrock, 44 al-
Sharif, DT, 393-5324 (maps,
art prints)
The Palm Press, 34 Mansur
Muhammad, 4th fl., apt. 10,
ZA, 736-5458, fax 736-3658

PUPPETS

See Children's Entertainment

QUILTING

See Needlework

RADIO STATIONS

Radio Cairo, Radio and TV
Building, Corniche al-Nil,
DT, 578-9407

REAL EASTATE AGENTS

Alfi Doss Services (apartment
rentals), 63 'Usman Ibn
'Affan, HE, 418-6516,
419-8772, fax 419-1876
Arabian American Real Estate
Co., 71 Rd. 9, and 19 Rd.
151, 6th fl., MA, 525-
5755/5618, 010 783-6913,
fax 358-6209
ASAP for Real Estate &
Investment, 1 al-Fardus, AG,
337-8086, 749-5884, fax
760-7638
Belanger and Issa, 794-5563/
1524
Betna (Coldwell Banker Egypt),
51 al-Nahda, MA, 359-1003,
fax, 359-1002,
www.coldwellbanker-eg.com
Bigger Builds Contracting Co.,
7 'Abd al-Latif Hamza, NC,
272-7961, fax 418-9352
Conserv, 17A Muhammad
Mazhar, ZA, 735-1811; 38
Nahda, MA, 358-3131,
359-8428
Diamond, 346-7366/5005
Excel Services, 69 'Umar Ibn
al-Khattab, HE, 290-7882,
679-339, fax 616-805
Foresight, 7 al-Shahid Mahmud
Husayn al-'Ashri, HE,
418-5684, fax 418-9352
Maadi Today, 23 al-Gulf, MA,
359-7562
Nile Services, 26 Rd. 81 and
Mustafa, MA, 358-3130
Sourya 'Abd El-Wahab, 12
Midan al-Misaha, DK,
748-2713

Suburban, 43 Surya, MO,
303-4035/2567

Sunny Home, 35 Rd. 13, MA,
358-2278

T.G. Real Estate, 22 Rd. 205,
Digla, MA, 516-6283,
010 108-8933

REPAIRS, HOUSEHOLD

Mohsen Gomaa, office 561-
6755, home 561-3741
(general, electrical, TV,
video, etc.)

RESTAURANTS

BYO Bring Your Own
DA Delivery Available
NA No Alcohol

DOKKI

Abou El Sid, 8 Midan
'Amman, 749-7326

Ciao, 10 Midan al-Misaha,
335-2482, *DA*

Il Cortigiano, 44 Mishil
Bakhum, 336-0620, 337-
4838, *NA*, *DA*

La Casetta, 32 Qambis, 748-
7970, *NA*

La Parisienne, corner of
al-Husayn & al-Tahrir

Le Carnival, 48 Michelle
Bakhoum, DK, 338-8902

Le Sandwicherie, 33 'Amman,
761-3389

Le Tabasco, 8 Midan 'Amman,
336-5583

Pizza Express, 52 Dr. Michel
Bakhum, 338-1838, *NA*, *DA*

Sapporo, Cairo Sheraton Hotel,
Midan al-Gala', DK,
336-9700/9800

Scoozi, 16 Midan al-Misaha,
748-2393/8668, 749-9765,
DA

Susana, 7 Iran, 760-5088

El Tekia, 12 Midan Ibn al-
Walid, 749-6673, *NA*, *DA*

DOWNTOWN

Absolute, Casino al-Shagara,
Corniche al-Nil, 579-6512

Abu Shaqra, 69 Rd. Qasr al-
'Aini, 19090, *NA*, *DA*

After Eight, 6 Qasr al-Nil,
574-0855, 576-5199

Alfi Bey, 3 al-Alfi, 577-1888

Aly Hassan El-Haty and Aly
'Abdou, 3 Midan Halim
Pasha, 591-6055

Arabesque, 6 Qasr al-Nil,
574-7898, *NA*, *BYO*

Asia House, Shepheard,
Corniche al-Nil, 792-1000

Bua Khao, Nile Hilton Mall,
578-0325 x754

Centro Recreativo Italiano
(Italian Club), 40 26th July

Club Hellenique (Greek Club),
Midan Tal'at Harb (above
Groppi), 575-0822

Estoril, 12 Tal'at Harb (near
Qasr al-Nil), 574-3102

Felfela, 15 Huda Sha'rawi,
392-2751/2833

Fu Ching, 28 Tal'at Harb,
575-6184

Kowloon, Cleopatra Hotel,
Midan al-Tahrir, 575-9831,
DA

La Chesa (Swissair), 21 'Adli,
393-9360/5768, *DA*

Le Bistro, 8 Huda Sha'rawi,
392-7694

Paprika, 1129 Corniche al-Nil,
Maspero, 578-7887/9447

Peking, 14 Saray al-Azbakiya,
591-2381, *DA*

S and P Thai Takeaway, 2
Champollion, 575-1308, *DA*

GARDEN CITY

Bird Cage, Semiramis Hotel,
Corniche al-Nil, 795-7171

Champollion, Grand Hyatt
Hotel, Corniche al-Nil

Hard Rock Café, Grand Hyatt
Hotel, Corniche al-Nil,
532-1277/81

Taboula, 1 Amrika al-Latiniya,
792-5261

GIZA AND AGOUZA

Al Fanous, Oman Center,
Riyadh Tower, 5 Wisa
Wasif, 570-1226/7

Fish Market, moored at 25 al-
Nil, 2nd fl., 570-9699

Flying Fish, 166 al-Nil, 749-
3234, 336-5111, *DA*

La Mama, Cairo Sheraton, 336-
9700

Mashrabia, 4 Ahmad Nasim,
348-2801

Pharaohs, 31 al-Nil, 570-1000,
fax 570-3737 (floating
restaurant)

Swissair Restaurants (Le
Chalet), al-Nil, el-Nasr
Bldg., 748-5321/6720

TGIF, moored at 25 al-Nil, 1st
floor, 570-9690, fax 570-
9691

HELIOPOLIS

Chantilly (Swissair), 11
Baghdad, 415-5620, *DA*

Chili's, 18 al-Sawra, 19002, *DA*

Cortigiano, 14 al-Safir Samir
Mukhtar, 414-2202/402,
NA, *DA*

La Sirena, 113 'Usman Ibn
'Affan, 415-8714

Peking, 115 'Usman Ibn 'Affan,
418-5612, 419-2247 *DA*

Pizza Express, 16 al-Marghani,
450-5871, *NA*, *DA*

Rossini, 66 'Umar Ibn al-
Khattab, 291-8282,
417-1401

KHAN AL-KHALILI

El Halwagi, Harat al-Busta
(between al-Azhar and Khan
al-Khalili) (best ta'miya)

Hotel El Hussein, top floor

Naguib Mahfouz, 5 al-
Badistan, 590-3788

MAADI

Abou El Sid, 45 Rd. 7, 380-5050, *DA*

Amsterdam, 17 Rd. 9B, 012 383-0453, 010 540-1417

Andrea, Corniche al-Nil

Asian Dragon, 32 al-Nadi al-Gidid (Satellite Area), 519-3739

Bua Khao, 9 Rd. 151, 358-0126, 378-3355, *DA*

Bukhara, 43 Misr-Helwan Rd., 380-5999, *DA*

Country Kitchen, 30 Rd. 213, 519-8443

Creperie des Arts, 30 Misr-Helwan Rd., 526-0082

Cue Club, 28 Rd. 7, 378-3300

Didos Al Dente, 1 Rd. 270 (off al-Nasr), 520-2255, *DA*, *NA*

Dragon House, 84 Rd. 9, 378-2928, *DA*

Fine Touch, 25 Misr-Helwan Rd., Borg al-Zeini, 380-5502, 750-9057

Fusion, Maadi Corniche, next to TGI Friday's

La Casetta, 11 Rd. 18, 358-7276, 359-9076

Lan Yuan, 84 Rd. 9, 378-2702

Le Tabasco, 45 Rd 7, 359-1222, *DA*

Lucille's, 54 Rd. 9, 359-2778

Maroush, 7/2 al-Nasr, 754-6406/4955, *NA*, *DA*

Maxie's Long Feng, Ghadat al-Maadi Towers, 358-3964

Mediterraneo, 78 Rd. 9, 380-5030, *DA*

Peking, 29 Rd. 257, al-Nasr, 516-4218, *DA*

Petit Swiss Chalet, 9 Rd. 151, 359-8328

Red Onion, 27 Rd. 276, 520-0240

Sea Horse, Maadi Corniche (opposite As-Salam Hospital),

Way Out Sushi, 14 Rd. 218, 754-3202, *DA*

MISCELLANEOUS

Mamoura Torz, 30 'Abd al-Aziz abu-l-Sa'ud, beside Qasr al-'Aini, Roda, 364-4091

The Virginian, Corniche, Muqattam Hills

MOHANDISEEN

Abu Shaqra, 17 Gam'at al-Duwal al-'Arabiya, 344-2299/4509, *NA*, *DA*

Amoudi, 4 Zamzam, 749-9694

Asmak Wadi El Nil, 88 Wadi al-Nil, 304-4188

Ataturk (Turkish), 20 Riyad, off Shahab, 347-5135, 305-5832, *DA*

Bakery Alain Le Notre, branches in MA, HE, MO, ZA, 335-8172

Bint Sultan, Midan al-Sawra and Suliman Abaza, 760-1213/6633

Bon Appetit, 21 Wadi al-Nil, 346-4637, 346-0393, *DA*

Charwood's, 53 Gam'at al-Duwal al-'Arabiya, 749-0893

Chili's, Midan Gami' Mustafa Mahmud, 19002, *NA*, *DA*

Chopsticks, 23B Surya, 304-8567/8/9, fax 304-8569, *DA*

Cortigiano, 44 Michel Bakhum, 336-0620

Creeks, 15 Ahmad Sami al-Sa'id (off Sawra), 760-7326, fax 735-9608, *NA*, *DA*

Flux, 2 Gama'iyat al-Nisr, 338-6601

Malik el Gambary (formerly Asmak el Dawaran) 71 Gam'at al-Duwal al-'Arabiya, 749-0021

Maroush, 64 Midan Libnan, 345-0972, fax 304-9680 *NA*, *DA*

Mint, 30 Gazirit al-'Arab, 302-3870/1, *DA*

El Omda, 6 Gaza'ir (behind Atlas Hotel), 346-2247, 202-3042/058, *NA*

Papillon, Tersana club wall, 26th July, 347-1672, *DA*

Paxy's, Amoun Hotel, Midan Sphinx, 347-3928

Peking, 26 al-'Ataba, 749-6713, 336-6734; 9 al-Kawsar, 749-9860, 336-6734, *DA*

Prestige Corner Pizzeria, 43 Gazirit al-'Arab, 347-0383, *NA*, *DA*

Raoucha & Kandahar, 3 Gam'at al-Duwal al-'Arabiya, 303-0615, *DA*

Tia Maria, 32 Jeddah, 335-3273

Tirol, 38 Gazirit al-'Arab, 344-9725, fax 303-0729

Wok-n-Roll, 21 Gam'at al-Duwal al-'Arabiya, 761-3253, 749-0092, *DA*

El Yotti, 44 Muhi al-Din Abu al-'Izz, 749-4944, 760-3682

PYRAMIDS

Andrea Maryoutia, 59–60 Maryutiya, 385-4441

Christo's Vue des Pyramides, 10 al-Haram, 383-3582, 386-0086

Inuka Ya, Sheraton Royal Gardens, Helmiyit al-Ahram, 781-2211

Moghul Room, Mena House Hotel, 383-3222/3444, fax 383-7777

Trader Vic's, Sheraton Royal Gardens, Helmiyit al-Ahram, 781-2211/3311

WTC

Absolut, Casino al-Shagara,
Corniche al-Nil, 579-
6511/12, 579-9701

Sangria, Casino al-Shagara,
Corniche al-Nil, 579-
6511/12, 579-9701

ZAMALEK

Abou El Sid, 157 26th July,
735-9640

Arabica, 20 Muhammad al-
Mar'ashli, 735-7982, NA, DA

Casino Cleopatra, 3 al-
Gabalaya, 736-4630/2921

The Cellar, President Hotel,
735-0652/0718

Chin Chin, 4 Hasan Sabri,
736-2961, 735-7510

Dar el Amar, Blue Nile Boat,
9A Saray al-Gazira, 735-
3114, 012 390-0256, DA

Deals, al-Sayyid al-Bakri
(behind Maison Thomas)

Didos Al Dente, 26 Bahgat
'Ali, 735-9117, fax 736-
9730 NA, DA

Don Quichotte, 9A Ahmad
Hishmat, 735-6415/736-
5496

Euro Deli, 22a Taha Husayn,
736-6112, DA

Five Bells, 13 Isma'il
Muhammad, 735-8980/8635

Florencia, Hotel Flamenco,
10th fl., 2 al-Gazira al-Wusta
(at Abu al-Fida),
fax 735-0815/0819

Hana Restaurant, 21 Ma'had
al-Swisri (at Muhammad
Mazhar), 735-1846, 736-
9734, fax 735-0220

Justine, 4 Hasan Sabri, 735-
1647, 736-5640, DA

JWS Steakhouse, Marriott
Hotel, 339-4678

L'Asiatique, Le Pacha 1901,
Saray al-Gazira, 735-6730

L'Aubergine, 5 al-Sayyid al-
Bakri, 738-0080
(Vegetarian)

L'Oasis, Le Pacha 1901, Saray
al-Gezira, 735-6730/3

La Bodega, 157 26th July,
735-0543, 736-1115

La Trattoria, 13 Muhammad
Mar'ashli, 735-0470

Le Steak, Le Pacha 1901, Saray
al-Gazira, 735-6730, fax
737-3168, DA

Le Tarbouche, Le Pacha 1901,
Saray al-Gazira, 735-6730,
fax 735-7905

Longchamps, 21 Isma'il
Muhammad

Maison Thomas, 157 26th July,
735-7057, DA

Peking, 23B Isma'il
Muhammad, 736-6167, DA

Piccolo Mondo, Le Pacha
1901, Saray al-Gezira, 735-
6730, fax 735-7905

Pub 28, 28 Shagarit al-Durr,
735-9200

River Boat, Le Pacha 1901,
Saray al-Gazira, 735-6730,
fax 735-7905, DA

Roy's Country Kitchen,
Marriott Hotel, 738-8888

Sequoia, end of Abu al-Fida,
735-0014

Tuscany, Marriott Hotel
738-8888

Zee, 47 Muhammad Mazhar,
735-7746, DA

RESTAURANTS, FAST FOOD

Chicken Tikka, 19099

Dominos, GZ, 338-5790; HE,
291-1717, 633-6836; MA,
358-8503 (Rd. 9), 520-0055;
MO, 305-4026; DK
338-5790

Ghanam, 16 al-Salih Ayyub,
ZA, 735-6671/1185

Hardee's, Midan al-Tahrir.,
DT, 19066

KFC, 19019

Kung Fu Express, 20
Muhammad Mahmud, DT,
795-6977

McDonald's, 19991

Pizza Hut, 19000

El-Tabaei (Egyptian), 17
Gam'at al-Duwal al-
'Arabiya, MO, 304-1123/4

Take Five, 4 Hasan Sabri, ZA,
735-1647,

Texas Fried Chicken, 31 26th
July, DT, 579-2047/2048

Winchell's, Nile Bowling
Center, 57 al-Nil, GZ, 336-
1637, 336-1638; 3 Wahib
Dos, MA, 378-5034/5032;
13 Baghdad, al-Kurba, HE,
418-9535, 291-9299; GZ,
336-1638/1637

SCHOOLS, ELEMENTARY & SECONDARY

El Alsson, Harraniya, GZ,
385-0661, 388-8512/0/3

American International School,
NC, 477-0044/0055,
262-3147, 617-4001 (for
kids with special needs)

British International School
Cairo (BISC), 5 Mishil
Lutfallah, ZA, 735-6674,
736-5959 fax 736-4168

British School Al Rehab, al-
Rehab City, Cairo-Suez Rd.,
New Cairo, 607-0291/2-5,
fax 607-0294, e-mail:
admin@the-british-school-
cairo.net

Cairo American College
(CAC), 1 Midan Digla, MA,
519-6665/6825, 358-1519,
755-5555, fax 519-6584,
www.cacegypt.org

Choueifat International School, Zone 5, New Cairo, 758-0001/2/3/4, fax 758-0006, e-mail: isccairo@sabis.net, www.isccairo-sabis.net

Maadi British International School, 9 Rd. 278, MA, 702-8211/8124

Modern English School, Zone 5, New Cairo, 617-0005/11, e-mail: mes@starnet.com.eg, www.mescairo.edu.eg

New Cairo British International School, Zone 5, New Cairo, 758-3071/2881/1710, fax 758-1360

SCHOOLS, NURSERY AND PRE-SCHOOL

El Alsson, Harraniya, GZ, 385-0661, 388-8512/0/3

AGOUZA
Reiltin, 16 al-Desuq, 347-7152

DOKKI
American Wonderland, 9 Babel, 760-9667

The Irish School, 64 al-Zahraa, 337-0399, 748-8144

Schweizer Kinder Garten, 65 Musaddaq, 337-2578

DOWNTOWN
Alf Leila Wa Leila Preschool (AUC Nursery), 24 al-Falaki, 797-5315

HELIOPOLIS
Busy Bees, 37 al-Shahid 'Abd al-Mun'im Hafiz, Almaza, 663-710

MAADI
Charlie Chaplin Nursery and Preschool, 13 Filistin, New Maadi, 702-4742

Maadi British International Nursery School, 10 Rd. 77, 358-5911

Maadi Nursery British School, 9 Wahib Doss, 702-8124

One World Childcare Center, Digla, 703-2467

Sindbad Al Bashaer School, 358-6803

Start Right Nursery, 9 Wahib Dos, 358-0626

Stepping Stones Nursery School, 702-3880

Tom and Jerry Kids, 21 Rd. 209, 702-8896

MOHANDISEEN
Prince & Queen, 52 al-Quds al-Sharif (off Shahab), 347-3725

Stepping Stones Nursery School, 519-3933, 347-8923

NASR CITY
Stepping Stones Nursery School, 401-0092

ZAMALEK
Stepping Stones Nursery School, 735-2054

SCHOOLS, SUMMER

The American University in Cairo, Junior Summer Program, Special Studies Division, 418-5653/54, 290-3128; campuses in HE and DT

SCHOOLS, UNIVERSITY-LEVEL

'Ain Shams University, Qasr al-Za'farani, 'Abbasiya, 482-0830, fax 682-6107

The American University in Cairo, 113 Qasr al-'Aini, PO Box 2511, 11511 Cairo, 794-2964, fax 795-7565, www.aucegypt.edu

Al-Azhar University, Midan al-Husayn, 262-3284/78, 263-3070, fax 261-1404

Cairo University, Orman, GZ, 348-3443

German University in Cairo, al-Tagammu' al-Khamis, New Cairo, 758-9990-8

Helwan University, Mudiriat al-Tahrir, Helwan, 344-6441, fax 345-5461

SEWING SUPPLIES & NOTIONS

Aseel, KK, 590-6847; 56 'Ammar Ibn Yasir, HE, 638-1858 (dressmaker & embroidery supplies)

Nomrossy Sons, 14 al-Muski, KK, 907-220 (buttons, beads, braid)

SHIISHA SUPPLIES

Mahmud Eid El-Qalamawy & Sons, 92 al-Mu'izz li-Din Allah (opposite Qasr Bishtaq), KK, 932-215

SHOEMAKERS, CUSTOM AND REPAIRS

'Abdel Mun'im Abu Zeid, 8 Brazil, ZA, 736-8263

Babel, Kodak Passage, off 'Adli, DT

El Aziz Shoes, 3 Isma'il Muhammad, ZA, 735-0911

SHOES

Al Baraem Co., 9 Libnan, MO, 303-5990; Yamama Center, ZA, 735-6631

Antonio, 41 Gazirit al-'Arab, MO. 347-7137

Atlas, Khan al-Khalili, 590-6139 (embroidered silk slippers)

La Scarpa, 10 Rd. 218, Digla, MA, 519-7389

Royal Fashions, Nile Hilton, DT (European and American designers)
Santana, 112 Commercial Ctr., Ramses Hilton, 575-2399; Yamama Ctr., ZA
T.A. Egypt, WTC; corner of Qambis and Midan Ibn al-Walid, DK, 580-4176
Vero Chic, 19 Tal'at Harb, DT, 393-1895

SHOES, MEN'S

Abbouda (Bally), 33 Ahmad Hishmat, ZA

SHOPPING MALLS

Al Serag Mall, Atiya al-Sawalhi, off Makram 'Ibeid, NC, 273-8855/44
Arkadia Mall, Corniche al-Nil, Bulaq, 576-9678, 579-2084
Bandar, 9 Palestine, MA, 516-8378
Bustan Center, DT
City Center, Makram 'Ibeid, NC, 273-8855/44
Citystars, 13 Rama Bldgs., Umar Ibn al-Khattab, NC, 480-0500/55
Digla Arcade, 11 Hasan Sabri, ZA
First Mall, 35 Giza, next to the Four Seasons, GZ, 571-7803/6
Florida Mall, Sheraton Buildings, HE, 268-4295
Geneina Mall, Badrawi, off 'Abbas al-'Aqqad, NC, 404-6261/3/4
El Horreya Mall, al-Ahram, HE, 452-1698
Maadi City Center, Carrefour, Kattamiya Rd, MA, 520-4212/4307
Maadi Grand Mall, Rd. 250, MA, 519-5380

Nile Hilton Commercial Annex, Corniche al-Nil, DT, 578-0444
Ramses Hilton Commercial Annex, Corniche al-Nil, DT, 575-2203
Egyptian Autistic Society, www.autismegypt.com
Enjoy Tours in Cairo (specializing in travel for the disabled), Dr. Mohamed Gamal, www.enjoytours.org
Flying Wheels Travel, www.flyingwheelstravel.com (specializing in travel for the disabled)
Sultan Center, 77 'Usman Ibn 'Affan, Midan Safir, HE
Tersana Center, 26th July, MO
Tiba Mall, al-Naser, NC, 402-9072/6
Wonderland, 'Abbas al-'Aqqad, NC, 260-0212
WTC, 1191 Corniche al-Nil, Bulaq; shopping center, 580-4000; business center, 578-8054
Yamama Center, 3 Taha Husayn, ZA, 736-1583/6/7

SOFTBALL
See Sports

SOUND & LIGHT
Schedule for Pyramids, 385-2880/7320/7738, fax 384-4257

SPECIAL NEEDS
Agency for Disabled Travelers, Barbara Jacobson, 143 West Bridge St., Box 382, Owatonna, MN, 55060; 1-800-535-6790 or 570-451-5005; e-mail: bjacobson@ll.net

Continental School of Cairo, al-Hay al-Sabi', Madinat al-'Ubur, 610-2222
The Learning Resource Center, 30 Rd. 252, Digla MA, 519-6119
MOVE Middle East, 23 Rd. 232, Digla, MA, 521-2321

SPORTING & COUNTRY CLUBS

Ahli Sporting Club, al-Gabalaya, ZA, 735-2112/3
Cairo Sporting Club, al-Nil, GZ, 748-9415
Gezira Sporting Club, ZA, 735-6000/6
Heliopolis Sporting Club, al-Mirghani, HE, 417-0065/75
Maadi Sporting Club, MA, 358-5455, 358-5455
Maadi Yacht Club, 8 Palmer, MA, 358-5169/5455/5693
El Nil Sporting Club, Manyal side of 'Abbas Bridge, 364-7626
Nile Country Club, 374-2211/3334
Qattamiya Heights, Zone 5, New Cairo, Ring Road, 758-0512 to 17, 758-0808
Saqqara Country Club, Saqqara, PO Box 72, al-Haram, GZ, 384-6115, fax 385-0571, e-mail: scch@ rite.com
Shams Sporting Club, HE, 622-3020
Shooting Club (Nadi al-Seid), Nadi al-Seid, DK, 337-4535/4678/6747
Tawfiqiya Tennis Club, off Ahmad 'Urabi, MO, 346-1930
Zamalek Sporting Club, Mit 'Uqba, MO, 263-3001

SPORTS

See also Health Clubs

AEROBICS

See also Exercise Classes *below*

BADMINTON

Contact Steven Dale, 536-2378

BILLIARDS/SNOOKER/POOL

British Community
   Association, MO, 748-1358
John Burgess, 336-5047

BOATING

Cairo Yachting Club, al-Nil,
   GZ, 748-9415
Maadi Yacht Club, Corniche
   al-Nil, MA, 380-2066
Ocean Classics, 582-0766,
   fax 582-0632

CHESS

Arab Contractors Club,
   683-2391
Gezira Sporting Club,
   735-6000/6
Al-Hurriya Café, Midan al-
   Falaki, DT

CRICKET

Contact Cairo Rugby Club,
   525-3841

DIVING

See also Desert & Diving
   Safaris
Atlantis for Scuba Diving
   Mobile 010 108-8090/010
   885-1439
British Sub Aqua Club;
   contacts: Steve Devereux,
   291-7892
Cairo Divers Group; contacts:
   Muhammad Mabrouk,
   735-0889, 266-6003; Amira
   Zeitoun, 760-8976

Diaa Shawki, 14 al-Nasser, HE,
   634-5147
SCUBA Plus, WTC, 580-4165
Seascapes, al-Lasilki (Satellite
   Area), MA, 519-4930,
   fax 519-4927,
   www.seascapesegypt.com

EXERCISE CLASSES (AND AEROBICS)

See also Health Clubs
Arthur Miller Dance Studio,
   Midan al-Mahatta Maadi
   Palace, MA Sarayat,
   751-5006/7
Community Services
   Association, 4 Rd. 21, MA,
   358-5284, 376-8232
Creative Dance & Fitness
   Center, 6 'Amr, off Surya,
   MO, 302-0572,
   fax 302-0571; 13B Rd.
   254, Digla, MA, 519-6575,
   fax 519-8378
Fitness and Dance Academy,
   Yamama Center, 3 Taha
   Husayn, 737-7500
Pyramids, GZ, 383-2571, 742-
   2980, 010 606-6181,
   www.step-center.com
STEP, Villa 13, Hadayik al-
   Ahram, off Cairo–
   Alexandria Desert Road,
   behind Movenpick Hotel

FISHING & HUNTING

Anglers Federation, 17
   Mahmud Basyuni, DT, fax
   570-1055
Fawzia Abu Dief & Co.,
   168 al-Tahrir, DT, 392-
   2634/ 5244

GOLF

British Golf Society, Capt.
   Keith Hardy, 739-8272, Vice
   Capt. Joe Divis, 736-4669
Mena House Ladies, Lalaine
   Noordhuis, 269-7650; Lynne
   Borghesius, 290-5055

GYMNASTICS

Gezira Club, 735-6000

HORSES & HORSEBACK RIDING

AA Stables, 385-0351; owner:
   'Abdul Aziz
El Boraq Stables and Breeding,
   Zawyat Abu Muslim, GZ,
   381-0349
Equicare Co., 2 Bahgat 'Ali,
   ZA, 735-6939
El Ferousseya, Gezira Club,
   ZA, 735-6000
Euro Stables, 385-5849
FB Stables, 385-0406; owner:
   Farouk Breesh
MG Stables, 385-3823; owner:
   Muhammad Ghoneim
SA Stables, 385-0629; owner:
   Salama Abou Aziza
Stables in/near Nazlat al-
   Simman on Gamal 'Abd al-
   Nasir at Giza Pyramids:
El Zahraa Stud Farm, HE,
   633-1733

ICE SKATING

Geneina Mall, Badrawi, off
   'Abbas al-'Aqqad, NC
Maadi Grand Mall, Rd. 250, MA

MARTIAL ARTS

Chao Min, 010 122-0053 (Tai
   Chi classes)
Number One Health & Beauty,
   Ghadat al-Maadi Towers,
   MA, 378-6256/7
Sports Mall, 80 Shahab, MO,
   303-0246/7 or 302-6432/3

ROWING

Egyptian Rowing Union, 3 al-
   Shawarbi, DT, 393-4350
El Nil Sporting Club, near
   Kubri 'Abbas, Corniche al-
   Nil, GZ, 393-4350

RUGBY

Cairo Rugby Club, Rds. 104
   and 161 (behind Maadi
   Military College), MA,

clubhouse 525-3841;
contact: Ben 010 184-4589,
Karl 010 638-3080,
www.cairorugby.com

RUNNING
Cairo Hash House Harriers,
Adrian, 010 129-8260,
Wesley 012 122-2864,
www.cairohash.com

SNORKELING AND SCUBA
See Diving, Desert & Diving
Safaris

SOCCER
www.Egyptiansoccer.com

SOFTBALL
Cairo American Softball
League, men's
commissioner Jon 012 279-
4225, women's
commissioner Monte, 012
724-8961

TENNIS
Maadi Ladies Tennis, Karen
Jones, 359-9744

SPORTS EQUIPMENT
A Sports, 14 Gumhuriya, DT,
near Midan Ubira, 390-9775,
Amr Khairy
Alfa Market (above
supermarket), Corniche al-Nil
Scuba Plus, 1st fl., WTC
Sports Mall, 80 Shahab, MO,
302-6432
Weider, 2A Bahgat 'Ali, ZA;
14 al-Mahrusa (off Ahmad
'Urabi near Midan Sphinx),
MO, 302-7993; 34A
al-Higaz, al-Tugariyin
Tower, Mahkama, HE, 632-
2227; Maadi Grand Mall,
MA, 518-1848
World Sport, 17 al-Mathaf al-
Zira'i, DK, 335-2778/3241

SPORTS FEDERATION
Angling, 17 Mahmud Basyuni,
DT, fax 570-1055
Athletics, Bahari Stadium, NC,
260-7788
Basketball, Bahari Stadium, NC
Billiards, 83 Ramsis, DT,
574-4934
Body Building, Higher Council
of Youth and Sports, Mit
'Uqba, MO
Boxing, 5 Tal'at Harb, DT,
392-2732
Chess, Arab Contractors Club,
683-2391
Croquet, Gezira Sporting Club,
794-4743
Cycling, Bahari Stadium, NC,
402-6724
Diving, 14 Autostrade al-
Bahari, Rabi'a al-'Adawiya,
NC, 260-5381
Egyptian Rowing Union, 3 al-
Shawarbi, DT, 393-4350
Fencing, Fencing Club, al-
Azbakiya Gardens (near
Midan Opera), 392-6120
Field Hockey, Bahari Stadium,
NC, 262-5052
Golf, Gezira Sporting Club,
ZAM, 735-6000/6
Gymnastics, 32 Sabri Abu
'Alam, DT, 392-3526
Handball, Bahari Stadium, NC,
261-0416/7
Horseback Riding, 261-6575
Horse Racing, 3 'Abd al-
Hamid Badawi (next to El
Salam Hotel), HE, 635-4090
International Equestrian Club,
Hassan Abdu Breash, 010
500-1103
Judo, Sumo, and Aikido,
Bahari Stadium, NC,
263-4367/8555

Karate, al-'Ubur Towers, Salah
Salim, NC, 269-1430,
260-7363
Katameya Tennis Center, el
Shafei Ranch, New Cairo
City Ring Road, 758-0512/7
Kung Fu, 3 al-Qaddarawi,
Bulaq al-Dakrur, 574-2195
Long-Distance Swimming,
Corniche al-Nil, GC,
794-7158
Olympic Committee, 261-1400,
263-2500, fax 260-5974,
e-mail: eo@idsc.gov-eg,
director Ahmed Dinar
Pole Vaulting, 16 al-Nuzha,
HE, 418-1839
Polo, 13 Qasr al-Nil, DT
(contact Olympic
Committee, above)
Power Lifting, 5 Musaddaq,
DK, 383-3799
Raquetball, 5 Montassir Bldg.,
Faysal, PY, 858-406, 852-
098
Rowing, el-Nil Sporting Club,
Corniche al-Nil, GZ, 393-
4350
Shooting, Bahari Stadium, NC
Soccer, 5 Gabalaya, ZA, 735-
3268/5560, 736-3730
Speedball, Higher Council of
Youth and Sports, Mit
'Uqba, MO, 346-0073
Squash, Cairo Stadium, NC,
262-4273, 401-0237
Swimming, 260-7375
Tae Kwon Do, 64 Ramsis, Apt.
2, HE, 263-1737, 261-7576
Table Tennis, 2 Abu Hif, Bab
al-Luq, DT, 392-5986
Tennis, 13 Qasr al-Nil, DT
Volleyball, Bahari Stadium,
NC, 262-1696
Weightlifting, Bahari Stadium,
NC, 260-9256/63
Wrestling, Bahari Stadium,
NC, 261-0608

Yachting, 82 'Abd al-'Aziz al-Sa'ud, MN, 364-6763, fax 983-679

STATIONERY

All along 'Abd al-Khaliq Sarwat, DT

El Fagre, Abu Bakr al-Siddiq (down from Kanzy Hotel), DK, 761-0131 (good office stationery)

Khodeir, 15 Nadi al-Seid, DK, 760-1842; 10 'Ilwi, DT; 20 Mansur Muhammad, ZA

STOPPEURS (RE-WEAVERS)

El Zayat, 4 Brazil, ZA, 735-1064

SUPERMARKETS

Abu Zikry, Muhi al-Din Abu al-'Izz (at al-Tahrir), DK; Rd 9, MA

Alfa Market, Riyadh Tower, Corniche al-Nil, GZ, 572-6203; Dalla Tower, 7a Corniche al-Nil, MA, 525-6400; 35 al-'Ubur buildings, Salah Salim, 'Ubur, HE, 405-0370; 4 al-Malik al-Afdal, ZA, 737-0801

Maadi City Center, Carrefour, Kattamiya Rd, MA, 520-4212/4307

Metro Market, DK, 338-9569; HE, 256-5365; MA, 526-4502; MO, 338-9567, 302-5035; NC, 263-3302; PY, 388-5121; ZA, 735-6902

Seoudi, 25 Midan al-Misaha, DK, 748-8225, 748-8441, 7488440; Quds al-Sharif and al-Higaz, MO, 346-3570, 346-0391; 20 Muhammad al-Mar'ashli, ZA, 735-0370, 735-9596, 736-3586; Rd. 214, MA, 754-6777

TAXI & LIMOUSINE SERVICES

Blue Cab, 760-9717/6, www.thebluecab.com

City Cab

Maadi Taxi, Rd. 9 and al-Nahda, MA, 358-1118

Muhammad Naguib, MA, 358-9123

Muhammad Selmi, MA, 702-8706

Mustafa Muhammad, Rd. 10, MA, 380-1961

Limousine Misr, 685-0625

TAXI DRIVERS

(English-speaking)

Alexander, 573-8068 (after 7pm)

Ashraf, 010 118-4282

Diaa, 330-7997 (English & Italian, 12–6pm)

Reda, 314-9924

Shouki, 318-3344 after 9pm

TELEPHONES

See Appliances

TELEPHONE DIRECTORIES

See Emergency and Other Important Numbers

Egypt Trade www.egtrade.com

Kompass Directory, www.kompassegypt.com, lists major companies

Telecom Egypt www.telecomegypt.com.eg/english/Home.htm, with directory assistance and emergency numbers, billing information, prepaid car service

Yellow Pages www.yellowpages.com.eg

TELEVISION: CABLE & SATELLITE

Cable Network Egypt (CNE) and Multi-Choice, 3 Rd. 262, Midan Gaza'ir, New Maadi, 519-2265/2355

Queen SAT, 519-7606; owner: Tarek Radwan 010 141-4982

V SAT, Tawfiq Tower, 29 Mustafa Kamil, MA, 358-0604, 012 246-8365

TELEVISIONS

See Appliances

TENNIS

See Sports

TENTMAKERS

All along Khayyamiya in Darb al-Ahmar near KK

Magdy & Salah Farghaly, 2 Khayyamiya, 517-737-9

THEATERS

(For movie theaters see Cinemas)

Balloon, al-Nil, AG, 347-1718, 347-7457

Bayt al-Harawi, behind al-Azhar mosque, 735-7001, 510-4177

Al-Fann, Ramsis, DT, 578-2444

Farid, Farid and 'Imad al-Din, DT

Al-Gezira Theater, 'Abd al-'Aziz al-Sa'ud, MN, 364-4160

Gumhuriya Theater, Gumhuriya, DT, 390-7707

Al-Hanager Theater, Opera Complex, Gezira, 735-6861

Al-Haram, al-Haram, GZ, 386-3952

Nasr City Theater, Yusif 'Abbas, NC, 402-0804

National Theater, Midan 'Ataba, 591-7783

Qasr al-Nil, Qasr al-Nil, DT, 575-0761

Ramses Hilton Theater, Annex, DT, 574-7435

Salah 'Abdel Sabour Hall, Midan al-'Ataba, 937-948

Al-Salam, Qasr al-'Aini, GC, 795-2484

Al-Tali'a, Midan Ataba, DT, 593-7848

Wallace Theater, AUC, Greek Campus, DT, 797-6373

Al-Zamalek, 13 Shagarit al-Durr, ZA, 736-0660

TILES

Ceramica Cleopatra, 38 al-Batal Ahmad 'Abd al-'Aziz, MO, 760-0581, 761-2442

Sharia al-Faggala, Ramsis (numerous dealers)

Sharia Salah al-Din, al-Qal'a (numerous dealers)

TOOLS

See Hardware

TOUR GUIDES

See Travel Agents *and* Desert & Diving Safaris

TOYS

Our Kids, Mustafa al-Nahhas (beside Pizza Hut), NC, 274-8741; 5 Midan al-Misaha, DK, 336-3602

Top Toys, 40 Musaddaq, DK, 335-3295

Toys & Joy, 3 Musaddaq, DK

Zero2Five, 13 Quroum, MO, 335-1032; Carrefour, City Centre, MA, 520-4412, will deliver large orders

TRANSLATORS

See Business Services Centers

TRAVEL AGENCIES

See also Desert and/or Diving Safaris

Abercrombie and Kent, Bustan Commercial Center, 10th fl., Bab al-Luq, DT, 393-6272/5179, fax 391-6255, www.abercrombiekent.com

Agency for Disabled Travelers, Barbara Jacobson, 143 West Bridge St., Box 382, Owatonna, MN, 55060; 1-800-535-6790 or 570-451-5005; bjacobson@ll.net

Akhnaton Travel, 70 al-Husayn, MO, 760-5683, 337-4831, fax 760-0934, 796-3632,

Basata, Sherif al-Ghamrawy, 358-1829 or, in Basata, at 069-500-481

Elegantes Voyages, 23 Yahya Ibrahim, ZA, 736-2145

Emeco Travel, 2 Tal'at Harb, DT, 574-9360, 390-7045, 578-5901/2, fax 574-4212

See Egypt–See the World, 26 Rd. 87, MA, 358-9146 (same fax), 378-0972

Ted Cookson (Egypt Panorama Tours), 4 Rd. 79, MA, 358-5880, 359-0200, fax 359-1199

Thomas Cook DT: 17 Mahmud Basyuni, 574-3955 GC: 12 Midan al-Sheikh Yusif, 796-4650/4651/4934-5-6, fax 796-4654 GZ: Le Meridien Pyramids, 382-2688, 384-5080, fax 382-1536 HE: 7 Baghdad, 417-3511-2, 290-7310, fax 291-6215 HE: (Heliopolis Club), phone/fax 418-23309, 417-2890 MA: 88 Rd. 9, Midan al-Mahatta, 359-1419/1438, 359-0232, fax 358-2651 MO: 10 26th

July, 344-0008, 346-2429/7187, fax 303-4530

Semiramis Hotel, 795-8544/8162, fax 795-7061

WTC: phone/fax 578-0808/9

Travco, 19 Yahya Ibrahim, ZA, 737-5737/1737, fax 735-4654

TUTORS

Check with Schools

UNIFORMS

See Sports Equipment

VACCINATION

See Schools, University-level

The Family Health Care Clinic, 71 Rd. 9, MA, 380-6766, 359-2048; Hotline 012 212-3665, 010 602-3118

Vacsera, MO, 761-1111

VCR & TELEVISION RENTAL

Ion Electric Fields, 34 Muhammad Mazhar (opposite Safir Hotel), ZA

Telehire, 3 Hasan 'Asim 1st fl., ZA, 736-0183, 263-8131

VETERINARIANS

Advanced Care Vet Clinic, 85 Rd. 199, MA, 754-4267, 010 505-8650, Dr. Adel A Amer

Dr. Berj Ya'qub, 40 Falah, off Midan Libnan, MO, 305-4806; 44 Ahram, HE, 415-0821

Brooke Hospital for Animals, 2 Bayram al-Tunsi, Sayyida Zeinab, DT, 364-9312

New Maadi Veterinary Clinic, 5 Rd. 278, New MA, 702-6693, 702-8882, Drs. Magdi & Magda Boutros

Dr. Osama Safar, PDSA Clinic, 577-2227, hospital 482-2294, home 684-3123

People's Dispensary for Sick
Animals (PDSA), 60 al-
Sikka al-Bayda, 'Abbasiya,
DT; clinic, 577-2227;
hospital, 482-2294, Dr.
Farouk, Dr. Osama Safar,
Dr. Ahmed Obeida

VIDEO RENTAL

Video Rack, 17 Dr. al-Mahruqi
(off Midan Aswan), MO,
304-5311/12; 23 al-Ma'had
al-Ishtiraki (Merryland), HE,
453-5503/4; 41 'Abd al-
Hamid Badawi (Nadi al-
Shams), HE, 240-4108; 15
Abu al-Atahia (International
Garden), NC, 273-6810; 1/5
al-Lasilki, MA, 754-3619

VOLUNTEERING

Awladi Orphanage, 29 Rd. 206,
Digla, MA, 359-0128
Befrienders Cairo, 209 26th
July, Midan Sphinx, MO,
344-8200; 303-6025/35
Caritas, Oasis of Hope Drug &
Rehabilitation Project, 010
522-1195
Center for Children with
Disabilities, 42 'Abdallah
Diraz, HE, 417-2084/5/6/7
Egyptian Red Crescent Society,
29 al-Gala', DT, 575-0558
Egyptian Museum Library,
Midan al-Tahrir, DT,
577-2352 (direct), 574-4267
Friends of Children with
Cancer, Betsy Munsey
519-6076
HOPE and IQRA'A (Help
Orphans Pursue Education
and Read), contact: Heba,
337-7930, Tamir 383-4269
and at Jameel Center, AUC,
797-5039
Hope Village Society, 14
Ahmad al-Khashab, NC,
272-4563

Al Nour Institute for Girls, 22
al-Kawsar, MO; director
Muhammad El-Zeidi,
748-0465 (blind children)
Al Nour Wal Amal (Light and
Hope Assoc. for Blind
Girls), 16 Abu Bakr al-
Siddiq, HE, Amal Hashem,
735-4991, or Malek El-
Sherbini, 634-1929.
SOS Children's Village, end of
'Abbas al-'Aqqad (next to
MB Petroleum Co.), NC,
274-3339/2286
UNICEF, 8 & 11 'Adnan
'Umar Sidqi (off Musaddaq
just past Club Med office),
DK, 761-6346

WALKING TOURS

See Organizations

WALL HANGINGS

See Arts & Crafts

WATCH & CLOCK REPAIRS

See Clock & Watch Repairs

WATER FILTERS

Laser, Ramses Hilton Annex,
2nd fl., 574-4400, 577-7444
Life Trend-Egypt (Instapure), 3
al-Diwan, GC, 796-4461, fax
795-6344

WATER PIPES

See Shisha Supplies

WEIGHT CONTROL

See also Health Clubs
Beauty Essentials, 14 Ahmad
Hishmat, 736-2927

WINDOW SCREENS

Hassan Hilmy, 50 Musaddaq,
DK, 748-1925

WINDSURFING

See Sports

WIRE SERVICES

See News Agencies

WOMEN'S GROUPS

See Organizations

WOOD

See Lumber

WROUGHT IRON (FER FORGÉ)

See also Furniture
Shops along al-Sabtiya and
Ramsis

X-RAYS

See Laboratories

YACHTING

See Boating

YOGA

Ashtanga classes, Charlie, 012
496-4480, 735-3247
CSA, 358-5284, 376-8232
Debra Desaulniers Yoga
Classes, 012 391-3313
Indian Cultural Center, 23
Tal'at Harb, 393-3396
Muhammad al-Naggar, 010
502-5051
The Swiss Club, al-Salam,
Imbaba, 736-2979
El Sawy Culture Wheel, 26th
July, ZA, 736-8881, 012
440-0100,
www.culturewheel.com

ZIPPERS

See Sewing Supplies

ZOO

Cairo Zoo, near Cairo
University, GZ, 570-8895,
572-6314

INDEX

Abu Simbel 61
accommodations 44
adoption 137
adultery 39
air conditioners 96, 111
air shipments 94
airline reservations, reconfirming 11
al-Alamein 61
alcohol 12, 13, 19, 20, 41, 52
allergies 21
alterations and tailoring 113
alternative medicine 73
ambulances 23
American Chamber of Commerce 31, 35, 134
American Research Center in Egypt 18, 54, 57, 74
American University in Cairo 17, 60, 101
Amideast 135
amusement parks 38, 46, 72, 99, 111
answering machines 32, 33
antibiotics 24
antiques 63, 116
ants 121
appliances 33, 62, 94, 111
appliqué work 63
Arabian Horse auction 61
archaeology 74
architecture 74
art classes 74
art galleries 79
artists 67, 74, 79
arts 79, 83
arts and crafts 63
Aswan High Dam 5, 6, 56
Ataba market 60, 62, 69, 119
Attarin 63
aviation 74
awnings 118

Bab al-Futuh 59
Bab al-Khalq 22, 58
Bab al-Luq 62
Bab Zuwayla 57
backgammon 74
bakeries 123
banking 26, 129, 133
bargaining 26, 143
bamboo chairs 119
bars 80

Basata 61, 86
baskets 63, 64, 117
bathing suits 93, 113
bathrooms 112
bawwaabs 96, 99, 100, 110, 111
Bayn al-Qasrayn 58
Bayt al-Sihaymi 59
BBC World Service 36
beads 66
beadwork 64
beauty salons 74
Bedouin market at al-Arish 61
beds and bedding 112
bedspreads 63
beer 13, 20, 45, 80
beggars 26
belly-dancing 81
beverages 50
bicycle repairs 86
birdwatching 61, 75
blankets 112
boating 85
bookbinding 64
books 64
bowling 72
brass 64
bread 48, 121, 123
bridge 75
British Community Association 18, 81, 84, 86
building services and personnel 110
buses xx, 11, 14, 15, 17
business service centers 33, 132
butchers 124

cable television 35
cafés 51, 81
Cairo Tower 59
calendars 40
camels 65; camel market 55
Capital Markets Authority 132
car and motorcycle rallies 75
carpentry and cabinets 112
carpets 65, 115
cars 104; accidents 105; alternatives to driving 107; classic 75; driving 107; duty free 104; fines 106; insurance 106; licenses 106; new cars 105; registration 104; rental 11, 106; traffic lights 107; used cars 105
cash machines 25

219